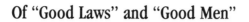

Of "Good Laws" and "Good Men"

Of
"Good Laws"
and
"Good Men"

*Law and Society
in the Delaware Valley,
1680–1710*

William M. Offutt, Jr.

University of Illinois Press   Urbana and Chicago

Library of Congress Cataloging-in-Publication Data

Offutt, William M. (William McEnery) 1956–
Of "good laws" and "good men" : law and society in the Delaware
Valley, 1680-1710 / William M. Offutt, Jr.
p.   cm.
Includes bibliographical references and index.
ISBN 0-252-02152-5 (cloth : acid-free paper)
1. Quakers—Legal Status, laws, etc.—Delaware River Valley
(N.Y.-Del. and N.J.)—History. I. Title.
KF4869.Q83037   1995
346.7301'3—dc20
[347.30613]   94-37980
                                                                   CIP

For Nancy

Contents

Acknowledgments

Much like the seventeenth-century clerks of courts and secretaries of
Quaker meetings, I am confronted with the task of conveying great complexity in a few words. What they wrote was informed not only by what
they saw and heard in written documents and oral testimony but also
by the contemporary legal, religious, and social forms of expression.
Though written by individuals, their records were collaborative products without which this study would not have been possible. Like those
scribes who were not mere scriveners, I have composed this work indi-
vidually, confronting not a blank parchment but a blank rectangular
screen with a profoundly annoying blinking prompt that has taunted
me for eleven years. Yet I am most humbly aware that this book is a
collaboration, informed not just by my own observations and under-
standings but by many disciplines, institutions, and people. To them I
give thanks.

There are my parents, with whom I am now in a small race to see
whose historical work gets into print first. They instilled in me a belief
common to those who began school in the 1960s—all things are possible, and learning, especially history, is the key. They supported my trans-
continental pursuit of education in the 1970s, where I learned the difference between the promises of process and the reality of power. They
encouraged my pursuit of the history profession in the 1980s, even
though it cost them their investment in my legal training; they bought
me the personal computer that made the whole project possible. Now,
as this book goes to press, I feel, to quote Bill Cosby, that "I started out
as a child."

There are my graduate school influences. Jack Greene sold me on
Johns Hopkins and himself in the spring of 1981, and I have never re-

gretted the purchase (even when I took his charge on the basketball court). He gave me room to run with this project and provided me significant editorial advice and substantial encouragement, especially through the years of my uncertain health. His graduate seminar read my ideas for four years and helped me immeasurably with the implications of the theories I used. Jack dedicated *Pursuits of Happiness* to twenty-two years of participants in that seminar, but the real debt runs the other way. Among the faculty, Ron Walters, Lou Galambos, Bill Freehling, and Toby Ditz were most helpful, while then-graduate students Stu McConnell, Jean Russo, Joyce Chaplin, Ane Lintvedt, Jane Sewell, Jeff Charles, Vinnie DeMarco, Ken Lipartito, Ken Ledford, Cliff Crais, and Mark Kornbluh made the work and my life better. The work also had support from Sharon Widomski, the History Department's funds, the Kenan Fund, the computer center, and the staff of the Eisenhower Library.

There are those who made the research in and around Philadelphia possible. The Philadelphia Center for Early American Studies provided the greatest assistance with a Mellon fellowship and with its seminars. The center's director, Richard Beeman; the codirector of the Penn Papers, Richard Dunn; all of the Penn Papers staff; and Lisa Wilson, also a fellow, made that year invaluable. Thanks to the center, I came to know Jean Soderlund, Jerry Frost, and Lucy Simler, all of whom provided significant leads and encouragement. The staffs of the Van Pelt Library at the University of Pennsylvania, the Historical Society of Pennsylvania, the Library Company of Philadelphia, the Friends Historical Society at Swarthmore College, the Chester County Archives, the Gloucester County Archives, and the Bucks County Archives guided me through their materials with unfailing patience. Finally, David Dauer, Paul Olk, Lisa Robinson, and Naomi Rogers enhanced my quality of life.

There are those who have worked with me to turn my manuscript into a polished book. Special thanks must go to those historians who have read and improved the entire manuscript at some point: John Modell, Stanley Engerman, David Thomas Konig, and Lois Green Carr (who has my undying gratitude for reading it at least three times). Cogent critiques of parts of this work have been offered by William Nelson, Eben Moglen, Bruce Mann, David Flaherty, John Murrin, the Baylor Scholarly Writing Seminar, and the New York University Law School Legal History Colloquium. Institutional support has come from many sources: the academic computing centers at Baylor University and Pace University; the deans of Arts and Sciences William Cooper at Baylor and Charles Masiello at Pace; and the scholarly research committee at Pace. At the University of Illinois Press, my thanks go to Richard Wentworth for sticking with this project when he did not have to, to Lisa Warne-Magro and Karen Hewitt for shepherding it through the process, and to Jane Mohraz for copyediting. Any mistakes that remain are my fault alone, for these people did all they could.

Finally, there is the one to whom this book is dedicated. Nothing I can ever write can express my thanks to Nancy Reagin, who has showed me places and taught me things I never would have seen or learned otherwise. She never lost faith, even when I had, and encouraged me page by page, even word by word, in the writing and rewriting. I only hope I can do as much for her work as she has done for mine.

Introduction

Let Men be good, and the Government can't be bad; if it be ill, they will cure it: but if Men be bad, let the Government be never so good, they will endeavour to warp and spoil it to their Turn.

I know some say, Let us have good Laws, and no matter for the Men that Execute them: But let them consider, that though good Laws do well, good Men do better; for good laws may want good Men, and be abolished or evaded by ill Men; but good Men will never want good Laws nor suffer Ill Ones.

—William Penn, 1682

The waters of the Delaware River chart a zigzag course as they meander south from their headwaters in New York to the Delaware Bay and then into the Atlantic. This wide river, accessible to ocean-going vessels for more than 150 miles, carved a valley that would attract seventeenth-century Europeans. The river and its tributaries provided the access for a small number of Dutch, Swedish, and Finnish settlers to begin encroaching on the Lenni Lenape Indians in the 1620s. European title to the valley's fertile soil, temperate climate, and transportation advantages passed into the hands of the English in the 1660s and attracted the attention of a small, unpopular group. Leading members of this group, the Society of Friends (Quakers), first acquired rights to the east bank of the Delaware (the western half of New Jersey), and a few years later they obtained rights to the west bank. Beginning in the 1670s and accelerating in the 1680s with Pennsylvania's establishment on that west bank by a leading Quaker, William Penn, the Delaware Valley swarmed with European settlers.[1]

As part or whole owner of three Delaware Valley colonies, William Penn sought a variety of goals in the New World. Penn wanted to shelter Friends from persecution and to provide sufficient land to enable those Quakers to practice their familial goals.[2] He sought personal gain through selling land and dominating the seaborne trade, but he also hoped for general prosperity through a well-ordered society "that would provide wide scope for the economic ambitions of its members."[3] Those members would be not only English Quakers but also people of other religious and ethnic backgrounds. Penn encouraged these disparate groups to immigrate, partly to enhance the value of his holdings and partly as a consequence of his commitment to liberty of conscience.[4] Another cornerstone of this edifice of land, toleration, prosperity, and diversity was Penn's determination to improve the common law and England's unwritten Constitution. Penn helped draft West Jersey's charter and fundamental laws of 1676, *The Concessions and Agreements of the Proprietors.* In 1681 and 1682, Penn wrote as many as twenty drafts of the *Frame of Government* and *Laws Agreed upon in England* for Pennsylvania, seeking the right rules of governance for Quaker colonies. Yet in the final, promulgated draft, Penn's preamble (quoted in the epigraph) emphasized not the "good laws" he had drafted in accordance with Whig principles but "good men."[5]

The "good men" he had in mind were Quakers. Retaining Quaker control was essential to maintaining a haven from religious prosecution and for freedom of conscience. According to Penn, Quakers were not to allow themselves to become "dissenters in our own Countrey," and the best way to ensure that was to retain Quaker control of government.[6] From the beginning, however, Quakers faced the inherent contradiction of opening the door to diverse immigrants in a spirit of toleration but wanting to restrict non-Quaker power in law and government. Animating Penn's *Frame* from his first to last draft was the belief that "the People of any Country should be Consenting to the laws they are to be governed by."[7] If the Quaker government lost the confidence of non-Quaker immigrants, their consent would be withheld, the government would lose legitimacy, and non-Quakers would take over.

As early as 1683, Penn confronted this fear. Quakers charged that his constitution contained no guarantees for maintaining Quaker control over Pennsylvania. Penn rejected calls to exclude non-Quakers from voting and government on the grounds that to do so would be hypocritical, yet he acknowledged that "in case they should outnumber us upon Vote, we are gone." Instead he proposed that Quakers govern in ways designed to keep the assent, and thus control, of non-Quakers: "If freinds here keep to god

& in the Justice, mercy equity & fear of the lord their enemys will be their foot stool, if not their heires & my heirs too will loos all." Penn recognized that Quaker "good men" would have to adhere to high standards of legal performance ("Justice, mercy equity") to retain authority even when Quakers constituted a majority. Should Quakers lose their majority, such performance might convince the non-Quaker population not to "outnumber us upon Vote" but to return Quakers to office.[8]

Penn's and other Quakers' theories on law and government came to life in both Quaker colonies on the Delaware River, since the boundary between West Jersey and Pennsylvania made little difference to the communication of political thought. On a broad range of other issues, settlers also acted with regional consciousness. Quakers saw their religious organization in regional terms, organizing a yearly meeting for the entire Delaware Valley. That yearly meeting, which coordinated the Society's hierarchy of quarterly and monthly meetings, alternately met in Philadelphia and Burlington, West Jersey.[9] Legally, both provinces recognized the validity of each other's warrants and hues and cries, perhaps the first legislated comity in British North America.[10] Culturally, residents sustained a sense of common interests across wide areas and sprawling townships. Cultural contacts were reinforced economically. The region's trade centered on Philadelphia, which collected produce from the rural farms and villages of Pennsylvania, West Jersey, and Delaware and funneled it into the Atlantic market. Settlers were not tied to a particular province; in their land purchases and economic dealings, they showed substantial geographic mobility within the region.[11]

Politically, though the provinces had leaders connected by blood and marriage, they were governed separately. Nonetheless, parallel patterns of political behavior were evident as both colonies saw pitched battles for control of government. Between 1682 and 1701, Pennsylvania had four different frames of government promulgated. Penn would lose his charter for Pennsylvania in 1692, regain it in 1694, and have to fight to maintain it through the early 1700s against formidable Anglican attacks. His appointed governors all faced concerted opposition from within the Society of Friends, and Penn, when personally present, could not maintain majority support within Pennsylvania's assembly.[12] West Jersey had five shifts in governmental structure between 1676 and 1703, when the colony merged with East Jersey under royal control. From 1685 to 1692, there were no meetings of the West Jersey assembly, and no legislation passed, whether under Governor Edmund Andros and the

Dominion of New England or during the four year period when West Jersey had neither governor nor legislature.[13] At the provincial level, the region's politics saw disruption, upheaval, confusion, and struggles for position and power.

Despite the turmoil at the top, contemporaries agreed that this region achieved dramatic economic and social success. In 1681, a report on West Jersey noted that "the Husband-Men have good Increase," "the Increase of their Corn being considerably greater than in England . . . For the Soyl it is Good, and capable to produce anything that England doth: [and] the Yearly Increase is far Greater."[14] Penn advertised in 1681 that immigrants to Pennsylvania would be greatly rewarded by the land and their industry in the new colony; by 1685, he claimed to have delivered on that promise, writing that lots in Philadelphia were now worth four to forty times their original price. Penn asserted, "The Earth, by God's blessing, has more than answered our expectation" of agriculture because of "so great an encrease of Grain by the dilligent application of People to Husbandry." Success, due to the fertility of land, was within reach "if Man use but a moderate diligence" in Pennsylvania.[15] Clearly, if these accounts are to be believed, new farmers established going concerns rapidly in the Delaware Valley.

The region's prosperity did not depend on agriculture alone. In 1698, Gabriel Thomas noted that "the true Reason why this Fruitful Countrey and Flourishing City advance so considerably . . . is their great and extended Traffique and Commerce both by Sea and Land." Thomas counted fifteen colonies in addition to England that carried on trade with the Delaware Valley and documented a long list of agricultural exports. Beyond the profits in trade were opportunities "for Poor People (both Men and Women) of all kinds, [who] can here get three times the Wages for their Labour they can in England and Wales." Blacksmiths, carpenters, shoemakers, tailors, sawyers—Thomas's list covered at least fifty skilled crafts that paid more than in England. Even "Labouring-Men" and "Maid Servants" did better than in England because Delaware Valley farmers who hired such workers paid less for land, got more for their produce, and had to pay more to prevent servants from setting up on their own.[16] If Thomas is to be believed, no colonial American region did so well economically so fast for such a wide variety of European settlers.

Historians do accept the thrust of Thomas's and Penn's accounts. Carl Bridenbaugh ascribed "the emergence in less than two decades of a new and strikingly successful society in the valley of the Delaware" to "the truly spectacular rise and growth that went on in the whole region."[17] James Lemon, echoing western European commentaries, called his book on southeastern Pennsylvania in the late seventeenth and eighteenth centuries *The Best Poor Man's Country* because "without doubt, the area was one of the most affluent agricultural societies anywhere."[18] Barry Levy, in discussing Quaker agriculture in the Delaware Valley, commented that "these were the most economically successful family farmers yet seen in North America, capable of sustaining a vibrant regional economy, who grew abundantly a crop [wheat] that did not require slave gangs or produce a 'boom psychology' during which European civility was almost entirely forgotten." Levy also credited farmers in New Jersey and non-Quaker farmers who followed the pace set by Pennsylvania Quakers.[19] Finally, in the most recent attempt at synthesis, David Hackett Fischer concluded that "Penn's system proved to be a highly efficient way of promoting settlement" that "prevented the growth of a small landowning oligarchy" and made wealth distribution more equal there than in other regions of colonial British America. Beyond agricultural settlement, "the Delaware Valley also became a hive of industry" and succeeded in making Philadelphia "the most important capital market in the New World" until the nineteenth century.[20] Historians have reached a remarkable consensus on the success of the early Delaware Valley economy and society.

That this region achieved a remarkable level of social peace and economic opportunity despite political turmoil can be better appreciated by comparing it with other British colonies. Virginia suffered through civil war with Bacon's Rebellion in 1676 and experienced further upheaval during the 1682 plant-cutter riots. Only at the end of the century, almost a century after its founding, did Virginia begin to achieve social stability. Massachusetts, having endured the upheavals of the Dominion of New England in the 1680s, found itself without a charter for three years. Unlike West Jersey, which peacefully lived through the same period without an established government, New England found itself convulsed in 1692 by the witchcraft trials. New York politics, suffering deep divisions between English and Dutch settlers, generated Leisler's Rebellion in 1689 and subsequent hangings of the losers in 1691.[21] The Delaware Valley, for all its political arguments, had no civil wars, no witchcraft hysterias, and no political hangings, nor would it up to the Revolution. Its settlers enjoyed relatively high levels of economic and social mobility while avoiding protracted food shortages and famines even in the earliest years of immigration.[22]

That immigration, so essential to Penn's economic plans, became both the cause and the effect of the Delaware Valley's success. During the first generation of Quaker rule, at least 23,000 Europeans of various ethnicities augmented the roughly 1,800 Dutch, Swedish, and Finnish settlers who had arrived before 1675. One early migrant noted in 1683 that "people come in so fast . . . about 1,000 people came in 6 weeks," which resulted in doubling the value of his land.[23] By 1685, Penn noted with pride that Pennsylvania held "a Collection of divers Nations in Europe: As, French, Dutch, Germans, Sweeds, Danes, Finns, Scotch, Irish and English; and of the last equal to all the rest: And which is admirable . . . they live like People of One Country, which Civil Union has had a considerable influence towards the prosperity of that place."[24] Coming from England, Ireland, Wales, Germany, and the Netherlands, Quaker immigrants themselves reflected this diversity. The proportions of the various groups changed over time, although it is believed that at no time did people of English descent ever constitute more than half the settlers. As of 1726, English and Welsh combined made up 60 percent of the European population; the rest were German (23 percent), Scots-Irish (12 percent), and Dutch or Scandinavian (5 percent).[25] Thereafter, the English percentage would decline as Germans and Scots-Irish poured into the Delaware Valley. Penn's encouragement of a diverse ethnic settlement, combined with the Quaker acceptance of religious pluralism (discussed later), created a climate that fostered remarkably little ethnic tension between 1680 and 1710.

Besides being divided ethnically, Quakers often fought among themselves over religious and political issues. Quakers in England had engaged in atomistic and anti-authoritarian behavior by, for instance, refusing to tip their hats to the social elite; this stance would not change simply by moving to a new region where Quakers were in control. Dissent within the Society of Friends and attempts by leading Quakers to instill discipline had been common from the beginning because of the "heterodox and argumentative" nature of the Society's membership.[26] Delaware Valley Quakers suffered through a divisive schism during the 1690s when George Keith called for greater doctrinal rigor, including a written creed. Keith built on previously existing grievances against Quaker leaders and acquired a following of perhaps a quarter of the Delaware Valley Quakers, concentrated among small farmers and merchants.

Such disputes naturally spilled over into a politics dominated by Quakers who had already engaged in "petty and acrimonious disputes among themselves and with others."[27] Besides the Keithian issues, Quakers divided themselves politically along ethnic lines and then into loose groupings, which hardened into parties that either favored or opposed the interests of the proprietor. They seemed to relish public participation, confrontation, and divisiveness as part of their religious duties, leaving Penn to rail against "scurvy quarrels that break out to the disgrace of the Province" and to plead that Quakers "be not so governmentish."[28] Despite their valleywide organization of hierarchical meetings for discipline, Quakers could not eliminate religious or political heterodoxy within their own ranks.

Perhaps the pluralism in Quakerdom enhanced their general commitment to tolerance and to treat a wide variety of Christian churches as legal equals. Mindful of the religious persecution Quakers had experienced, West Jersey's *Concessions* and Penn's *Laws* provided for freedom of conscience in the hope that all Protestants would live together peacefully.[29] Regardless of the theoretical relationship between church and state on such issues as oaths, Quaker pacifism, and the moral basis of criminal law, the practical result was a population that belonged to a wide variety of churches. Anglicans were perhaps the most prominent of the non-Quaker groups. Christ Church was founded in Philadelphia in 1696, and George Keith's conversion brought ex-Quakers into the Church of England. Anglicans played a substantial irritant role in Pennsylvania in their opposition to Quaker rule, and they achieved enhanced social and political status in West Jersey following the 1703 royal takeover of that colony.[30] Other substantial religious groups included Swedish and German Lutherans, Presbyterians, and Baptists. Later, Huguenots and a variety of German sects would join the mixture.[31] Compared with other British colonies, the Delaware Valley saw unparalleled diversity of religious adherents because of freedom of conscience.

What percentage of the settlers was Quaker as opposed to other denominations was unclear then and remains so today, partly because of the lack of a census and partly because of the ambiguity over who was a Quaker. Richard Vann's estimates are at the low end. He suggests that Quakers who were in touch with their meetings and conformed to the norms of the Society constituted only 10 percent (approximately two thousand) of all immigrants to Pennsylvania before 1700. Vann believes there were substantially more settlers who fell between adherence and hostility to the Society and that a majority of Delaware Valley Quakers were "made in America."[32] Nonetheless, his figures suggest substantially less than a majority of Pennsylvania residents—perhaps only a third—were Quakers. At the other extreme, J. William Frost contends that Quakers were "the overwhelming preponderance of the colonists" in the 1680s and 1690s and that non-Quakers had "no choice but to follow Friends' practices." Although this view reflects the consensus of past historians, Frost does not provide statistical support for his estimate.[33]

Taking a middle position, David Hackett Fischer tries to avoid defining the Quaker population precisely by contending that "the majority of these emigrants were either Quakers or Quaker sympathizers. . . . Together, these two groups of Quakers and Quaker sympathizers came to constitute a majority of English-speaking settlers in the Delaware Valley by the end of the seventeenth century."[34] By his own terms, Fischer's Quaker group might not have constituted a majority if the non-English speaking European settlers (German, Dutch, Scandinavian) were included. Furthermore, his dependence on the category "Quaker sympathizer" to support his finding that a Quaker majority existed prior to 1715 suggests that *members* of the Society of Friends were indeed a minority and illustrates the fluidity of religious attachments in the Delaware Valley. When this analysis is combined with known Quaker tendencies toward infighting and schism, it is probable Quakers could not claim that a majority of the Delaware Valley's first generation of settlers would submit to their rules and discipline.

Diversity of ethnicity and religion produced diversity of cultural and land-settlement patterns. Barry Levy has shown that Quaker families saw in their new land a chance to practice fully their ideals of child nurturing and domesticity. The quantity and quality of land available in the Delaware Valley allowed Quakers to combine their interest in profits with their doctrinal desires to ensure that their children adhered to the "Holy Conversation" of the Society of Friends. To provide for their sons' economic and spiritual well-being, Quakers followed strategies designed to acquire more land per family than their non-Quaker neighbors did.[35] Settlers of all faiths and strategies sought the best land for farmsteads and ended up living not in clusters of the like-minded but in dispersed rural farmsteads, often with neighbors of diverse backgrounds and cultures. Delaware Valley migrants had a high rate of short-distance geographic mobility, as settlers moved within the region to better their holdings. A majority of Quaker sons would be set up on land not contiguous with their parent's holdings but in a different town. This combination of cultural imperatives and "unruly individualism" resulted in a centrifugal pattern of land occupation that rapidly destroyed Penn's plans for corporate control over well-organized, tight-knit, communal townships. For such a diverse and dispersed society to achieve economic success and social peace, not just Quakers but all groups would have to go beyond mere tolerance. They would have to consent to some authority for resolving the inevitable disputes that would arise within groups, between individuals of different groups, and between individuals and the society's norms (however those norms might be set).[36]

The locus of that authority would lie not in the powerless townships or in the often divided and often paralyzed provincial governments. Rather, county courts, controlled by justices of the peace with the assistance of sheriffs, clerks, constables, highway overseers, grand and trial jurors, and a variety of lesser officers, would have jurisdiction over civil cases, criminal cases, and most administrative functions.[37] Control of these courts was supposed to remain with the Quakers who Penn believed were the "good men" of justice, mercy, and equity. Whatever the size of the Quaker population in either colony, the true effectiveness of the legal system would depend on whether the residents would grant the courts legitimacy through their active participation. From their own contentious history, Quaker leaders knew they could not expect unswerving loyalty from English Quakers; they could not possibly demand such loyalty from settlers of disparate ethnicities and religions. Only through voluntary participation could local courts, as instruments of Quaker government, achieve decision-making power over the population. If substantial numbers of the population, Quaker or non-Quaker, chose nonparticipation, the level of coercion available to the fledgling Delaware Valley governments was insufficient to force such recalcitrants into line. Only if individuals chose to bring cases, testify, prosecute, record deeds, serve their road-clearing duty, and accept the judgment of the court on these and other matters could titular Quaker authority be made real.

The idea that participation was necessary for local government to function was not new. English local government in the seventeenth and eighteenth centuries depended on the obligation of eligible males to serve regularly in some capacity. Included was an obligation among the propertied ranks to participate in prosecutions; in one shire in 1642, about half the eligibles were involved with the criminal courts. The compulsory nature of this system could break down, however, if the community was weak, the small population was dispersed and sometimes transient, and the demand for basic seventeenth-century governmental services—legal and otherwise (e.g., new highways and bridges)—was great.[38] Despite such limitations, British colonies sought to mobilize, if not compel, participation by "private persons to carry out public ends" in government and county courts. Studies of counties in colonial Maryland and Virginia have noted obligatory service and the widespread distribution of that service.[39] Furthermore, as with English quarter sessions, colonial county courts assembled the county residents and provided them cases that served as morality plays on court day. From Massachusetts to Virginia, courts wanted spectators from scattered farmsteads to view the organization of authority, to comprehend community norms and values, to accept the outcomes of civil and criminal cases as just, and to engage in the ceremonies and rituals that tied together the great and the small.[40] The need for voluntary participation of many sorts to legitimate courts was not confined to the Delaware Valley.

Yet three aspects of this need for legal participation distinguished the Delaware Valley. First, the pluralism of the initial settlers was more diverse than it was in any other colony and thus required that no group be excluded or even feel excluded, lest its omission or boycott bring on a social earthquake that diverse social faultlines suggested was possible. The insulation of Puritan Massachusetts from nonbelievers, the exclusion of freed servants from Virginia's polity, or the English dominance of the Dutch in New York could not be models for success in the Delaware Valley. Second, law would be critical to establishing social cohesion right from the start. While colonies like Virginia and Massachusetts would evolve certain levels of legal consensus to replace or modify their initial social order, the Delaware Valley founders and leaders consciously depended primarily on the rule of law to create social order.[41] Third, Quaker leaders had a sophisticated strategy for and understanding of the content of the rule of law that implemented English law-reform theories from their colonies' inceptions. The Delaware Valley was not alone in its interest in law reform; Massachusetts and Virginia adopted many reforms before West New Jersey and Pennsylvania existed. Those colonies, however, approached reform piecemeal, often as adaptations to local circumstances, which took years or decades to become recognized statutorily.[42] Only Quaker West Jersey and Pennsylvania codified a comprehensive set of law reforms for both civil and criminal issues at the outset of governance and maintained those reforms through the early years of settlement. These reforms, discussed at length later, enhanced the social significance of legal participation.

This study argues that the legal system of the Delaware Valley regulated and restrained the scope of social conflict among the region's diverse groups, thus providing the necessary stability that made the region's success possible. In much the same way David Konig described for Massachusetts, county courts integrated residents into the legal system by attracting their active participation in the real and symbolic applications of legal norms. The norms—the "good laws" of law reform—formed a legal ideology, a framework for resolving interpersonal disputes, defining and controlling deviants, and persuading those of different backgrounds and interests to accept the decisions of county courts. Whether as litigants, criminal defendants, witnesses, or mere spectators, those accepting the decisions conferred legitimacy on the decision-makers, who remained overwhelmingly Quaker (the "good men") in this plural society. The study also argues that the legal system of the Delaware Valley was manipulative. From the beginning to the end of legal processes, personnel choices, litigation choices, and prosecution choices reflected and reinforced the power of Quakers as the leaders of this region. Not merely integrative, the law established winners and losers through the choices of participants and decision-makers. Because of "good laws," the diverse society was willing, through continued participation, to ratify and legitimate Quaker leaders as "good men" who deserved to rule.

The analysis is based on an examination of the legal system from multiple perspectives. Multiple perspective analysis evaluates, for example, the demography of who held legal offices (a systemic perspective) as well as the chances members of various groups had of achieving office (a second perspective from the point of view of potential aspirants). Multiple perspective analysis looks at civil disputes in terms of the options available to disputants, the choices made, and the outcomes produced from the perspective of the litigants (which differed for plaintiffs and defendants) as well as the overall pattern of cases. For criminal matters, this approach evaluates patterns of accusation and conviction across demographic traits (a systemic perspective), but it also examines what chances members of various groups had of being charged and what alternatives they preferred among the choices available (the perspective of the criminal defendant). This study also examines the law from the perspective of the crowd that gathered on court day to discern what impact the case might have had on those spectators' assessment of the legitimacy of the system. Multiple perspective analysis of the choices available and the choices made illuminates the integrative and manipulative aspects of the law in the Delaware Valley.

The evidence for this study derives primarily from the court records from 1680 to 1710 of four counties that surrounded Philadelphia like a horseshoe.[43] To the north of Philadelphia lay Bucks County, and to the south was Chester County; in West Jersey, across the river from Philadelphia, were Burlington and Gloucester counties. From the beginning, the justices of the peace in these counties, sitting as courts of common pleas, had virtually unlimited original jurisdiction over civil cases arising under common law (including land issues). The same justices were given broad control over cases arising under equity, and in criminal matters, they sat as a court of quarter sessions and had power over all but specified capital offenses. Administratively, county courts raised and collected taxes, laid out and maintained roads, regulated servants' time and service, recorded land transactions, erected public facilities, cared for orphans, and licensed taverns, among other duties. Such governmental functions that required attendance at court created a large potential audience of residents to view civil and criminal cases.[44] Given such wide jurisdiction, county courts could see hundreds of settlers at the quarterly court days, when settlers in a county numbered in the hundreds. In the courts' quest for legitimate authority, the question was whether those people who came would empower the courts with real decision-making authority by participating in and accepting the outcome of cases.

Roads, essential to the prosperity of the dispersed farmers, provide one small example of how courts gained or lost authority through mobilizing residents. West Jersey and Pennsylvania courts first tried central control over road courses and construction by having the justices appoint committees or grand juries drawn from throughout the county to lay out the routes. This ineffective top-down method was quickly replaced with one that emphasized bottom-up participation. Local inhabitants would determine the road's path, and the course would be announced and confirmed publicly in court. Roads were built to meet local needs more quickly when locals participated, while courts retained symbolic authority through the court-day ceremony and delivered this essential public service at no public cost.[45] The limits of legal authority, however, appeared when courts tried to mandate road maintenance. County courts appointed overseers of the highways, who, in their yearly tour of duty, had to ensure that all residents performed their required days of road building and clearing. Those who failed to perform their road duty faced harsh criminal fines, but in reality, they rarely suffered. Instead, townships and sometimes even the whole county were cited for road neglect, without any individual liability; those individuals cited for nonperformance were almost invariably given a second chance without penalty.[46] Even on such important economic issues as roads, courts could rarely command obedience, but they could induce it through broad-based participation.

Legitimacy so conferred could just as easily be withdrawn, illustrating that the public attends to the quality of justice.[47] Dramatic shifts in court personnel can undermine confidence in the justice system, leading to nonparticipation on the part of the public and catastrophic losses of authority for the new officers. Such a shift and loss occurred in Gloucester County in 1698–99. In 1698, the new governor of West Jersey, Jeremiah Basse, replaced all Gloucester County's justices and sheriffs in a court that had had citizen participation and public acceptance. At the first court session under the new regime, all of Gloucester County's constables boycotted the proceedings. At the next session, all summoned jurors, whether veteran participants or newcomers, refused to serve. In December 1698, the new court officers, desperate to ensure participation, levied wholesale fines against those who refused jury duty. Despite this effort, by March 1699 the court still could not constitute a trial jury, because the recalcitrants claimed that the new sheriff was unlawful when he summoned them. By June 1699, Gloucester County's court was out of business. "For Sundry Considderations," the justices continued all the cases before them, repeating the blanket continuances in September and December. Only a new governor's return of three previous justices and the previous sheriff enabled Gloucester County's court to regain popular support and resume making decisions. Its first order of business in March 1700 was undoubtedly popular; the court suspended all criminal prosecutions from the previous regime, thinking "fitt to take no further notice thereof."[48]

This attempted use of criminal sanctions to compel public participation is part of a pattern sociologists of law have discovered. When a legal system and its personnel are seen as legitimate, public participation and compliance with court orders accord with self-interest and are voluntary; when legal personnel lose legitimacy, a higher percentage of court business will involve criminal sanctions at the expense of the civil docket. Using law to settle private disputes is an act with tremendous political implications. Litigation is a form of political participation that reflects individual choices and judgments about the decision-makers and serves to confer legitimacy on them.[49] Gloucester County's experience matched this theory. In 1697, thirteen civil cases were filed, but in 1698 and 1699, the filings dropped almost in half, to an average of seven cases per year. Upon the return of the old, legitimated personnel, the civil caseload reverted to its earlier level, with twelve cases in 1700 and thirteen in 1701. The ability to get individuals to use court processes to resolve their disputes was a clear marker for legitimacy.

This phenomenon of declining civil usage as a commentary on court personnel was also found in another study of seventeenth-century colonial law and society. David Konig observed that civil filings dropped in Essex County courts in Massachusetts from an average of 160.4 cases in 1680 to 1684 to 72.2 cases in 1685 to 1689. Konig suggests this 55 percent decline was partly because of legal changes instituted by the Dominion of New England, such as unfamiliar common-law procedures and higher costs; however, he found "demonstrable proof" for only one explanation for the decline in litigation: "the composition of the new bench." The newly appointed justices and clerk were not Essex residents, and their decisions caused "no little antagonism." When the appointed sheriff began choosing jurors instead of letting the town elect them, county residents lost both control of and trust in the legal system, and litigation declined. Only the overthrow of the Dominion's illegitimate legal system and legal personnel, Konig suggests, returned the role of law to its preeminent place in protecting the "contentious and well-ordered people" of Essex.[50]

The behavior of court personnel dominates a controversial theory of how the English elite of the eighteenth century maintained its hold without large doses of coercive force. Douglas Hay's paradigm required majesty, justice, and mercy in courtroom drama. Majesty meant elegant trappings and ceremonies so court officers could "impress the onlookers by word and gesture, to fuse terror and argument into the amalgam of legitimate power in their minds." Justice depended on courts' paying meticulous attention to procedural forms and regularities, convincing spectators that the law's "absurd formalism" could rein in the powerful. Mercy allowed courts to pardon half of the multitude sentenced to death, reinforcing paternalism, popular gratitude, and patronage connections. These parts composed "the rule of law," as outlined by John Brewer and John Styles: "'The law' was used as a standard by which to judge the just exercise of authority. Authorities therefore chose to limit themselves in order to acquire greater effectiveness: they traded unmediated power for legitimacy."[51]

This theory has been challenged regarding England.[52] Although this study takes no position on that controversy, it is clear that the Delaware Valley's elite possessed *none* of the elements Hay described as necessary in the English setting for legitimating authority. These courts lacked majesty because new justices were not disproportionately wealthy and had only recently settled. Other elements that supported the English elite, such as an established church or hierarchical relations extending back generations, were similarly lacking. Majesty in the courtroom itself suffered because of the general inability to get the newly arrived Pennsylvanians and Jerseyites to pay taxes for the construction and repair of courthouses and prisons.[53] As for "justice" consisting of "absurd formalism" and technicalities, this legal system demanded simple, easily understood processes (described below), aided and abetted by the absence of lawyers. As for "mercy" to be shown those about to be executed, very few judges had the opportunity to demonstrate it because reforms had so limited the applicability of the death penalty that few were condemned. Without these trappings of authority, and without the coercive force of the police or army (a true impossibility given Quaker pacifism), how would a Quaker legal elite gain legitimacy?

Although Delaware Valley Quakers lacked those props, they did believe generally in the rule of law. The idea of using legal rules to restrain the power of the legal elite came naturally to a sect that had often protected itself from prosecution by manipulating legal norms. Penn's jury acquittal in 1670, based on a defense that invited jurors to decide both law and facts, set the precedent that jurors could not be prosecuted for their verdicts.[54] Penn remained consistently dedicated to restraint of authority by the rule of law even when he was in power: "For the matters of liberty and privilege, I propose . . . to leave myselfe & successors noe power of doeing mischief, that the will of one man may not hinder the good of an whole country."[55] Yet Penn also believed his government had to be controlled by a select group of Quakers, those "good men." How could these elite Quakers convince average Quakers and non-Quakers alike that the rule of law ruled, that "good men" were so bound by the law that their judgments would be legitimate? The answer rested in changing the processes and substance of English law in the Delaware Valley. By creating a new set of "good laws" that would generate participatory incentives, the diverse settlers would have ample opportunity to observe and judge how the "good men" implemented the new procedures. This theory was well known, for it had been discussed in England for decades by Quakers and others. What would create a new rule of law was law reform.

The ferment of the English Civil War that had spawned the Society of Friends had also accelerated the movement for law reform. From 1640 to 1660, an extensive pamphlet literature promulgated a thorough critique of civil and criminal law and proposed massive changes. Levellers and lawyers alike participated in this debate, which was ultimately squelched by the Restoration and its triumph of conservative legal forces.[56] Partly out of self-defense, Quakers were well aware of the potential of law reform. Edward Byllynge, a Quaker who drafted West Jersey's first constitution and laws, wrote a leading pamphlet on law reform in 1659. In 1670, William Penn's defense that juries had the power to find both fact and law reflected the thinking of Leveller law reformers. The relentless prosecution of Quakers in the 1660s and 1670s left them with an appreciation of the English legal system's injustices and an intimate understanding of legal complexities.[57] Quakers were thus hardly legal primitives when they contemplated settling the Delaware Valley; instead, they possessed a well-considered legal agenda grounded in both reform theory and personal experience.

The best evidence for the influence of law reform on Quaker notions of governance exists in the initial laws passed for West Jersey and Pennsylvania. The *West Jersey Concessions* of 1676, to which Byllynge and Penn contributed after the Quaker takeover and which was promulgated in 1677 just prior to the Quaker migration to the Delaware Valley, Penn's *Laws Agreed upon in England* that accompanied his *Frame of Government* in 1682 prior to his embarkation, and *The Great Law* passed by Pennsylvania's first assembly in 1682 all revealed Quaker leaders to be the intellectual heirs of the law reformers of the English Civil War. Delaware Valley colonies adopted various law reforms, as indicated in Table 1. Despite Penn's theoretical preference for personnel over procedure, the acts passed for West Jersey and Pennsylvania manifested a belief that Quaker rule required "good laws" on legal procedure to help those "good men" achieve legitimacy.

The law-reform brief against English law was extensive, covering vast areas of the civil and criminal law. A prime goal was to make the law accessible to the average person, demystifying it and thus eliminating

Table 1. First Legislative Enactment of Law Reforms

	West Jersey	Pennsylvania
General legal process		
law in English		1682
law in plain language		1682
laws to be printed		1682
laws to be read regularly	1676	1682
local county courts handle cases	1676	1683
juries to be from neighborhood	1676	1682
jury verdict to be final	1676	1682
creation of land registry	1676	1682
popular election of justices		1682
justice arrived at openly	1676	1682
Civil law		
peacemakers/arbitrators	1682	1683
reduce technicalities		1682
allowed to plead own cause		
(no need to have lawyer)	1676	1682
small claims before justices out of court	1682	1683
fees set, to be moderate and posted	1681	1682
timetable for process and trial		1682
same court to handle law and equity		1684
Criminal law		
capital punishment only for		
murder and treason		1682
restitution as punishment	1676	1682
two witnesses to convict	1676	1682
right to jury trial	1676	1682
no prison fees	1676	1682

absurd formalities. Law reforms sought to eliminate Latin and Law French and replace them with English for all legal transactions. Oaths, required throughout the legal process, prohibited by Quaker dogma, and used to exclude Quakers in England, were replaced by affirmations.[58] The laws themselves were to be written simply and clearly, codified, put into books, and read aloud frequently. George Fox, founder of the Society of Friends, proposed all law be "drawn up in a little short volume, and all the rest burnt."[59] To simplify the law of land conveyancing, a registry of land ownership and transactions was to be kept. Justice was to be decentralized, because reformers decried the cost, time, and difficulty of trying most cases at Westminster. As part of that decentralization, juries were to be drawn from the neighborhood of the case, and civil and criminal jury verdicts, even when they decided both fact and law, had to be enforced by judges. Finally, reformers sought greater accountability in justice through electing judges and opening all courts to the public.[60]

Quaker laws followed these recommendations closely. Penn's *Laws* required "all Pleadings, Processes and Records in Courts shall be short, and in English, and in an ordinary and plain Character, that they may be understood." West Jersey followed this rule in practice, and subsequent Pennsylvania legislatures reaffirmed Penn's commitment. Byllynge's *Concessions* demanded a reading of the laws four times a year in the courts, while Pennsylvania required a yearly reading (but their laws were printed). Both provinces set up land registries and penalties for transactions not recorded within six months, and Pennsylvania extended this recording requirement to servants' indentures and commercial paper transactions (e.g., bonds) greater than five pounds. County courts were granted original jurisdiction over all civil and most criminal cases, and in Pennsylvania, the governor would choose the county's justices of the peace from a double list (twice as many names as spaces) elected by the residents. In the county courts, juries came from the neighborhood, their judgments were final, and justices were required to implement them. Finally, "that Justice may not be done in a corner nor in any Covert manner," the courts were to be open for all to attend.[61]

Particular practices in the trying of civil cases followed law-reform recommendations and served to make Delaware Valley legal dispute resolution easier for the average litigant to use. Simple forms in English of deeds, bills, arrests, summons, attachments, replevins, and execution were set forth in law to be copied and used by litigants, secure in the knowledge of their meaning, applicability, and enforceability.[62] Small claims, set at either twenty or forty shillings, did not even have to go to court but could be decided out of court by an individual justice of the peace, with the loser able to appeal to the full bench of justices at the next court day. In an attempt to reduce costs and avoid a potentially nasty battle in court, reformers wanted cases referred to arbitrators after they were filed; Pennsylvania tried to institutionalize this process by creating "peacemakers" in 1683 to arbitrate cases.[63] Lawyers were a particular bane to law reformers. Edward Byllynge criticized them as "terrible and law-less lawyers, under whose oppression the whole nation smarts," while George Fox referred to them as "black . . . like unto a black pit" and railed, "Away with those lawyers."[64] In the Delaware Valley, litigants could plead their own cause or have friends (regardless of legal train-ing) appear for them. No one was required to pay a lawyer to go to tri-al. Fees for English court officers (e.g., sheriffs, clerks, justices) in liti-gation were high, often based on a percentage of the award, and an invitation to corruption; Delaware Valley fees were to be moderate, fixed by legislation, and posted in court.[65] As for speed, Pennsylvania set strict timetables for processing cases and, while not abolishing the distinction between law and equity as reformers desired, required county courts of quarter sessions to serve in both roles.[66]

In the language of economists, Delaware Valley reforms reduced the information costs of resolving private disputes through law by simpli-fying legal language and forms. They reduced threshold costs by mak-ing lawyers less necessary (if not totally unnecessary), streamlining small claims procedures, and diverting some cases to arbitration. They reduced processing or transaction costs by reducing fees (and reducing court of-ficers' extortion of additional fees), establishing timetables that reduced delay, and breaking down the barrier between law and equity courts. When the price of a good declines, demand for it will rise. Both law reformers and Delaware Valley Quaker legislators knew that by reduc-ing legal costs and complexities, there was a danger of overuse; regis-tries were an attempt to reduce the need for litigation over land, ser-vants, and commercial transactions. Pennsylvania passed laws against malicious, repetitive suing (called barratry). Quakers held a doctrine against suing other Quakers, a rule more often honored than observed in the Delaware Valley.[67] The overall, and desired, result of reformed civil law, however, would be *more* opportunity for average disputants to litigate, resulting in *more* business for the legal system.

Law reformers and Quakers took on criminal law as well. One of their primary concerns was proportionality. Punishment should fit the crime to avoid, in George Fox's words, laws and lawyers "that will throw men into Prison for a thing of nought."[68] Most attention focused on the death penalty, especially for theft. Reformers believed that overly harsh penal-ties led to a breakdown in law enforcement and a subversion of the law by juries that would refuse to convict thieves or would undervalue goods stolen to avoid a death sentence.[69] The death penalty was therefore limited to treason and murder, and other crimes were punished by a combination of restitution, fines, whipping, and imprisonment. Restitution was set based on a multiple of the value of the property lost plus the nature of the offense; simple theft in West Jersey resulted in twofold restitution, while burglary in Pennsylvania required fourfold restitution and three months' imprisonment. Rape, sodomy, and bestiality, all capital crimes in England, were to be punished in Pennsylvania by whipping and imprisonment, while such moral offenses as swearing and drunkenness would receive fines. Prisoners were to be free of fees and humanely treated.[70] Until 1700, when Pennsylvania drastically toughened its punishments, the Delaware Valley had the most lenient penal policies in the English world.

As the Quakers implemented this new approach to criminal penalties, they also focused on ensuring procedural fairness. In line with the Bible, any conviction would require two witnesses.[71] All criminal trials would require a jury drawn randomly from the neighborhood pool, and defendants could challenge and remove jurors for cause and peremptorily (up to thirty-five peremptory challenges in West Jersey).[72] The victim of the crime could take over as "master" of the criminal process, not just to make sure the perpetrator was prosecuted but to "have full power to forgive and remit the person or persons offending."[73] Finally, Delaware Valley justices revitalized the common-law practice of requiring recognizances, or peace bonds, from those thought to pose a criminal threat. The conditions of the bond included the period for which the peace had to be kept, plus the specific sum of money to be forfeited by the defendants or their sureties if they misbehaved.[74] The bond would usually be pronounced on court day, adding public pressure to the monetary pressure. Peace bonds attempted to prevent crime and thus avoid full-blown prosecutions.

Quaker criminal law reforms were based on the belief that the criminal was reformable. Peace bonds, victim control of prosecution with its desire for conciliation, and restitution penalties were all efforts to resolve the problem in ways that repaired and rehabilitated deviants and their social relationships. In the event these methods failed, Quakers' experiences with English prosecution led them to increase the safeguards against innocents' being convicted, and, if the accused were guilty, to decrease the public's fear of conviction by reducing the penalties. In the same way that civil law reforms decreased the costs of taking disputes to court, so too criminal law reforms reduced the costs of prosecution to the victim, deviant, and society alike. When costs decline, in criminal no less than civil disputes, demand increases. By making the criminal law less absolute, less terrifying, and more focused on rehabilitation, Quaker law reforms sought to increase the range and amount of criminal business brought to court.

Until now, most colonial historians have not regarded the role of law, reformed or unreformed, as very important in explaining the success of the Delaware Valley colonies in general and the Delaware Valley Quakers in particular. Rather, two broad rationales for this region's long-term success under a Quaker elite have been proffered. The first concentrates on the alleged preponderance of Quakers in the early years of English settlement. According to this theory, Quakers held a substantial numerical majority, which gave them undisputed hegemony over Pennsylvania and West Jersey until at least 1700; under this Quaker rule, increasing social stratification and cultural dominance enabled a Quaker elite to consolidate its social, economic, and political power. The most recent exponent of this view has been David Hackett Fischer, who believes that despite the influx of "un-Friendly" immigrants after 1716, Quaker domination "continued long enough to imprint a large part of their culture and institutions upon this region." Quakers' role in law was that of social referee, administering primarily criminal laws to ensure the social peace created by the settlers' mutual tolerance for each other's rights.[75] Leaving aside whether there was in fact a majority of Quakers, this theory begs the question of how an elite within the Quakers established and maintained the support of average Quakers and non-Quakers to legitimate its rule. In short, Fischer has not answered why people chose to use the social referees they did, not just for criminal cases but also for civil disputes.

The other major rationale looks to cultural forces to explain Quaker control. Some historians, such as James Lemon, Mary Schweitzer, and D. W. Meinig, have explained it in terms of a cultural of individualism that centered on acquisitive influences and produced "dense networks of collective obligation" under the tolerant policies of Quakers. Alan Tully has looked at Quakers' political culture in the 1700s, finding their ability to act like a modern party key to resolving tensions and maintaining authority in the face of the growing non-Quaker majority. Barry Levy has combined many of these cultural forces in his comprehensive analysis of the Delaware Valley settlements. Levy believes that Quaker family practices, called "domesticity" and emphasizing land acquisition and grain farming, produced "a new kind of ruling American middle class which joined wealth, effective child-rearing, and spiritual innocence." By 1720, the Quakers' "acceptance of pluralism, disciplined privatism, child-centeredness, and wealth" had become a "trouble-free vehicle of early North American social, economic and political development." Because of the Quaker farmers' success in producing "virtuous and industrious children and significant wealth on the expanding frontier without expensive and corrupting institutions," non-Quakers, a majority of the population, supported Quaker hegemony for decades.[76] Levy recognizes that non-Quakers had a choice about whether to accept Quaker hegemony, but he skips over the choices of the first generation of Quaker and non-Quaker settlers, who, he believes, had relatively equal access to resources. Levy's approach cannot explain any legitimacy conferred on early Quaker governance, before the results of domesticity could have persuaded non-Quakers.

This book offers a third alternative to explain the relative social peace of the pluralistic Delaware Valley: the Quaker legal ideology—"good men" operating within the "good laws" of law reform—legitimated Quaker rule from the start. This approach does not depend on whether Quakers were a majority of the settlers at any particular time, nor does it depend on the long-term effects of domesticity. Rather, it depends on an analysis of alternatives available and the choices settlers made in using or not using the law to resolve disputes and control deviance. Law reforms, by encouraging use of the law in ways unavailable in England, created the fertile soil in the Delaware Valley for diverse and regular legal participation to grow. That initial choice to participate conferred power on the decision-makers; decision-makers' adherence to reformed processes perceived to be fair enhanced their legitimacy in the eyes of spectators and participants alike; and subsequent participation reflected a vote of confidence for that legal elite. The success of law was not the only buttress for Quaker rule, but it was the pivotal support, one that was established at the start and the only one of Penn's plans for Quaker governance that survived intact the political struggles of early West Jersey and Pennsylvania.

Choices in the use of law reveal not only the attitudes of participants toward the courts but also the attitudes of litigants toward each other and the attitudes of society toward certain behaviors. Such choices help reveal the relative social power of individuals and groups. The outcomes of such choices reveal how the law not only drew in participants but also made winners of some, made losers of others, and helped arrange compromises for still others. Process mattered but so did results, since certain Quakers managed to make choices within the law's boundaries that both reflected and reinforced their status. The meaning of such choices and outcomes, however, must always be placed in the context of the Quaker elite's overall quest for legitimacy. The subtle patterns of how settlers used the law and how the law used settlers reflected sophisticated strategies and complex relationships at every level of Delaware Valley society. As Roberto Unger has written, "each society reveals through its law the innermost secrets of the manner in which it holds men together."[77]

This analysis links people and power; it works at the intersection of social history and political/institutional history on those critical problems—interpersonal disputes and perceived deviance—which have the potential either to divide or to unite a society. Chapter 1 examines the diversity of the participants in this legal system and the attributes of the elite that occupied the positions of power. Chapter 2 focuses on the litigants—who chose to come to court to resolve disputes, who sued whom, and what the cause of the suit was. Chapter 3 then traces the choices of those litigants, closely examining every path to every type of outcome, to determine the strategies behind and the meaning of those choices and outcomes. Chapter 4 recognizes there were significant alternatives to courts for processing disputes. Quaker meetings took on the responsibility for resolving intra-Quaker disputes; chapter 4 brings the same analysis used for civil litigation to bear on the choices made in this alternative to law. Chapters 5 and 6 extend the analysis to criminal justice—who were the accused, what charges did they face, what choices did they make in confronting the charges, and what were the results? As with disputes, the parallel Quaker system for controlling acts considered deviant is analyzed, using the same methods as the criminal justice analysis.

The result is a comprehensive picture of a legal system that succeeded in roughly the way its founders intended. In Connecticut, it took until the eighteenth century for the formal legal system to establish its hegemony over how people resolved their differences. In Massachusetts, the same process took decades to overcome church and community-based decision-makers.[78] In the Delaware Valley, the law's dominance and the dominance of those in charge of the law were in place from the beginning. The "good laws" brought into court residents of all stripes, committing them to processes that protected social peace under Quaker rule. The "good men" of Penn's preamble, restrained from excess and exploitation by their new rule of law, maintained their hold on governance because of the legitimating participation of diverse groups. At the same time, these men subtly manipulated the law's choices to protect their status and position and that of their fellow Quakers. Finally, the law infiltrated and began to capture the Quaker alternatives, making the courts the first place to turn for intra-Quaker disputes and making the meeting processes less a choice and more an echo of the law. In the end, Penn did not have to choose between "good laws" and those he defined as "good men" to ensure social peace for his settlers. The Delaware Valley colonies had both.

The Demography of the Law

In the new Quaker legal system, John Hollinshead of Burlington County flourished. As a yeoman farmer, Hollinshead owned land and prospered in this fertile valley, accumulating by the time of his death in 1699 an estate of 541 pounds, which ranked in the top 20 percent of all inventoried estates during West Jersey's first fifty years. He was an active participant in the Burlington Men's Monthly Meeting of Quakers, performing so many of the tasks of arbitration, authority, and representation that he was certainly a leader in that meeting. Such activities in the Society of Friends would likely have marked him for jail in England and at least disqualified him from officeholding, but in the Delaware Valley he could also play a leading role in public life. From 1695 to 1699, he served his county as justice of the peace, a position English gentry strove for, which may account for his occasionally calling himself "gentleman." Before that stint, Hollinshead served as constable, overseer of highways, and representative to the provincial assembly. Six times he was a grand juror and twenty-one times a trial juror; nineteen times he was a civil plaintiff, twice he was sued, twice he was a witness, and three times he was a criminal defendant.[1] Here was a public man, by any standard a member of the legal elite of the Delaware Valley.

Few residents of the Delaware Valley participated in court as much as Hollinshead, but the number of those involved in the courts was large. As in other colonies, court days, which coincided with market days, "assembled the county" four times a year for legal and economic transactions essential to this nascent society.[2] Regularly appearing were such people as Francis White of Middletown, Bucks County, a solidly established landowning yeoman farmer of slightly above average wealth, a member of Middletown's Quaker meeting in the 1690s. White served on grand and petit juries; supervised highways and, as constable, over-saw behavior; he sued, was sued, and faced a criminal prosecution for not performing his highway duty.[3] White once sued another court reg-ular with very different attributes—James Allman of Bucks County, who was not a Quaker, or a landowner, or a legal officer, or a juror. Allman found his way to court primarily in adversarial roles, twice suing, three times as a criminal defendant (twice for assault), and seven times as a civil defendant.[4] Others made appearances much less frequently and left more elusive paper trails. In Chester County, Annakey Peterson, a Swede from Ridley, was called as a witness, while Mary Thorley, a servant in Concord, suffered prosecution for fornication in 1705, illustrating the two most common routes that brought women into the legal system.[5] Harry, "the Negro man Servant of Isaac Marriott" in Burlington Coun-ty, appeared once in court, to be tried and convicted for buggering a cow, but he avoided execution by escaping.[6] These six individuals, plus 3,776 others, participated in the legal process as officeholders, jurors, litigants, criminal defendants, and witnesses. Together, they constituted these four counties' *legal population.*

This legal population provides the most complete picture yet com-posed of the rural population around Philadelphia in the first genera-tion of English settlement. Its signal significance is that it allows statis-tically valid comparisons across a wide range of personal attributes (religion, occupation, landownership, wealth) and legal roles (officehold-er, juror, litigant, criminal defendant). In short, the legal population provides a baseline, a control group for examining the individuals, groups, and legal processes of this society. Nonetheless, the legal popu-lation is not a perfect reflection of the whole society. It significantly un-derrepresents certain groups of adults, omitting most women, servants, and slaves, who were generally denied participation in legal roles of au-thority. It includes some who were not residents, since suits could in-volve those from other counties, other colonies, or England. Finally, it does not identify those who, by choice or by chance, avoided the legal system entirely despite the efforts of Quaker law reform. These limits and biases notwithstanding, this legal population creates the most in-clusive base yet available for analyzing the residents of this region.

One way to measure how many Delaware Valley residents were in-cluded in this legal population is to examine the names of individuals on lists compiled for taxes and by Quaker meetings. Of Pennsylvania's 1693 tax list, which covered all property owners and freemen, 83 percent of the names listed in Bucks County and 90 percent of the names for Chester County participated in the courts. Those taxed members made up only 19.1 percent of all the legal population of Bucks and Chester counties from 1680 to 1710, indicating that the legal population identified a far wider range of the society than the tax list did. In 1699, 83 percent of the names on Chester County's tax list were members of the legal population.[7] Regarding Quaker participation in the legal system, 94 percent of the males who subscribed to the Chester Monthly Meeting in 1688 became legal participants, while in Burlington's Monthly Meeting the figure was 89 percent in 1683.[8] Clearly, free adult white males, whether Quaker, propertied, or not, participated in the legal system at extraordinarily high rates. This legal population thus almost completely incorporates that group and also covers all others who were legally active in this society.

With the legal population in place, it is possible to obtain not only absolute numbers but also statistical comparisons of various groups. Some personal attributes of the legal population can be determined fairly precisely: Quakers and non-Quakers; landowners and nonlandowners; men and women. For other attributes, unknowns must make the analysis more tentative and less precise: analysis of the occupation of males or the wealth of individuals (by tax list or inventory). Statistically valid comparisons examining which groups held which attributes are possible *within* the legal population, identifying not only gross numbers and percentages but also statistical significance using a measure known as *chi-square.*

When we compare the landownership of Quakers and non-Quakers, for example, it is not enough to know that 83 percent of identified Quakers owned land while only 41 percent of non-Quakers did. Chi-square determines whether that frequency distribution is *normal*—that is, whether the results mirror the population percentages in each category. If the chi-square probability is greater than .05, the distribution is regarded as normal, that is, within the range of results likely produced by chance as much as by design. If the chi-square probability falls below .05, however, the results are regarded as a statistically significant deviation from the normal predicted value. One can therefore conclude that the pattern is skewed or biased in some way; it is not produced by chance. In such a case, chi-square cell numbers identify which parts of the pattern deviated the most from a random distribution and whether that deviation was higher or lower than the expected result.[9] Only with this population comparison is it possible to conclude that Quakers in this legal population were disproportionately landowners and that non-Quakers were disproportionately nonlandowners. The statistic raises the inference that land distribution in this society was skewed; it does not explain why such statistical bias existed, which is the analytical job of the historian.

These personal attributes can then be matched against the distribution of authoritative positions within this system to determine whether statistical bias existed in the selection of legal personnel. There were three broad categories of such roles, presented here in descending order of importance. High legal officers—justices of the peace, court clerks, sheriffs, coroners, and attorneys general, plus provincial assemblymen and councillors—were the legal elite. They functioned with the most discretion, the most power, and the most authority in judicial and administrative matters in the county. Lesser officers—primarily constables and overseers of highways, plus tax officials, fence-viewers, packers, and rangers, who never attained a high office in this period—were the foot soldiers of the legal system. They were poorly compensated and had limited discretion, power, and jurisdiction; they often did not desire to serve in the office. At a third level of legal authority were the jurors, supposedly drawn at random from the freeman population of the county. Grand juries were responsible for taxing and administration as well as for presenting criminal violations, while trial juries decided contested criminal or civil cases.[10] The distribution of such offices and duties, examined for evidence of statistical bias between social groups, reveals who made it into the legal elite—and at what level—and who did not.

This chapter presents two portraits, one of the whole legal population and one of a subset, the legal elite. Since these colonies were founded by Quakers using the precepts of Quaker law reform, it comes as no surprise that the legal elite was Quaker; historians have long confirmed the predominance of Quaker leadership in the Delaware Valley, especially in Pennsylvania, long after the Quaker population had declined to a minority.[11] What is surprising is how soon Quakers became a minority in the population and how much legal control rested with a minority within that minority, the Quaker leaders. The exclusion of the vast majority of non-Quakers from positions of authority raises questions about how Quakers legitimized their rule, how they maintained the voluntary assent of their neighbors to a legal system that had packed bench and jury box with Quakers.

The Legal Population

Within the Society of Friends, membership was not a settled concept. For the purpose of identifying Quakers in the legal population, participation in a Quaker meeting as recorded therein or confirmation in a Quaker genealogical work was required.[12] Religion in Gloucester County could not be analyzed because its Quaker meeting records for this period have not survived. This definition obviously may undercount Quakers, but it does focus attention on Quakers who were active in their faith at some minimal level. This study has rejected the concept of Quaker sympathizers, whose numbers might pad the Quaker totals and who might have acceded genially to Quaker rule.[13] There is no empirical evidence or quantitative test for such a notion, and, as will become clear, Quakers identified here and non-Quakers had substantially different personal and legal profiles. Like membership, leadership within the meeting was not precisely defined, yet some men and women, like Hollinshead, were regularly appointed such positions as arbitrator of disputes, elder, overseer, treasurer, representative to other meetings, and clerk. Repeat appointments qualified one as a Quaker leader.[14] The legal population was thus divided into Quakers and non-Quakers, and within the Society of Friends, into average Quakers and Quaker leaders.

Information about other personal attributes was similarly gleaned, occasionally from the court records but more often from a variety of collateral sources.[15] Landownership was attributed to all individuals who appeared in a land transaction recorded in court; were noted in a road survey, petition, tax return, or probate record as having land; or appeared in a county's deed and survey book. Even though some might have avoided this recording net, those without such evidence of ownership were denoted nonlandowners. Occupation was the most difficult to trace and could be determined for only 51 percent of the males. Classification schemes for the recorded self-descriptions vary from historian to historian, but for purposes of this study they were divided into seven groups (see table 2).[16] As for wealth, only three tax lists survived for this period—Bucks County and Chester County in 1693 and Chester County in 1699. Although there were many inventories of wealth at death in Chester, Burlington, and Gloucester counties up to 1730, they covered only 25 percent of those counties' legal population. These sources all have substantial biases and many unknowns. Wealth analysis is therefore limited to the slice of the population whose wealth can be identi-

Table 2. Attributes of the Legal Population, by County

Attributes	Bucks	Chester	Burlington	Gloucester	Total
Women (%)	7.4	11.2	11.0	7.4	9.9
Men (%)	92.6	88.8	89.0	92.6	90.1
n	705	1289	1288	500	3782
Quakers (%)	40.3	36.7	40.8	—	39.1
Non-Quakers (%)	59.7	63.3	59.2	—	60.9
n	705	1289	1288		3282
Quaker leaders (%)	9.9	14.7	9.0	—	11.4
Average Quakers (%)	30.4	22.1	31.8	—	27.7
n	284	473	525		1282
Landowners (%)	59.3	57.1	56.9	61.2	58.0
Nonlandowners (%)	40.7	42.9	43.1	38.8	42.0
n	705	1289	1288	500	3782
Occupations (males only)					
Farmer (%)	53.1	51.4	44.6	49.3	49.0
Artisan (%)	16.8	17.6	21.4	14.6	18.3
Farmer-artisan (%)	8.4	5.9	11.3	9.3	8.9
Merchant (%)	8.7	7.6	9.0	8.6	8.5
Self-described gentry (%)	2.7	6.1	5.1	10.0	5.6
Servant/slave/ laborer (%)	7.3	6.5	3.7	2.9	5.1
Other (%)	3.0	5.0	4.9	5.4	4.6
n	369	461	630	280	1740
1693 Pennsylvania tax assessment (in pounds)					
100+ (%)	16.5	12.9	—	—	14.2
50–99 (%)	24.1	14.5	—	—	17.8
1–49 (%)	59.4	72.6	—	—	68.0
n	133	248			381
Inventoried wealth (in pounds)					
500+ (%)	20.3	21.0	18.6	14.9	19.0
100–499 (%)	64.4	55.2	56.7	57.0	56.8
1–99 (%)	15.3	23.8	24.7	28.1	24.2
n	59	252	328	114	753

fied. Furthermore, by dividing the wealth values into three broad wealth groups, the problems associated with means are avoided; the impact of large disparities of wealth on legal behavior can thus be identified.[17] Finally, the easiest attribute to identify was gender, done from first names, which revealed that less than 10 percent of the legal population was female. Because women were excluded from authoritative roles and only a few owned land, were taxed or left inventories, statistical analysis of gender must be confined to an examination of women's civil and criminal case participation in later chapters.

Quakers constituted 39 percent of the legal population, and 11 percent of the legal population (29 percent of the Quakers) were Quaker leaders. As is apparent in table 2, the percentages of Quakers and Quaker leaders were similar across county lines, reaffirming the notion of a regional culture. The population percentage agrees with estimates made regarding Philadelphia's Quaker population in the 1690s (40 to 42 percent), with a census of all West Jersey in 1699 (32 percent Quaker, including Gloucester, Salem, and Cape May), and with a claim by Anglicans in 1701 that non-Quakers outnumbered Quakers throughout Pennsylvania. It also agrees with Richard Vann's estimate that only a minority of Pennsylvania immigrants, perhaps as low as 10 percent, were British Quakers in good standing.[18] Other historians, however, have regularly estimated that the Quaker population in the Delaware Valley during this period was much higher. For example, Chester County was supposedly almost entirely Quaker; West Jersey was virtually all Quaker at the start (declining to one-half in the early 1700s); overall a majority of inhabitants were Quakers or Quaker sympathizers (lasting perhaps through the first forty years of settlement); and this "overwhelming preponderance" meant that those who were "not Quakers had no choice but to follow Friends' practices."[19] If true, Quakers' ability "to imprint a large part of their culture and institutions upon this region" is easily explained as a function of time and numbers.[20]

These high estimates are erroneous, though. The legal population indicates clearly that Quakers identifiable through meeting records had lost whatever numerical advantage they might have had within the first generation of settlement. Even if the total number of Quakers were undercounted by 25 percent, they would still not represent a majority of the legal population. To conclude that Quakers nonetheless constituted a majority of the population would require accepting one of two assumptions. First, Quakers could be massively underrepresented if one assumes a higher percentage of Quakers than non-Quakers avoided the legal system. Given identified Quakers' rates of landownership and participation in offices, juries, litigation, and criminal cases (described later), which are equal to or greater than the rates of those identified as non-Quakers, it is not plausible to assume that other Quakers avoided the legal system at a rate greater than non-Quakers. A second assumption would be that a high percentage of Quakers somehow avoided being registered in meeting records. Although these early meetings were often haphazard in their record-keeping, to accept this assumption would mean that the dragnet of birth, death, marriage, census, certificates of good standing, "clearness" for marriage (i.e., they are Quakers in good standing and not married to anyone else), and meeting participation records the Society of Friends created missed a large number of silent, uninvolved, backbench Quakers. That some were missed is probable; that enough were missed to account for a Quaker majority in this first generation is improbable. Furthermore, it is implausible that backbenchers that had (at best) tenuous allegiance to the Society of Friends would be reliable supporters of Quaker power. The explanation for Quaker political, cultural, and legal dominance must therefore lie elsewhere: in a mixture of power, organization, and legitimized authority.

Analysis of other attributes of the legal population tends to challenge some established views regarding early Delaware Valley settlers. Landownership was indeed widespread (58 percent of the legal population owned land), yet only 49 percent of the males described themselves as engaged solely in farming (yeoman, husbandman, or planter). At the other end of the occupational spectrum, only 5 percent were described as servants, slaves, or free laborers, a number far lower than other historians' estimates; those whose occupations were unknown probably account for this difference.[21] Artisans, at approximately 18 percent of the legal population, formed the second largest occupational group. The rest of the occupational distribution reveals an economy in which residents often pursued more than one occupation. Almost 9 percent of the legal population practiced both agricultural and artisanal arts, while about half the merchants and self-described gentry (primarily "gentleman") also had farming pursuits. The "other" category, about 5 percent of the legal population, includes innkeepers, millers, and other professions, revealing a small service sector. Despite, or perhaps because of, this diversification, extremes of wealth were rare compared with England's. The vast majority of the taxed and inventoried fell into the middle and lower brackets, which were not that far removed from the wealthiest. The question to be answered now is whether landownership, occupation, and wealth were distributed evenly across the population.

Between and within religions, those assets were clearly not randomly distributed (see table 3). Quakers were the clear winners in the scram-

Table 3. Comparison of Quakers and Non-Quakers

Attributes	Quakers	Non-Quakers
Total *n*	1282	2000
Percentage of total	39.1	60.9
Landowners (%)	83.0	41.2
Nonlandowners (%)	17.0	58.8
n	1282	2000
Chi-square probability = .000		
Occupations (males only)		
Farmer (%)	53.4	42.9
Artisan (%)	17.0	21.8
Farmer-artisan (%)	12.5	3.9
Merchant (%)	8.0	9.2
Self-described gentry (%)	3.9	5.9
Servant/slave/laborer (%)	2.4	9.6
Other (%)	2.8	6.7
n	837	623
Chi-square probability = .000		
1693 Pennsylvania tax assessment (in pounds)		
100+ (%)	15.5	11.1
50–99 (%)	18.6	16.2
1–49 (%)	65.9	72.7
n	264	117
Chi-square probability = .386		
Inventoried wealth (in pounds)		
500+ (%)	24.2	11.2
100–499 (%)	57.3	54.3
1–99 (%)	18.4	34.5
n	374	206
Chi-square probability = .000		

Table 3, continued

Attributes	Quakers	Non-Quakers
Legal roles		
High officer (%)	19.7	3.3
Lesser officer (%)	35.3	16.3
Nonofficer (%)	44.9	80.5
n	1282	2000
Chi-square probability = .000		
Grand juror (%)	55.3	16.4
Never grand juror (%)	44.7	83.6
n	1282	2000
Chi-square probability = .000		
Trial juror (%)	50.2	16.2
Never trial juror (%)	49.8	83.8
n	1282	2000
Chi-square probability = .000		

ble for land in the Delaware Valley, acquiring real estate over twice as often as non-Quakers, a statistically significant difference as measured by chi-square. Part of the explanation for that difference can be seen in the different occupational distributions between Quaker and non-Quakers; a disproportionate number of Quakers were farmer-artisans, while a disproportionate number of non-Quakers were servants/slaves/laborers. Other less significant differences found non-Quakers to be farmers less often and artisans more often than Quakers were, which also contributed to non-Quakers' lower rate of land acquisition. An additional explanation, derived from a much smaller survey of Quaker and Anglican families in the Delaware Valley that had similar initial assets, suggests that Quaker "domesticity" regarding providing for children led them to invest more heavily in land and by so doing to become more prosperous than Anglican families.[22] Yet such an explanation would account for disparities only after a generation of accumulation; this difference in landownership occurred in the first thirty years. Such a discrepancy, appearing so quickly, meant that non-Quakers and Quakers could not have started out with equal access to land. One need only note that for non-Quakers the combined farmer and farmer-artisan percentage (46 percent) is higher than their landowning percentage (41 percent), suggesting that some non-Quaker farmers could not obtain their own land. Figures for Quakers, on the other hand, indicate 66 percent were in farming and 83 percent owned land, suggesting they had no trouble obtaining land. From the outset, more Quakers than non-Quakers had access to land and the opportunity it provided.

That this disparity might have had significant long-term implications for wealth is apparent from the tax and inventory brackets. Quakers and non-Quakers fell into a statistically identical pattern in the 1693 tax, but by the time of death some years later, Quakers left their heirs disproportionately large estates while non-Quakers' estates fell disproportionately into the lowest bracket. Put another way, Quakers owned 80 percent of the top-bracket estates. This pattern occurred despite the fact that non-Quakers claimed to be merchants and members of the gentry more often than Quakers did, occupations that produced disproportionately large estates, as is discussed more fully later. The statistically significant occupational disparities must also have influenced opportunities for wealth acquisition. Between diversification of income opportunity, the overwhelming Quaker advantage in obtaining land (perhaps a result of Quakers' having greater assets on arrival than non-Quakers had), and the use of a primarily non-Quaker bound-labor force, Quakers might not have needed much "domesticity" to prosper.[23] Social and legal power, whether brought or acquired, produced a multitude of skewed opportunities favoring Quakers, regardless of any other strategies.

Such differences in opportunity persisted within the meetinghouse as Quaker leaders significantly outstripped average Quakers economically (see table 4). Delaware Valley Quakers never lost their belief in hierarchy, and traditional English notions of wealth as a precondition for leadership seem to have been applied.[24] Quaker leaders owned land at a significantly higher rate and more often died possessing a relatively large estate than average Quakers did; nearly half (48 percent) of all estates valued at over 500 pounds belonged to Quaker leaders. In terms of occupation, the most statistically significant difference between average and leading Quakers lay in the farmer-artisan category. Quaker leaders were almost twice as likely to be farmer-artisans than average Quakers were. In contrast, Quaker leaders were only slightly more likely to be farmers than were average Quakers and were less likely to be simply artisans, while they were just as likely to call themselves merchants or gentry.

Table 4. Comparison of Quaker Leaders and Average Quakers

Attributes	Quaker Leaders	Average Quakers
Total *n*	374	908
Percentage of Quaker population	29.2	70.8
Landowners (%)	94.4	78.3
Nonlandowners (%)	5.6	21.7
n	374	908
Chi-square probability = .000		
Occupations (males only)		
Farmer (%)	57.4	51.3
Artisan (%)	9.6	20.9
Farmer-artisan (%)	17.9	9.7
Merchant (%)	7.2	8.4
Self-described gentry (%)	3.8	4.0
Servant/slave/laborer (%)	1.0	3.1
Other (%)	3.1	2.6
n	291	546
Chi-square probability = .000		
1693 Pennsylvania tax assessment (in pounds)		
100+ (%)	18.1	12.5
50–99 (%)	20.8	15.8
1–49 (%)	61.1	71.7
n	144	120
Chi-square probability = .193		
Inventoried wealth (in pounds)		
500+ (%)	33.8	17.2
100–499 (%)	55.6	58.6
1–99 (%)	10.6	24.2
n	159	215
Chi-square probability = .000		
Legal roles		
High officer (%)	40.1	11.3
Lesser officer (%)	42.3	32.5
Nonofficer (%)	17.7	56.2
n	374	908
Chi-square probability = .000		

Grand juror (%)	81.3	44.6
Never grand juror (%)	18.7	55.4
n	374	908
Chi-square probability = .000		
Trial juror (%)	71.9	41.2
Never trial juror (%)	28.1	58.8
n	374	908
Chi-square probability = .000		

Furthermore, as noted later, farmer-artisans whose wealth can be identified were not significantly richer than farmers or artisans separately, so extra wealth was not likely to be the hidden factor here. Quakers seem to have valued economic diversification in their leadership as much as they did their accomplishments as grain farmers.[25] Whether leadership was related to the avoidance of being disciplined by the meeting on certain issues will be examined later, but it is clear that wealth and occupation played a large role in establishing the Quaker elite within the membership.

If the landed are compared with the nonlanded, Quaker advantages stood in stark relief (see table 5). The majority of landowners (56 percent) were Quakers, which, under English tradition and political principles that lacked religious disqualifications, advanced them over the first threshold in obtaining authoritative positions. The vast majority of nonlanded (84 percent) were non-Quakers, revealing again the skewed na-

Table 5. Comparison of Landowners and Nonlandowners

Attributes	Landowners	Nonlandowners
Total *n*	2193	1589
Percentage of total	58.0	42.0
Quakers (%)	56.4	15.6
Quaker leaders (%)	18.7	1.6
Average Quakers (%)	37.7	14.1
Non-Quakers (%)	43.6	84.4
n	1889	1395
Chi-square probability = .000		

Table 5, continued

Attributes	Landowners	Nonlandowners
Occupations (males only)		
Farmer (%)	52.3	22.0
Artisan (%)	17.7	23.6
Farmer-artisan (%)	10.0	0.0
Merchant (%)	8.3	10.0
Self-described gentry (%)	5.3	8.4
Servant/slave/laborer (%)	2.9	22.5
Other (%)	3.5	13.6
n	1549	191
Chi-square probability = .000		
1693 Pennsylvania tax assessment (in pounds)		
100+ (%)	14.9	4.2
50–99 (%)	18.5	8.3
1–49 (%)	66.7	87.5
n	357	24
Chi-square probability = .103		
Inventoried wealth (in pounds)		
500+ (%)	20.0	4.3
100–499 (%)	57.4	48.9
1–99 (%)	22.7	46.8
n	706	47
Chi-square probability = .000		
Legal roles		
High officer (%)	16.7	1.7
Lesser officer (%)	31.0	11.2
Nonofficer (%)	52.3	87.1
n	2193	1589
Chi-square probability = .000		
Grand juror (%)	48.3	13.0
Never grand juror (%)	51.7	87.0
n	2193	1589
Chi-square probability = .000		
Trial juror (%)	44.6	10.0
Never trial juror (%)	55.4	90.0
n	2193	1589
Chi-square probability = .000		

ture of opportunity in the Delaware Valley. As might be expected, the majority (52 percent) of the landed were farmers, although 22 percent of the nonlanded also called themselves farmers, possibly because of squatting, tenancy, or underrecording of land transactions. Not surprisingly, the groups most often without land were artisans and servants/slaves/laborers, the latter group perhaps further disadvantaged by its preponderance of non-Quakers. Also unsurprisingly, landownership and inventoried wealth had a statistically significant relationship; landowners were almost five times as likely to be in the top bracket of estates, and nonlandowners were twice as likely to be in the lowest bracket. Although analysis of chances for mobility in terms of groups acquiring land later is not possible using this cross-sectional analysis, clearly the benefits of this fertile region were unevenly distributed in its first thirty years.

The final attribute examined in this portrait of the legal population was self-described occupation (see table 6). Quakers and Quaker leaders were disproportionately farmer-artisans, again reflecting an interest within the Society of Friends in occupational diversity. Non-Quakers made up three-quarters of the servants/slaves/laborers group, underlining the class distinctions associated with religion. Most interesting was that a majority of those describing themselves as gentlemen were non-Quakers, perhaps indicating a need to bolster non-Quakers' titular status in the absence of real authority. In terms of land, every identified farmer-artisan owned some, while only 51 percent of the servants/slaves/laborers ever owned any. Merchants, who might seem to have the least need for land, nonetheless owned land at a rate behind only farmer-artisans and farmers. These merchants were the most likely to own estates of five hundred pounds or more at death, while artisans were the most likely non-bound occupation to die poor. As with religion, Quaker leadership, and land, one's occupation influenced one's economic and social opportunities in statistically significant ways.

The critical brushstrokes on the portrait of the legal population are now in place. Despite their rapid decline from majority to minority status (if indeed they ever were a majority), Quakers held economic advantages disproportionate to their numbers. Within the meetinghouse, the minority of Quakers chosen to lead their Society of Friends held a larger share of those benefits, leaving average Quakers often little better off than their non-Quaker neighbors. To understand how such advantages translated into tangible positions of legal power requires painting a second picture using the same palette, a portrait of the legal elite within

Table 6. Comparison of Occupations

Attributes	Farmers	Artisans	Farmer-Artisans	Merchants	Self-described Gentry	Servant/Slave/Laborer
Total n	852	319	155	148	98	88
Percentage of total	49.0	18.3	8.9	8.5	5.6	5.1
Quakers (%)	62.6	51.1	81.4	54.0	47.1	25.0
Quaker leaders (%)	23.4	10.1	40.3	16.9	15.7	3.8
Average Quakers (%)	39.2	41.0	41.0	37.1	31.4	21.3
Non-Quakers (%)	37.4	48.9	18.6	46.0	52.9	75.0
n	714	278	129	124	70	80
Chi-square probability = .000						
Landowners (%)	95.1	85.9	100.0	87.2	83.7	51.1
Nonlandowners (%)	4.9	14.1	0.0	12.8	16.3	48.9
n	852	319	155	148	98	88
Chi-square probability = .000						
1693 Pennsylvania tax assessment (in pounds)						
100+ (%)	15.3	2.9	13.3	62.5	50.0	0.0
50–99 (%)	20.9	20.0	13.3	0.0	37.5	0.0
1–49 (%)	63.8	77.1	73.3	37.5	12.5	100.0
n	163	35	30	8	16	14
Chi-square probability = .000[a]						

Inventoried wealth (in pounds)						
500+ (%)	15.4	5.9	22.7	50.0	47.2	0.0
100–499 (%)	66.0	47.1	61.4	44.4	41.7	22.2
1–99 (%)	18.6	47.1	15.9	5.6	11.1	77.8
n	312	85	88	54	36	9
Chi-square probability = .000						
Legal roles						
High officer (%)	17.5	6.9	28.4	30.4	58.2	1.1
Lesser officer (%)	37.1	31.7	33.6	6.1	4.1	19.3
Nonofficer (%)	45.4	61.4	38.1	63.5	37.8	79.6
n	852	319	155	148	98	88
Chi-square probability = .000						
Grand juror (%)	57.3	44.8	71.6	19.6	35.7	25.0
Never grand juror (%)	42.7	55.2	28.4	80.4	64.3	75.0
n	852	319	155	148	98	88
Chi-square probability = .000						
Trial juror (%)	52.2	43.6	68.4	18.9	28.6	23.9
Never trial juror (%)	47.8	56.4	31.6	81.1	71.4	76.1
n	852	319	155	148	98	88
Chi-square probability = .000						

a. Chi-square may not be a valid test because more than 20 percent of the cells have expected counts of less than 5.

the legal population. In the dispersed settlements of the rural Delaware Valley, the legal officers of court and county had to resolve disputes, punish deviance, and produce governmental functions despite lacking sufficient resources to compel compliance. Who the legal elite were and how they performed their duties would provide the foundation for legitimizing Quaker rule.

The Legal Elite

By the seventeenth century, the ancient office of justice of the peace had reached its high point of power and prestige in the counties of England; it was a high legal office signifying legal elite status. Drawn from the local gentry and relied on by the Crown as a bulwark against disorder, justices of the peace had increased their summary jurisdiction over minor criminal offenses, had regulated behavior by requiring bonds to keep the peace, had expanded their control over local government, and had displaced many manorial courts. They were under constant political pressure from central authorities who wished to control their autonomy (often by wholesale replacement) and from other local gentry who either competed to replace the justices or desired patronage positions.[26] In the colonies, justices of the peace were central to county courts and governments from New England through the Chesapeake to North Carolina. As colonies increased the justices' power by adding civil jurisdiction to criminal and administrative roles, it was not surprising to find intense political competition for these powerful positions. Furthermore, colonial governors sought to use justices to implement central policies, paralleling contemporary English institutional development.[27] The Delaware Valley's founders could build on a long institutional history on both sides of the Atlantic when they made justices of the peace the linchpins of their legal system.

A variety of formal and informal sources existed to educate these untrained selectees for the proper performances required of a legal elite. From England came manuals and form books, such as Michael Dalton's *The Countrey Justice* and Richard Chamberlin's *The Complete Justice,* reference works that would later be edited, published, and circulated intercolonially.[28] More directly, both Pennsylvania and New Jersey required justices to attest to do "equal right to the poor & rich" and not to be "Counsel of any matter or cause depending before thee" or to sit on their own cause; litigants successfully removed justices who had taken sides before trial.[29] In pursuit of regularity and impartiality, both colonies promoted behavioral propriety among justices, prohibiting them from granting licenses outside of court and fining them double for drunkenness or absence from court. Such efforts were not always successful, since sessions sometimes lacked a quorum and some justices drank and abused their authority.[30] In session, Delaware Valley justices served with mixed competence. They ruled complaints failed to state a legal cause of action (but once took two years to decide this, and in another instance handed the case back to attorneys to arbitrate), aided juries in construing laws (a difficult proposition when justices occasionally lacked copies of the laws), and served as a court of equity.[31] Their most important informal responsibility was political, for shifts in central governments often resulted—as in England—in wholesale personnel replacements; one new group of justices in Gloucester County decided "to take no further notice" of the actions of their predecessors.[32] The role of justice demanded that justices adhere to formal legal norms and possess political skills; it was never so simple or primitive as the story of a New Jersey justice holding court on the tree stumps in his meadow might have suggested.[33]

Delaware Valley justices shared certain attributes. In both West Jersey and Pennsylvania, the people initially had a role, at least on paper, in electing justices, but in practice justices were appointed by representatives to provincial assemblies and by governors.[34] Virtually all were landowners (96 percent) but so was the majority of this legal population, so, unlike England, land was not so determinative of office. The critical attribute was religious leadership: 50 percent were Quaker leaders, and another 29 percent were average Quakers, making 79 percent of the justices Quaker. The Quaker dominance was so pronounced that from 1683 (after Penn was fully established) until 1703 (when West Jersey was ceded to the Crown), there were only 10 non-Quakers out of a total of 134 justices. Moreover, these non-Quakers often did not stay on the bench as long; non-Quakers served 3.4 years on average, while Quaker leaders averaged 5.8 years.

Just as leadership in the Society of Friends aided one's chance to become a justice, so too did wealth, suggesting that the quantity of land and other personal property mattered. Fifty percent of those whose taxable Pennsylvania property was 100 pounds or more in 1693 served as justices; however, 5 percent of those with 50 pounds or less also served (all were Quakers). Fifty-six percent of justices were assessed at 100

pounds or more, roughly four times the legal population's average, meaning that 44 percent were assessed at under 100 pounds. Large amounts
of wealth helped gain an appointment, but they were clearly not abso-
lutely necessary or sufficient. Such non-Quakers as George Heathcote
and Henry Marjorum, who had the second and fifth highest taxable estates in Bucks County, were left off the bench, while in Chester County, James Sandilands, Jr., a non-Quaker who had the fourth highest assessment, also never became a justice. Regarding inventories, the
relationship between wealth and being a justice was similar; 45 percent
of justices but only 19 percent of the population died owning estates
valued at more than 500 pounds. The average justice's wealth was almost double that of the population average.[35] As with taxed wealth, rich
non-Quakers found it difficult to obtain appointments; Israel Taylor and
John Nields, Chester County's richest non-Quakers, who had estates of
1,744 and 851 pounds, respectively, did not become justices. At the other end, poor non-Quakers had virtually no chance of becoming justices, even though a few poor Quakers could. Wealth added years to one's
tenure on the bench, but it added more to Quakers' tenure; rich Quaker leaders averaged 8.2 years, while rich non-Quakers averaged only 5.7
years. The amount of land and property one owned was relevant to appointment, but not nearly as important as religion.

As for the source of that wealth, justices claimed gentry and merchant
professions far more often than did the general population. Yeomen and
artisans made up barely 50 percent of the justice population, and Chester
County never seated someone who claimed merely artisanal pursuits.
Those claiming gentry status at some point (the court records do not
refer to them as gentlemen merely because they appeared on the bench)
constituted 28 percent of justices (five times their population percentage), while merchants claimed 18 percent of the seats (more than double their population percentage). Some, but not all, of the Delaware
Valley's justices were proclaiming themselves an elite.

Court officers were a second type of high officer. Their performance
often determined the success or failure of a legal action and thus a resident's perception of the courts. Clerks of the court not only recorded
events in court but also drew up the warrants, summonses, arrests, and
attachments in civil and criminal cases; they entered all civil complaints,
answers, appeals, bonds, and transcripts and acknowledged every valid
deed in the court records.[36] Inadequate clerks who lost bonds or kept
poor records threatened the administration of justice, in one case lead-

ing to the loss of a litigant's chance for an execution on the goods of his defaulting debtor.[37] Competent clerks, such as Phineas Pemberton, who was Bucks County's clerk for sixteen years, acquired such additional offices as recorder of deeds and register of wills and in the process earned statutory fees for their services.[38] Without formal legal training, clerks relied on statutes, attorneys, and their own experience to provide proper legal forms, become repositories of legal information, and mediate many legal problems.[39]

Pemberton's performance as clerk showed his critical role and his talent for mediation. John Tatham, a contentious landowner on both sides of the river, wrote Pemberton asking him to draft a declaration against Claus Johnson for impugning his land title in Bucks County. Tatham knew it should be cast as an action in trespass, but he wanted Pemberton's legal talent "because I would have my Worke well done . . . knowing you to be the only Person in all that County capable to serve in that fashion."[40] Similarly, Pemberton was consulted on the validity of a will, was regarded by the attorney David Lloyd as the most competent person to arbitrate a land dispute, and was asked by Joseph Growden to draw up a deed when Growden feared that he would not get a good title.[41] In other cases, Pemberton used his position to delay having disputes become lawsuits. He slowed a case against his cousin Joseph Pemberton on the pretext that he would not enter the action without ready money from the plaintiff's attorney. In another instance, Pemberton told a plaintiff to forbear suing on his bond because the defendant would soon pay; however, the plaintiff was not paid and sent an angry letter to Pemberton demanding that he now file the suit. In a third case, Pemberton delayed filing papers from an absent plaintiff against Jacob Hall to aid Hall, but when the plaintiff returned Pemberton hurriedly wrote Hall that he should pay within twenty days.[42] As a clerk, Pemberton was far more than a scrivener; he was both a mediator and a translator of people's needs into the proper legal forms necessary to resolve problems.

A second court officer, the sheriff, implemented decisions made by litigants and the court, using papers often drawn by the clerk. Sheriffs selected the jury pool, made arrests, served summonses, executed judgments, and ran elections. Statutory fees, covering every action entered, judgment made, execution ordered, appeal desired, and prisoner discharged, made the office extremely lucrative; in one case in Bucks County, the sheriff's fees totaled nearly twenty-five pounds.[43] Like all law officers, sheriffs often encountered hostility from unwilling subjects of the legal process. In 1694, Burlington County's sheriff Thomas Bibb pursued a fleeing prisoner to Jacob Perkins's house. When he identified himself as "their Majesties Officer" and charged Perkins to aid him, Perkins declined, stating "thou the Sheriffe, thou a turd" and thrusting a fist in Bibb's direction. (Perkins was convicted and fined fifty pounds for this contempt, but the fine was suspended.)[44] Sheriff Christopher Wetherill went to serve a summons on Thomas Roberts. Not finding anyone on the obviously inhabited farm, Wetherill stuck the summons in the keyhole, whereupon Roberts's wife and children called out from inside saying they would burn the paper. The court "adjudg'd that the Summons was well serv'd," and the absent defendant lost by default.[45] Despite such inconveniences, the position remained so politically powerful and lucrative that terms were limited to three years to rotate the office and restrain competition.[46]

Other court officers appeared irregularly when their services were needed. Coroners viewed dead bodies to determine probable cause of death (for a fee of ten shillings), summoned inquests to investigate suspicious deaths, and incarcerated misbehaving sheriffs when necessary.[47] Most investigations determined death was the result of natural causes or accident, but some brought charges of willful murder. Coroner John Cook, fully earning his ten shillings by viewing the body of an unknown man who had died six weeks earlier, investigated "Several Streames" of blood on the wall of Derrick Johnson's house, resulting in Johnson's indictment.[48] Another court officer was the peacemaker, an innovation in Pennsylvania. Each county was to choose three men to act as official arbitrators, whose decisions would be legally binding. Such peacemakers were selected only three years, however, and in only one case in Chester County was a peacemaker's judgment recorded. By 1692, lack of use had led to the position's abolishment.[49] Finally, the position of king's or queen's attorney for criminal prosecutions on trial appeared as early as 1687 in Bucks County, but it was apparently appointed ad hoc, sometimes for a single court session. Much of the local professional legal talent held the job, but its irregular nature and the lack of statutory fees inhibited the growth of this office until late in this period.[50]

On the whole, court officers had the lowest percentage of elite attributes of the three types of high officers, although they were usually well above the legal population's averages. As with justices, these offices were initially designed to be responsive to elections but ultimately became appointive.[51] Only 69 percent of court officers were Quakers, a slightly lower level of Quaker dominance than among justices (although still disproportionately high considering 39 percent of the population was Quaker), and 89 percent of court officers recorded landownership, again less than justices. Sixty-five percent described themselves as farmers or artisans, while only 29 percent claimed merchant or gentry pursuits (far lower than the 48 percent of the justices who were merchants or self-described gentry). These positions, especially that of clerk, required both legal knowledge and a substantial time commitment, which might have limited the available pool of candidates. Another likely cause was the recognition that ability was critical; yeoman Pemberton virtually monopolized the Bucks County clerkship until his death in 1702. Although on the whole they possessed lower socioeconomic status than justices, these men clearly possessed attributes sufficiently above the masses to entitle them to membership in the legal elite.

Provincial officers, the final group of high officers, were the elected representatives of the freeman electorate and sat as assemblymen or councillors in the legislative bodies of Pennsylvania and West Jersey. They were not involved in the day-to-day functioning of county courts, but their election marked these individuals as members of the legal elite. Assemblies and councils acted as central directors of the legal system by establishing rules of jurisdiction and laws of entitlement and prohibition and by serving as forums for processing legal problems through appeals, petitions, hearings, and legislation. For present purposes, these provincial officers, whose duties and attributes have recently been explored in great depth,[52] are not separately analyzed but are included, along with justices and court officers, as high officers for the analysis below. These three groups constituted the legal elite, clearly identifiable by position and attributes.

Of the lesser legal officers, the constable held the least desirable job and was on the fringe of the legal elite. Described as "the workhorse of the English law enforcement establishment" for each township, the constable served warrants, assisted in tax assessment and collection, and presented to the grand jury offenders and offenses ranging from breach of peace to breach of Sabbath.[53] The fees he received were meager—a shilling for each warrant served, a penny per mile for travel, nothing for police duties—during his one-year appointment. That term could be extended indefinitely, since the office was such an dubious honor that constables had to find their own replacements or "soe fayling stay in another year."[54] Sometimes even presenting a successor was insufficient to gain relief from constable duty. John Snape, Springfield's constable, failed to execute a warrant properly and was punished by the court, not by removal but by continuance in office. Unwilling successors often refused to appear or to be certified, risking a fine in hopes of avoiding the office.[55]

Getting out of the office was often the least of a constable's concerns; getting out alive was often more important. Samuel Paul, the Greenwich constable, was assaulted by Edward Eglington while serving a warrant. Edward Beazer and William Freeman "did beate wound & evilly entreat against the Kings peace" Robert Barber, Chester's constable, while seven men looked on and refused to help Barber. John Hendrickson, Ridley's constable, while investigating a charge of murder of a bastard child, found the woman's relatives "with knives & staves in their hands," and they "swore the death of man or women that should touch their sister." Hendrickson, exercising the better part of valor, retreated and later used the court's criminal process against his besiegers, as did Paul and Beazer. Court results showed less than stunning support from the bench. Eglington was fined a mere five shillings, Beazer was discharged after promising to behave himself, and Hendrickson's attackers apparently suffered no penalty; there is no subsequent prosecution of their indictment.[56] High officers' support of constables was not always as slight as it was when the sheriff was acquitted of contempt after refusing to aid a constable and "bidding him to Kiss his Brich," but constables clearly got little respect from either justices or evildoers, a finding consistent with the English experience.[57]

In seventeenth-century Anglo-America, historians have generally assumed constables were weak because they came from the lower ranks of society.[58] Such suggestions about their relatively low status can be tested by examining 776 Delaware Valley constables. Quakers held a majority (62 percent) of the constable positions, but there were more non-Quakers in that office than in any higher office. Furthermore, only 27 percent of constable positions were occupied by Quaker leaders, the lowest level of that group's participation in any legal position. Eighty-three percent of all constables owned land, a higher percentage than found in the population but lower than for any other officer group. In taxed wealth, constables in 1693 were less often found in the highest bracket and more often in the lowest; in inventoried wealth, constables were the least propertied officers at death. Of the constables whose occupations were identified, 89 percent were farmers, artisans, or both, and only 4 percent claimed merchant or gentry status. In fact, self-identified gentry avoided the position so successfully that there were as many servant as gentry constables. Finally, in terms of social mobility within the legal system, constables were less likely to serve as a high officer than were highway overseers or jurors, and only 14 percent ever advanced. In short, by every measure, constables were at the bottom of the social ladder among those who held legal positions, but in the middle of society in such attributes as religion, landownership, and wealth. They had just enough status to be tapped by the system but insufficient status to avoid this dubious privilege or to command respect.

Overseers of highways had similarly difficult duties, yet overseers were clearly of higher status and received more respect. Each township's court-appointed overseer supervised the maintenance of highways and bridges for one year; like constables, they also retained the job so long as they did not find an acceptable replacement.[59] Overseers, however, had far more court support at their command than did constables, for the law required all inhabitants to work on the roads as the overseer directed each year (e.g., six days in Burlington), on pain of fines up to twenty shillings. Though overseers risked the court's displeasure and fines if they neglected their duties and ignored complaints to clear and mend roads, high officers had no problems finding volunteers, and, in Burlington County, justices fought hard to preserve their patronage powers of appointment against inroads by towns wishing to choose their own overseers.[60]

The demography of overseers reflects the higher status accorded that office, but it also shows that rank to be still less than that of the high officers. Quakers filled 73 percent of the positions, and Quaker leaders accounted for 35 percent of the whole. Eighty-eight percent of overseers were landed, and tax and wealth indices showed they had more in the top bracket and fewer in the low bracket than the legal population did. Turnover was slower than for constables; even though each township was entitled to new lesser officers each year, only 377 individuals served as overseers, less than half the number of constables. Perhaps this longevity derived from a higher potential for advancement; 29 percent of overseers also served in high offices, more than double the rate for constables. That the status of overseers should be higher than that of constables implied a high social value imputed to roads, a recognition of their economic significance to dispersed farmers. In an area where roads had to be carved out of virtual wilderness, it made sense for the legal system to assign its higher-status personnel to jobs that facilitated the flow of people and goods and to promote those overseers who had shown that they could get things done.

The attributes of high officers in the legal system, lesser officers who never became high officers, and those who never became legal officers in this period appear in table 7.[61] All personal attributes significantly

Table 7. Officeholding Status

Attributes	High Officers	Lesser Officers	Nonofficers
Total *n*	394	858	2530
Percentage of total population	10.4	22.7	66.9
Quakers (%)	79.6	58.2	26.4
Quaker leaders (%)	47.2	20.3	3.1
Average Quakers (%)	32.4	37.9	23.3
Non-Quakers (%)	20.4	41.8	73.6
n	318	778	2186
Chi-square probability = .000			
Landowners (%)	93.1	79.3	45.3
Nonlandowners (%)	6.9	20.7	54.7
n	394	858	2530
Chi-square probability = .000			
Occupations (males only)			
Farmer (%)	45.2	61.2	43.3
Artisan (%)	6.7	19.6	21.9
Farmer-artisan (%)	13.3	10.1	6.6
Merchant (%)	13.6	1.7	10.5
Self-described gentry (%)	17.3	0.8	4.1
Servant/slave/laborer (%)	0.3	3.3	7.8
Other (%)	3.6	3.3	5.7
n	330	516	894
Chi-square probability = .000			
1693 Pennsylvania tax assessment (in pounds)			
100+ (%)	34.3	5.7	8.5
50–99 (%)	27.6	15.5	11.0
1–49 (%)	38.1	78.9	80.5
n	105	194	381
Chi-square probability = .000			

Inventoried wealth (in pounds)			
500+ (%)	39.8	14.4	10.6
100–499 (%)	50.8	67.0	51.3
1–99 (%)	9.4	18.5	38.1
n	181	270	302
Chi-square probability = .000			

influenced the chance for and level of officeholding. As would be expected in any English-based legal system of the era, landownership was a necessary but not sufficient prerequisite for high office. Membership in the Society of Friends was nearly as important as owning land; nearly 80 percent of the high officers were Quakers. Within that group, Quaker leaders disproportionately went to the top, producing a close association between control of the meetinghouse and control of the court house. Regarding occupation, high officers were disproportionately merchants or self-described gentry, while disproportionately few artisans and servants achieved high office. Simple farmers attained high office nearly as often as expected, but farmer-artisans did disproportionately better, calling again into question whether Quakers preferred their leaders to farm or to have occupational versatility. Finally, high officers were disproportionately more likely to fall into the highest wealth bracket, whether measured by tax assessment or inventory at death.

Measures of the likelihood of serving as a high officer for each group paints this legal elite in sharper tones. While nearly one in five Quakers became a high officer (and nearly two in five Quaker leaders did so), the legal system used only one of thirty non-Quakers in these elite roles (see tables 3 and 4). One in six landowners became high officers, whereas one in sixty nonlandowners did (see table 5). The self-described gentry accurately assessed themselves; 58 percent of their members served in high offices. Between a quarter and a third of the identified merchants and farmer-artisans claimed roles in this legal elite, while artisans were disproportionately ignored for such roles (see table 6). Regarding wealth, a majority of those with inventories greater than 500 pounds and two-thirds of those with 1693 tax assessments greater than 100 pounds became high officers; for the poorest bracket, the percentages were 9 percent and 15 percent, respectively. John Hollinshead, the landed Quaker leader who called himself a gentleman as well as a farmer and whose inventory totaled 541 pounds, was almost destined to be a high legal officer, whereas James Allman, a non-Quaker who owned no land, had no appreciable chance of becoming a high officer.

Lesser officers possessed attributes at rates that fell between those of the high officer legal elite and those who never held an office. These lesser officers had disproportionately higher percentages of landowners, Quakers, Quaker leaders, and large inventories than did nonofficers but disproportionately lower percentages than high officers did. As expected from the social hierarchy evident in the legal population, nonofficers were disproportionately nonlandowners, non-Quakers, and small estate owners at death. Some with high status occupations, however, preferred not serving at all rather than serving in a lesser office. A majority of those describing themselves as gentry (58.2 percent) occupied a high office, and a majority of those never occupied a lesser office. Only 4 percent of the self-described gentry occupied a lesser office and never moved up. Merchants followed a similar pattern: most of those who became high officers jumped straight into that role without first serving in a lesser office; only 8 percent of merchants served as lesser officers and never went higher. Farmers, farmer-artisans, and artisans were disproportionately drafted into these lesser offices. For over 75 percent of these groups, a lesser office was as high as the legal system would allow. Similarly, those with high tax assessments in 1693 avoided lesser office when high office eluded them, leaving the vast majority of lesser offices to those with the least taxable wealth. While constables and overseers might have been vital to the efficient operation of the legal system, for some, the status of such offices seems to have been beneath them. This statistical distribution of offices reflects a clear and convincing hierarchy of offices and attributes, established both socially and legally throughout the Delaware Valley. Yet the legal elite had still more critical roles within the system to fill and still needed, somehow, to be legitimized.

Grand and Trial Jurors

Jurors constituted this final authoritative group in the legal system. Juries have been seen as having two main roles in colonial America: mobilizing a group of "lawworthy" men to participate in the system and helping form a behavioral consensus in society. These roles suggest that legal elites co-opted the middling sort of colonial society into making decisions in court to achieve social stability under elite rule and elite rules. Such middling men were found on juries from Middlesex, Massachusetts, to Middlesex, Virginia, and many places in between, which gave jurors a stake in their colony's legal system.[62] Once on a jury, either grand or trial, jurors "played their mediatory role between authority and community" and "established recognizable boundaries around their communities by marking out the limits of acceptable behavior for members."[63] Such bodies of men represented both an opportunity and a threat to the Quaker legal elite's authority; its solution, jury packing, maximized opportunity and avoided any threats.

The grand jury, whose origins dated back to the twelfth century, was described as "the body of the county" in seventeenth-century England. Grand jurors, numbering thirteen to twenty-three, presented to the court persons and matters dangerous to the county. Such dangers included licensing alehouses and ordering roads repaired, but of greatest importance was the grand jury's judgment on criminal accusations, drawn from its members' own knowledge or from evidence and testimony laid before it. These collective judgments determined whether an accused would have to stand trial (a "true bill") or could be discharged on a bill found "ignoramus" (meaning insufficient evidence to find the charge true).[64] From New England to the Chesapeake to North Carolina, colonial grand juries carried over many of their English functions, serving as watchdogs of morals and drawing in many lawworthy men who otherwise might not have played a role in the legal system.[65]

In the Delaware Valley, grand juries played a significant governmental role. One 1697 Bucks County grand jury presented the need for having a ferry, building bridges, collecting tax arrears, and erecting a new township. Grand juries were also responsible for setting the county budget and raising taxes (independently or in conjunction with justices), ordering the building of a courthouse or prison, obtaining a book of laws, auditing the county treasurer's books, and straightening roads.[66] These functions gave Delaware Valley grand juries far more power than comparable grand juries in Virginia or Maryland, where grand jury authority generally was limited to criminal offenses, orphans, roads, and bridges.[67] The reason for this expansion of grand jury administrative power is unclear, but it might have been because of the general Quaker and law-reform preference for juries. Regardless of its source, this expansion would make control of the grand jury pool significant for political as well as legal reasons.

Delaware Valley grand jurors' most unfettered power lay in their discretion to define and prosecute (or not prosecute) criminal deviance. Summoned supposedly at random from among the freemen of the county, grand jurors could and did present (what today would be called indict) defendants on the basis of their own knowledge, ignore calls from the bench to inquire into breaking the Sabbath, charge officers with offenses to control their excesses, and block undesired prosecutions by refusing to find "true bills."[68] Although justices could drop prosecutions and could use their summary powers over contempt and peace bonds, grand jurors' broad charge to "present the truth, the whole truth & nothing but the truth" of "all such matters and things" made them the prism through which the legal elite had to examine behavior for its criminal content.[69]

All criminal defendants presented by grand juries and all civil litigants had the right to trial by jury in the Delaware Valley. In some cases, provincial laws, inspired by law reform and Quaker principles regarding juries, seemed to require them—a Pennsylvania freeman could not be imprisoned, dispossessed of freeholds, exiled, damnified, destroyed, hurt, or condemned without the lawful judgment of his equals. Twelve men of the neighborhood were to be selected from the county's freeman population by a child pulling names from a hat. To increase the perception of a fair jury, criminal defendants were allowed thirty-five peremptory challenges in West Jersey (Pennsylvania allowed only removals for cause).[70] The role of justices was to instruct juries in law, and Pennsylvania even prescribed specific instructions on such difficult issues as defalcation (where each party was indebted to the other). In practice, however, jurors had a virtually free hand to decide cases regardless of law and testimony, reflecting again experience with English juries that had protected Quakers in spite of the law and judicial bullying of jurors. West Jersey's *Concessions* mandated that jury judgments be implemented by the justices regardless of the verdict and that the bench decide cases only if the defendant refused a jury, a stricture also followed in Pennsylvania except for a small number of equity cases.[71] The goal was not only to protect jury decisions but also to encourage principled decision making. When a Bucks County jury flipped a coin to decide a case, both the court and monthly meetings disciplined the offenders, and William Penn used these punishments as a defense for his government before the Board of Trade.[72]

Despite a jury pool that by law was to include all of a county's freemen and despite the legal requirement of random selection from that jury pool, sheriffs, following an old English habit of jury packing, clearly chose the jury.[73] The 1693 tax list recorded all freemen in Bucks and Chester counties and thus presumably the entire jury pool at that time. Yet only 49 percent of those listed in Bucks County and 66 percent in Chester County ever found themselves on a grand jury; 49 percent of those listed in Bucks County and 61 percent in Chester County served on trial juries. Delaware Valley's legal elite culled those lists for those who would probably do more for Quaker justice than just act as a mobilized group of the middling lawworthy. As with officeholders, jurors overwhelmingly owned land, the most common way to achieve the status of freeman necessary to qualify for jury service and thus of little predictive value (see table 8). More critically, disproportionate numbers of Quakers served on grand and trial juries, approximately two-thirds of each category. Even though Quakers in the legal population accounted for 56 percent of the landowners, and thus could be expected to constitute the majority of those chosen for juries, the disparity persists when landowning is factored out. Quakers accounted for 74 percent of all landowners who served on grand juries and 72 percent of all landowners who served on trial juries, rates which chi-square reveals as statistically significant (.000). This stark differential on its face raises the inference of jury packing by Quakers for Quakers.

Table 8. Jury Service Comparison

Attributes	Grand Juror	Never Grand Juror	Trial Juror	Never Trial Juror
Total *n*	1266	2516	1138	2644
Percentage of total	33.5	66.5	30.1	69.9
Quakers (%)	68.4	25.5	66.5	27.6
Quaker leaders (%)	29.3	3.1	27.8	4.5
Average Quakers (%)	39.1	22.4	38.7	23.1
Non-Quakers (%)	31.6	74.5	33.5	72.4
n	1037	2245	967	2315
Chi-square probability	= .000		= .000	
Landowners (%)	83.7	55.0	86.0	45.9
Nonlandowners (%)	16.3	45.0	14.0	54.1
n	1266	2516	1138	2644
Chi-square probability	= .000		= .000	

Table 8, continued

Attributes	Grand Juror	Never Grand Juror	Trial Juror	Never Trial Juror
Occupations (males only)				
Farmer (%)	57.2	41.0	56.3	42.8
Artisan (%)	16.8	19.8	17.6	19.0
Farmer-artisan (%)	13.0	5.0	13.4	5.2
Merchant (%)	3.4	13.4	3.5	12.6
Self-described gentry (%)	4.1	7.1	3.5	7.4
Servant/slave/laborer (%)	2.6	7.4	2.7	7.1
Other (%)	2.9	6.2	2.9	6.0
n	853	887	790	950
Chi-square probability	= .000		= .000	
1693 Pennsylvania tax assessment (in pounds)				
100+ (%)	14.1	14.4	14.5	13.5
50–99 (%)	18.0	17.6	18.2	17.3
1–49 (%)	68.0	68.0	67.3	69.2
n	125	256	133	248
Chi-square probability	= .993		= .934	
Inventoried wealth (in pounds)				
500+ (%)	18.8	19.3	22.2	15.4
100–499 (%)	62.5	49.2	59.6	53.8
1–99 (%)	18.8	31.5	18.2	30.8
n	432	321	396	357
Chi-square probability	= .000		= .000	

Table 8 reveals other factors regarding those selected for juries. First, there was little statistical difference between grand and trial juror profiles. Although English courts had begun to seek out grand jurors with higher status commensurate with their functions and bemoaned the low status of trial jurors, such a gap did not appear here, a finding that parallels colonial Maryland.[74] Second, farmer-artisans were called disproportionately often for both grand and trial juries, while merchants avoided such calls, much as they had avoided service in lesser offices. Although farmers were also called more often than expected, diversity of occupation seems to have helped qualify one as lawworthy, whether for office or for a jury. Finally, one's bracket in the 1693 tax list had no statistical influence on being chosen as a juror, indicating that for this group of freemen other factors determined whether they were called.

A better method for evaluating jury service involves not merely looking at those who participated on juries but also counting *within* groups the percentage who served versus those who were not called. As expected, landowners were 3.7 to 4.4 times as likely to be called for jury duty as nonlandowners were; the surprise may be that so many nonlanded were called (see table 5). The most striking differentials were denominational and within that denomination. Quakers were more than three times as likely to serve on a grand jury or a trial jury (see table 3). If we look at the combination of religion and landowning, a Quaker landowner was still more than twice as likely as a non-Quaker landowner to serve on a grand jury or a trial jury.[75] When selecting jurors from within the meetinghouse, the system clearly preferred Quaker leaders. Nearly 90 percent of all Quaker leaders served on some jury, and those men were twice as likely as average Quakers to sit on grand juries and 75 percent more likely to sit on trial juries (see table 4). Finally, farmer-artisans were the most likely occupational group to be called, while merchants' risk of serving on a jury was even less than that of servants, slaves, or laborers (see table 6). Clearly, those "good men" for juries were the most respected members of the founders' faith, and there was a definite preference for diverse pursuits. It is equally clear that those "good men" on juries could not have been chosen randomly by a child from a hat filled with the names of all the eligibles.

This pattern of packing extends to a third level of juror analysis: the distribution of assignments among those who did serve on juries (see table 9). The question asked here was, did a juror's attributes influence the number of assignments that juror received? The number of assignments was divided into those who served only once (the mode), those who served two to four times, and those who served five or more times (this group accumulated the majority of all assignments). Wealth as measured by the 1693 tax and by an inventory at death did not make a statistically significant difference in the number of assignments. Other factors, however, did play a significant role. The majority of jurors who owned no land or were non-Quakers served once and were never called again. Those of higher status—the landed, Quakers, and Quaker leaders—served repeatedly. Of grand jurors with five or more assignments, 98.9 percent were landowners, 85.8 percent were Quakers, and 52.1 percent were Quaker leaders; for trial jurors, the figure for landowners

Table 9. Distribution of Jury Assignments

Attributes	Grand Jury				Trial Jury			
	Once	2–4	5+	n	Once	2–4	5+	n
Overall[a]	40.0%	39.3%	20.6%	1266	42.4%	37.1%	20.5%	1138
Quakers	32.7%	44.3%	23.0%	709	35.0%	40.1%	24.9%	643
Quaker leaders	24.3	43.1	32.6	405	24.1	39.6	36.3	269
Average Quakers	39.0	45.2	15.8	324	42.8	40.6	16.6	374
Non-Quakers	62.5	29.3	8.2	328	58.8	31.3	9.9	324
Chi-square probability	= .000				= .000			
Landowners	33.5%	42.2%	24.3%	1060	35.9%	40.4%	23.8%	979
Nonlandowners	73.8	24.8	1.5	206	83.0	17.0	0.0	159
Chi-square probability	= .000				= .000			
Occupations (males only)								
Farmer	30.1%	41.8%	28.1%	488	39.1%	39.6%	21.4%	445
Artisan	38.5	40.6	21.0	143	37.4	38.9	23.7	139
Farmer-artisan	16.2	40.5	43.2	111	18.9	35.9	45.3	106
Merchant	31.0	51.7	17.2	29	28.6	46.4	25.0	28
Self-described gentry	51.4	22.9	25.7	35	21.4	35.7	42.9	28
Servant/slave/laborer	31.8	54.6	13.6	22	52.4	28.6	19.1	21
Other	40.0	36.0	24.0	25	34.8	34.8	30.4	23
Chi-square probability	= .000				= .000			

1693 Pennsylvania tax assessment (in pounds)

100+	30.6%	36.1%	33.3%	36	16.7%	41.7%	41.7%	36
50–99	23.9	45.7	30.4	46	22.2	48.9	22.2	45
1–49	26.4	44.8	28.7	174	31.7	40.7	27.5	167
Chi-square probability	= .890				= .231			

Inventoried wealth (in pounds)

500+	30.9%	37.0%	32.1%	81	26.1%	39.8%	34.1%	88
100–499	28.9	40.4	30.7	270	30.1	36.9	33.1	236
1–99	45.7	28.4	25.9	81	37.5	36.1	26.4	72
Chi-square probability	= .075				= .591			

Legal roles

High officer	28.3%	37.0%	34.8%	230	21.3%	37.6%	41.1%	202
Lesser officer	28.5	46.0	25.5	530	33.4	40.6	26.0	497
Nonofficer	57.5	33.4	9.1	506	62.4	32.8	4.8	439
Chi-square probability	= .000				= .000			

a. Percentages may not add across to 100 due to rounding.

was 100 percent, for Quakers 83.3 percent, and for Quaker leaders 51.0 percent. Within the Society of Friends, Quaker leaders, such as John Hollinshead (who served on six grand juries and twenty-one trial juries), accounted for the vast majority of jury regulars. Finally, in terms of occupation, farmer-artisans were disproportionately likely to get such multiple service.

Grand jury packing was so institutionalized in Burlington County in the 1690s that a rotation system can be observed; the favored individuals served once a year, usually at the same session each year. For instance, the Quaker William Righton served on the August grand juries in 1691, 1694, 1695, and 1696; John Paine, a leader in the Burlington Monthly Meeting, was on a grand jury in May 1695, May 1696, and May 1697; and Samuel Bunting, a Chesterfield Monthly Meeting leader, served on six juries between 1692 and 1702, five of them at the November session. Burlington County rotated its trial jurors as well; for example, the Quaker John Abbott served in August 1695, 1696, and 1697, while the Burlington Meeting leader William Hunt served seven years in a row, six of them at the February or May sessions. The Quaker legal elite had juror selection figured out.

So long as the Quaker legal elite retained power, they packed juries with an aplomb that English sheriffs would have envied. The expression "a jury of one's peers" takes on an ironic twist when one looks at the profile of litigants and criminal defendants who came before the court (done in depth in subsequent chapters). Sixty percent of all plaintiffs were not Quakers, and 67 percent of civil defendants and 64 percent of criminal defendants were not. These figures were in keeping with the percentage of non-Quakers in the legal population (61 percent). For these non-Quakers, their peers on an average thirteen-man grand jury would be five Quaker leaders, five regular Quakers, and three non-Quakers. On average, their trial jury would be made up of five Quaker leaders, four regular Quakers, and three who were not Quakers. The Quaker elite might have achieved control of all the legal levers of power, but they still faced a majority of the population that was not under the Society of Friends' control. That majority could potentially become hostile and was possessed of the numerical power to thwart Quaker courts by merely boycotting the system. Procedure and performance would be critical to whether and how this legal elite gained legitimacy.

Litigants and Their Causes

Courts need cases to have authority over a society. A court may be granted power to resolve disputes and to punish deviants, but unless human beings come before it for judgment, that power is meaningless. Although courts have some control over prosecuting crimes and bringing reluctant defendants to justice, the Anglo-American legal system does not force individuals to bring their civil complaints to court. A court that sees no civil cases does not sit over a dispute-free society; rather, other methods and institutions have assumed authority over such issues. Litigation therefore reflects choices by the plaintiff and, to a lesser extent, by the defendant, to participate voluntarily in the legal system to resolve an interpersonal dispute. Such choices reveal the scope of authority residents grant to courts and the law over their daily lives.

All litigation begins with a grievance, a feeling by the aggrieved that the defendant-to-be has done something wrong, for example, not paying a debt, taking something that the aggrieved owns, calling the aggrieved names, or causing the aggrieved accidental harm. The aggrieved must decide whether to confront the offending party with the grievance and demand some recompense or to ignore it. Many grievances are too slight to argue about, others are not worth endangering an otherwise happy relationship and are thus set aside, and still others are such that the parties simply avoid each other in the future (e.g., not returning to a tavern that served stale beer). If the aggrieved confronts the offending party and receives no satisfactory response, subsequent choices include returning a grievance for a grievance (an eye for an eye), dropping the matter, avoiding the offending party, seeking a third party to mediate or arbitrate, or turning to a community dispute-resolution mechanism. Or the aggrieved can go to court—lawsuits represent an unknown fraction of all disputes—if these other methods failed or were deemed inappropriate for this problem or this opponent. By choosing to sue, the aggrieved may have revised attitudes (such as seeing a former friend now as an intractable adversary) and will see the dispute transformed by legal procedures into language and arguments not always understood.[1] It is through this translation that a dispute becomes a case, the aggrieved becomes a plaintiff, the opponent becomes a defendant, and the courts acquire authority.

The transformation of a dispute into a legal case in the Delaware Valley began with the plaintiff's filing a declaration with the court at least fourteen days before the next court day.[2] Though plaintiffs might be generally familiar with such requirements, most would not know the specifics necessary for an acceptable declaration. They would probably request a knowledgeable neighbor, the court clerk, or one of the few lawyers who circulated through the Delaware Valley to help them frame the facts and use the right phrases. Not all grievances were justiciable (i.e., acceptable for courts to hear under appropriate jurisdictional and substantive law), and plaintiffs needed to know that their grievance was of the sort that courts would try. Furthermore, plaintiffs needed to believe not only that their cause was just but also that they had a good chance to win, which would justify the costs of drafting, filing, and summoning the defendant.[3] Once a case was filed, the bargaining position of the parties shifted in the plaintiff's favor, because the defendant now had to take some action or risk a default judgment. "Under the shadow of the law," the defendant assumed this role in the legal system; he or she now had choices to make regarding direct negotiation with the plaintiff, settling out of court, running away, confessing judgment in court, or contesting the case with all available legal resources and tactics.

Most litigants sued or were sued as individuals; only 11 percent of the cases involved more than one plaintiff or defendant. Similarly, no matter what legal advice litigants might have garnered beforehand, in 89 percent of the cases there was no attorney for either party, since most litigants pleaded their own cause. Law reforms, as part of the antagonism toward lawyers, had specifically provided that litigants need not "fee" attorneys but "that all persons have free liberty to plead his own cause."[4] Litigation was thus a personal choice that reflected a variety of dispute-processing options and a set of evaluations about oneself, one's opponent, the state of the law on a particular subject, and the chances for success in front of a particular court with a particular set of decision-makers. A legal system's authority over civil disputes reflects the aggregate of those individual choices. Each option for ending the case once begun, whether inside or outside the legal system, whether exercisable by plaintiff, defendant, or both, represents a branch on a decision tree. It is possible to draw inferences about power within both society and the court system by comparing groups of individuals regarding the branches they followed among the legal options.

Bringing a Case

Once a plaintiff decided to bring suit, one of the first choices was what process to use to begin the case and to inform the defendant of the suit. Rules of civil procedure deriving from statute, common law, and custom in the Delaware Valley circumscribed a plaintiff's options. If the amount in dispute was less than forty shillings, the plaintiff could avoid written formalities by making an oral complaint to one justice of the peace (two were required in Pennsylvania until 1693), who could summon the defendant, hear evidence, and determine the case. At first, such decisions were binding only if approved by the county court, but by 1700 a single justice could render a final judgment along with an execution without further review.[5] For amounts greater than forty shillings and issues involving equity or land, the plaintiff had to file a written complaint at the courthouse at least fourteen days before trial, and notice was given to the defendant, along with a copy of the declaration, at least ten days before trial.[6] The plaintiff chose what type of notice to give defendants. This choice revealed a change in attitudes toward defendants and the law over time.

There were three ways to require the defendant's presence at court. The simplest and least intrusive method was a summons. After informing the defendant of the adversary's name and the court date, this form merely threatened the defendant to "fail not at thy peril" to appear.[7] It was much more threatening to the defendant (thus improving the plaintiff's bargaining position) to begin the case by a replevin (in the narrow circumstance where the plaintiff claimed specific chattels had been wrongfully taken and should be returned before trial) or more commonly by an attachment, whereby the sheriff seized some of the defendant's assets before trial. Initially, West Jersey law allowed attachments only if defendants failed to respond to a summons, and Pennsylvania did not provide for them at all. In practice, courts on both sides of the Delaware allowed attachments against nonresidents and those regarded as bad risks.[8] Pennsylvania's assembly, concerned that there was no law to "direct the proceedings on attachments," codified existing practice in 1699, retroactively approving all previous attachments and allowing them in the future against nonresidents, those about to leave the province, and those who refused to give sufficient security to the complainant.[9]

In contrast, the third method—arresting the defendant—was heavily regulated from the outset to avoid imprisoning debtors, a prime goal of the law-reform movement.[10] Freeholders in both provinces were not to be arrested without evidence that the defendant was about to flee; arrests were permitted for nonfreeholders and nonresidents only where potential flight and lack of security were proved.[11] For those arrested, Pennsylvania required the plaintiff to call a special court the next day to limit the defendant's time in prison, and both colonies refused to confine debtors who had an unpaid judgment against them, requiring defendants to pay their debt by servitude instead.[12] Despite these restrictions, courts generally deferred to the plaintiff's judgment on the advisability of an arrest, even when a freeholder defendant challenged the arrest, thereby strengthening the plaintiff's hand.[13]

Plaintiffs' choices between the simple yet weak summons and the more complex yet more secure attachments and arrests were based on not only an evaluation of the opponent but also the contradictory influences of the processes, rules, and the legal culture that combined to form the Delaware Valley's legal system.[14] On one side lay the legal processes that originated in the law-reform agenda the Quaker elite carried to the New World (described in the Introduction) and that became embodied in the region's earliest laws and practices. The most important procedural reforms covered pleadings, which were to be short, written in English in an ordinary and plain manner, easy to read and understand, and devoid of fictions and color; forms (statutorily laid out in English) of deeds, bills, arrests, summons, attachments, replevins, and executions for litigants to copy, secure in their enforceability; attorneys (unneeded in court since litigants could represent themselves or use a friend as their lawyer, regardless of legal training); and fees, which were set by law for particular documents and functions at "moderate" levels and posted in every court to avoid overcharges.[15] The legal processes were speedier, cheaper, easier to understand, and detached from the eccentricities and incomprehensible terminologies of the English common law. Plaintiffs were encouraged to use the courts by lowering the threshold barriers, making the law less intimidating for all parties, and influencing plaintiffs to choose the less intimidating summons. The overall result of procedural reform would necessarily give Delaware Valley courts a higher percentage of society's disputes for adjudication than English common-law courts would see. The Delaware Valley legal elite, lacking the attributes that gave the English legal elite power, needed those extra cases to establish true decision-making authority that could, in turn, legitimate their rule.

Yet these reformed processes faced the corrosive presence of common-law language and complexity, an influence that grew over time. Though all proceedings and pleadings were to be in English, proper understanding of such terms as *nihil dicit, assumpsit, quantum meruit, scire facias, capias ad satisfaciendum,* and *fiere facias* was needed to comprehend fully court proceedings.[16] Defendants in the early 1700s flooded court dockets with terms previously unseen in the Delaware Valley—*oyer* (a reading of the written instrument stated in the plaintiff's declaration), *imparlance,* and *special imparlance. Imparlance,* which often followed an oyer, was a pleading for the defendant "to have a longer and further day to answer the matter." These pleadings began to appear at the same time that the number of continuances granted increased. Suddenly, causes that previously had been resolved in a single court session were being delayed through legal tactics.[17] This clash between law reform and the rigor of the common law was never so apparent as in the confused drafting of Pennsylvania's Judiciary Act of 1701 by David Lloyd, then perhaps the best legal mind in the Delaware Valley. This act instructed county court justices to observe as nearly as possible "the methods and practice of the King's court of common pleas in England," yet in the very next words it told the justices to have "regard to the regular process and proceedings of the former county courts; always keeping to brevity, plainness and verity in all declarations and pleas, and avoiding all fictions and color in pleadings."[18] That English standards were mentioned at all was a significant change from previous laws, which had described procedure only in law-reform terms. Clearly the issue was becoming unsettled and left room for plaintiffs to prefer the harsher, more complex attachments and arrests.

Yet the legal system's substantive rules sent a second, contradictory message to plaintiffs, one that told them to avoid court if at all possible. Bringing too many harassing suits (called barratry) was a criminal offense punishable by fine, imprisonment, and dismissal of the suit.[19]

Statutes required the public recording of all land transactions and all written debt instruments on pain of having such transactions become null and void. This harsh provision, later relaxed, was designed to reduce lawsuits by establishing clear entitlements to those who recorded transactions while denying enforceability to those who did not.[20] Similarly "to prevent Differences and unnecessarie Law-suits about Dealing," all business accounts were to be balanced yearly and the net paid if one party owed more than forty shillings.[21] Preferring arbitration to litigation, Pennsylvania created "peacemakers" for each county and encouraged disputants to use them as binding arbitrators by giving their awards the status of a court judgment.[22] The "moderate" fee system escalated costs dramatically if the case actually reached trial, where witnesses, juries, and a multitude of documents cost far more than the cost of withdrawing the case.[23] Going to court became cheaper, simpler, and more understandable, but the reformed legal system also signaled plaintiffs to go slow in utilizing these benefits.

Along with processes and rules, a legal system contains a legal culture, which, according to Lawrence M. Friedman, refers to "ideas, attitudes, expectations and opinions about law," a "network . . . which determines when and why and where people turn to law or government or turn away." For Kermit Hall, a legal culture reflects two elements: "a manifestation of ideology" about legal expectations and experience plus a "response to individual and group interest."[24] Two groups within this legal system, subcultures that crossed jurisdictional borders, illustrate this concept with their opinions regarding the law and their members' disputes. Quaker doctrine discouraged Quakers from suing non-Quakers, an attitude born of religious conviction and the necessity of keeping a low profile in an England that regularly prosecuted Quakers.[25] Should attempts to accommodate the dispute with a non-Quaker fail, however, a suit violated no Quaker norm. Nonetheless, a Quaker was not to sue another Quaker without consent of the meeting; to do so was an offense so grievous that doctrine demanded the offender be disowned. In place of litigation, an elaborate mechanism (discussed in chapter 4) for arbitrating and deciding all intra-Quaker disputes in the meeting was developed so "that the World may not know of our Differences."[26] Similarly, the merchant community looked askance at merchants suing other merchants, but for practical rather than moral reasons. In the late seventeenth century, English merchants abandoned the common law because of its expense, its lawyers, and its principles, all of which seemed less attuned to their needs than arbitration by their peers was. With their own dispute-settlement institutions that were knowledgeable in customary business practices, merchants thought they could improve predictability and rationality of decisions.[27] Though law reforms might have eased the threshold costs of suits in the Delaware Valley, contradictory elements in the overall legal culture could reduce the practical effect of these reforms.

Suing with simplicity, suing with complexity, or not suing at all—despite the contradictions, this legal system encouraged all three for dispute resolution. It is impossible to know how many disputes were resolved before a case was filed; this "dark number," if known and compared with the number of litigations, would illuminate how successful the no-suit message was in the legal system. It is, however, possible to learn what happened once cases were filed and what they revealed about how parties integrated the various messages into their choices. The decision to use summons rather than arrests or attachments was not affected by cost since fees were identical. In Bucks and Gloucester counties (the only counties that recorded more than 50 percent of the process used in cases), 75 percent of the cases in each court's first decade that had recorded the process used the summons. After 1693, Bucks County saw a reversal, with only 24 percent using summons from 1693 to 1710; from 1698 to 1710, Gloucester County saw a decline to 57 percent. In Chester County from 1708 to 1710, the only period when the Chester County clerk recorded significant numbers of processes, 53 percent used summons, while 43 percent used attachment or arrest (4 percent were unrecorded). The trend clearly was for plaintiffs to move toward a stronger initial legal process, which reflected their judgments about their opponents and the law.

The choice of a summons over an attachment or arrest was only one of many choices in the litigation available for analysis. Sixty-three percent of the adjudicatory business of these courts was civil litigation, while only 37 percent involved criminal issues. In terms of cases that utilized the full resources of the legal system—those with jury trials—civil juries occurred more than twice as often as criminal juries (313 to 145), even though penalties were usually more severe for criminal offenses than for most civil losses. Voluntary participation in civil procedures was roughly double that of involuntary participation in criminal cases, a measure of this system's success in drawing litigants to court and thus enhancing court authority and legitimacy.

Overall, 1,092 plaintiffs brought 2,017 cases against 1,176 defendants in this period. Yet 71 percent of the legal population never brought a case, and the majority of the legal population never appeared as either plaintiff or defendant. Furthermore, 84 percent of all plaintiffs and all defendants sued or were sued only once or twice. From the perspective of the individual, a suit was a seldom-if-ever phenomenon, though by participating as witnesses, jurors, or spectators on court day, the average resident undoubtedly observed many. Although the "dark number" of overall disputes remains elusive, once litigation began it is possible to identify who sued, who was sued, who sued whom and for what, and what the outcomes were. In those choices, plus the distinctive legal strategies followed by litigants in resolving the contradictions in the legal culture regarding dispute behavior (discussed in chapter 3), social power and legal authority revealed themselves.

The Litigants: An Overview

The simplest method to evaluate litigants is to compare the subsets of those who sued or were sued with nonlitigants—that 51.5 percent of the legal population that never engaged in litigation (see table 10). This statistical portrait examines the attributes of gender, landownership, religion, occupation, and wealth; the authoritative legal roles of officeholding and jury service; and other legal roles in litigation, criminal prosecution, and witnessing. Evaluating the litigants required an initial examination of those who sued or were sued at any time and a further examination of the characteristics of those who sued multiple times. Plaintiffs and defendants were divided into three groups for this second evaluation: those who appeared only once or twice in a litigant role, repeat players who appeared three to five times, and megaplaintiffs or megadefendants who sued or were sued six or more times. Table 10 displays this last group, but the analysis below is based on all three groups.

The vast majority of all litigants were male. Only 7.4 percent of plaintiffs and 6.3 percent of defendants were women, and an even smaller percentage of women were plaintiffs or defendants in three to five cases and six or more cases. Women appeared as the sole or first-named party less frequently than they appeared as coplaintives, and most often they appeared in cases with their husbands. Occasionally clerks did not even record the woman's first name, her identity reduced to that of "wife of" or "uxor," especially in cases involving land where she was an indispens-

Table 10. Demography of Litigants and Nonlitigants

Attributes	Plaintiffs (all)	Plaintiffs (6+ times)	Defendants (all)	Defendants (6+ times)	Nonlitigants	Legal Population Rate
Women (%)	7.4	4.2	6.3	0.0	12.2	9.9
Men (%)	92.6	95.8	93.7	100.0	87.8	90.1
n	1092	49	1176	46	1951	3782
Quakers (%)	40.3	64.4	32.8	53.5	42.7	39.1
Quaker leaders (%)	11.9	28.9	8.7	7.0	13.6	11.4
Non-Quakers (%)	59.7	35.6	67.2	46.5	57.3	60.9
n	959	45	1023	43	1686	3282
Landowners (%)	69.1	91.8	64.7	91.3	53.1	58.0
Nonlandowners (%)	30.9	8.2	35.3	8.7	46.9	42.0
n	1092	49	1176	46	1951	3782
Occupations (males only)						
Farmer (%)	39.6	23.3	45.6	37.8	58.0	49.0
Artisan (%)	16.3	9.3	21.9	29.7	17.2	18.3
Farmer-artisan (%)	10.4	2.3	10.2	8.1	7.4	8.9
Merchant (%)	15.9	30.2	6.9	2.7	3.9	8.5
Self-described gentry (%)	9.6	23.3	5.7	13.5	3.0	5.6
Servant/slave/laborer (%)	3.5	0.0	4.4	2.7	6.7	5.1
Other (%)	4.9	11.6	5.4	5.4	3.8	4.6
n	637	43	636	35	766	1740

Table 10, continued

Attributes	Plaintiffs (all)	Plaintiffs (6+ times)	Defendants (all)	Defendants (6+ times)	Nonlitigants	Legal Population Rate
1693 Pennsylvania tax assessment (in pounds)						
100+ (%)	23.9	52.4	16.3	21.4	10.6	14.2
50–99 (%)	24.6	38.1	19.9	42.9	15.9	17.8
1–49 (%)	51.5	9.5	63.8	35.7	73.5	68.0
n	130	21	141	14	189	381
Inventoried wealth (in pounds)						
500+ (%)	24.7	55.0	18.6	41.7	17.2	19.0
100–499 (%)	52.9	40.0	54.6	50.0	59.8	56.8
1–99 (%)	22.4	5.0	26.9	8.3	23.1	24.2
n	263	20	242	12	373	753
Legal roles						
High officer (%)	15.8	70.8	11.4	28.3	9.3	10.4
Lesser officer (%)	17.5	16.7	20.7	26.1	27.6	22.7
Nonofficer (%)	66.8	12.5	67.9	45.7	63.0	66.9
Grand juror (%)	29.8	58.3	28.0	47.8	40.1	33.5
Trial juror (%)	30.3	64.6	31.2	67.4	34.0	30.1
Plaintiff (%)	100.0	100.0	37.1	82.6	0.0	28.9
Defendant (%)	40.0	81.3	100.0	100.0	0.0	31.1
Criminal defendant (%)	27.7	64.6	32.1	71.7	30.0	27.9
Witness (%)	29.2	72.9	29.5	65.2	28.3	26.9
n	1092	49	1176	46	1951	3782

able party. Some women did use the courts independently, such as Anne Mayes, who filed eight suits in 1710, and Mary Beakes, a landed widow who successfully brought three cases in four years. For the most part, however, the rules of coverture limited such opportunities.[28] Because authoritative roles were closed as well, 60 percent of the women in the legal population participated only as witnesses or criminal defendants.

The relationship, displayed in table 10, between land, wealth, and legal officeholding status, on the one hand, and litigants, on the other, can be expressed in a few straightforward sentences. Those who sued were on average better off than those who did not sue. Those who sued often were likely even better off. Those who were sued were better off than those who never litigated, although they were worse off than the average plaintiff. If an individual was sued a lot, he or she was probably better off than the average plaintiff, although not as well off as those who sued often. Finally, the average nonlitigant was less likely to own land, hold high office, and be wealthy at tax time or at death than was the average litigant, whether plaintiff or defendant. Litigation did involve some of the marginal members of the legal population, but they were not the civil court's biggest customers;[29] rather, society's most established groups flocked to the courts with their disputes.

Another factor apparent in the use of courts was occupation. Merchants (despite their attitudes about the common law) and self-described gentry appeared as plaintiffs more often than their relatively small legal population percentage would have suggested. Constituting the majority of megaplaintiffs, they showed a remarkable propensity for litigiousness. Farmers', artisans', and farmer-artisans' percentages of megaplaintiffs are far below their percentage of plaintiffs and proportion of the legal population. The pattern for defendants is reversed for both merchants and artisans. Merchants formed a smaller percentage of the megadefendant pool than their overall rate, while artisans' percentage of repeat and megadefendants increased. Across the board, simple farmers never became litigants at their population rate, while servants, slaves, and laborers were even less likely to be involved in a suit. The wide variation among occupational groups' propensity to become plaintiffs, along with the statistics on landowning, officeholding, and wealth, suggests that civil courts served the interests and responded to the needs of those groups that disproportionately sued.

That inference must be tempered by two factors that logically must have entered into court usage. The first factor, called *transactional den-*

sity, represents the idea that those who engaged in more economic transactions were more likely to have transactions that failed and thus were more likely to end up in court. Merchants and artisans, who in the normal course of business engaged in substantial buying and selling, logically should have had a larger absolute number of transactions than did farmers or servants, whose market involvement was more limited, and thus a greater chance for a dispute. Transactional density may well account for some of the extra litigation by the landed, high officeholders, and wealthy. A second factor, labeled here *deep pockets* (wealth), might also have played a role. Rarely would a rational plaintiff sue a judgment-proof (i.e., broke) defendant, whose assets could not possibly cover the claim; rarely would an assetless plaintiff (in an era before contingency fees) have the wherewithal to launch a suit, even given the lowered barriers to litigation. Identifying the role played by social power, as opposed to transactional density and deep pockets, requires a more subtle examination of the litigation pattern from the point of view of both plaintiffs and defendants.

The pitfalls of monocausal explanations become most apparent in discussing Quakers. Quakers might have dominated legal authoritative roles, but they did not dominate the pool of litigants. Quakers overall and Quaker leaders were plaintiffs at a rate barely above their proportion of the population (see table 10), and they became defendants at significantly less than expected rates. As for multiple appearances, Quakers did form a majority of those suing or being sued six or more times, but Quaker leaders were less likely to be megadefendants. Given their clear control of legal power and their deep pockets, as shown in chapter 1, why did Quakers not tread the well-worn path to the bar of justice as often as the landed, the wealthy, or the high officers? First, as noted above, Quaker dogma required Friends to arbitrate disputes against other Friends within the monthly meeting and discouraged Quakers from suing the "world's people."[30] Furthermore, transactional density would argue Quakers should have had a lower proportion of plaintiffs because more of them were farmers and fewer of them were merchants, artisans, and gentry (see table 3). Yet, by suing as often as their general population percentage and by dominating the megaplaintiff category, Quakers revealed a propensity for litigation that balanced such cultural and occupational forces. Second, deep pockets as well the lack of constraints on the majority non-Quakers from suing Quakers would suggest that Quakers should have been more vulnerable to the legal process. Yet there were relatively few Quaker defendants, which suggests that some combination of Quaker social power and Quaker transaction patterns worked to insulate some Quakers from lawsuits. Only a statistical examination comparing litigation rates *within* groups and comparing who sued whom (matchups—analyzed later in the chapter) can provide inferential answers for these subtle questions about choices.

The final observation regarding table 10 is that the more one participated in litigating roles, the more likely one was to participate in other legal roles as well. On the whole, plaintiffs appeared as grand jurors, trial jurors, criminal defendants, and witnesses at rates close to the overall legal population rates for those roles. The more suits plaintiffs filed, however, the greater the likelihood of their performing those four roles. Similarly, civil defendants as a whole were jurors, witnesses, and criminal defendants roughly equivalent to their population percentage. Yet, as with plaintiffs, those who were defendants in many cases participated in legal roles more often than defendants who were sued only once. Additionally, suing begot getting sued, since plaintiffs and defendants were more likely to be on the other side of a declaration at some point. Megaplaintiffs were almost three times as likely to have been defendants, and the same was true for megadefendants having been plaintiffs. Litigation and overall legal involvement were thus closely linked. Though the legal system was open to all, in practice its roles were disproportionately filled by members of this same core group who reappeared with great regularity before and behind the bar on court day.

This overlapping of roles and attributes has already been seen in chapter 1. John Hollingshead, a Burlington County Quaker leader and justice of the peace, was a megaplaintiff (nineteen cases), twice a civil defendant, and three times a criminal defendant, who also served twenty-seven times as grand and trial juror. The Quaker James Allman was a repeat plaintiff and once a civil defendant, all of which was sandwiched around his service as a constable, overseer of highways, and juror. Other members of this core group included William Biles, a Quaker leader, wealthy merchant, yeoman farmer, justice in Bucks County for eighteen years, and a six-term assemblyman, who sued twelve times, was sued twice, testified twice, and served on one grand jury. This pattern held even for non-Quakers. Jeremiah Collett, a Chester County Anglican, launched thirty-nine suits, more than anyone else in this period. He served as justice, sheriff, overseer, and tax appraiser and collector before his death in 1706. This wealthy gentleman, merchant, and yeoman was also a defendant eight times, a witness seven times, a trial juror seven times, and a criminal defendant twice. It was people like Hollinshead, Allman, Biles, and Collett who disproportionately held legal power, used the legal process, and, perhaps because of their legal visibility, had cases brought against them. Closer analysis using the chi-square test can reveal whether these first estimates possess statistical significance, and if so, where the probable causes for such discrepancies may lie.

The Litigants: A Closer Look

Three different statistical questions arise in evaluating the litigants in the colonial Delaware Valley. The first question, access to civil justice, occupied the minds of Quaker legal theorists. Law reforms, designed to increase all residents' access to the courts, can be tested by looking at groups within the legal population to see if any were excluded. The total or near total absence of a group among the plaintiffs could have dire consequences for legal legitimacy because courts could exercise no power over that group's disputes. A second question was, even if all groups had some access, did some groups have more access than others? The answer here can suggest groups' perceptions of how courts would receive their problems. A second measure, vulnerability, looks at the percentage within groups who became defendants, and again suggests power differentials. Were certain groups not exposed at all to suits, or were certain groups more vulnerable (or less vulnerable) to suits? Access and vulnerability lend themselves to chi-square analysis. Finally, the third measure, usage, evaluates appearance in litigation in two ways. Usage analyzes the percentage of megaplaintiffs and megadefendants found among each group's litigants, suggesting, like access, which groups' members found the courts most receptive to their disputes. Usage also analyzes a ratio of all cases involving a group's members, dividing the number of cases in which a member of a group was the plaintiff by those cases in which a group member was the defendant. This last measure allows comparisons of each group's relative experience and perspective in litigation. Access, vulnerability, and usage paint a portrait of an uneven playing field for disputants.

As table 11 indicates, the legal system succeeded in attracting as plaintiffs members from all groups in the legal population. Twenty-one percent of all nonlandowners sued at some point, which was the lowest rate for any group; even 25 percent of identified servants, slaves, and laborers brought suits to courts. Access, however, was not identical for all groups, since five of the seven categories showed statistically significant differences in the propensity to sue. Landowners were disproportionately likely to sue, as were men, merchants, the self-described gentry, the wealthy, and high legal officers. Those significantly less likely to sue

Table 11. Access and Vulnerability in Civil Litigation

Attributes	Plaintiff	Never Plaintiff	Defendant	Never Defendant
Total *n*	1092	2690	1176	2606
Percentage of total	28.9	71.1	31.1	68.9
Male (%)	29.7	70.3	32.4	67.7
Female (%)	21.6	78.4	19.7	80.3
Chi-square probability		= .001		= .000
Quakers (%)	30.1	69.9	26.2	73.8
Quaker leaders (%)	30.4	69.6	23.5	76.5
Average Quakers (%)	30.0	70.0	27.3	72.7
Non-Quakers (%)	28.7	71.4	34.3	65.7
Chi-square probability		= .390		= .000
Landowners (%)	34.4	65.6	34.7	65.3
Nonlandowners (%)	21.3	78.7	26.1	73.9
Chi-square probability		= .000		= .000
Occupations (males only)				
Farmer (%)	29.6	70.4	33.9	66.1
Artisan (%)	32.6	67.4	43.3	56.7
Farmer-artisan (%)	42.6	57.4	42.5	57.5
Merchant (%)	68.2	31.8	29.9	70.1
Self-described gentry (%)	62.2	37.8	37.1	62.9
Servant/slave/laborer (%)	25.0	75.0	31.8	68.2
Other (%)	38.8	61.3	43.0	57.0
Chi-square probability		= .000		= .012
1693 Pennsylvania tax assessment (in pounds)				
100+ (%)	57.4	42.6	42.6	57.4
50–99 (%)	47.1	52.9	41.2	58.8
1–49 (%)	25.9	74.1	34.7	65.3
Chi-square probability		= .000		= .407

Table 11, continued

Attributes	Plaintiff	Never Plaintiff	Defendant	Never Defendant
Inventoried wealth (in pounds)				
500+ (%)	45.4	54.6	31.3	68.8
100–499 (%)	32.5	67.5	30.8	69.2
1–99 (%)	32.4	67.6	35.9	65.3
Chi-square probability	= .000		= .449	
Legal roles				
High officer (%)	43.7	56.4	34.0	66.0
Lesser officer (%)	22.3	77.7	28.3	71.7
Nonofficer (%)	28.8	71.2	31.6	68.4
Chi-square probability	= .000		= .085	

were women, the nonlanded, farmers, servants/slaves/laborers, the poor, and the lesser officers. Only between Quakers and non-Quakers and between average Quakers and Quaker leaders were there no statistically significant differences in becoming a plaintiff. That Quakers dominated the bench and jury did not deter non-Quakers from bringing their suits to court; concomitantly, that Quakers (and particularly Quaker leaders) dominated the bench and jury did not encourage Quakers and their leaders to overwhelm courts with their suits. Access, which tilted toward those with assets, status, and power in the secular world, was equal between and within religions. The Quaker legal elite succeeded in attracting to its courts a fair share of the non-Quaker majority and of the average Quaker population, who expressed, through their choice to bring a case, their belief that the forum would at least treat their cause fairly.

Vulnerability statistics reveal whether higher-status individuals could avoid being sued. Overall, no group wholly avoided becoming defendants, though women were the least likely to be sued. Men, in control of the vast majority of the colony's assets because of patriarchy and the rules of coverture, were much more likely to be sued than women were. Similarly, landowners were significantly more vulnerable to being sued than were the nonlanded, illustrating how widespread distribution of land made landowners' pockets deeper and encouraged plaintiffs. Deep-pocketed high officers were more likely to be sued than were lesser officers or those who never held office, but, unlike for men and landowners, this difference was not statistically significant. Furthermore, neither taxed wealth nor wealth at death was significantly related to vulnerability. These attributes of land, gender, office, and wealth did not insulate the more privileged from civil litigation. Their appearances would reinforce legitimacy by showing the crowd that all could be called to account for their civil (or uncivil) relationships.

The more significant vulnerability findings relate to merchants, Quakers, and Quaker leaders. While many of them did appear as defendants, the number of such defendants was statistically significant in being less than their percentage of the legal population would have predicted. Among occupations, merchants showed the lowest propensity to be sued, despite their transactional density and deep pockets, while artisans, the other occupation with a high number of transactions, were sued more often than any other group. Similarly, the deep pockets of Quakers and Quaker leaders did not attract judgment-seeking plaintiffs, because these groups successfully avoided their proportionate share of the defendant role. This finding contrasts with the earlier access statistics, which showed no difference between Quakers, Quaker leaders, and non-Quakers in suing and showed merchants the most likely plaintiffs. The clear inference is that Quakers and merchants arranged their relationships such that they disproportionately escaped having to defend suits. Such arrangements logically suggest that, before and during an economic deal, they kept one eye on the law's requirements regarding performance and potential liability. The other eye probably focused on the other party so, should that potential plaintiff have cause to sue, he or she might be convinced by the socioeconomic power of Quakers and merchants that such litigation would not be in his or her best interest. It is also interesting to note that these groups maintained extralegal dispute-resolution mechanisms, which suggested legal outcomes might have been subtly skewed to augment these groups' advantages so they would stay within the court system, thereby encouraging their suits and discouraging those of their opponents.

The third statistical variable, usage, reveals a legal system heavily involved with the disputes of the leading members of the society (see table 12). Examinations of the propensity to become megaplaintiffs and megadefendants reveal a higher percentage of the higher status joining the parade to court on both sides, with all but gender and the defendant's occupation being statistically significant. Such a finding reconfirms that, although the court system provided access and vulnerability for all, litigation involved the leading members of the society most heavily. Because these higher-status members predominated in both roles, access and vulnerability statistics alone cannot tell whether a group's experience with lawsuits was more active or reactive, more positive than negative, in short, more plaintiff than defendant. The fourth column of table 12 provides that answer with a ratio of plaintiff to defendant appearances. A ratio of 1 is a neutral value, indicating a group was as likely to sue as be sued. A ratio greater than 1 indicated positive court usage for a group, while less than 1 reflected an overall negative litigation posture. Merchants, self-described gentry, taxed wealthy, high officers, and Quaker leaders had the highest usage ratios, in that order, while the servant/slave/laborer group, the poorest group in 1693's tax, artisans, and nonlanded had the lowest ratios. Together, these three measures show a litigation system accessible to all yet used by some more than by others; all were vulnerable to suits, yet some were more vulnerable than others.

Table 12. Relative Usage of Civil Litigation

Attributes	Mega-Plaintiff	Mega-Defendant	Plaintiff Cases/Defendant Cases	Ratio
Total *n*	49	46	2017/2017	1.00
Percentage of litigant population	4.5	3.9		
Male	4.7%	100.0%	1945/1960	.99
Female	2.5	0.0	72/57	1.26
Chi-square probability	= .573	= .060		
Quakers	7.5%	6.9%	790/616	1.28
Quaker leaders	11.4	8.1	289/136	2.13
Average Quakers	5.9	3.4	501/480	1.04
Non-Quakers	2.8	2.9	1001/1175	.85
Chi-square probability	= .000	= .000		
Landowners	6.0%	5.5%	1613/1490	1.08
Nonlandowners	1.2	1.0	404/527	.77
Chi-square probability	= .000	= .000		
Occupations (males only)[a]				
Farmer	4.0%	4.8%	466/567	.82

Artisan	3.9	7.9	182/295	.62
Farmer-artisan	1.5	4.6	128/121	1.06
Merchant	12.9	2.3	312/73	4.27
Self-described gentry	16.4	13.9	223/84	2.65
Servant/slave/laborer	0.0	3.6	28/60	.47
Chi-square probability	= .000	= .431		
1693 Pennsylvania tax assessment (in pounds)				
100+	35.5%	13.0%	173/77	2.25
50–99	25.0	21.4	113/94	1.20
1–49	3.0	5.6	120/208	.58
Chi-square probability	= .000	= .044		
Inventoried wealth (in pounds)				
500+	16.9%	11.1%	254/125	2.03
100–499	5.8	4.6	272/236	1.25
1–99	1.7	1.5	94/107	.88
Chi-square probability	= .000	= .023		
Legal roles				
High officer	9.7%	19.8%	663/296	2.24
Lesser officer	4.9	4.2	376/478	.79
Nonofficer	2.6	1.0	978/1243	.79
Chi-square probability	= .000	= .000		

a. The category "other" has been omitted to ensure that chi-square is a valid test. Litigation analysis will use only six occupational categories.

Litigation Matchups: Who Sued Whom

The legal population, in filing its civil suits, behaved in ways that revealed a clear hierarchy during these years, a hierarchy that paralleled the one found for authoritative roles in chapter 1. Yet these indices do not by themselves prove the oppression of vulnerable groups; they do not indicate who was vulnerable to whom and do not suggest why. Historians and sociologists of law have suggested two hypotheses that relate the litigation choices of legal populations to the status of the litigants. First, legal elites rarely should have invoked the formal mechanisms of law against status equals but instead should have disproportionately sued more vulnerable adversaries. If such a pattern held, the logical inference would be that those of high status used legal institutions to maintain and reinforce their positions of influence. Second, nonelite members of the legal population should have been inhibited from filing suit against those legal elites, despite the likely deep pockets of such potential defendants. As with the first theory, if such a pattern held, it would suggest that hierarchical status relationships controlled litigation to the benefit of the elite by insulating them from suits.[31]

To test these hypotheses of litigation as oppression, in each individual case, the attributes of the plaintiffs were matched against the attributes of the particular defendants they sued, and the results were analyzed, using chi-square, for skewed patterns of litigation. Despite the theory, many attributes showed no statistical evidence of bias in the plaintiffs' choices. The defendant's gender (chi-square probability = .983), level of taxed wealth (.132), level of inventoried wealth (.494), and occupation (.109) cannot be said to have influenced the choices of this group of plaintiffs in their decisions to sue. In accordance with the second hypothesis, land-ownership does appear to have had a significant effect on litigation (see table 13). Nonlandowners sued nonlandowners disproportionately more often and sued landowners disproportionately less often than expected. Landowners, however, sued other landowners with relative abandon, choosing to litigate with the landed more than three times as often as they did with the nonlandowners. This result suggests that while nonlandowners were inhibited from suing the richer, more powerful landed, the landed did not possess any sort of solidarity that led them to refrain from suing each other. Nor apparently did the landed see any great benefit in using litigation against those without land. While the first thesis thus did not hold true, it must be noted that landowners might have had a hierarchy of litigation choices based on the amount of land held at a particular time, something not examined in this study.

Statistically significant results also appeared upon examination of the litigation matchups of officeholders, average Quakers, and Quaker leaders. If officeholding is taken into account for plaintiffs, the pattern of suits was not random (see table 13). Lesser officers disproportionately focused on other lesser officers in their suits, despite their likely high transaction rates with high officers and the deep pockets of high officers. This pattern parallels the finding that nonlanded plaintiffs disproportionately sued other nonlanded, in accordance with the second hypothesis, and indicates status weakness for these constables and overseers. High officers disproportionately avoided suing other high officers, instead suing lesser officers and nonofficers more often than expected. This result supports the first hypothesis, that elites will use legal process against status inferiors while trying to keep intra-elite disputes out of sight.

Table 13. Litigation Matchups: Who Sued Whom

Plaintiff Attributes	Defendant Attributes	
	Landowners	Nonlandowners
Landowners (%)	75.9	24.1
Nonlandowners (%)	65.8	34.2
Percentage of cases	73.9	26.1
Defendant *n*	1490	527
Chi-square probability = .000		

	High Officer	Lesser Officer	Nonofficer
High officer (%)	11.9	24.4	63.7
Lesser officer (%)	13.8	29.8	56.4
Nonofficer (%)	16.9	20.9	62.3
Percentage of cases	14.7	23.7	61.6
Defendant *n*	296	478	1243
Chi-square probability = .001			

	Quakers	Non-Quakers
Quaker (%)	38.0	62.0
Non-Quaker (%)	31.6	68.4
Percentage of cases	34.4	65.6
Defendant *n*	616	1175
Chi-square probability = .005		

	Quaker Leaders	Average Quakers	Non-Quakers
Quaker leaders (%)	4.2	32.2	63.7
Average Quakers (%)	9.2	29.7	61.1
Non-Quakers (%)	7.8	23.8	68.4
Percentage of cases	7.6	26.8	65.6
Defendant *n*	136	480	1175
Chi-square probability = .001			

Note: This table is to be read across: e.g., in the first cross-tabulation, landowner plaintiffs sued other landowners in 75.9 percent of their cases and sued nonlandowners 24.1 percent of the time.

Yet there were seventy-nine cases of high officers' suing high officers, which means about two such cases in each jurisdiction every three years, making it a much more common phenomenon than the theory implies. Such cases ran the gamut of causes and resolutions. Edward Hunloke, a justice for ten years in Burlington County, sued fellow justice John Tatham, but Tatham had Hunloke's case thrown out of court for failing to file the declaration on time. At the next session, Tatham consented to arbitration on the condition that Hunloke pay half of Tatham's charges in the earlier case.[32] William Clayton and Jeremiah Collett, both justices of the peace in Chester County, argued a land dispute in 1691.[33] John Brock, a former sheriff and then a justice in Bucks County, obtained a default judgment against Gilbert Wheeler, a former assemblyman who was about to become a justice, on a debt in 1690.[34] Because, as chapter 1 showed, those who held high offices were richer, more landed, and more likely to be merchants or self-described gentry, it is probable that such intra-elite battles arose from a higher level of transactions among themselves. Officers did succeed in keeping most such disputes out of court, but the number of such cases reveals that this segment of the legal elite had yet to eliminate such intra-elite disputes from the public view.

Analyzing Quaker litigation choices in terms of litigation theory is made more difficult by Quaker dogma regarding disputes and courts. George Fox, the London and Philadelphia yearly meetings, and various quarterly and monthly meetings firmly enjoined Friends not to sue other Friends. Filing a civil case against a fellow Quaker without first utilizing the dispute-resolution procedures of the meeting and without then gaining permission to sue was a disownable offense.[35] Given these strictures and heavy Quaker usage of courts, one would expect Quaker plaintiffs to sue non-Quakers, a matchup that would cause no doctrinal difficulties and would match litigation theory. Yet Quakers disproportionately chose to sue other Quakers. In 38.0 percent of their cases Quaker plaintiffs sued Quaker defendants, while non-Quakers sued Quakers in only 31.6 percent of their cases (see table 13). The Quaker plaintiff practice thus was precisely contrary to what their alleged legal culture would have predicted and what the first litigation theory would predict for this higher-status group. By contrast, the pattern of non-Quaker plaintiffs, unconstrained by religious injunctions, fit the second hypothesis, which postulated that plaintiffs with lesser status would avoid litigation when faced with a higher-status adversary.

At the risk of digression, this Quaker litigation pattern requires additional comment because it was a totally unexpected finding. Despite Quaker dogma, Quaker plaintiffs chose other Quakers as defendants in 302 cases. Quaker records were largely silent on whether meetings actually approved specific suits as required; only seven Quakers were given permission to go to court against other Quakers, and there were only two cases of discipline for litigation.[36] Given that Quakers controlled the courts and would have obviously observed such intra-Quaker suits, such silence implies the Quaker community consented to this trend to litigate rather than to arbitrate in meeting.

Was this intra-Quaker resort to courts a phenomenon that existed roughly evenly across the region or did some monthly meetings ignore this rule more than others? Of the cases in which both Quaker parties could be identified as members of a particular meeting, 46 percent were intrameeting conflicts, in other words, both the plaintiff and the defendant belonged to the same monthly meeting, where an arbitrated resolution would most likely occur. For these cases, a comparison was made between the percentage of Quakers who belonged to that meeting and the percentage of intra-Quaker cases that involved members of that meeting. Members of the Chester, Middletown, and Burlington monthly meetings engaged in intrameeting litigation at rates greater than their population percentage, while members of Darby, Radnor, and Falls meetings rarely engaged in intrameeting litigation.[37] Further evidence of the higher litigiousness in Chester and Burlington meetings was the distribution of plaintiffs in all Quaker versus Quaker cases, including the 54 percent of cases that involved litigants from different meetings. These two meetings provided 80 percent or more of those plaintiffs. This evidence suggests that to speak of *the* Quaker community or *the* Quaker legal culture oversimplifies the Delaware Valley experience. Although Quakers widely flouted the no-litigation doctrine, meetings varied considerably in the amount of noncompliance.

These findings carry certain implications relating to the economic and social power of Quakers in this society. Quakers were noted for "keeping their Trade within themselves,"[38] which, when combined with their virtually universal landownership, deeper pockets, and control of authoritative positions in the legal system, made it likely that Quakers would have more transactions with other Quakers than with non-Quakers. Should a dispute arise, such Quakers likely had enough at stake and enough confidence in the Quaker-run courts to make a suit a better choice than an informal arbitration in meeting, which might not be enforceable. For non-Quakers, these same factors—fewer transactions with Quakers, less at stake because of less wealth, and a court system controlled by Quakers—suggest why they sued Quakers at significantly lower rates. Finally, on the issue of intra-Quaker suits, doctrine and practice diverged widely, suggesting that Delaware Valley Quakers saw less need to avoid exposing their differences to the "world's people" when, unlike the situation in England, they controlled the legal system.

Of all the attributes analyzed in terms of litigation theory, power relationships became most apparent when the Quaker elite was separated out from average Quakers. In a three-way matchup of Quaker leaders, average Quakers, and non-Quakers, there was a statistically significant relationship between the elite's litigation patterns and those of the rest of society, which both theories predicted (see table 13). Quaker leaders disproportionately avoided suing other Quaker leaders, despite their deep pockets and likely high number of transactions with each other. Only 12 of the 302 Quaker versus Quaker cases saw Quaker leaders in both roles. Spectators would rarely if ever see an in-court fight between Quaker elites, who were thus more successful in maintaining an unbroken front than high legal officers were. Furthermore, Quaker leaders sued average Quakers disproportionately more often than they did non-Quakers, a result even more baffling in light of Friends' dogma (to which the leaders should be more willing to adhere) but right in line with the theory of using courts to control those below. Finally, non-Quakers disproportionately avoided suing average Quakers, a pattern of litigation deference predicted by the second theory. In a hierarchy of litigation, the elite (defined as Quaker leaders) thus found ways to avoid exposing its differences in public while using litigation against the next highest group (average Quakers), whereas those lowest in religious status (non-Quakers) avoided stepping up to sue those just above them.

This matchup analysis suggests how litigants perceived their social standing when it came to pursuing disputes in court. Oppression through lawsuit did not often come from the highest-status individuals hauling those at the bottom before the bar of justice; the lack of deep pockets of such defendants might have made such cases more trouble than they were worth. Rather, social power manifested itself in litigation when those lower-status nonlandowners, nonofficers, and non-Quakers did not take on those above them, despite the fact that such potential defendants likely had deep pockets. These lower-status potential plaintiffs, when faced with a higher-status adversary, chose to resolve disputes without the bargaining advantage of filing a suit or chose to "lump it." Either way, those of lower status found their options constrained by the social standing of the potential defendant. Once again, power in this system was most revealed by looking at individuals and groups when they occupied or avoided the role of defendant.

The Causes of Action

No legal system can regulate all disputes in a society; no legal system has the resources even to try. Rather, legal systems send out signals through their procedures and decisions that indicate which disputes are controlled by law and are therefore justiciable. Certain recurring interactions established reciprocal expectations of conduct that were enforceable under the seventeenth-century English system of common law. For these selected issues, which were called "causes of action" and were a critical aspect of common-law civil procedure, individuals could call on the power of the courts. These causes of action influenced, albeit indirectly, the ways members of this society structured their dealings and their thinking about disputes.[39] To analyze these choices requires, first, a short primer on the complex world of causes of action and, second, an examination of which plaintiffs used which causes and which defendants faced them.

Under common-law pleading, each dispute had to be fit into one of a limited number of causes of action, each cause of action having its own theories on which recovery could be based. Using a cause of action that did not fit the facts, using an incorrect theory under an appropriate cause of action, omitting essential elements, or combining two or more separate causes of action in one declaration were grounds for dismissing a case. So the unwary might avoid these traps, formbooks and advice manuals proliferated with explanations and models of successful declarations containing the precise language or *formula* that would get plaintiffs over the pleading threshold and into court on their merits. Delaware Valley's justices, laymen, and lawyers relied on such sources in striking a balance between law-reform simplicity and common-law complexity in plaintiff's declarations.[40]

Though each cause of action derived from a single theory that would entitle a plaintiff to recovery in certain situations, in practice and over time, the theories and resulting formulas mutated to give plaintiffs relief in new situations. For example, the action of trespass, begun under the theory of a breach of the king's peace, initially covered only wrongs committed with violence, actual or implied, against people and things, denoted by the formula *vi et armis* (with force and arms). Yet whether the damage was to a person's body (assault and battery), to a person's things (*de bonis asportatis,* or carrying away goods), or to a person's land (*quare clausum fregit,* or unlawful entry, cutting trees, etc.), the requirement of physical force became so weak that the term *force and arms* became, in most cases, a legal fiction, and the breach of peace was not always alleged. A wrongful step on land or a wrongful touch to a person or a person's chattels was force enough to allow plaintiffs to recover under trespass.[41]

Trespass, in addition to the three types of damage to person or property just noted, developed in the late Middle Ages additional forms to cover different types of harms. From the standpoint of seventeenth-century practice, the most important expansion had been "trespass on the case," or more simply, "case." Case acquired its name from the requirement that the writ not use one of the three stylized forms of trespass (above) but rather lay out particular narrative details of the "special case." Case became an elastic, residual action that covered injuries to a person or the person's property by a wrongful act of another unaccompanied by actual or implied force, or where the injury was the indirect or secondary effect of a wrongful act accompanied by actual or implied force. Broken promises could thus be a trespass on the case, under the theory that the defendant, in promising to do something for the plaintiff and then failing, had induced the plaintiff to rely on the defendant. By breaking the promise, the defendant had injured the plaintiff by "contriving and fraudulently intending craftily and subtly to deceive and defraud the plaintiff in and by his mere act of disregarding his promise."[42]

Although this formula on deceit continued to live on in the declaration regardless of its truth, case broadened to include the general area of *assumpsit,* which was an obligation undertaken or assumed by an individual without a sealed document and which covered many different forms of what today would be called contracts. Case covered in special assumpsit a debtor's refusal to pay an expressly promised sum (often embodied in a promissory note); *indebitatus assumpsit* covered implied promises to pay sums certain, such as when the debtor refused to return to the plaintiff money "had and received by the defendant to his use" or refused to pay for goods "sold and delivered," for "work done," or "money due on an account stated" (account book). If the indebtedness was not made in a precise sum, another variety of assumpsit for goods delivered (*quantum valebant*) or services rendered (*quantum meruit*) was available.[43]

Case was not limited to indebtedness, although that was by far its most common usage. The two most important other uses for case in the Delaware Valley involved defamation (injury to personal reputation or sometimes to land title) and conversion (deprivation of property). Case for defamation required that plaintiffs specifically plead the allegedly defamatory words (guidebooks contained long lists of actionable words) and that the good name of the plaintiff had been materially damaged.[44] For goods the defendant had allegedly taken from the plaintiff and refused to give up, "a distinct species of case developed—the action of trover." Etymologically derived from the French word *trouver,* meaning "to find," trover relied on the legal fiction that goods that the defendant detained were actually "casually lost" (formula) by the plaintiff and found by the defendant, who then "converted" the goods to his or her own use by refusing to return them though "often requested" to do so.[45] Other available uses of case included for nuisance and for negligence, but these uses were rare in the Delaware Valley.

Just as case did not simply include debt, so too it did not cover all debts. The common law also provided the action of debt, most commonly used in the Delaware Valley for recovering money loaned. The circumstances for debt were narrow, requiring a written instrument that contained the defendant's explicit promise to pay a fixed sum and that had been affixed with a legal seal. A common practice involved the defendant's having to pass a sealed obligation or bond agreeing to pay the plaintiff a sum of money unless a certain condition was performed, such as repaying a loan or building a house. To allow for damages or penalties, the sum would often be greater than the underlying value. The advantage of sealed, conditioned bonds was that few defenses were allowed; courts would not look behind the bond to any legal problems with the underlying transaction. Debt could also be used for arbitration bonds (sealed obligations by disputants to pay a sum usually well in excess of the controversy, conditioned on accepting the arbitrators' award), statutory penalties, or prior court judgments. The disadvantage of debt was its strict formal requirements for the sealed written obligation, an inconvenience and an implicit statement that at least one party was not entirely comfortable with informality and was doing business with one suspicious eye cocked toward a potential day in court.[46]

Other common-law actions appeared less frequently. One particularly convoluted form of trespass, designed to try title to land without having to use the ancient real actions, was called *ejectione firmae* (spelled
firme in the Delaware Valley) or ejectment. The declaration invoked the
names of two fictitious people, each of whom possessed a fictitious lease
from one of the true parties contesting who held proper title. One of
the fictitious lessees fictitiously ejected the other fictitious lessee, leaving the court to decide on the rights of the rival fictitious lessees based
on the underlying title claims of the real parties in interest, who had to
consent to all the untruths to protect their claims.[47] Ejectment was an
extreme example of common-law rules that deviated from common sense
but had to be mastered to sue successfully in England and that in practice revealed the tensions between law reform and common-law tradi-
tions. Other common-law actions that appeared only rarely in Delaware
Valley courts included covenant (for breach of sealed instruments that
did not involve a specified sum); detinue (for the recovery of specific
things unjustly detained, which was less popular than trover because it
allowed defendants to return the property at the end of the case, however damaged, without paying damages); and account (for a fiduciary
to render an account).[48]

Once plaintiffs had filed their declarations under a particular cause,
defendants, if they chose not to default or confess judgment (admit liability), now had to plead. One choice would not go to the merits of
the dispute but would attack the plaintiff's declaration. The defendant's
plea could claim that the plaintiff's grievance was not actionable at law
(a demurrer) or that the plaintiff's writ contained a technical error (plea
in abatement). When such requests were made on some grounds, Delaware Valley's justices would dismiss the cases. Defects, such as omitting
one of the parties, not filing papers on time, suing in the wrong name,
not making the content of the declaration consistent with the accom-
panying writ, writing a declaration without providing particulars, failing to have one's witnesses ready for trial, and failing to appear, were
grounds for judgment for the defendant, often called a nonsuit.[49] Yet
these dismissals were without prejudice, allowing the plaintiff to bring
the suit anew at a subsequent session, as John Tatham did in his long-
running dispute against Joseph Growden over land in 1691.[50] Furthermore, justices had the discretion to waive defects in the pleading and
to allow amendments "gratis" to an improper declaration. Not once was
a cause of action disqualified for containing more than one theory of

recovery, for lacking the name of the proper cause, or for failing to contain the proper formula. Justices (or clerks) were so lax that declarations in case one session could suddenly appear in debt at the next.[51] By allowing plaintiffs to start over or amend their complaints for egregious errors and by ignoring other deviations from English procedure, courts found practical compromises between the tenets of law reform and the tenets of the common law.

When the issue involved a question of the substance of the common law rather than a procedural question, justices had to make legal decisions, although few had any formal legal training. Some issues of law were easy. Where no consideration was pled, actions of case on assumpsit were readily nonsuited, yet the justices could distinguish that a bond served as good consideration in case as well as in debt.[52] In most instances, however, the court would finesse hard questions by simplifying the pleading or inducing the parties to come to trial by consent, regardless of the niceties of common law. In an action of case in 1694, the defendant, Lewis Levalley, put in a "plea Speciall" against the plaintiff's declaration; the court denied the plea, stating "that in regard of the infancy of the Province, advantage may not be taken against the formality of a Plea." John Budd pleaded that an action of *scandalli magnat* brought against him by John Tatham did not lie; the court decided to proceed on the declaration as if it were a simple action of case for defamation, avoiding the issue of whether the plaintiff's status as a justice entitled him to special protection of his reputation.[53]

Trying land titles provided these courts with their most obvious conflict between common-law complexity and law-reform simplicity. Debates over the proper role, if any, for the action of ejectment in the Delaware Valley were recurring. When defendants did not challenge the plaintiff's use of *ejectione firme,* courts followed the consent rule, instructing the defendant to "by rule of Court Confess the lease Entry & Ejectment & Insist only upon the tittle."[54] Many defendants, some represented by the attorney David Lloyd, did object to such fictions, however. Lloyd vehemently contended that ejectment was inconsistent with the law reforms of the province and succeeded in writing this view into statutes prohibiting fictions. Courts never failed to accept such arguments and always required rewriting of such challenged declarations. Courts thus forced litigants to try land titles by consent or under a variety of other causes of action, including land, case, and trespass.[55]

When complex legal issues on causes of action could not be recon-

ciled in such a manner, courts were often at a loss. Confusion intensified when there was clearly more knowledge at the bar than on the
bench. In a 1692 Chester County case, two attorneys appeared for each
side, and the court, "after a great Debate Concerning ye Leagallness and
unLeagallness of ye Declaration," finally granted a nonsuit in a divided
opinion. In the case of Israel Taylor versus Nicholas Gottava in 1703,
attorneys again appeared for both sides contesting the sufficiency of the
declaration at law, but this time the Chester County court retired to
consider its verdict. Such consideration took more than two years before the justices finally ruled for the defendant.[56] Legal institutions might
have preferred simplicity based on law-reform philosophy, but a desire
to avoid exposing the justices' lack of legal expertise might well have
influenced decisions that restrained litigants' desire for more complex
legal proceedings.

While courts consistently allowed (and even desired) great deviation
from the strictures of common-law pleading, litigants moved in the opposite direction, toward greater complexity in their declarations and
pleas. In the 1680s, pleas in case to recover money on contracts did not
use the word *assumpsit* or the formula on deceit. Rather, the critical terms
appeared in easily understood English, words like *due, oweth,* and *indebted,* in declarations that could contain less than a hundred words.[57]
A 1686 trover declaration in Gloucester County contained no allegation that the defendant "found" the plaintiff's bull but instead stated
that the defendant "hath wrongfully and unjustly taken away [the bull]
and the same Detaines, keeps, and converts to his owne use."[58] Even
when plaintiffs tried to use ejectment to try title, the fictitious parties
did not appear, raising the possibility that, for example, in the case of a
landowner living in New York, there was a real lease and eviction instead of one by collusion.[59]

This early simplicity did not mean that convoluted legal language was
dead in the Delaware Valley. Through formbooks and advice from clerks
and attorneys, plaintiffs quickly acquired and used common-law pleading. As early as 1686, a declaration in case long-windedly alleged that
the defendant "did then Contract and bargain with and engaged to pay
and deliver to the sd plaint or his order, upon a valluable Consideration
by ye sd defend in Hand received [63 buckskins] good and merchant-
able," yet "notwithstanding his aforesd Contract promise and agreement"
he "hath not paid nor delivered . . . but hath Refused or neglected, and
doth still Refuse or neglect to pay or deliver the same, allthough by ye

said plaint he hath since the day and year Abovesaid been thereunto offten required."[60] Here were all the formal elements in common-law language—agreement in the form of promises between parties, consideration, performance by plaintiff, and breach by defendant that continued despite the plaintiff's repeated entreaties and willingness to accept performance. After about 1695, a majority of plaintiffs used this formulation, even though courts still accepted simpler forms. The deceit formula infiltrated slightly later; a declaration having the defendant "Intending and subtilly Designeing . . . to Defraud and Craftily to Deceive" the plaintiff was first recorded in Gloucester County in 1694 and Bucks County in 1697. By the early 1700s, virtually all appropriate contract cases contained variations on this theme.[61] Damages likewise became standardized, with little regard to real loss; debt cases always asked for roughly twice the principle owed (as expressed in the underlying bond), and in case, plaintiffs seemed harmed only in round numbers (five, ten, twenty, or fifty pounds).[62] Though courts still allowed roughhewn declarations, a sort of Gresham's law of pleading took place—by the early 1700s, plaintiffs' preferences for complex English forms were driving out the simple forms.

Over time, defendants trod a similar path in adopting more complex forms of pleading. By 1692, defendants were pleading the "general issue" to contest the case on its merits by using the term *non assumpsit* to defend against contract claims; by the 1700s, pleas *nihil debet* or *non cull* had replaced simple English statements that a defendant owed nothing or was not guilty.[63] Pleas in the alternative—there was no consideration; even if there was, the debt was fully paid; but even if it was not, nothing was owed the defendant according to the manner and form of the declaration (a negative pregnant, begging the question of whether the defendant owed the plaintiff in some other manner or form)—and demurrers to test the sufficiency of the pleading at law became commonplace.[64] The most significant defendant pleading change was the introduction of the oyer, the imparlance, and the special imparlance (discussed earlier) in the early 1700s. Plaintiffs in debt cases, who previously could expect the defendant to admit the bond and resolve the case in one court meeting, now were faced with defendants who had discovered the requirement of reading the bond in court (oyer), which was naturally followed by defendants' requesting an imparlance to respond to what they had heard. Such tactics were so popular that 50 percent of the court business on Chester County's docket from 1704 to 1710 consisted of cases continued, most of which had started by using such pleas.[65] Despite the founders' law reforms designed to keep civil justice simple, quick, and in English, litigants brought more complexity, more delays, and more legal French and Latin into their cases. Delaware Valley civil procedure evolved a working compromise, which was keyed to the level of legal information that litigants were willing to use and which resulted in legal practice that was controlled by common law, not law reform, after 1710. Law reform would die the death of a thousand cuts inflicted by increasingly complex pleadings, but law reform's legacy was the legitimacy conferred on the legal elite by attracting cases on all causes from all sectors of this pluralistic society.

The Causes of Action Used

Discovering which plaintiffs used which causes illuminates the relative concerns of each group and thus suggests the level of legal sophistication, the kind of transactions, and the type of behavior each group believed courts would view favorably. Examining which defendants had which causes filed against them reveals which groups suffered from what sort of civil attacks and, if possible, why. The causes of action have been divided into four categories. The first, case, was by far the most common action recorded, but its catch-all nature makes it too amorphous to be useful analytically. Case as used hereafter will therefore refer to causes where an underlying debt or contract was indicated or implied in the dockets (the most common usage) or when the cause recorded was case without any other information given. When case was used for trover, defamation, or other nondebt/contract issues, those cases have been reclassified. The second type of cause, debt, because of its narrow applicability, reflects all causes so named, plus those where no cause was cited but the declaration referred to the formula of writing obligatory under seal for a sum certain. The third category covers other indebtedness or contract causes, including covenant (16 cases), account (1), equity (7), court fees (10), and no recorded cause but which indicated a contract or indebtedness was at issue (180). The final category is a residual, covering all nondebt, noncontract issues (i.e., trespass, defamation, trover, detinue, assault and battery, land/ejectment, and similar cases that had no cause recorded). Eight attributes—officeholding status, religion, Quaker leadership, landownership, wealth, male occupation, gender, and multiple usage—were matched up (from both plaintiff and defendant sides) with the four categories to identify any statistical deviations and, if possible, the probable cause of those differences.[66]

Overall, 62.1 percent of civil cases filed (1,253 of 2,017) could be classified. Only 52.4 percent of the cases (1,057) had a specific cause of action recorded (another 9.7 percent could be classified by context), an indication of law-reform leniency (or possibly the clerk's laxness) regarding the formalities of common-law pleading. Of those 1,057 cases that recorded a specific cause of action, case totaled 487 (46.1 percent), and debt constituted 330 (31.2 percent). When cases that had identifiable issues without specific causes named are included, cases that involved debts and contracts made up 82.3 percent of identifiable issues (see table 14). As in other colonies, the civil workload consisted mainly of vol-

Table 14. Plaintiffs' Causes

Attributes	Case	Debt	Other Debt/ Contract	Nondebt/ Contract	N
Total *n*	487	330	214	222	1253
Percentage of total causes	38.9	26.3	17.1	17.7	
Male	39.1%	26.3%	17.5%	18.2%	1219
Female	29.4	29.4	14.7	26.5	34
Chi-square probability = .465					
Quakers	37.3%	25.1%	20.0%	17.5%	474
Quaker leaders	33.3	29.2	22.2	15.2	171
Average Quakers	39.6	22.8	18.8	18.8	303
Non-Quakers	36.0	28.6	18.5	17.0	578
Chi-square probability = .651 (average Quakers vs. leaders chi-square = .220)					
Landowners	38.1%	26.6%	17.1%	18.2%	1036
Nonlandowners	42.4	24.9	17.1	15.7	217
Chi-square probability = .643					
Occupations (males only)[a]					
Farmer	42.5%	18.5%	17.2%	21.8%	308
Artisan	37.6	23.9	23.9	14.7	109
Farmer-artisan	35.6	27.8	20.0	16.7	90
Merchant	36.1	37.6	16.6	9.8	205
Self-described gentry	36.0	30.7	14.7	18.7	150
Servant/slave/laborer	58.8	11.8	11.8	17.7	17
Chi-square probability = .001					

Table 14, continued

Attributes	Case	Debt	Other Debt/ Contract	Nondebt/ Contract	N
1693 Pennsylvania tax assessment (in pounds)					
100+	37.0%	32.4%	17.6%	13.0%	108
50–99	51.6	15.6	20.3	12.5	64
1–49	26.5	26.5	20.6	26.5	68
Chi-square probability = .016					
Inventoried wealth (in pounds)					
500+	31.7%	32.3%	17.1%	19.0%	158
100–499	41.1	24.7	19.2	15.1	146
1–99	31.5	20.4	25.9	22.2	54
Chi-square probability = .245					
Legal roles					
High officer	37.9%	29.5%	18.7%	13.8%	427
Lesser officer	33.3	23.1	16.9	26.7	225
Nonofficer	41.6	25.3	16.0	17.1	601
Chi-square probability = .002					
Number of cases brought					
1–2	40.7%	25.5%	17.7%	16.1%	639
3–5	34.3	26.1	15.5	24.1	334
6+	39.6	28.3	17.4	14.8	247
Chi-square probability = .047					

a. The category "other" has been omitted to ensure that chi-square is a valid test. Litigation analysis will use only six occupational categories.

untary economic transactions in which one party had failed to perform and now was being sued by the person deprived of the benefit of the bargain.[67] Of the 222 identifiable nondebt/contract cases, the most common was trespass (without assault and battery, 67 cases), followed by defamation (61), trover and conversion (35), land/ejectment (27), assault and battery (22), detinue (5), replevin (3—not technically a cause but used as such), and wrongful imprisonment (2). If the different economic causes reflected how plaintiffs and defendants structured their economic relationships, the propensity for nondebt/contract causes disclosed the relative significance of what were usually personal harms as opposed to market harms among groups.

When officeholding ranks of plaintiffs were matched against causes, the results were statistically significant (see table 14). The greatest deviance was lesser officers suing far more often in nondebt/contract causes than expected; the second largest contributor was high officers suing less than expected in these same noncontract causes. Lesser officers sued less often than expected in case, and high officers sued more often than expected in debt. Lesser officers thus used the courts disproportionately often to protect themselves against nondebt harms than against indebtedness. This finding is consistent with the low status and lower esteem in which constables, for example, were held; lesser officers were most concerned about protecting their reputations, their bodies, and their property from harm. High officers needed the law proportionately less to protect themselves against such nondebt slights, indicating a security of position and place. To protect their economic deals, high officers structured their transactions using the law's more certain method for recovery, the sealed bond, which allowed them to sue in debt rather than in case. Finally, nonofficers deviated little in terms of the overall average of causes, indicating that legal information had been transmitted to this two-thirds of the legal population.

This pattern for officeholding—higher-status plaintiffs seeking the certainty of sealed instruments and suing in debt more often, lower status suing disproportionately often in nondebt/contract causes—persisted for half of all attributes at statistically significant levels. In terms of the occupations of male plaintiffs, the causes used deviated significantly: merchants sued disproportionately in debt, merchants sued disproportionately less in nondebt causes, and farmers used nondebt causes more often. Those calling themselves gentry were second only to merchants in the percentage of their suits in debt. For taxed wealth, the poorest group sued more often in nondebt causes, the middle group sued more often in case and less often in debt, and the highest percentage of debt suits came from the wealthiest group. Regarding the number of suits brought, the megaplaintiffs (noted in chapter 1 as having higher-status attributes) sued less often in nondebt causes and had the highest percentage of debt usage, while repeat plaintiffs sued more often in nondebt and less often in case. Inventoried wealth and landownership did not show statistically significant results, but the pattern held there as well; the richest group used debt more often than the less fortunate did.

Unlike high officers and others of higher status, Quaker plaintiffs did not choose causes of action that differed statistically from those used by non-Quakers, nor did Quakers use debt more often than non-Quakers. Quaker leaders did not differ from average Quakers in their suing habits, although they did use debt slightly more often, but only at a rate virtually identical with that of non-Quakers. It was in the defendant's role that Quakers showed significant deviation from the expected pattern of causes of action (see table 15). Quaker defendants were sued dis-

Table 15. Causes against Defendants

Attributes	Case	Debt	Other Debt/ Contract	Nondebt/ Contract	N
Total *n*	487	330	214	222	1253
Percentage of total causes	38.9	26.3	17.1	17.7	100
Male	38.9%	26.6%	15.9%	18.6%	1217
Female	38.8	25.4	20.9	15.0	36
Chi-square probability = .432					
Quakers	37.5%	22.0%	19.7%	20.8%	341
Quaker leaders	34.9	19.3	19.3	26.5	83
Average Quakers	38.4	22.9	19.8	19.0	258
Non-Quakers	36.2	29.4	19.0	15.5	711
Chi-square probability = .034 (average Quakers vs. leaders, chi-square = .517)					
Landowners	38.9%	26.6%	15.9%	18.6%	946
Nonlandowners	38.8	25.4	20.9	15.0	307
Chi-square probability = .156					
Occupations (males only)[a]					
Farmer	41.2%	24.5%	15.8%	18.5%	379
Artisan	39.5	31.8	18.5	10.3	195
Farmer-artisan	31.7	28.1	8.5	31.7	82
Merchant	42.6	23.4	19.2	14.9	47
Self-described gentry	44.7	23.4	21.3	10.6	47
Servant/slave/laborer	31.4	25.7	22.9	20.0	35
Chi-square probability = .020					
1693 Pennsylvania tax assessment (in pounds)					
100+	34.6%	32.7%	11.5%	21.2%	52
50–99	47.6	36.5	9.5	6.4	63
1–49	38.5	23.1	20.5	18.0	117
Chi-square probability = .016					

Inventoried wealth (in pounds)
500+	42.4%	25.4%	10.2%	22.0%	59
100–499	38.6	22.1	18.1	21.3	127
1–99	34.9	25.4	15.9	23.8	63

Chi-square probability = .870

Legal roles
High officer	43.9%	25.7%	11.7%	18.7%	171
Lesser officer	39.9	21.8	18.4	19.9	266
Nonofficer	37.5	27.9	17.8	16.8	816

Chi-square probability = .169

Number of cases against
1–2	38.5%	24.6%	15.9%	21.0%	672
3–5	36.5	28.1	19.2	16.2	334
6+	42.9	28.7	17.4	10.9	247

Chi-square probability = .016

a. The category "other" has been omitted to ensure that chi-square is a valid test. Litigation analysis will use only six occupational categories.

proportionately less often in debt and more often in nondebt causes, while non-Quakers were sued more often in debt. There was no statistical difference between average Quakers and their leaders as defendants. The debt results suggest either that Quakers did not like to do business with sealed bonds (perhaps fearing there was a chance they might not perform and would then be sued) or that they took such bonds more seriously than did their non-Quaker counterparts so that the Quaker performance rate was actually higher than that of non-Quakers. Of these two inferences, it is more likely that Quakers did not use sealed written instruments very often, because as plaintiffs they showed no preference for suing in debt, especially when compared with others of high status. Quaker dogma in business dealings also reinforced the idea that oral agreements, especially with other Quakers, should be no less binding than written ones.[68] As for the disproportionately high number of nondebt suits against Quakers and Quaker leaders, this result indicates that they were giving more personal than economic offense to their neighbors. It cannot be determined whether plaintiffs were more on guard against slights by Quakers or Quakers pressed their status advantages too far in such areas as defamation and trespass. Finally, one sees that despite the large degree of overlap between officeholding and membership or leadership in the Society of Friends, the patterns of litigation experience were quite different.

With the exception of Quakers who were sued more in nondebt causes, the causes used against other defendants did not clearly differ by status. Whether one held a legal office during this period did not statistically alter a defendant's likelihood of facing any of the types of suits. Neither did the level of wealth at one's death show a statistical bias regarding what one was sued for while alive; the richest group and the poorest were sued at identical rates (25.4 percent) in debt. Gender and landownership likewise showed no bias regarding defendants' causes. The distribution of causes for occupation of male defendants was significant as were tax level and number of cases, but no common pattern emerged. Farmer-artisans were sued disproportionately more often in nondebt causes, but artisans were sued disproportionately less in nondebt. Those in the lowest tax group defended against debt claims more often outside of case and debt, while the middling group faced other or undesignated debt causes as well as nondebt cases less often. Megadefendants faced fewer cases in nondebt and more cases in case, while once or twice defendants faced more nondebt actions. The pattern of megadefendants indicates they had encountered economic difficulties, and anxious creditors, having extended them relatively small amounts of credit that did not warrant sealed bonds in the normal course of business, now flooded the courts in case. In conclusion, except for Quakers, the use of debt was distributed statistically evenly across the defendant population, and except for megadefendants, so was the use of case.

Conclusions in this area must be considered tentative because in many cases no cause could be identified, facts about the underlying transaction were often unrecorded, and the ambiguity inherent in common-law causes could be used for very different sorts of transactions.[69] Comparing usage of case, even when stripped of actions in trover and defamation, with usage of debt in the Delaware Valley may be revealing, but it is a crude tool to examine the impact of law on society. Nonetheless, sealed debt instruments underlying debt cases seem to have played a significant role in this region's economic transactions from the start, a role that expanded over time. In the 1680s, there were 118 debt cases compared with 231 in case; debt represented 34 percent of the total case and debt cases. In the 1690s, there were 143 debt cases, 41 percent of the total of case and debt cases. In the first decade of the 1700s, there was an overall decline in recorded causes of action, but the 69 debt cases constituted 58 percent of case and debt cases. By way of comparison, a study of colonial Connecticut (which used the underlying transaction, not the cause of action, for classification) found sealed bonds that could underlie a debt action constituted only 3 percent of suits that involved book debt, bonds, or notes in the decade of the 1700s and 22 percent in the 1710s.[70] Delaware Valley litigation suggests that neighborly transactions played a lesser role than they did in Connecticut; perhaps because the neighbors were of such diverse backgrounds, arm's length market transactions through sealed bonds became more important.

The relation between attributes and causes of action illustrated how this legal system both reflected and reinforced power and status relationships. In the plaintiff role, high officers, the wealthy, and merchants seem to have disproportionately formalized their economic transactions, with apparent knowledge of the legal advantages of sealed instruments should a deal go bad. Merchants' disproportionate avoidance of courts for nondebt issues (such as defamation, which accounted for only 4 of 205 suits) suggests a security of place not found in other colonies.[71] Conversely, farmers, the most numerous, were less formalized in their economic litigation, but they saw courts as a favorable forum to air their nondebt grievances. As will be seen in chapter 3, the social and economic power that enabled some groups to compel a debtor to sign a sealed bond is rewarded by the legal system. The rewards of debt will be spread evenly against all defendant groups, with one exception, suggesting that sealed bonds were not reserved for specific high-risk transactions or debtors but part of the regular course of business. The exception, Quakers, avoided being sued in debt, and also, despite their high status, did not prefer debt when they sued, suggesting their business practices diverged from those of non-Quakers, who were more formal and less reliant on trust. But Quakers' and Quaker leaders' appearances as defendants revealed that they possessed a disturbing tendency to create nondebt grievances and that Quakers' opponents believed the courts might just correct those grievances.

These litigants had just begun their choices in a system that all groups were using. By inducing disputants of all kinds to use legal processes and to frame disputes in terms of legal rules, the Quaker legal system had crossed its first threshold toward legitimacy. Resolving the case still remained, with each step affected by the law, the facts, and the relative power position of each litigant.

THREE

Strategies and Outcomes
in Civil Litigation

When the dispute became a case on a court's docket, private individuals took on new personas. They became litigants, whose choices
were shaped by the legal system. Already, as noted in chapter 2, the aggrieved had had to transform their understanding of a transaction, whose
objectives might have had little or nothing to do with legal norms, into
the language of civil procedure, which framed the dispute in obscure
terms.[1] Even after this transformation, an ambiguity remained about
whether the aggrieved's interpretation of the entitlement due from the
defendant was correct, an ambiguity the court could resolve through an
adversary process allowing for opposing witnesses, physical evidence,
arguments, and resort to legal authorities. Yet, then as now, such full-
blown trials were but one option among many, which required litigants
to weigh several variables. For instance, they had to consider the likely
outcome of this type of case in court, since some causes would be easy
to win and others more difficult. Plaintiffs and defendants responded
to such cues in their litigation choices and thus helped shape the likely
results and likely behavior of future litigants on similar issues. In other
words, the choices related to a particular grievance, and its chances for
legal remedy were part of an interactive process that determined as well
as reflected social norms.[2]

    This chapter examines the variety of litigation choices available for
disputes that became cases in the Delaware Valley. As noted earlier, these
suits represent only a fraction of all justiciable disputes in a society. By
the time a case appeared on a legal docket, the individuals involved in
the dispute had ignored, discarded, or found wanting possible extralegal alternatives for resolving the grievance, such as direct confrontation,
mediation, informal arbitration, avoidance, and "lumping it." Now a

new set of choices appeared, because the law rewarded plaintiffs for coming to court by enhancing their bargaining positions against defendants for these transactions. Should the defendants now make no response, they would lose by default and put themselves and their property at the mercy of the court's judgment. The "shadow of the law" now influenced the parties' choices, since the legal system sanctioned and rewarded some choices, tolerated others, and discouraged or punished a third set that dwelt outside the law's accepted channels for dispute processing (such as violence). Desirable choices included whether to bargain and settle the case out of court, seek formal arbitration, confess judgment to the opponent (i.e., admit liability in court), or fight immediately in court using available legal weapons. Other choices, less desirable but nonetheless available, included running away, hiring an attorney, and stalling. Such decisions would be influenced not only by legal rules (i.e., whether the case was strong or weak) but also by the personal and power relationships between the parties, by the claims of other behavioral norms (e.g., religious), by the relative skill of the parties in manipulating the options to their own advantage, and by the wider legal culture. If the disputants chose to fight their case to an in-court verdict, society, as represented by jury or justices of the peace, would decide whether a claim merited enforcement, supposedly according to legal norms but potentially influenced by those same extralegal attributes that affected the parties' choices.[3]

These practical strategies of dispute resolution revealed the basic values of the legal system as tied to the wider society, how the new, pluralistic Delaware Valley society revealed "through its law the innermost secrets of the manner in which it holds men together."[4] Not only did the pattern of causes of action illustrate what members of this society valued, but also how those issues were disputed indicated which transactions were routine and which were divisive. The divisive cases had special potential for serving integrative and symbolic functions, influencing the wider legal culture while legitimizing courts as decision-makers.[5] Whether such integration would occur depended on how law reformers' promise of open and equal access to fair justice would fare in the hands of the Delaware Valley's social and legal elite. Litigants also had to integrate in their choices conflicting messages, deriving from legal processes and legal culture, which on the one hand said that suing should be simpler, easier, and cheaper while on the other hand proclaimed that lawsuits should be avoided entirely. Overall, the pattern of choices in dispute processing would reinforce the initial choice made by the Quaker elite, to use "good law" to keep "good men"—themselves—in power in an increasingly diverse society.

Defining the Completed Civil Case

The basic analytical unit for this chapter is the *completed* civil case, a subset of all cases recorded for a county's court of common pleas. Chapter 2 considered all cases *entered*, but not all those cases revealed a result that could shed light on litigation choices. To be considered completed, a case must have had a recorded final outcome, which fell into three categories. First, a case could have been determined by the parties themselves or by the parties' agreement to arbitrate their dispute formally. In some cases, courts clearly recorded an outcome of accommodation, since the parties "agreed" or referred their case to "indifferent men" for arbitration, both of which could occur anytime between the filing of the case and the rendering of an in-court verdict.[6] In other cases, the docket's notation of a case being "withdrawn," "ended," or "discontinued" indicated that the plaintiff had accepted, at least for now, a final resolution of this dispute. The two most probable inferences from such notations are that the plaintiffs reached an accommodation with their adversaries or that they recognized that the suit would fail and gave up. In either case, the case ended without an in-court contest, without a public confrontation. All these cases are therefore defined as completed and *settled*.[7]

The second category of completed cases were those in which the court determined the rights of the parties without a contest on the substantive merits of the dispute, called here *uncontested*. Plaintiffs won uncontested when summoned defendants failed to appear (default judgment) or when they confessed judgment, stood silent, or entered no defense. Defendants won uncontested in nonsuits when plaintiffs failed to appear to prosecute their complaint or when the court dismissed the complaint for a technical failure in the plaintiff's pleadings. The final category of completed cases were those that were *contested*, cases in which both parties appeared or were represented in court, substantive real issues of fact or law were in dispute, potentially large numbers of witnesses appeared for the parties, and a jury verdict or a bench judgment was reached. These cases represented the greatest potential for court-day drama and integration of social norms through law.[8] Conflicts with the greatest intensity and the most significance for the legal system's perceived fairness as well as for litigants involved jury trials, which is dealt with separately and at length.

Of the 2,017 cases filed in these courts from 1680 to 1710, 1,642, or 81 percent, were completed. Some unfinished cases reflected the defendant's deliberate choice to avoid justice by leaving the county. Bartholomew Thatcher, a farmer-artisan and long a resident of Bucks County, fled in 1698 when he was sued separately by John Carter and Joseph Kirkbride, who had anticipated his flight by attempting to have him arrested.[9] Jeremiah Basse succeeded in serving his warrant on John Powson in Burlington County in 1695, but "Powson made his escape," and the case languished. The defendant Benjamin Devell, a landed yeoman, escaped three times from plaintiffs in West Jersey, twice by avoiding service of process and once with outside help as he was "rescued" from custody.[10] Other defendants who were "not found," and thus likely escaped, were geographically, economically, or socially marginal. Most incomplete cases, however, did not result from such runaways but were cases where the record went silent. Undoubtedly, some of these cases did have in-court outcomes that either were not recorded or were lost, while other cases were incomplete because the parties settled the issue without a court record being entered, as has been suggested occurred often in English courts of the sixteenth and seventeenth centuries.[11]

To determine whether incomplete cases might reveal a true litigant choice of avoidance, the distribution of completed versus incompleted cases was matched up with various attributes and legal roles for both plaintiffs and defendants. For all groups, the only statistically significant difference on the plaintiff side was on the issue of landownership (chi-square probability = .011), where nonlandowners participated in disproportionately more unfinished cases than landowners did. The incomplete cases of all other plaintiff groups were statistically normal, a result that merely reflects that plaintiffs were unlikely to abandon the jurisdiction and their case when they held a clear legal advantage over the defendant. The analysis as viewed from the defendant angle turned up three groups that were more likely to have incompleted cases. Nonlanded defendants were less likely to have final results (.037), as were one-time defendants (.030), a group with similarly low levels of status and wealth. That these groups might run away rather than face civil justice seems logical, but it is less clear why average Quaker defendants, as opposed to Quaker leaders and non-Quakers, had disproportionately more incomplete cases (.006). Given the lack of causal information on whether settlement, running away, or record failure was at work, and given that most categories showed no statistical difference, these results barely suggest that litigant choice, not some other factor, was at work. Therefore, although all litigants and causes could be analyzed in chapter 2, understanding the interaction among litigants, causes, and outcomes must be limited to completed cases with known outcomes.

Distribution of Causes and Outcomes

To analyze litigants' choices during litigation, one can begin with the outcome and work backward. The causes of action discussed in chapter 2 reflected the values of litigants as well as the values of the legal system that attracted such cases. Table 16 examines the disposition of that civil workload for the three types of outcomes—contested, uncontested, and settled—which reflected three different litigant strategies. Table

Table 16. Causes of Action, by Outcome

Cause	N	Contested	Uncontested	Settled/ Arbitrated
For completed cases with causes specifically identified by the court records				
Case	424	24.3%	22.4%	53.3%
Debt	276	18.1	31.9	50.0
Trespass	57	61.4	8.8	29.8
Defamation	55	49.1	7.3	43.6
Trover/conversion	32	40.6	21.9	37.5
Assault/battery	19	68.4	5.3	26.3
Land/ejectment	16	68.8	31.3	0.0
Total *n*	879 (53.5% of all completed cases)			
For completed cases by category of cause of action, including those cases where no specific cause was recorded				
Case	424	24.3%	22.4%	53.3%
Debt	276	18.1	31.9	50.0
Other debt/contract	169	37.9	46.2	16.0
Nondebt/contract	200	55.5	14.0	30.5
Total *n*	1069 (65.1% of all completed cases)			
All cases	1642	24.2%	24.9%	50.9%

17 identifies the percentage of cases plaintiffs won, either contested or uncontested, for various causes. These two indices combine to reveal levels of consensus within the legal system regarding certain transactions and behaviors. The premise here is that when consensus has been achieved, only rarely would plaintiffs bring cases if they expected to lose, and only rarely would defendants choose to contest suits when the outcome was clearly and predictably against them. If the system had achieved a high degree of consensus, one would therefore expect to see higher levels of uncontested and settled cases, since the parties avoid real conflict by accommodating the dispute beforehand or having the defendant confess judgment (an uncontested plaintiff victory). For those few cases that were contested, higher percentages of plaintiff victories would be expected. When there was less consensus on standards of behavior or genuine disagreements to be resolved—that is, when defendants did not feel the law or facts were so against them that in-court resistance was hopeless—one would expect a higher percentage of cases

Table 17. Plaintiffs' Victories, by Cause

Cause	Overall *N*	Contested	Uncontested	Overall
For completed, unsettled cases with causes specifically identified by the court records				
Case	198	74.8%	73.7%	74.2%
Debt	138	84.0	93.2	89.9
Trespass	40	71.4	0.0	62.5
Defamation	31	77.7	0.0	67.7
Trover/conversion	20	38.5	28.6	35.0
Assault/battery	14	53.8	0.0	50.0
Land/ejectment	16	63.6	60.0	62.5
Total *n*	457 (56.6% of all completed, not settled cases)			
For completed, unsettled cases by category of cause of action, including those cases where no specific cause was recorded				
Case	198	74.8%	73.7%	74.2%
Debt	138	84.0	93.2	89.9
Other debt/contract	169	84.4	89.7	87.3
Nondebt/contract	139	67.6	28.6	59.7
Total *n*	644 (79.8% of all completed, not settled cases)			
All cases	807	75.4%	72.6%	74.0%

to be contested and the plaintiff victory percentage to be closer to 50 percent, indicating that defendants won nearly as often as plaintiffs. Contested cases that went before juries could also display divisions in society that uncontested and settled cases could not. Arguments, evidence, and witnesses would be mustered to convince jurors, who theoretically would then help formulate a consensus judgment on the questionable behavior. Where consensus exists, cases are low-intensity, predictable, and routinely dispatched; without consensus, cases more often involve high-intensity, in-court conflict, and unpredictable results.[12]

Actions in debt, relying on formally sealed bonds, clearly revealed such a consensus. Debt cases were settled or arbitrated half the time, were the least often contested and the most often uncontested of all causes, and had the highest percentage of plaintiff victories in contested and uncontested cases; plaintiffs won nine cases for each one lost (see tables 16 and 17). Courts served as a routine debt collection agency for plaintiffs who could produce the appropriate documents necessary to plead in debt. The high rate of uncontested cases in debt and the 93 percent plaintiff victories for such cases reflected the courts' routinization of the procedure for chancering bonds. It was a common business practice for creditors to force their debtors to sign penal bonds, which entitled the creditor to an amount double the principle should the debtor not pay the agreed sum on time or on demand. In common law (at least until 1697 when Parliament outlawed such penalties), the creditor could recover the full amount of the bond, forcing the debtor to initiate a second action in a court of equity to chancer the bond down to the principle plus interest. Delaware Valley's courts, possessing both law and equity powers, reduced this process to a single step, completing an uncontested case. The plaintiff would declare in debt for the bond, the defendant would acknowledge the bond and confess judgment in court, the plaintiff would then remit the penalty on the bond, and the court would pass judgment only for principle and interest.[13] This procedure became so routinized that those defendants who defaulted or took the case to a jury and lost still had the penalty remitted, while plaintiffs who might have wished to recover the face amount of the bond discovered courts would issue executions only for principle and interest.[14] There was so little doubt about rights that public participation was hardly needed; only 16.3 percent of completed debt cases required a jury, only 12.7 percent required witnesses, and only 3.3 percent utilized more than the two witnesses required by statute to prove a case.[15] Clearly, the legal system had reached a firm consensus about cases in debt.

Case actions, for the purposes of this analysis confined primarily to contracts and debts less formally evidenced than in debt, were settled or arbitrated more often than not and even more often than debt. Case actions were slightly more likely to be contested than actions in debt, and plaintiffs' overall victory percentage trailed debt by 15 percentage points. Plaintiffs in case, however, did win nearly three cases to every one they lost, higher than every other specific cause of action. The lower percentage of uncontested plaintiff victories accounted for most of the difference between case and debt, because of a wider range of potential issues and a lower level of routinization in case. Contract issues, such as failure to pay for work performed, fraud, inadequate quality of goods, and insufficient performance, were matters that required an interpretation of evidence and intent instead of merely reading a standardized bond.[16] In 22.8 percent of actions in case a jury was called. Litigants called witnesses in 17.2 percent of these cases, and in 8.9 percent of the cases they used three or more witnesses. Yet the higher level of contentiousness in such causes relative to debt should not obscure the high level of consensus achieved. High levels of settled cases, high levels of plaintiff victories, and low overall levels of contested cases reflected a consensus on appropriate economic behavior even without routinized and sealed bonds.

That economically aggrieved plaintiffs could rely on courts is further substantiated by the results of other cases where a debt or contract was involved. Most of those cases had no specific cause recorded, but facts in the record revealed the issue. Because of this method of identification, obviously few (16 percent) were settled; such cases decided out of court usually left little clue about the subject matter. These cases involving economic behavior confirm the above consensus through their high plaintiff victory percentages—84.4 percent in contested cases and 89.7 percent in uncontested ones. Only 18.3 percent of these cases involved juries and witnesses, and only 2.4 percent had three or more witnesses. Overall, plaintiffs won in 82.3 percent of the completed cases identified as dealing with a debt or contract (case, debt, and other). With such predictability, it is no surprise that a majority of defendants would reach a settlement with plaintiffs in case and debt to avoid adding court costs to their almost certain liability.

Statute law added to such reliability and further encouraged plaintiffs to consider potential lawsuits when structuring their economic transactions. Pennsylvania dealt with the least formal deals in its "Law about Verbal Contracts," stating, "all Promises, Bargains, and Agreements, about buying and Selling, being made appear by Sufficient Evidence, shall stand good and firm." Violators of verbal contracts were to pay double the value involved should they lose in court, a clear incentive to litigate. Other laws encouraged the recording of all written contracts to establish clear entitlements to recovery for the recorders should the contract be breached.[17] These rules, when combined with the law reforms enacted on process, fees, and attorneys, opened wider the law's door to those aggrieved by unkept bargains and unpaid debts. Plaintiffs acquired the leverage they needed at little cost and effort and with great predictability, while the legal elite acquired the cases and therefore the allegiance of those participants in Delaware Valley's burgeoning market.

Little to no consensus was apparent in litigant behavior involving nondebt/contract matters that we would now call torts (involuntary transactions resulting in alleged damage to person or property) and infringement of land titles. The majority of these cases were contested, in contrast to case and debt, where half or more cases were settled. Of those cases brought to decide land titles, not one was settled. Three causes—trespass, defamation, and assault and battery—had less than 10 percent uncontested. Obviously, when there were more contests, more of the population became involved in litigants' conflicts: 49.1 percent involved juries, 42.3 percent had witnesses, and 27.0 percent used three or more witnesses. Clearly such participation showed a high level of divisiveness in the community stemming from the behavior in dispute, a division manifest in the lack of a legalistic consensus on such issues. Moreover, that plaintiffs won victories in only 28.6 percent of the uncontested nondebt/contract cases—plaintiffs actually *lost* more than twice as many uncontested than they won—suggests that defendants, seeing no consensus about their behavior, rarely surrendered. Finally, the overall victory percentage (see table 17) for plaintiffs in nondebt/contract cases was less than 60 percent, including one cause (trover) where plaintiffs lost more often than they won and another (assault and battery) where the plaintiffs' chances for victory were the same as the defendants'. Although this legal system predictably validated plaintiff expectations for debts and contracts, appropriate standards of behavior in other areas were less certain. The higher percentage of contests and the reduced incidence of settlements, the intensity of in-court conflict, and the close distribution of verdicts prove that these cases were not routine; courts had to resolve real disputes without a clear consensus for guidance.

When decisions on cases were unpredictable, the room for manipulation by litigants increased, both in and out of court. Many defamation cases allowed the plaintiff to gain the initiative against those whose accusations, if unchallenged, represented a far greater danger to the plaintiff.[18] Henry Reynolds's maid died suddenly, and Justa Anderson said that he had seen Reynolds beat her the night before she died. Reynolds sued Anderson and introduced four witnesses who had heard Anderson's slander and two others who had seen no evidence on the maid's body of her having been beaten. The jury, however, turned against Reynolds when Anderson produced three witnesses who had actually seen Reynolds threaten her with a pair of tongs and beat her with a "broom staff." The defendant won, but Reynolds may have avoided a criminal trial by his preemptive strike.[19] Similarly, John Tatham, a justice in Burlington County, felt his authority threatened by John Budd's repeated accusations that Tatham had poisoned Budd's brother. Public interest in Tatham's defamation suit ran high; the "press of people" even prevented one witness's testimony from being heard. The bulk of the evidence went against Tatham. Witnesses testified that they saw the brother's swollen and black corpse (a symptom of poison), that they heard the brother express fear for his life, and that Tatham had a potential motive—a large debt he owed Budd's brother. Nonetheless, the jury found Tatham damaged in the sum of twenty pounds, the highest sum ever awarded in this period.[20] We cannot know if Tatham was truly defamed and Reynolds was not, but such dissimilar results in cases with similar fact situations illustrate the lack of predictability on what constituted defamation, a case-by-case approach that encouraged court fights.

Phillip Yarnell's defamation case against Moses Musgrove never revealed exactly what Musgrove said, although the testimony intimates Musgrove had accused Yarnell of rape or fornication. The outcome revealed an ambiguity regarding sexual behavior. Elizabeth Woodward, testifying for Musgrove, claimed that Yarnell had asked to feel her to find out "whether she was a woman," had forced her to put her hand in his "Codpise," and had kept her awake for three nights so that when she fell asleep he would (as John Jones put it) "see what he could Doe with her." The plaintiff's witnesses did not exactly paint Yarnell as a model of decorum. One said she saw Yarnell force Elizabeth on the bed, and another said Yarnell claimed to have "scattered from him which was his seed" as Elizabeth "did not know what was In his mind." Yarnell's most effective evidence came from two men who heard Elizabeth say that though Yarnell might have tried to force her, he did not succeed. Such testimony convinced a jury that Musgrove did defame Yarnell, but it assessed him only two pence for damages.[21] Though Musgrove appealed and had the verdict overturned in equity, this case, like the other two, illustrated the variety of litigant strategies, the resulting hard-fought cases, and the less than definitive outcomes.

Juries often tried to balance conflicting testimony through compromise verdicts, which could leave observers wondering just what the community approved or disapproved. John Calowe sued Thomas Wright for calling him a "forsworne Rogue" in a bitter dispute over a mare with a walleye; the jury found that the plaintiff had been defamed but awarded him only two pence.[22] Joel Bayly tried to stop a servant from speaking contemptuously of the new sheriff, whereupon the ex-sheriff, Thomas Withers, siding with the servant, "fell violently with Blowes upon ye said Joel so that he fell to ye ground and Bled all that night." In an action of assault and battery, Bayly produced four witnesses, while Withers's witnesses attacked Bayly's physiology to minimize damages—"Joel Bayly did usually Bled before he had any Difference with Thomas Wither." The jury found Withers culpable but gave Bayly only two pence.[23] Samuel Coles sued William Evans in an action of trover for a horse, and both sides introduced persuasive testimony claiming the horse was rightfully theirs. The jury, unable to decide between the claims, gave a special verdict that both parties accepted: the defendant kept the horse but paid the plaintiff fifty shillings, and court costs were split evenly.[24] It has been said that hard cases make bad law; in the Delaware Valley, they made for uncertainty that produced ad hoc compromises and further incentive for both parties not to surrender.

This is not to suggest that legal decision-makers could never make hard choices when confronted with conflicting evidence. Trespass issues, such as cutting and carrying away grass and timber or damaging crops by fire, and trover cases that involved ownership claims to ranging animals were hotly contested and utilized many witnesses (e.g., sixteen to establish the markings on a boar). Yet most reached a clear-cut verdict.[25] Nor is it to suggest that this legal population condoned the beating of servants, poisoning, public affray, vicious slander, or extramarital sexual activity, topics of criminal prosecutions discussed in chapters 5 and 6.

What is clear is that the courtroom was where the legal system attempted to articulate and reinforce norms, which it did consistently for debts and contracts, and to mediate conflicting values in the face of often conflicting evidence, as it did with other disputes. It is also clear, however, that while this legal system often failed to integrate the community in the nondebt/contract arena, it was still used by disparate members of the community to attempt to resolve those grievances.

The statistical significance of these differences in completed cases, including both the level of contested cases and the differential victory patterns, is confirmed by chi-square analysis. As in chapter 2, the number of categories of cause has been reduced to four to allow valid statistical analysis: case; debt; other debt/contract actions, including those without a specific cause named; and nondebt/contract causes (i.e., trespass, defamation, trover, assault and battery, land/ejectment, and similar cases that had no specific cause named). Regarding results in completed cases, the following distribution covers all the litigants' options, including the propensity to accommodate, the propensity to fight, and the chance of success: settled/arbitrated, plaintiff won contested, plaintiff won uncontested, defendant won contested, and defendant won uncontested. This distribution is also used for subsequent chi-square analyses of attributes' statistical significance regarding outcomes.

When these four types of actions were matched against these five types of outcomes, the results noted earlier from the descriptive statistics and stories were confirmed: different causes produced different outcomes in a statistically significant pattern (chi-square probability = .000). The next question is, which results deviated most from the values expected if the outcomes had been statistically normal? For this distribution, the four most deviant outcomes did not involve actions in case or debt. Rather, cases in the other debt/contract category saw plaintiffs winning more uncontested cases and settling fewer cases than expected. More important, in those cases without a debt or contract at issue, defendants won more contested cases, and plaintiffs won fewer contested cases than expected. Chi-square thus confirms that the outcomes of nondebt/contract causes were significantly different from those involving a debt or a contract. The next question that logically follows is, who were those defendants who engaged in so many contests of nondebt/contract causes and who won a disproportionately high share? The answer was given in chapter 2 in the analysis of causes of action and attributes. Defendants who disproportionately faced suits with nondebt/contract causes were average Quakers, Quaker leaders, and farmer-artisans (who were disproportionately Quakers).

This association between cause of action, defendants who were average Quakers or Quaker leaders, and contentious results suggests that one reason for the lack of societal consensus on nondebt/contract cases lay with those who established this legal system. In this one example, Quaker behavior produced particular grievances, particular strategic choices by litigants followed, and outcomes of suits based on these complex interactions favored the Quaker defendants. Clearly, a complete integration into a legalistic consensus on some causes was impossible because of all those choices by plaintiffs, defendants, and decision-makers.[26] Thus, legal conflict was not necessarily integrative, nor did it invariably produce social divisions. Legal cases were, however, always manipulative, since legal results were a function of power attributes, legal skill, and conscious strategy. This manipulative nature can best be seen by examining what strategies were available, which strategies were employed by which groups, and who won.

Strategies Available in Disputes: A First Look

The strategies plaintiffs and defendants embraced after a case had been filed revealed their perceptions and their attitudes toward legal conflict and toward their adversary. Some of these strategies have already been discussed—defendants could avoid the case by leaving the jurisdiction; litigants could script a legal play in cases of penal bonds whereby defendants would appear as the confessing debtor and plaintiffs would respond by remitting the penalty; or litigants in nondebt actions could (and often did) assume confrontational postures and insist on full-scale, in-court contests with witnesses and juries. Litigants' approaches varied, depending on their attributes, their role (plaintiff or defendant), the attributes of their opponent, and the cause of action. This section examines the choices made and the results that followed for the three methods of completing a case—out-of-court resolution, noncontested court verdict, and contested court verdict. These choices revealed how litigants tried to resolve the tension created by the legal system's conflicting goals of making litigation easy yet discouraging litigation, all the while attempting to obtain the result they wanted.

This legal system's officially preferred resolution of these contradictory messages was arbitration. Arbitration relied on the disputants' voluntary submission of their problem to outside parties for resolution, usually two chosen by each side and an agreed-upon fifth person to act as umpire in the event of a tie. English common law did not recognize the enforceability of such arbitration awards until 1698, but this problem had been evaded by having each party execute a penal bond to the other conditioned on the performance of the arbitration award. Failure to perform gave rise to an action in debt (always subject to removing any penalty by chancering the bond), but any practical advantages of arbitration depended on voluntary compliance to make a court fight unnecessary.[27] Delaware Valley courts tried to avoid this problem by making arbitration references from the bench while promising to confirm any award later in court and, in Pennsylvania, by establishing "peacemakers" as a standing arbitration board, whose awards, once registered at the court, would be as binding as an in-court judgment. Despite this encouragement, only thirty-five cases, or 2 percent of completed cases, had an arbitration reference. Though this low rate may underestimate the actual frequency of arbitration because much might have occurred either without a lawsuit or without court sanction once one had been filed, the failure rate of those who accepted such references might have accounted for litigants' limited use of this method of accommodation. Official arbitration thus was an insignificant feature of legal dispute resolution in the Delaware Valley.[28]

Some court-backed arbitrations succeeded in their purpose of accommodating the parties without an in-court fight. In the suit of Samuel and Sarah Harrison against Edward Eglington and Elizabeth Tomlinson, which involved accusations of theft on one side and defamation on the other, the arbitrators for "ye ending of all Differences from ye beginning of ye world to [this day]" awarded only court costs and got both sides to acknowledge that they were sorry for the accusations.[29] Other suits merely recorded an arbitration reference, and the silence of later records or a notation of "withdrawn" suggested a successful arbitration.[30] There was, however, only one specific reference of a case to the much-touted peacemakers, and Richard Crosby was still asking the Chester County court to execute that award thirteen years later.[31] Losing parties often reneged, and the winners were forced to sue in debt, occasionally requiring a full jury trial. A most dramatic case of such backtracking came when John Hugg, distressed that arbitrators had not awarded him possession of a servant, sued John Burroughs, claiming the award had not been made within the agreed-upon time limits. Eight witnesses convinced a jury that the arbitrators had beaten the clock, whereupon Hugg appealed to the Court of Appeals for West Jersey.[32] Altogether, 41 percent of arbitration cases required further court enforcement. The reason for such a low rate of usage and high rate of failure lay in the pluralistic nature of the Delaware Valley. Successful arbitration relied on a strong community to enforce voluntary agreements through informal social pressure; the merchant community and certain colonial New England communities successfully used arbitration so long as a tight-knit community basis for enforcement existed.[33] The Delaware Valley never had such a unified community, though. As a result, reality lagged far behind rhetoric; legal arbitration never touched the vast majority of litigation.

Perhaps another reason formal arbitration occurred so infrequently was that litigants adopted strategies that allowed them to accommodate cases on their own. Of all completed cases, 49 percent were recorded as agreed, ended, discontinued, or withdrawn before trial, which, when combined with arbitrated cases, meant that a majority of completed cases were resolved without any court decision. That such behavior reflected an adaptation to the conflicting positions of these legal rules and culture about litigation can be seen by comparing the Delaware Valley cases with those of two other nearby jurisdictions operating under the same legal heritage and at approximately the same time. The court at Upland, operating from 1675 to 1681 under the jurisdiction of the Duke of York and using the common law, covered approximately the same amount of territory that Chester County did. Upland saw only 33 percent of its civil cases settled before trial in the six years prior to the time William Penn and the Quakers assumed control of government. Kent County, Delaware, which Penn would also take over in 1682, revealed virtually the same low accommodation rate Upland had between 1680 and 1682 (32 percent settled). The clear inference is that changes in the makeup of the laws and the law-using population led to a greater than 50 percent increase in litigants' willingness to decide cases out of court. Furthermore, other jurisdictions had similarly low settlement rates, such as Suffolk County, Massachusetts, where only 15 percent were withdrawn in the 1670s. Examinations of some early 1700s civil cases in Connecticut and Virginia, while not differentiating between uncontested and settled cases, imply a rate of settled cases far less than 50 percent. Delaware Valley's legal system appears to have encouraged a much higher rate of out-of-court accommodation than other contemporary colonial legal systems did.[34]

A second descriptive statistic reveals that the propensity to settle cases was remarkably constant for *plaintiffs* of differing attributes (see table 18). With only three exceptions, all attribute groups accommodated at least 46 percent of their cases, regardless of religion, landownership, number of cases filed, officeholding status, occupation, or wealth. Less likely to settle were merchants and the poor, whether measured by inventories or taxes. On the other end, the only groups that settled at a rate far above the average were Quaker leaders and women, who settled 60 percent of their cases. Such a relatively constant response by such different groups of participants in the legal system suggests that a com-

Table 18. Settled Case Percentage, by Attributes

Attributes	As Plaintiff	N^a	As Defendant	N^a
Males	50.5%	1585	50.9%	1596
Females	59.7	57	47.8	46
Quakers	51.4%	644	46.3%	482
Quaker leaders	59.9	242	36.4	118
Average Quakers	46.3	402	49.5	364
Non-Quakers	48.6	809	51.6	971
Landowners	50.0%	1331	49.6%	1229
Nonlandowners	54.7	311	54.5	413
Occupations (males only)[b]				
Farmer	50.1%	383	51.0%	473
Artisan	50.0	146	54.6	242
Farmer-artisan	49.5	103	52.9	104
Merchant	42.5	247	39.3	56
Self-described gentry	55.4	186	49.3	71
Servant/slave/laborer	56.0	25	52.4	42
1693 Pennsylvania tax assessment (in pounds)				
100+	53.3%	152	42.7%	68
50–99	49.0	92	51.3	80
1–49	44.9	98	45.1	164
Inventoried wealth (in pounds)				
500+	52.3%	199	42.7%	87
100–499	49.0	192	48.8	164
1–99	34.7	72	62.9	89

Table 18, continued

Attributes	As Plaintiff	N^a	As Defendant	N^a
Legal roles				
High officer	51.6%	549	38.5%	244
Lesser officer	49.2	309	51.5	400
Nonofficer	51.0	784	53.6	998
Cases				
1–2	51.5%	828	53.3%	876
3–5	46.8	402	46.1	451
6+	53.6	412	50.8	315
Overall	50.9%	1642	50.9%	1642

a. *N* refers to the total number of cases involving each attribute in the role indicated
   by the column heading; the percentage is the number of cases defined as settled
   out of that *N* number.
b. The category "other" has been omitted to ensure that chi-square is a valid test. Litigation analysis will use only six occupational categories.

mon, cultural influence was at work. Quaker leaders were more likely
to settle because of Quaker doctrine. The lower settlement rate for merchants and the poor, the extremes of economic occupation and status,
may have something to do with what their opponents thought about
their chances of victory, a question to be addressed later. In summary,
over half the plaintiffs reconciled the legal system's messages of making
litigation easy while hoping that litigation would be avoided entirely by
ending the case out of court after gaining the advantage over their opponent through filing suit.

A few surviving letters illustrate this pretrial accommodation strategy in action. John Smith wrote the Bucks County court to "Stop the
Suit, for James Allmand and I have agreed for he is at work for me and
is to worke it out." The Bucks County court clerk Phineas Pemberton
intervened on several occasions to give a defendant more time to satisfy
the plaintiff before trial.[35] Since court records did not document pretrial negotiations that produced an "agreed" case, most qualitative evidence
for accommodative desires must come from cases that reached court and
were then settled. In 1685, Ann Milcome had had enough of Martha
Wheeler's calling her "cheat" for the past year and sued in scandal and
defamation for two hundred pounds. After a jury had been summoned

and witnesses called, both parties asked to defer the trial so they might end the matter. Mathew Allen obtained a judgment against Samuel Cole in Burlington County to gain title to land Cole had sold him at least four years earlier, a judgment that was reconfirmed even after Cole obtained a new trial because he had "other Evidence than what hee produced at the Tryall formerly." Cole still wanted to appeal to England, but the court refused this request when it emerged that Allen, who had won twice, had offered Cole four different alternatives to settle the dispute. John Clark in Gloucester won a fifteen-pound judgment after the defendant cut down Clark's trees; Clark then forgave the judgment. Seven witnesses testified about whether James Stanfield or John Orion rightfully owned a mare, but just before the jury could decide, the parties agreed to share court costs and let the matter rest.[36] When these anecdotes are combined with the statistics and placed alongside accommodation rates in other colonies, it is clear that, compared with plaintiffs from other colonial legal systems, Delaware Valley plaintiffs were much more likely to find ways to accommodate the dispute. This propensity is evidence of the development of a unique legal culture among the residents of this region.

That litigants responded to the legal system's mixed signals by settling cases is clear from the accommodation rates during times of political upheaval. In Chester County's first ten years, from 1681 to 1692, the rate of settled cases, calculated as a five-year moving average, never dropped below 36 percent and was usually between 44 percent and 52 percent. Beginning in 1693 and continuing through 1699, however, the rate of settled cases dropped to less than half the former average. The new decade saw the return of accommodation; in no year from 1701 to 1708 did settled cases constitute less than 46 percent. Similarly in Burlington County, no year prior to 1699 averaged less than 50 percent settled cases, but in 1699 to 1704 the rate declined sharply, to as low as 5 percent. This collapse was followed by a steady climb in the number of disputes settled, until these once again made up the majority. The periods of decline in both counties coincided with the years of maximum political unrest in which the legitimacy of the leadership and the structure of the legal system were under constant challenge. That litigants responded to uncertainty by becoming less willing to end cases out of court further indicates how individuals translated the legal culture into their litigating strategies. When norms and decision-makers were uncertain, litigants would try to gain advantage by proceeding into court;

when legal stability returned, plaintiffs could again compromise without fear of losing a legal advantage.

Plaintiffs would not relinquish their enhanced bargaining power gained by bringing suit without some agreement or concession from defendants (unless the plaintiff for some reason simply gave up); it took both parties to settle a case. Unlike plaintiffs' strategies, the strategies of *defendants* varied considerably, depending on certain attributes. Members of higher-status groups were considerably less accommodating when they were sued than when they sued (see table 18). Every group with high-status attributes—Quaker leaders, high officers, merchants, self-described gentry, and the wealthy—showed a lower propensity to settle as defendants than as plaintiffs. Quaker leaders, who constituted the group most likely to accommodate as plaintiffs (60 percent settled), were willing to settle only 36 percent of the cases brought against them. This dramatic decline in the propensity to settle cases when litigation roles were reversed made them the least likely defendant group to accommodate. Even excluding nondebt/contract cases, which were disproportionately filed against Quaker leaders and which had disproportionately fewer settled, Quaker leaders still settled only 40 percent of the cases brought against them. The other high-status groups, which were not so prone to more nondebt/contract actions, similarly showed a stark decline in their percentage of cases settled. High-status defendants across the board disproportionately chose to force their opponent into public view on court day. These results confirm that the cause of action was but one factor that determined strategies and reveals the power of multiple perspective analysis.

In contrast to the behavior of high-status defendants, most lower-status groups in this population—non-Quakers, lesser officers, nonofficers, farmers, artisans, farmer-artisans, and those poor in taxed or inventoried wealth—showed at least a slight increase in the propensity to settle when they were defendants compared with when they were plaintiffs. Again, when nondebt/contract cases were excluded, non-Quaker defendants settled more often (53 percent) than Quaker defendants in general (49 percent). Clearly, legal strategies depended not only on the strength of litigants' legal position but also on the strength of their socioeconomic position. High-status defendants probably believed that forcing their opponent into court would produce a better outcome than the one that might be achieved by direct negotiation and accommodation with the plaintiff. The reverse inference is also true; lower-status civil defendants, feeling less confident about their legal and social positions, more often sought to settle rather than to risk a public fight. As will be seen in the next section, such a nonaccommodationist strategy worked to favor higher-status litigants.

Despite the popularity of accommodation, litigants did choose other strategies, reflecting their evaluation of their bargaining power and legal position, in the 49.1 percent of cases (24.9 percent uncontested, 24.2 percent contested) that went to court. When a case reached court unsettled, litigants could act in ways that either minimized or intensified the dispute. Uncontested cases bore similarities to cases that were settled in that there was no real conflict in front of the court. As earlier noted, defendants could confess judgment, as in debt cases that became a nonconfrontational play, or they could appear but fail to present a defense. That a plaintiff required a public confession or appearance, plus a recorded court judgment, indicated a level of coercion and mistrust not present in settled cases; an uncontested judgment could be followed by an execution against a recalcitrant, whereas a settled case could not. Litigants could also choose not to appear when the case was called, leading to an uncontested judgment against them. Such nonsuits and defaults, while not presenting a contest on the merits, differed from settled cases in that a court, not the parties, put an end to the dispute. If a case was not settled and was not uncontested as defined above, it was defined as contested. As noted earlier, this definition of contested cases is expansive and may slightly overemphasize the level of contention, since the category includes cases where the record of a fight on the merits was ambiguous. In most contested cases, however, litigants chose to fight with arguments, witnesses, and evidence before the bench or, more often, before a jury of their peers. Although such cases represented only a small minority of court cases, which were themselves a minority of all disputes, their significance was magnified by the court drama and their potential messages about legally acceptable behavior.

Hiring an attorney, which occurred most often in cases that were not settled, had been discouraged by the Delaware Valley's law reforms. In addition to allowing litigants to plead their own cause or to employ any friend, regardless of legal training, to plead it for them, there were attempts to ban lawyers from taking fees and to require them to take attestations far more detailed than those demanded of any justice or court officer.[37] In the early years, friends appeared as attorneys for litigants much more often than did those with professional training. Most often, litigants called on those whose familiarity with the law came from appearing in many cases (e.g., John Tatham, Edward Hunloke, Jeremiah Collett) or from serving as court clerks (e.g., Phineas Pemberton, Thomas Revell, Patrick Robinson).[38] By the early 1700s, however, a few professionally trained lawyers—David Lloyd, Thomas Clark, George Lowther, John Moore, Alexander Griffith, and John White—had virtually evicted amateurs from litigation. Because of staggered court dates, these attorneys were able to ride a Delaware Valley circuit, attending to clients in various counties and undoubtedly spreading a higher level of legal knowledge throughout the entire society. Finally, though the small number of attorneys led to complaints by one litigant that he could not obtain a lawyer because his opponent had retained all the region's attorneys, the ratio of lawyers to population was probably no worse than 1 to 4,000, which was the estimated ratio in England in 1606.[39]

The greater part of these attorneys' business derived from drafting and filing legal documents, such as wills, deeds, bonds, and contracts.[40] In part, this lesser emphasis on trial work occurred because so few litigants used attorneys when going to court, although the number that might have gotten aid in drafting the documents remains unknown. Only 7.5 percent of plaintiffs and 4.7 percent of defendants used attorneys in completed cases. As might be expected, the rate of settling such cases was very low; only 22 percent of plaintiffs and 15 percent of defendants with attorneys ended the case before trial. Rarely would one hire an attorney if the case was not to be fought, since attorneys existed to exploit opportunities for the best outcome possible for the client. The results of employing an attorney in contested cases were mixed, however, indicating that attorneys might have been called on to try to bail out a weak case or that their legal advice might not have been very practical. Plaintiffs with attorneys won a lower percentage of contested cases than did plaintiffs overall (72 percent versus 75 percent), while defendants with attorneys won contested cases at approximately the same rate (24 percent) that unrepresented defendants did. The only clear advantage came in uncontested cases; plaintiffs and defendants had higher uncontested victory percentages than the unrepresented did. Perhaps sharp-eyed lawyers caught technical errors that led to nonsuit victories for defendants, convinced justices to declare default rather than continue cases in which the defendants did not appear, or impressed defendants so well with the strength of the case against them that they confessed judgment. For this period, however, those advantages did not prove a sufficient incentive for the vast majority of litigants to hire an attorney.

Although only 24 percent of all completed cases were contested, this statistic should not obscure the fact that a wide variety of strategies was available to litigants with very nonaccommodating legal personas. As noted before, pleas by defendants gradually became more sophisticated; the appearance of the oyer and imparlance, along with sufficiency pleas (e.g., making the plaintiff first prove his or her title in trespass cases) and negative pregnants showed the influence of the emerging legal talent in the region. However, one of a defendant's most potent weapons, the countersuit, could neutralize some of the plaintiff's bargaining power without any sophisticated pleading. When Godfrey Hancock and Thomas Revell sued Thomas Mann in trespass in Burlington County, Mann replied by suing Hancock, which Mann dropped when the first action was agreed. Such a pattern of aggressive countersuits occurred in every county.[41] When an out-of-court agreement could not be obtained, juries could apportion blame, such as the jury did in the paired slander actions of the Eglingtons and the Harrisons, where it awarded the Eglingtons five pence and the Harrisons twenty shillings, a judgment that confirmed the wisdom of the Harrisons's countersuit tactic.[42]

In a few instances, litigants went against the grain of the legal culture's developing attitude favoring settlements and adopted a confrontational and litigious stance. Thomas Wood acknowledged that he owed William Beakes, Jr., nine pounds, but he boasted that he could get Beakes to accept only six pounds and that "if he [Beakes] sue me he shall get nothing by it." Wood's defiant attitude backfired, because Beakes did not accept the partial payment, did sue, and convinced a jury to award the full nine pounds plus the cost of the suit.[43] Abraham Hewlings testified against Thomas French in a land case that French lost. Immediately afterward, French began accusing Hewlings of false testimony, and, at the next grand jury on which French sat, he "said unto the said Jury if they would not present Abraham Hulings for perjury he would not Consent to them In other matters." Hewlings was able to halt this bitter attack by suing in defamation and obtaining a five-pound damage award.[44]

Perhaps the best example of litigiousness was John Tatham, who doggedly pursued a dispute against Joseph Growden, a neighboring Bucks County landowner, for twelve years, to no avail. A 1687 attempt to arbitrate failed, because the dispute was, in the words of Phineas Pemberton, "the most railing and reviling business yt ever I saw."[45] Tatham's 1691 suit against Growden was first nonsuited when Tatham did not appear, and its follow-up had to be withdrawn when Growden made use of the law immunizing magistrates and councilmen. Tatham then simmered seven years, finally filing another action in case on the same facts, which came to trial in 1699. Voluminous accounts from as far back as 1685 were introduced into evidence, producing a verdict again for Growden. Tatham desired an appeal in equity, which he was granted, but he also was named by the grand jury for taking a false attestation in the case.[46] These cases ended with Tatham's death in 1702, but he had clearly adopted one of the most litigious personas in the valley. Such legal personas were chosen rarely and often, as above, produced poor results,[47] but the legal system offered them strategic opportunities nonetheless.

If litigants decided to contest the case, the final strategic choice before trial was whether the case should be decided by the justices of the peace *en banc* or a jury. Such a choice required the assent of both parties to forego a jury and leave the case to the justices. Though the laws seemed to require jury trials in all contested cases, only once, in an assault case in Burlington County, did the justices refuse the litigants' request for a judgment from the bench without a jury trial.[48] Judgments from the bench were usually not as contentious as jury trials were, because justices often heard no witnesses in deciding issues based on the pleadings submitted or in reviewing the awards of single justices in small disputes made between sessions. Some contested cases before the bench were more difficult, requiring an actual judgment on the facts as well as the law. Furthermore, justices could modify a jury award by interpreting its "true meaning"—setting aside the verdict temporarily so that a defendant could pay the debt on a schedule or overturning the award entirely as a court of equity, as they did when the evidence was "so inconsistent" that the jury's verdict could not be upheld.[49] In 30 percent of contested cases, litigants received a judgment from the justices rather than, or sometimes in spite of, a jury verdict.

The defendant, having discarded the options of defaulting or confessing judgment and being unable to agree with the plaintiff about settling the case out of court or having the justices hear the case, could enter a defensive pleading (a general denial) to the plaintiff's declaration. In early Delaware Valley practice, this pleading was usually the only one defendants made when they wished to contest the case on its merits. Assuming the plaintiff wished to continue with the suit, the defendant's general denial would "joyne issue"—"of this he puts him Self upon the Cuntry"[50]—and launch a jury trial. Although in more complex back-and-forth pleadings under common law plaintiffs could submit a factual point raised by the defendant's pleading to a jury, in the simplified and shortened pleadings employed under law reform, a jury trial almost always reflected the defendant's strategic choice. Rather than accept the plaintiff's terms, the defendant chose to fight the plaintiff to remove the shadow of the plaintiff's suit. In 70 percent of contested cases, the jury would determine if the defendant had made a wise choice.

The fee structure made this contest before a jury a potentially costly gamble. Summoning and swearing jurors, calling and recording witnesses, and recording the verdict were additional costs not usually present in an uncontested or even a contested bench proceeding.[51] Additional social costs were at stake as well, for testimony that could be damning as well as exculpatory would emerge before the crowd assembled on court day. Furthermore, juries were risky, having a dynamic of their own, which sometimes resulted in peculiar decisions, as seen previously in nondebt/contract cases. The most notable example of jury randomness occurred in the case of Francis White against James Allman over rightful ownership of a horse. The testimony of five witnesses for White and seven for Allman so confused and divided the jury that jurors decided for the defendant by flipping a coin.[52] Despite such risks, defendants who felt confident enough of their case to fight the plaintiff did much better when they went to a jury verdict (27 percent won) than when they got a bench judgment (where they won only 18 percent). If defendants were able to produce many witnesses, they would further increase their chances for success.[53] Such choices in trial were the final chances for litigants to manipulate the legal system to their advantage. The outcomes of these choices reveal whether law reform's success in encouraging access to justice actually led to equal justice.

Litigants adopted different attitudes regarding whether to settle cases according to whether they were in the plaintiff or defendant role; such differences recurred in those cases that were not decided out of court. For plaintiffs, the percentages of uncontested and contested cases for most attributes fell in a statistically normal pattern close to the overall averages (24.9 percent uncontested, 24.2 percent contested). The distribution of contested, uncontested, and settled cases was not significantly affected by the plaintiff's gender (chi-square probability = .099), landownership (.271), religion (.237), occupation (.067), officeholding status (.181), taxed wealth (.247), inventoried wealth (.113), or multiple appearances as plaintiffs (.187). Only Quaker leaders showed a statistically significant preference for disproportionately fewer contested cases, compared with average Quakers (.000). With that exception, these attributes did not affect plaintiff choices for contested court fights in any consistent pattern.

Attributes did have a consistent and statistically significant influence on *defendants'* choice for a contested court fight. Within each set of attributes, except for taxed wealth, the high-status defendant group had the highest percentage of contested cases. High officers contested 34 percent of all cases when they were defendants (chi-square probability = .000); nonofficers contested only 21 percent. Quaker defendants contested 29 percent of their cases as opposed to non-Quakers' 22 percent (.003), and Quaker leaders contested 37 percent of cases when they were sued, whereas average Quakers contested only 27 percent (.027). Excluding the contentious nondebt/contract cases that were disproportionately brought against Quakers, the same discrepancy held. Quaker defendants contested 26 percent of all other cases (case, debt, etc.), while non-Quakers contested 18 percent (.006); Quaker leaders contested 32 percent. Merchant defendants fought 36 percent of the cases brought against them, while artisan defendants' 20 percent contested rate was barely half the merchants' rate (.046). Landed defendants contested 26 percent, while the nonlanded fought only 19 percent (.008). Wealthy-at-death defendants contested 34 percent of cases brought against them, fighting the plaintiff in court almost twice as often as poor defendants (18 percent) (.022). These are the same groups that had the lowest rates of settlement; since the uncontested rates for these defendants fell close to the average, it is clear that these higher-status defendants chose public conflict when, if they had been in the plaintiff's chair, they might have accommodated. The question is why those of higher status, so accommodating as plaintiffs, not only refused to settle but also disproportionately chose to force their adversary to put the full case on display for all the assembled public to see.

The answer lies in an examination of who won these nonsettled cases, particularly the uncontested ones. Major determinants of success as a plaintiff or defendant were litigants' attributes of status and power within the legal system and society, although other factors, such as acquired skill in the law, apparently had some influence. Table 19 lists the victory percentages for plaintiffs by attributes in contested cases, uncontested cases, and overall. Regarding overall victories by plaintiffs, a high-status group had the highest rate of success for each particular set of attributes. That margin over those of lower status stemmed from higher-status groups' maintaining the highest rate of victory in uncontested cases, suggesting that defendants were evaluating their opponent's status and giving up in court more easily to those of higher status. Contested cases, however, revealed a mixed pattern of successes; artisan, women, non-Quaker, and nonlandowner plaintiffs won more often than merchants, men, Quakers, and landowners, respectively. These results lend insight into the quality of justice juries dispensed, which is explored later, and suggest that the system was open to all plaintiffs who learned how to gauge the quality of their cause and thus avoid taking losing cases to trial.[54] High-officer and multiple plaintiffs, who did far better in contested cases than others did, achieved some of their advantage by not suing in the difficult nondebt/contract causes (see table 14). Whatever

Table 19. Plaintiffs' Victories, by Attributes

Attribute	N^a	Contested	Uncontested	Overall
Males	784	75.2%	73.0%	74.1%
Females	23	85.7	62.5	69.6
Quakers	313	73.6%	77.5%	75.7%
Quaker leaders	97	85.7	80.7	82.5
Average Quakers	216	69.7	75.7	72.7
Non-Quakers	416	77.8	69.6	73.8
Landowners	666	74.7%	73.6%	74.2%
Nonlandowners	141	78.1	67.7	73.1
Occupations (males only)[b]				
Farmer	191	68.9%	67.1%	68.1%
Artisan	73	93.1	70.5	79.5
Farmer-artisan	52	75.0	67.9	71.2
Merchant	142	76.3	90.4	84.5
Self-described gentry	83	70.0	86.1	78.3
1693 Pennsylvania tax assessment (in pounds)				
100+	71	75.0%	89.7%	83.1%
50–99	48	66.7	66.7	66.7
1–49	54	66.7	66.7	66.7

Table 19, continued

Attribute	N^a	Contested	Uncontested	Overall
Inventoried wealth (in pounds)				
500+	95	69.4%	84.8%	76.8
100–499	98	66.0	72.9	69.4
1–99	47	61.9	73.1	68.1
Legal roles				
High officer	266	81.3%	83.3%	82.3%
Lesser officer	157	62.9	72.1	66.9
Nonofficer	384	77.1	66.0	71.1
Cases				
1–2	402	78.3%	69.7	74.1
3–5	214	64.8	67.9	66.4
6+	191	81.4	82.9	82.2
Overall	807	75.4%	72.6	74.0

a. *N* is the number of cases that were not classified as settled.
b. The category "other" has been omitted. "Servant/slave/laborer" has also been omitted because of an extremely low *n* (11). Litigation analysis will normally use six occupational categories.

social advantages plaintiffs of higher status held seem to have had little impact once a case reached trial; social power convinced defendants to concede defeat before trial.

A more dramatic version of this pattern held for defendants' victory percentages (see table 20), which showed defendants generally winning roughly one-fourth of their cases. These victories were not distributed equally; with two exceptions (gender and usage), the highest-status group for each attribute had the greatest overall victory percentage. Legal maneuvering, combined with social power, obviously mattered, which was apparent again in the results of uncontested cases. In a legal system where defeating a plaintiff on a nonsuit depended on the court's discretion, even when the plaintiff did not appear (which constituted the vast majority of nonsuits), defendants who described themselves as gentry or had high tax assessments in 1693 were able to win more uncontested cases than they lost. Merchants, the inventoried wealthy, high officers, Quakers, Quaker leaders, and landowners also outpaced those of lesser status in uncontested victories. These differences persisted even when

Table 20. Defendants' Victories, by Attributes

Attributes	N^a	Contested	Uncontested	Overall
Males	783	24.2%	27.6%	25.9%
Females	24	40.0	21.4	29.2
Quakers	259	25.5%	33.1%	29.0%
Quaker leaders	75	34.1	38.7	36.0
Average Quakers	184	21.7	31.0	26.1
Non-Quakers	470	22.8	23.9	23.4
Landowners	619	24.2%	29.2%	26.7%
Nonlandowners	188	26.3	22.2	24.0
Occupations (males only)^b				
Farmer	232	24.1%	23.3%	23.7%
Artisan	110	20.4	27.9	24.6
Farmer-artisan	49	41.9	22.2	34.7
Merchant	34	20.0	42.9	29.4
Self-described gentry	36	17.7	57.9	38.9
Servant/slave/laborer	20	25.0	12.5	20.0
1693 Pennsylvania tax assessment (in pounds)				
100+	39	30.0%	52.6%	41.0%
50–99	39	27.8	23.8	25.6
1–49	90	23.5	15.4	20.0
Inventoried wealth (in pounds)				
500+	49	32.3%	38.9%	34.7%
100–499	81	25.6	34.2	29.8
1–99	33	23.5	18.8	21.2
Legal roles				
High officer	150	31.0%	42.4%	36.0%
Lesser officer	194	26.5	18.5	22.7
Nonofficer	463	21.2	26.7	24.2
Cases				
1–2	409	31.9%	28.3%	30.1%
3–5	243	20.8	26.0	23.5
6+	155	10.8	27.2	19.4
Overall	807	24.6%	27.3%	26.0%

a. N is the number of cases that were not classified as settled.
b. The category "other" has been omitted. Litigation analysis will use only six occupational categories.

the distribution of causes of action is taken into account. For example, excluding the nondebt/contract cases, where Quakers and Quaker leaders were sued disproportionately often, Quaker leaders won 34.6 percent of uncontested cases, Quakers overall won 31.1 percent, average Quakers won 29.8 percent, and non-Quakers won only 26.7 percent. For defendants, as with plaintiffs, contested cases revealed again a mixed pattern of success. Farmer-artisan defendants had the highest percentage of victories.

Whether litigants were plaintiffs or defendants, status and power played a clear role in determining the chances for success, but not at every stage of the process. Higher-status plaintiffs, with the weight of the law added to their own social weight, convinced the vast majority of their adversaries to avoid a public display of their civil failings at trial. These defendants either would sue for peace (settled) or give up (uncontested plaintiff victory). By refusing to settle, however, higher-status defendants were in effect calling their adversary's bluff. Many plaintiffs, thinking that their suit would bring them a bargaining advantage, must have felt the tables had turned. They would now have their dealings, their conflict, and their case publicly exposed before decision-makers clearly like the defendant. Such plaintiffs then often folded their hands, giving up their suit, which resulted in an uncontested victory for the defendant. Higher-status defendants' strategy of refusing to settle many suits thus makes perfect sense, not because they necessarily believed they would win more often at trial but because merely forcing a plaintiff to public trial made many surrender without a fight.

Strategies Available in Disputing: A Closer Look

As with the statistics for causes of action, the descriptive statistics regarding outcomes and attributes just discussed can be examined more closely using the chi-square test on the population of completed cases. The five possible outcomes reflect the spectrum of litigants' final choices and results: settled, plaintiff won contested, plaintiff won uncontested, defendant won contested, and defendant won uncontested. When a matchup between attributes and outcomes was statistically significant, the most significant contributors to that result are listed in order of importance. The percentages in the previous section described a picture of social and legal power operating to influence some outcomes, but more detailed statistical analysis can identify those inequities that could not have been due to chance. This analysis becomes somewhat more complicated, however, because the cause of action, which is itself statistically significant, influenced the pattern of outcomes. Some potential plaintiffs apparently anticipated likely legal alternatives and outcomes if a transaction failed and thus altered the ways they structured their relationships to maximize their chances if they sued. Therefore, for those plaintiff attributes where matchups to both cause of action and outcome were statistically significant, it was necessary to examine the cause of action relative to the attribute's influence on results. In English, the question can be posed, did some plaintiffs win more often because the system favored them or did they win more often because they had, for example, more debts to collect (for which they could use, depending on how the transaction was structured, the most pro-plaintiff causes of case or debt)?

Plaintiffs' outcomes reveal that four attributes—officeholding, Quaker leadership, multiple usage, and male occupations—showed statistically significant biases (see table 21). In the test of the relationship between officeholding and plaintiffs' outcomes, lesser-officer plaintiffs lost more

Table 21. Plaintiffs' Outcomes, by Attributes

		Contested		Uncontested		
Attributes	N	Won	Lost	Won	Lost	Settled
Males	1585	18.6%	6.1%	18.1%	6.7%	50.5%
Females	57	10.5	1.8	17.5	10.5	59.7
Chi-square probability = .215						
Quakers	644	16.5%	5.9%	20.3%	5.9%	51.4%
Non-Quakers	809	20.4	5.8	17.6	7.7	48.6
Chi-square probability = .155						
Quaker leaders	242	12.4%	2.1%	20.7%	5.0%	59.9%
Average Quakers	402	18.9	8.2	20.2	6.5	46.3
Chi-square probability = .001						
Landowners	1331	18.3%	6.2%	18.9%	6.8%	50.0%
Nonlandowners	311	18.3	5.1	14.8	7.1	54.7
Chi-square probability = .423						
Occupations (males only)[a]						
Farmer	383	19.1%	8.6%	14.9%	7.3%	50.1%
Artisan	146	18.5	1.4	21.2	8.9	50.0

Table 21, continued

Attributes	N	Contested Won	Contested Lost	Uncontested Won	Uncontested Lost	Settled
Farmer-artisan	103	17.5	5.8	18.5	8.7	49.5
Merchant	247	18.2	5.7	30.4	3.2	42.5
Self-described gentry	186	15.1	6.5	19.9	3.2	55.4
Servant/slave/laborer	25	20.0	0.0	16.0	8.0	56.0

Chi-square probability = .001

1693 Pennsylvania tax assessment (in pounds)

100+	152	15.8%	5.3%	23.0%	2.6%	53.3%
50–99	92	13.0	6.5	21.7	10.9	47.8
1–49	98	20.4	10.2	16.3	8.2	44.9

Chi-square probability = .123

Inventoried wealth (in pounds)

500+	199	17.1%	7.5%	19.6%	3.5%	52.3%
100–499	192	17.2	8.9	18.2	6.8	49.0
1–99	72	18.1	11.1	26.4	9.7	34.7

Chi-square probability = .264

Legal roles

High officer	549	19.9%	4.6%	20.0%	4.0%	51.6%
Lesser officer	309	18.1	10.7	15.9	6.2	49.2
Nonofficer	784	17.2	5.1	17.6	9.1	51.0

Chi-square probability = .000

Cases

1–2	828	19.6%	5.4%	16.4%	7.1%	51.5
3–5	402	16.9	9.2	18.4	8.7	46.8
6+	412	17.0	3.9	21.1	4.4	53.6

Chi-square probability = .003

Overall	1642	18.3%	6.0%	18.1%	6.8%	50.9%

a. The category "other" has been omitted to ensure that chi-square is a valid test. Litigation analysis will use only six occupational categories.

often than expected in contested cases, high officers lost less often in uncontested cases, nonfficers lost more often in uncontested cases, and high officers lost less often in contested cases. Because officeholding status also had a statistically significant relationship to plaintiffs' choice of cause of action, a second-level chi-square test was done, which evaluated outcomes by controlling for cause of action. In these tests, case, debt, and other debt/contract causes showed no significant relationship between attribute and outcome. Nondebt/contract causes did reveal a significant bias in favor of high officers. In short, these results indicate that high officers' greater number of debt and contract cases was not essential to their advantage. The largest advantage for high officers came in nondebt/contract causes, the hardest type to win, while lesser officers who had filed more nondebt/contract cases fared less well.

Similarly, being a Quaker leader gave a plaintiff a tremendous statistical advantage in achieving a satisfactory outcome. Quaker-leader plaintiffs lost fewer contested cases and had more cases settled than expected, while average Quakers lost more contested cases than expected. Because there was no statistically significant relationship between Quaker leadership and the choice of cause of action, this result cannot mean that Quaker leaders' advantage stemmed from suing more often in causes most favorable for victories. Rather, these results strengthen the inference that defendants, realizing their relatively weak social and legal position vis-à-vis Quaker leaders, chose to avoid court fights and accommodate whatever dispute had brought the Quaker leader to sue them. Quaker leaders, in turn, accepted those offers to settle, revealing an accommodative stance when in the plaintiff's chair that conformed to the legal culture they had helped create. That this disparity in outcomes favored this narrow element of society was reflected in the fact that merely being a Quaker did not give a plaintiff a statistically significant advantage when compared with non-Quakers. The legal system did not disproportionately favor all Quakers who sued; rather, the most successful outcomes went to a small, favored few at the top of the Society of Friends, and litigants against such plaintiffs chose to switch rather than fight.

Regarding the number of suits brought, there did appear to be a learning curve that enhanced plaintiffs' chances in litigation, but that may reflect not legal skill but the power of the officers and Quaker leaders. Those who sued three to five times suffered more contested losses than expected, a predictable result expected because this group filed a disproportionate number of nondebt/contract cases. Megaplaintiffs, however, lost fewer uncontested cases and fewer contested cases than expected, despite no disproportionate filing of case, debt, or other debt/contract issues. As was discussed in chapter 2, these megaplaintiffs were more likely to be high officers and Quaker leaders (as well as landowners and wealthy). It can be inferred that the legal system recognized a plaintiff elite narrowly drawn from the top of society, that positive outcomes encouraged such plaintiffs to use the system, and that defendants realized that they fought such plaintiffs at their peril.

The final statistically significant attribute for plaintiffs was occupation. Merchants won a disproportionate number of uncontested cases, lost fewer uncontested cases, and settled fewer cases. These results were clearly associated with merchants' disproportionate use of debt (reflecting their practice of doing business in writing) and their avoidance of those causes most contested, the nondebt/contract causes. Merchants thus found Delaware Valley law a congenial system, especially in the courts' practice of chancering and enforcing bonds after a defendant confession in a single court session, which was an uncontested victory. Law reform seems to have persuaded merchants not to abandon the legal system (as they had the English common-law system) by providing predictable and efficient court results. Another significant contributor to this result was artisans' disproportionately fewer losses in contested cases. Artisans, like merchants, had many transactions but, unlike merchants, did not arrange their dealings to be able to sue in debt. Rather, their actions were disproportionately in the category of other debt/contract causes. That they lost so few of these cases reveals again the success of law reform in attracting the legally unsophisticated, who did not organize their dealings with an eye cocked toward filing a suit in debt or case. Plaintiffs who presented courts with debt and contract grievances in whatever form found their deals enforced. Farmers, who filed disproportionately more nondebt/contract actions, had disproportionately fewer uncontested victories and more uncontested losses. The proportion of all these outcomes that can be attributed to stronger cases, better strategies, bias in the process, or some combination of all three cannot be established with certainty. It is certain that the legal experience of those who had many market transactions, regardless of how those transactions were organized, was more positive than the experience of those who used courts for remedying more personal harms.

More surprising than those attributes that seemed to benefit plaintiffs were those attributes that made no statistical difference. None of the three wealth measures seemed to affect plaintiffs' outcomes. Although the wealthy did slightly better, neither landowning, inventoried wealth at death, nor taxed wealth in 1693 showed a statistically significant relation to outcomes. Wealth conferred no apparent benefit. Nor was there a statistically different pattern of outcomes favoring men over women plaintiffs. A class of privileged plaintiffs was created by individuals who had positions of power in the courts and the meetinghouse and by merchants (Quaker and non-Quaker alike) who engaged in large numbers of transactions and had the ability to organize their dealings so that they were virtually guaranteed success.

For defendants, the legal system produced a similar set of results; in these cases the privileged made choices designed to minimize the chance of losing, choices that were rewarded. Of all the attributes tested, inventoried wealth, 1693 tax assessments, land, and gender were not statistically significant for defendants (see table 22). Frequency of being a

Table 22. Defendants' Outcomes, by Attributes

| Attributes | N | Contested | | Uncontested | | |
		Won	Lost	Won	Lost	Settled
Males	1596	5.9%	18.4%	6.8%	17.9%	50.9%
Females	46	8.7	13.0	6.5	23.9	47.8
Chi-square probability = .685						
Quakers	482	7.5%	21.8%	8.1%	16.4%	46.3%
Non-Quakers	971	5.1	17.1	6.3	20.0	51.6
Chi-square probability = .013						
Quaker leaders	118	12.7%	24.6%	10.2%	16.1%	36.4%
Average Quakers	364	5.8	20.9	7.4	16.5	49.5
Chi-square probability = .034						
Landowners	1229	6.3%	19.6%	7.2%	17.3%	49.6%
Nonlandowners	413	5.1	14.3	5.8	20.3	54.5
Chi-square probability = .054						
Occupations (males only)[a]						
Farmer	473	5.7%	18.0%	5.9%	19.5%	51.0%
Artisan	242	4.1	16.1	7.0	18.2	54.6
Farmer-artisan	104	12.5	17.3	3.9	13.5	52.9
Merchant	56	7.1	28.6	10.7	14.3	39.3
Self-described gentry	71	4.2	19.7	15.5	11.3	49.3
Servant/slave/laborer	42	7.1	21.4	2.4	16.7	52.4
Chi-square probability = .044						

Table 22, continued

Attributes	N	Contested		Uncontested		
		Won	Lost	Won	Lost	Settled
1693 Pennsylvania tax assessment (in pounds)						
100+	68	8.8%	20.6%	14.7%	13.2%	42.7%
50–99	80	6.3	16.3	6.3	20.0	51.3
1–49	164	7.3	23.8	3.7	20.1	45.1
Chi-square probability = .128						
Inventoried wealth (in pounds)						
500+	87	11.5%	24.1%	8.1%	12.6%	43.7%
100–499	164	6.7	19.5	8.5	16.5	48.8
1–99	89	4.5	14.6	3.4	14.6	62.9
Chi-square probability = .169						
Legal roles						
High officer	244	10.7%	23.8%	11.5%	15.6%	38.5%
Lesser officer	400	6.8	18.8	4.3	18.8	51.5
Nonofficer	998	4.5	16.7	6.7	18.4	53.6
Chi-square probability = .000						
Cases						
1–2	876	7.4%	15.9%	6.6%	16.8%	53.3%
3–5	451	5.5	21.1	7.1	20.2	46.1
6+	315	2.5	21.0	7.0	18.7	50.8
Chi-square probability = .009						
Overall	1642	6.0%	18.3%	6.8%	18.1%	50.9%

a. The category "other" has been omitted to ensure that chi-square is a valid test. Litigation analysis will use only six occupational categories.

defendant was significant, but being a repeat defendant did not bring benefits, despite the fact that repeat defendants had greater wealth and status. Megadefendants won fewer contested cases than expected, while one-shot defendants won more of those contested cases than expected and lost fewer. These results reinforce the conclusion that wealth in all its forms was virtually irrelevant to the civil results of this legal system. The legal elite might have been wealthier, but that wealth was not the factor that brought them advantages in court.

While wealth was insignificant in skewing outcomes, high officehold-ers' and Quaker leaders' strategies and status combined to bring these defendants disproportionately positive results. Defendants who were high officers won more often than expected in contested cases, won more of-ten in uncontested cases, and settled less often. High officers' strategies included a lower level of accommodation; their excess victories were more a function of more often choosing to force the cases to court than a function of explicit bias, since they also had an excess of contested loss-es. Lesser-officer defendants lost more often than expected in uncon-tested cases, while nonofficers lost more often in contested cases. Such results cannot be attributed to differences in causes of action each of-ficer group defended; for example, high officers did not disproportion-ately defend against nondebt/contract actions (the easiest for defendants to win) to garner disproportionate victories.

Quaker defendants held a statistically significant advantage as well, primarily because they too chose to force the plaintiff into court. In con-tested cases, Quaker defendants won more than expected and lost more because they settled disproportionately fewer cases. Compared with av-erage Quakers, Quaker leaders held that same advantage, winning more contested cases and settling fewer cases brought against them. Exactly as it was for high officers, here was the interaction of strategy (Quaker and Quaker-leader defendants avoiding settling) and result (producing more victories but also more losses in the contested categories). Simi-larly, regarding defendants' occupational status, the self-described gen-try led the statistically significant results by winning far more uncon-tested cases than expected. Here were the winners, the legal elite, who—whether as plaintiffs or defendants—knew how to play the law.

The strategic choices in litigation were thus inextricably bound up with the perspectives of the litigants, perspectives formed by their roles as plaintiffs or defendants, their own social standing, the social stand-ing of their opponent, and the court's likely reaction to them and their cause. In general terms, those of higher social status—such as high of-ficers, Quaker leaders, and merchants—arrived at the following strate-gy: as plaintiffs, convince defendants to settle the case out of court, but as defendants, settle reluctantly and force your opponent into court if at all possible. Justices would, if at all possible, give those of higher sta-tus the benefit of defaults and nonsuits to produce more uncontested victories before trial. The bias was not gross, but it was there, lying in the discretion of a bench that favored the few.

Those of lesser status learned the opposite message. As defendants, they would try to settle rather than go to court. Aiding such a strategy was the legal system's preference for accommodation over confrontation. If a settlement was not possible, then such defendants, especially in debt cases, often preferred to confess judgment, accepting an uncontested loss rather than undergoing the expense and potential embarrassment of a trial. As plaintiffs, they must have been uneasy launching a case, especially if their opponent was of higher status. If a settlement could not be reached, such plaintiffs often abandoned their cases rather than fight through a trial.

"Good laws" brought in cases and gave all a forum; the "good men" encouraged the development of a legal culture in which most disputes would be resolved by the decisions of the parties themselves according to their bargaining power. Yet bargaining power in this society, as in any society, was unequal, and those with legal knowledge could gain further advantages. Some bargaining power derived from the law's protection of economic transactions involving contract and debt, but power reflected far more than legal rights. The law's forum gave those of greater social power and higher legal position (but not necessarily those of greater wealth alone) the processes and rituals by which their choices would produce a greater chance of success and by which their opponents would accept their less successful fate. The bargaining power of such as high officers, Quaker leaders, and merchants produced disparate results even though fair processes were fully enforced. From the perspective of the losers, such results were unfortunate but not unfair; because they derived from the choices available, which had been fairly chosen, the outcomes the system produced were legitimated.

From the perspective of the crowd, most of which had no suits on a given court day, settled cases were virtually invisible. Nonsuits and default judgments were only slightly more apparent, and if anyone paid attention, few would deny that these litigants who did not appear deserved to lose. Confessed judgments might draw more attention about who was up and who was down in the local economy, but those cases would likely not bring murmurs about the fairness of a result where the defendant admitted liability. It was conflict, the play of a contested case, that would draw the crowd's close attention. The vast majority of contested cases unfolded in front of juries, and the level of conflict in those cases exceeded the average bench trial. Jury trials thus assumed an importance to the perceived fairness of the system far out of proportion to their numbers, and it was those cases that would allow the spectators to evaluate the quality of Quaker justice.

Jury Trials

Jury trials were (and are still) the most dramatic of Anglo-American court proceedings. Litigants brought before juries witnesses, impassioned arguments, and other evidence of social conflict not produced in settled or uncontested cases and less often produced for bench trials. Quaker law reformers, from Penn on down, had emphasized the significance of juries when they protected the right to a jury trial in civil as well as in criminal cases and the right of jurors to have their verdict confirmed, free from prosecution for that verdict. That freedom from prosecution, however, apparently covered only principled verdicts and did not extend to verdicts done by chance. In the Bucks County case of Francis White versus James Allman, a deadlocked jury flipped a coin to find for the defendant White but later reconsidered and collectively reimbursed the litigants. Despite the parties' announced satisfaction with this outcome, the jurors were fined the large sum of two pounds and ten shillings, and seven Quakers who sat on the jury were condemned by their monthly meetings for their action. This case echoed all the way to London. Penn's opponents, as part of their attempt to obtain a royal charter, cited the coin flip as an example of corruption and shoddy justice, while Penn used the punishment of the jurors as part of his successful defense.[55] Clearly, these colonists paid close attention to the quality of justice delivered in jury trials.

For the parties, especially the defendant, electing to present their case before a jury often meant a conscious rejection of the legal culture's preference for accommodation in favor of public confrontation. Although the plaintiff had a hand in deciding whether to reach an out-of-court resolution, once that choice was eliminated, such public confrontation generally represented a defendant's strategic choice not to give up, not to let the case go by default and not to confess judgment in court. Whether civil defendants chose a jury depended on their attitudes toward their opponent, the case against them, and their perceived chances for success.

Of all civil cases entered, 15.5 percent went to a jury; of all completed civil cases, 16.8 percent received a jury verdict. It is hard to determine whether this percentage was high or low since there have been no comprehensive studies of civil jury usage.[56] Nonetheless, such a figure is misleadingly low regarding what the public saw in court, because 51 percent of completed cases were settled and removed from public view. Of the civil cases that made it to court, 38.8 percent went to a jury. Of all contested cases, 70 percent were decided by juries. Even this figure is deceptive because justices often decided cases where there was little controversy and the records often do not reveal much. Though jury trials were infrequent, the records suggest that jury trials, both civil and criminal, occupied the bulk of a court's time on court day. These dramatic cases therefore presented the legal system's greatest opportunities and greatest dangers for social integration. From the litigants' perspective, however, jury trials were clearly not the preferred way to resolve disputes; their preference stemmed not from official opposition to juries but from the success of other methods of dispute resolution.[57]

Defendants' choices for jury trials reflected the level of consensus that the legal system had reached about certain behaviors. As discussed generally for all contested cases, when a consensus existed and defendants could reasonably predict what a jury would say about their behavior, jury usage would be low. Rational defendants would not risk the expense and public humiliation of a jury trial if they could foresee a negative verdict. If defendants could not predict the verdict with certainty, they would more likely risk a public airing of the cause because they could reasonably think their behavior was legally in the right *and* because they could believe a jury would agree. Plaintiffs, having already gone to the trouble of making a claim of right in the declaration, would most likely go forward and present evidence and argument supporting their claim to the jury rather than back down. Obviously, for these types of cases, no clear consensus has yet emerged, yet it is inherent in the integrative theory of law that juries in such hard cases will create a societal consensus about the behavior.[58] It is also clear that jury verdicts did not always make behavioral standards any clearer, for juries had a dynamic of their own.

The pattern in contested cases overall was equally apparent for juries. Debt (13.9 percent of identified filings) and case (19.9 percent) revealed the lowest jury usage of specific common-law causes. Overall, only 16.9 percent of cases where an economic transaction had gone wrong (regardless of the cause of action) ended in front of a jury. Defendants had to feel very sure of their case to force a jury trial in the face of the consensus for enforcing certain transactions. In contrast, nearly half (49.1 percent) of nondebt/contract cases went before a jury. Trespass causes had the highest percentage of juries (59.7 percent), followed by assault and battery (54.6 percent), land causes (51.9 percent), trover (42.9 percent), and defamation (42.6 percent). It is important to consider the various perspectives in evaluating these percentages of juries and causes of action. Litigants, especially defendants, saw nondebt/contract causes as lacking a predictable outcome compared with case or debt; therefore, both sides could fight through a trial in the reasonable belief that they would win before a jury. Because cases overwhelmingly dealt with economic transactions, however, juries saw more cases on issues where there was a clear consensus on behavior. Spectators saw almost as many juries in case (97) as in *all* nondebt/contract causes (109); when case, debt, and other debt/contract cases are combined, these economic issues totaled more jury trials (174) than nondebt/contract issues did. Court-day crowds thus regularly saw juries reinforce economic consensus by finding overwhelmingly for plaintiffs in all cases dealing with economic issues (78 percent), while defendants' choices for juries in nondebt/economic issues (lacking a clear behavioral consensus) were reinforced when juries rewarded defendants with victories in 32 percent of such cases.

Litigants' perceptions of their chances to win were determined by more than the cause of action; they were also influenced by calculations of whether the jury would likely be sympathetic to the defendant. Choosing to go before a jury partly reflected defendants' beliefs regarding their own social standing vis-à-vis the opponent and the jury of peers. Civil cases were not merely confrontations over a standard of behavior but also tests of social strength. When this possibility is combined with the fact that defendants usually made the strategic choice for a jury trial, some predictions logically follow and can be tested statistically. Defendants of higher status should have chosen jury trials more often than those of lower status in the belief that their social standing might sway the result. Conversely, plaintiffs of lower status should have faced jury trials more often than those of higher status, for the defendant (of whatever status) would more likely believe such a plaintiff would be easily beaten. In testing these hypotheses, it is important to remember who disproportionately served on juries—legal officers, landowners, Quakers, Quaker leaders, and farmer-artisans—and which attributes had little to no impact on jury service—taxed wealth and inventoried wealth. If the groups did exhibit differences in their preferences for jury trials along the lines predicted, once again chi-square is be used to measure whether these differences were statistically significant. In general, defendants of higher status did choose juries more often than those of lesser status, although the differences were not always significant (see table 23). Men chose juries slightly more often than women, and the poorest in

Table 23. Choice for Jury Trial and Jury Victories by Defendants

Attributes	Civil Cases with Jury (%)	Civil Defendants Who Won Jury Cases (%)
Percentage of all cases	15.5	27.2
Total n of jury trials	312	277
Male	15.5	27.0
Female	14.0	42.9
Chi-square probability (n)	.761 (312)	.354 (277)
Quakers	17.5	28.9
Non-Quakers	13.9	26.4
Chi-square probability (n)	.040 (271)	.672 (241)
Quaker leaders	23.9	46.7
Average Quakers	15.6	20.9
Chi-square probability (n)	.006 (108)	.029 (69)
Landowners	17.1	26.6
Nonlandowners	10.8	31.4
Chi-square probability (n)	.001 (312)	.486 (277)
Occupations (males only)[a]		
Farmer	16.9	25.3
Artisan	10.5	25.0
Farmer-artisan	23.1	42.3
Merchant	21.9	21.4
Self-described gentry	14.3	25.0
Servant/slave/laborer	11.7	14.3
Chi-square probability (n)	.012 (190)	.538 (170)
1693 Pennsylvania tax assessment (in pounds)		
100+	22.1	33.3
50–99	16.0	38.5
1–49	15.9	32.1
Chi-square probability (n)	.438 (65)	.922 (56)

Inventoried wealth (in pounds)

500+	28.8	27.3
100–499	17.0	30.3
1–99	15.0	28.6
Chi-square probability (*n*)	.010 (92)	.964 (80)

Legal roles

High officer	24.7	32.8
Lesser officer	16.5	29.0
Nonofficer	12.9	24.3
Chi-square probability (*n*)	.000 (312)	.423 (277)

Cases

1–2	15.8	32.9
3–5	15.8	26.3
6+	14.5	10.4
Chi-square probability (*n*)	.812 (312)	.009 (277)

a. The category "other" has been omitted to ensure that chi-square is a valid test. Litigation analysis will use only six occupational categories.

the 1693 tax assessment chose juries less often than those who had higher tax assessments, but in neither case was the difference statistically significant. Inventoried wealth, however, was a statistically significant factor; those with greater wealth at death sought jury trials more often than those with less wealth. Similarly, landowners, farmer-artisans, and merchants disproportionately preferred juries when they were civil defendants. Not coincidentally, these landowners and farmer-artisans were the same ones that disproportionately served on juries. Overall, those who served as jurors also tended to prefer juries when they were civil defendants, which probably reflected their experience as well as the fact that "good men," similar to them, were sitting in the jury box.[59] A logical inference is that these defendants thought they would have an advantage with juries composed of men like them.

Three key attributes—officeholding status, religion, and Quaker leadership—also showed a statistically significant pattern of choices regarding civil juries in accord with the first prediction. Here were the elite of Delaware Valley society—legal officers, Quakers, and their leaders—choosing to place their defense before a jury significantly more often than those of lesser status. Their implicit claim was one of power; this preference loudly proclaims their belief that jurors would be more receptive to their case because of who they were. Affinity with those who sat on juries might also have encouraged this behavior, which again reflects the power of these groups to pack their members on juries. It is critical to note that all those who were disproportionately packed onto juries disproportionately chose to use juries when the choice was theirs. Those disproportionately excluded from juries disproportionately chose other methods to resolve their civil problems. Power expressed in one sphere redounded throughout the legal system to skew individuals' choices.

Members of the officeholding and Quaker elite were not the only ones who shared the belief in their power, as can be seen in the distribution of jury trials among different groups of plaintiffs. The second prediction stated that socially weak groups would face more jury trials when they were plaintiffs, while disproportionately fewer juries would decide the cases of higher-status plaintiffs because defendants, fearing defeat because of their opponent's status, would seek other methods of dispute resolution. In the case of officer litigants, lesser-officer plaintiffs faced juries disproportionately often (20.5 percent), while high officers disproportionately avoided them (12.7 percent).[60] For Quaker leaders, the results were even starker—as plaintiffs, they faced juries in only 6.9 percent of their cases (versus 16.3 percent for non-Quakers and 17.6 percent for average Quakers),[61] revealing that Delaware Valley society believed Quaker leaders to be so strong that a jury trial against them would probably be futile. Most plaintiff groups, however, showed no statistically significant difference in their having to face a jury to prove their case. In litigation, it was primarily the choice of defendants, which reflected not only their views of juries but also their assessments of how their own status might affect the outcome.

Because such choices reflected to some degree internalized perceptions about power, the hierarchy of Delaware Valley society must have been visible to those on the bottom as well as to those on top. The question then becomes how did Quakers, particularly Quaker leaders, packing themselves onto juries and then disproportionately choosing such juries to resolve their disputes, maintain their system's legitimacy? David Fischer's idea that Quaker sympathizers behaved and were treated like "real" Quakers cannot be true, given the evidence regarding jury packing, officeholding, and differential behavior in litigation. The legal system treated identifiable Quakers (especially Quaker leaders) and non-Quakers differently. Non-Quakers could not have had a large subset of Quaker sympathizers blending in with the plurality of Quakers because if they had, the numbers would not have shown statistical significance.[62] Maintaining legitimacy therefore required that the majority non-Quakers continue to use the courts and to obey those courts' decisions voluntarily. Yet how could a population that clearly recognized inequities in power within the legal system, as evidenced by their choices for jury trials and other options, be convinced of that system's legitimacy?

The answer lies in the behavior of juries. With two exceptions, all groups received statistically neutral, unbiased distributions of verdicts from juries in civil cases (see table 23). No matter what the gender, landowning status, occupation, wealth, officeholding history, service on a jury, or religion of litigants, jurors seem to have lived up to their oath to "well and truly try the issue . . . according to your evidence."[63] As table 23 shows, juries might have slightly favored higher-status defendants, but that advantage was statistically insignificant. The results were similar for plaintiffs—there were statistically neutral results for all categories but one.

Juries did show a statistically significant bias in favor of Quaker leaders in civil cases, whether they were defendants or plaintiffs. A Quaker leader was more than twice as likely to win as a defendant than an average Quaker was. As plaintiffs in jury trials, Quaker leaders never lost, winning sixteen times (chi-square probability = .019). These benefits that juries conferred on litigants who were Quaker leaders were significant yet rare. Only forty-six times in these thirty years did Quaker leaders face a civil jury, an average of roughly one time every two years in any particular county. Unless one was the opponent of a Quaker leader in litigation, such a pattern might easily be unremarked upon in a system that delivered such statistically neutral justice for the vast majority of litigant groups. The other category where there was a significant difference was in defendant's usage, where megadefendants won disproportionately few cases. Those who were sued repeatedly might not have been able to judge the strength of the cases against them, or they might have been extraordinarily contentious, which would perhaps account for why they were sued so often in the first place.

The advantages for high-status groups in litigation stemmed primarily not from decisions made by jurors but from the choices made before a case reached a jury. By refusing to settle as often as they had when they were plaintiffs, defendants who were high officers or Quaker leaders chose, in effect, to call their opponents' bluff. Those opponents, now facing a potential trial against a powerful adversary before judges and juries that had attributes very similar to the defendant's, often gave up; those uncontested decisions provided a substantial portion of these defendants' higher percentage of success. Plaintiffs could try to avoid a jury trial with a bench decision, but such a choice seemed to gain them little advantage. Defendants who were high officers won 25 percent of contested cases before the bench, which was not very different from the average for all defendants who went to jury trials. Finally, the fact that high officers and Quaker leaders disproportionately chose jury trials reveals that at least they thought their chances for a positive outcome were better served by a full-fledged, in-court contest as opposed to a settlement of the dispute that would have probably required compromise. Even though juries did not fully comply with their expectations, these choices were a powerful commentary on the power relations of the parties involved.

Two conclusions are inescapable. First, in a system where juries were packed, those jurors seemed to decide without evident bias. Jurors, facing dramatic disputes and functioning in front of an observant throng on court days, provided a concrete and observable rationale for the non-Quaker majority to accept voluntarily the authority of the Quaker minority's rule over the legal system. In a reformed system that provided litigants maximum opportunity to control personally the presentation of their evidence and arguments, jurors seemed to be trying hard to be fair by deciding cases consistently and without regard to social standing. Party control over the process, consistency of the results, the ability to suppress bias in the process, and a perceived effort by decision-makers to be fair and to judge according to ethical standards—modern social scientists have identified these as potential keys to a public's evaluation of whether procedures produce "justice" and are thus legitimate.[64]

The performance of the civil justice system, especially the performance of juries, provides a key to unlock the mystery of Quaker power and social peace in the rapidly expanding and diversifying Delaware Valley society. The legal system, established in accordance with the ideology of law reform and Quaker principles, produced public dramas that produced visible affirmation of those facets of procedural justice needed to legitimize Quaker power over the legal system. Penn's "good men" on juries had justified his faith in them, and in so doing, they helped protect Quaker authority. Yet juries were but one part of the edifice of Quaker authority. Jury trials decided few cases, albeit cases that had maximum public impact. Other choices, made primarily out of court, enabled

Quaker leaders and others of high status to manipulate that system using their knowledge and social power to gain disproportionately positive outcomes in resolving their disputes. The law's integrative and manipulative aspects combined to confer both legitimacy and concrete advantages on the Delaware Valley's Quaker elite.

FOUR

Quaker Dispute Processing

Courts do not have a monopoly on dispute resolution in any society. In addition to individuals' resolving their own disputes, communities produce values, rules, and processes designed to resolve their members' disputes.[1] In the colonial Delaware Valley, the Quaker community provided a specific dispute-resolution alternative to legal institutions. Quakers believed disputes between members undermined the harmony of the whole Quaker community and therefore required community-determined and community-controlled processes to end the dispute and restore "unity." Such "differences" between members were not to be resolved by outsiders—who were present in common-law courts—without approval of the community's corporate organ, the monthly meeting. Quaker doctrine thus sought a monopoly on decisions within a specific subset of all social disputes—those between Quakers—and gave meetings the authority to enforce that monopoly by "disowning" (expelling) those disputants who refused to conform to the meeting's processes and decisions. Because good records from eleven monthly and quarterly meetings' handling of Quaker differences in Bucks, Chester, and Burlington counties exist for this period, this alternative can be compared with the legal system's processing of Quaker disputes.[2]

Many aspects of legal dispute resolution paralleled the doctrines designed to resolve differences between Quakers. Quakers believed that in certain recurring interactions between members, norms established by the community should be followed, as they were in the legal system. Though the line was often ambiguous, there was an operational distinction between differences between individual Quakers who felt their interpersonal expectations had been violated (analogous to civil cases) and disciplinary cases where the behavior offended the entire community (criminal cases). When aggrieved individuals chose to bring their disputes with another Quaker to the meeting, requirements of procedure and standardized, specialized language transformed their claim of entitlement, increased the number of participants, challenged the parties' perceptions of each other, and took the outcome at least partially out of the parties' hands. Though their processes of dispute resolution were mediation and arbitration rather than adversarial confrontation, Quaker decision-makers also relied on norms to determine the rights of the parties; they developed and pronounced acceptable boundaries of behavior within the community and reinforced their decisions with sanctions against recalcitrant losers. The analysis of disputes within the Quaker community, as with disputes in courts, is a study of choices that reflected the power of the community, the bargaining position of the parties, and the definition of conformity to community norms.[3]

The analytical framework applied to civil litigation can thus be applied to this parallel structure, and valid comparisons can be made. What drove the Quakers to establish these procedures as an alternative to the legal system? How efficient and successful were meetings in achieving their goals of harmony in the community and control over intra-Quaker disputes? What were the implications of changes in dispute processing over time for this community's power over its members? What influence did legal procedures and norms have on Quaker procedures and norms? What goals did disputants possess, what strategies did they employ, and to what advantage? What types of differences were brought to the meeting, and how did this docket differ from the legal system's civil docket? Demographically, who brought differences to the meeting, and were these "plaintiffs" different from those with whom they had the differences or from Quakers in general? Setting aside panegyrics composed of anecdotal evidence on alternative, community-based dispute-resolution systems,[4] this chapter rigorously examines the actual functioning of the Quaker alternative to law.

The Gospel Order

As noted in the Introduction, the Society of Friends' political and religious radicalism produced a thorough critique of the English legal system and proposed reforms. Beyond these general criticisms, however, Quakers had specific grievances that led the Society of Friends to reject courts as forums to resolve their disputes. According to Craig Hor-

le, "Quakers had developed a collective set of principles which threatened the foundation of the English legal system. They were a large and
expanding group of potential criminals. . . ." Quaker doctrinal pronouncements, ironically entitled "testimonies," demanded open meetings for worship; utilization of ministers traveling even on the Sabbath;
interruptions of sermons in Anglican churches; and refusals to bear arms,
to doff hats to magistrates in court, and to contribute through tithes to
the established church, all of which constituted clear conflicts with English law. A quarter-century of legal harassments, imprisonments, and
distraint of goods for payment of fines and tithes left Quakers skilled
in legal technicalities, experienced in maintaining support networks for
those suffering at the hands of the law, and determined to resist legal
oppression without abandoning principles.[5] The most difficult legal
problem facing Quakers was their refusal to take an oath, under the biblical injunction to "swear not at all." In refusing, Quakers disqualified
themselves from holding public office and serving on juries, from engaging in many trades, and, most important, from suing for debts, giving evidence, and answering suits in equity.[6]

If Quakers were to avoid taking oaths, alternatives to common-law
courts had to be developed in England. Although extralegal Quaker procedures for resolving disputes among themselves were a necessary response to the oath controversy, early Delaware Valley jurisdictions under Quaker control rendered this problem moot by allowing attestations
and affirmations in place of oaths for official business. Anglican agita-
tion about oaths would later disrupt Pennsylvania and force the new
royal colony of New Jersey, at least nominally, to remove the affirmation option in the early 1700s.[7] Regardless of the oath situation, the
Delaware Valley Quakers' method for dispute resolution, called the "Gospel Order," was supposed to be more than a vestigial remnant of adaptations to legal circumstances prevailing in England.

If their refusal to take oaths pushed Quakers out of the English legal
system, they were equally pulled into the Gospel Order by their faith's
community-building measures. Organized from the top down into a
system of monthly, quarterly, and yearly meetings, the Society of Friends
after 1660 rapidly developed a singular community for members' legal
protection, spiritual and physical sustenance, and moral education and
discipline. The monthly meeting, made up of several smaller meetings
that met weekly for worship, was the cornerstone of a structure designed
to knit Quakers on both sides of the Atlantic into one people through

the regular flow of travelers and information. In these monthly meetings, the "sense of the meeting"—a consensus judgment influenced by epistles from authoritative Friends and other meetings—determined doctrine and behavior. Quarterly meetings covering a county oversaw the various monthly meetings and were attended by representatives from each. The Philadelphia Yearly Meeting, alternately meeting in Burlington and Philadelphia as a symbol of the region's unity, included all the quarterly meetings of the Delaware Valley and served as the apex of an organization through which information passed from and to English Friends.

A critical issue facing Delaware Valley meetings was defining the membership of their new community. Meetings established among immigrants who were "strangers" to one another often relied on certificates of "clearness," issued by the collective judgment of the bearer's old meeting, that he or she was in good standing and should be accepted into the new meeting.[8] A great many Friends, however, might not have bothered to get a certificate before emigrating, and others (perhaps a majority of all early Delaware Valley Quakers) might have joined the Society only after arrival.[9] Membership decisions were thus corporate, in that the local Quaker community approved and the principles on which these decisions were based had been passed down through a hierarchy. The ironic result was that in a religion dedicated to the primacy of individual conscience, Quakers all held roughly the same beliefs wherever they lived, even to the point of codification of "discipline" in the Delaware Valley by 1704.[10]

As anthropologists of law have long noted, mechanisms of dispute resolution build and consolidate community boundaries by allowing insiders to resolve their disputes through community-based methods inaccessible to outsiders, by ostracizing insiders who take their dispute outside community bounds, and by reclassifying an insider as an outsider when community norms are violated.[11] George Fox, the founder of the Society of Friends, quoted St. Paul in providing the doctrinal groundwork for Quaker dispute resolution: "Dare any of you who have a matter against another go to law before the unjust, and not before the saints?" According to Fox, litigation subverted the purposes of "love, order and unity of brethren."[12] The evil was conflict about secular issues; the solution lay in religious-based mechanisms independent of the secular law. The London Yearly Meeting's epistle in 1697, recorded in both the Chester Monthly Meeting and Quarterly Meeting and presumably read throughout the valley, counseled against "Reflections one upon another . . . that may tend to beget an uneaseyness or Dissatisfaction among friends about outward things" that could lead to "the hurte of truth and Greef of many friends" by a lawsuit. Official doctrine even discouraged Friends from suing non-Quakers because "it is our duty to seek peace with all men and to avoid giving provocation or just offense with any."[13] Contention in this world distracted good Quakers from concentrating on the next world, and lawsuits with anyone only exacerbated the problem.

A second, and more pragmatic, rationale was the desire to keep up the facade of a united community for the outside world. Friends feared their enemies might exploit any known dissension. In an epistle distributed in the late 1680s, the Philadelphia Yearly Meeting desired not only that "there may be no strife amongst us" but also that there be no "endeavoring to uncover the nakedness one of another by presenting matters and things before the unjust . . . by goeing to Law one with another," laying "open one anothers nakedness in the sight of the worst of men." Despite the fact that the courts were overwhelmingly Quaker, disputants and their monthly meeting were to determine the controversy within the bounds of the Quaker community so "that the World may not know of our Differences for the time to come Or that there is disunion amongst us."[14] To sue a fellow Quaker without the meeting's consent or to resist a decision made within the community put the offender at risk of the most severe sanction—disownment, the public declaration that a member was "out of unity," that an insider was now an outsider.[15] Throughout the Society of Friends, dispute processing established behavioral boundaries so the community could keep its defenses strong against the outside world.

The essentials of Gospel Order procedure for dispute resolution between Friends first appeared in the Delaware Valley in 1681 in Burlington's Meeting. The first injunction was that Quakers "do not go to Law before they first lay itt before ye particular Monthly Meeting yt they do belong to." As subsequently elaborated, the procedure demanded that the parties try to end the controversy between themselves, and "if they cannot . . . then to refer it to two friends or more to see if they can end it then if not to bring it to ye Monthly Meeting there to be ended."[16] Although no penalty for failure to comply was mentioned, as early as 1683 the procedure in cases of prolonged resistance became clear. The Burlington Monthly Meeting leader Daniel Wills, a landed gentleman who served as justice of the peace for thirteen years, was threatened with "the necessity of the Meeting giving testimony against him for refusing" to perform (i.e., comply with or execute) a Quaker arbitration award.[17] Such disownment was ultimately unnecessary because Wills apparently performed the award, but the precedent had been set.

The informality of such procedures allowed meetings to make minor alterations within the general framework. The Radnor Meeting established standing two-man arbitration committees in each local meeting, giving them authority to determine and end differences between Friends, to request help from additional people if necessary, and to refer intractable differences to the full monthly meeting.[18] The Chester Quarterly Meeting instructed the disciplinary overseers for each monthly meeting to intervene if they found any personal differences.[19] The London Yearly Meeting's epistle of 1697 sought to make the procedure more rigorous by imposing responsibility on neighboring Friends to attempt to mediate a dispute, responsibility on arbitrators chosen by the parties to serve, and responsibility on the parties to "bind themselves to stand to the award." Failure to perform any of these duties without good cause was a disownable offense.[20] Delaware Valley Friends codified the procedure in 1704, when the yearly meeting ordered aggrieved Quakers to try direct reconciliation first, followed by the use of disciplinary overseers as mediators. If that failed, then the disputants were to appoint arbitrators, whose decision the monthly meeting could then review and implement. Appeals to the quarterly meeting and then to the yearly meeting were possible. Disownment was reserved for recalcitrant parties, and the innocent party could then go to court to enforce the claim.[21] Yet even as Quakers rationalized the Gospel Order, the substance remained as informal and flexible as ever in practice.

The goals, procedures, and sanctions available in the Gospel Order stood in stark contrast to those established by law. In place of a publicly adversarial court structure designed to identify winners and enforce judgments, the Quakers sought to preserve the community's harmony and insularity by accommodating disputants privately "by Gentle means in a brotherly and loving manner." Unlike civil procedure (even in its reformed version), that gentle manner knew few formal constraints, and the execution of a Quaker decision rested not on seizing person or property but on an indirect sanction, removal from the community. Because the Society of Friends opposed using the courts for dispute resolution between Quakers, comparative analysis of the two mechanisms becomes possible. The monthly and quarterly meeting records were geographically conterminous with Bucks, Chester, and Burlington counties and were nearly unbroken for this period, paralleling the legal records. Private disputes (analogous to civil cases) usually included the word *difference* in the record or mentioned a claim, such as a debt owed. The identified "plaintiff" was the one who first brought the difference to the meeting, lodged a claim of right against another (the "defendant"), or was listed first when the record followed the pattern of "in the difference between x and y."[22] By these definitions, there were 187 differences involving 150 Quakers as Gospel Order plaintiffs and 164 Quakers as defendants (a total of 279 disputants) between 1681 and 1710 to compare with the civil litigants and civil cases.

The Gospel Order versus the Law

As noted in chapter 2, the Gospel Order failed miserably in its stated goal of keeping Quakers from "going to law" against each other. Quakers filed suit against other Quakers 302 times, 61 percent more often than they took their disputes to meetings. Of the three counties, only Bucks County saw more disputes between Quakers brought to meetings than were brought to court (71 were brought to meetings and 49 were taken to court).[23] Almost half of all intra-Quaker cases were between members of a single monthly meeting, who presumably had the most to lose by disrupting the community through a lawsuit. For example, of the lawsuits the Quaker leader John Hollinshead brought, three were against average Quakers from his own Burlington Meeting; he never brought these or any other differences to his meeting for resolution. Amidst this cascade of litigation, Quaker leaders were more confrontational than any other litigant group and were less likely to accommodate a case, whether facing a Quaker or non-Quaker plaintiff, than the rest of the defendant population. If Quaker meetings had given approval for such suits, either before or after Gospel Order proceedings, such procedures would not have been out of order, and Delaware Valley Quakers would have met their goals regarding dispute resolution. However, in no meeting was there any concerted effort to question Quakers for taking their disputes to court, and rarely was permission given or discipline imposed for such suits.

These three counties and their associated meetings had different propensities regarding where to resolve Quaker disputes. Bucks County Quakers used the Gospel Order (71 differences) more often than Chester County Quakers (70) or Burlington County Quakers (46) did, despite the fact that Bucks County had far fewer Quakers than the other two counties. Outside of Bucks County, Quaker dispute-resolution choices depended on who controlled the courts. In Burlington County, Quaker use of courts against other Quakers peaked between 1680 and 1685 (the period of greatest Quaker power), and each successive five-year period found fewer Quakers suing other Quakers. At the same time, the number of differences handled by meetings remained relatively constant, except for the period of 1701–5, when the number tripled to 15, only to return to its previous level (5) in 1706–10. Overall, there were more than three times as many intra-Quaker suits in the courts than there were differences recorded in meetings from 1680 to 1703. From 1704 to 1709, however, this overall pattern reversed itself; Quakers went to meetings 50 percent more often than they went to court (12 to 8) to resolve their differences. This shift followed the royal takeover of the colony in 1703 and the subsequent exclusion of Quakers from justice-ships and juries because of their politics and their refusal to take oaths. These trends support an inference that Quakers, with or without meeting approval, went to court so long as the saints controlled the system, but they withdrew from that system when the non-saints increased their authority. As Quakers' hold over the legal system loosened, the courts steadily lost control over Burlington County's intra-Quaker disputes; the legitimacy of this secular forum could not be assumed when saints were no longer judging saints.

In Chester County, disputants' choices also seem to have responded to political challenges. During the first ten years, meetings took on 25 intra-Quaker differences, while the courts saw 26. Both systems suffered major challenges to their authority between 1691 and 1695—the Quakers with the Keithian schism and the legal system with the suspension of Penn's charter and the consequent replacement of many legal personnel.[24] In both systems, the number of disputes brought declined, but the Quaker system lost more ground than the legal system. (Similarly in Bucks County, 1691 to 1695 was the only period in which legal resolution of intra-Quaker disputes was more popular than meeting resolution.) After 1695, however, the Quaker community saw a sharp surge in differences brought to meetings, while the legal system, embroiled in political power struggles over control of the judiciary until 1701, showed no such increase. Quaker meeting usage then declined over the next ten years, while legal resolution of intra-Quaker disputes grew and exceeded meeting resolution. Changes within each system correlate well with this result—leading Friends were losing their unchallenged authority while the government and legal system in Pennsylvania stabilized.[25] In Chester County, Quakers' choices of the dispute forum corresponded to the perceived legitimacy and authority of the institutions.

These counties in this regional legal system contained Quakers who deviated wildly from doctrine in their choice of dispute forums. Yet, as a matter of principle, these meetings maintained an allegiance to the stated doctrine. Five times between 1700 and 1702 meetings in Chester County called on their members to use the Gospel Order and not to go to court.[26] Apparently, these missives were attempting to reverse a trend, because court usage was then increasing while meeting usage was declining. Burlington County's meeting gave its members similar instructions in 1681 and 1685, at the peak of legal usage in Burlington County.[27] Though intra-Quaker court cases declined thereafter, meeting usage did not increase, and only after the 1703 royal takeover did Burlington County Quakers resolve a majority of formal disputes between members inside their own bounds. Bucks County's Quakers, who settled the largest percentage of disputes within meetings, never recorded such a pronouncement. These epistles were thus likely hortatory efforts to remedy known deficiencies, not statements of social fact, as historians have often interpreted them.

Since Quakers and Quaker leaders dominated the legal system throughout this period, it was impossible for Quaker meetings to have been unaware of over three hundred intra-Quaker disputes brought to county courts. Yet in only a handful of instances did Quakers receive reprimands for going to court against another Quaker, and none resulted in the ultimate sanction of disownment. Chester's Quarterly Meeting heard Cornelius Empson's complaint against George Harlin and Robert Way for destroying Empson's old mill without his permission. Even before the meeting heard this difference, however, Empson had won his case in court, a victory confirmed by the meeting, which forced Harlin and Way to acknowledge that they were "too forward in doing what they did without Empson's leave." Yet Empson acknowledged his "forwardness in prosecuting them by law" and had to pay most of Harlin and Way's court costs. With both parties apparently satisfied, no further discipline followed.[28] In Walter Faucett's difference with Edward Pritchett, the meeting found Faucett's complaint just, but he was reprimanded for "fetching a warrant" against Pritchett though not disciplined.

Similarly, Robert Heaton and Thomas Thwait differed over the disposition of the Thwait estate and the appointment of Thomas's guardian. Before Middletown's Meeting could rule, Heaton was accused of "proceeding in a legal way without the advice and approbation of Friends." Heaton simply acknowledged his sorrow, and the meeting went forward to "do best for the young man" by giving Heaton what he wanted—control over the estate and guardianship over Thwait.[29]

As opposed to cases where the legal behavior came out when one party brought the dispute to the meeting, three cases, all in Bucks County, arose where the meeting intervened on its own initiative. William Paxson, Jr., and Jon Scarbrough engaged in an "untruthlike quarrel," and Scarbrough "without having regard to truth's order went to a magistrate to desire justice." When both condemned themselves and forgave each other, there was no further discipline.[30] William Biles, a Quaker leader, had to condemn himself for not "owning" (admitting to) a bill in court presented at the suit of another Quaker, Simon Rouse, who suffered no penalty for bringing the case in the first place.[31] Finally, emissaries asked Robert Carter why his difference with Henry Paxson, a Quaker leader, was not placed before the meeting. Carter replied that Paxson had already filed a suit against him (the case was filed one month before the meeting intervened) and that "he thought it improper or needless to trouble the meeting with it."[32]

That the meeting took no further steps in this last dispute illustrated not only the laissez-faire attitude taken toward suits contrary to doctrinal injunction but also meetings' primary concern with the parties' attitudes. The mere fact of going to court did not bother meetings; disputes in court that subverted harmony did trouble meetings. In the first three cases, the parties proceeded on both tracks at the same time, a clear challenge to the Quaker claim of authority over intra-Quaker disputes. The next two cases involved egregious public behavior that threatened public exposure of community disunity, which the Quaker alternative was designed to conceal. Most Quaker cases, however, were like the Carter-Paxson case, where the parties apparently preferred the legal forum but did not want a confrontation between law and meeting. Because most of the justices and jurors were Quakers, the spirit of the doctrine about not going before the "world's people" could be de facto preserved. By ignoring and tacitly sanctioning such cases before legal decision-makers from the Society, disciplinary struggles over intra-Quaker litigation were avoided. If historians have concluded that there were few offenses and disownments prior to 1720, it was true only because Quakers closed their eyes to such litigation offenses.[33]

If disputes taken first to court rarely brought meeting discipline, tacit approval of those cases did not imply blanket permission to go to court for every dispute. Once the dispute was inside the Gospel Order proceedings, parties found it very difficult to get meeting approval to begin a suit against a recalcitrant Quaker opponent, even in clear-cut cases. John Worrall obtained an order from his meeting for Joseph Carter to pay Worrall his "Just Debt," yet it took a full year before the meeting determined that Carter was not going to pay and allowed Worrall "to take his course with him att Law." Despite his opponent's refusal to submit the dispute to arbitration, Ephraim Heaton had to "forbear prosecuting his bond" until the quarterly meeting could arbitrate the case.[34] George Gray of Philadelphia faced greater difficulties. He came to Burlington's Meeting in early 1706 complaining that Samuel Gibson had long owed him money, and the meeting agreed that Gibson should pay or else face a lawsuit. By the beginning of 1707, Gibson had not yet paid, and the meeting again threatened to allow Gray to sue if Gibson did not pay. By October 1709, more than three-and-a-half years after the initial complaint, even the meeting's patience had worn thin, and Gray was finally given permission to sue if Gibson did not pay by the next monthly meeting.[35]

The Quaker leader Robert Barber might gladly have accepted even such a delayed solution in his dispute with William Smith, Smith's wife, and the wife's son, Phillip Pritchett. Barber obtained an arbitration award against the three for trespassing on his land, yet three months later, Pritchett had not left but instead was sowing new crops on Barber's property. The meeting arranged a new agreement by which Pritchett was to remove the old fence that enclosed twenty acres of Barber's land, which should have been done five months earlier. Three months later, with this second agreement unfulfilled, the good Quaker Barber asked meeting permission to go to court, which was denied. Barber then appealed to the Chester Quarterly Meeting to give him such permission, and that body, one year after the original decision, proclaimed that although Barber "had cause to appeal," he and Pritchett should try arbitration again. Barber then appealed to the yearly meeting to get permission to sue, also apparently unsuccessfully because a case never appeared for trial.[36] Starting a dispute inside the meeting meant that taking it to court would be difficult; all told, only eight pairs of disputants whose issue began in a Quaker forum later became adversaries in a court of law.[37] Meetings, by acting to keep the disputes already brought before them from going to court, preserved the sense of their doctrinal monopoly, but those same meetings did not attempt to pull in disputes that had already bypassed the Gospel Order and gone to court. Such a pattern reveals that image might have triumphed; so long as the conflict between rhetoric and reality in intra-Quaker disputes did not appear in a meeting, everyone could pretend it did not exist.

Why was there such reluctance to allow Quakers who had won a meeting's verdict to sue their adversaries who had flaunted the decision? Doctrine required the disownment of the offending party prior to such a suit so the litigants would not both be saints. With such extreme retaliation the only sanction available, meetings would bluff the recalcitrant with the double threat of disownment and subsequent suit to coerce compliance, a bluff that was sometimes called. John Rutledge won an arbitration award, sponsored by the Middletown Meeting, against Jonathan Cooper in the summer of 1707. In the summer of 1708, the meeting threatened to disown Cooper unless he performed the award. He promised to do so, but seven months later the award was still not performed, and again the meeting threatened disownment to allow Rutledge to sue. Again Cooper promised, again he failed, again he was threatened, and again he promised. But this time the meeting waited to "see how far they can believe the reality of it." Finally, in late 1709, the difference ended when the meeting accepted Cooper's acknowledgment of his sorrow, but how satisfied Rutledge was with finally receiving his long-delayed award went unrecorded.[38]

Despite the rhetoric of harmony, single community, and a common set of rules, Quakers often disregarded doctrine concerning intra-Quaker disputes and the law. Broad generalizations about Quaker behavior derived from simply reading important Quaker directives and assuming that the organization automatically achieved compliance are thus suspect.[39] Quaker communities were as diverse as New England towns. While some meetings were more effective than others in resolving disputes, all were selective and inconsistent in their approaches to prescribed behavior. Their tacit concession of control over disputes, even though they maintained their formal doctrine, ultimately made the Gospel Order into an echo of the law. The attractiveness of the Delaware Valley legal system to Quakers, with its formal yet reformed procedures and consistent norms, meant that Quaker meetings had surrendered not just their monopoly but much of their real authority over their members.

Quaker Dispute Procedures

The paramount goal of the Gospel Order was to restore and preserve harmony among members of the Quaker community. Determining how well the process resolved the 187 differences brought to meetings first requires comparing these procedures and legal procedures. Perhaps the most significant difference was the Quaker requirement of a personal appearance before the meeting. Avoidance of a personal appearance was possible in the courts: 19 percent of cases were unfinished, others were defaulted or nonsuited because a party did not appear, and still others saw litigants appear only through attorneys. In contrast, in none of the differences entered at a meeting was a defendant ultimately able to avoid answering the complaint. Some disputants took more persuading than others, but the meeting's repeated pressure took its toll and always elicited a face-to-face confrontation with the meeting.

Such pursuit of reluctant Gospel Order defendants occurred even when such resistance indicated that prospects for satisfactory accommodation were slight. After three months of John Eastborne's refusal to answer John Naylor's complaint, Middletown Meeting's threat to disown Eastborne finally resulted in his appearance, but it only delayed the inevitable—he was disowned four months later for his "refractory . . . disorderly and contentious" behavior in this dispute.[40] Thomas Kirle was not present when Joseph Henbury brought a difference against him, so two leaders were sent to tell Kirle to appear next time. Kirle refused, so the meeting sent the same men back to tell him of its dissatisfaction. Kirle still kept his distance, so several were ordered to speak to him, including two "weighty" Friends, all just to obtain his presence to face the complaint. Finally, Kirle relented and appeared, beginning a process that ended nearly three years later with Kirle's disownment.[41] The goal of retaining members meant that the aggrieved party's interest in prompt redress was subordinated to the community's desire to restore unity and harmony by face-to-face persuasion; no one lost by default in the Society of Friends.

Forcing a personal appearance to resolve differences did not imply that the confrontation was to be public, another way in which Quaker procedures differed from legal procedures. As early as 1684, the judgment of the Chester Meeting regarding George Gleve and John Nixon was "that there difference Should not be made publick" by the arbitrators chosen.[42] All meetings followed a variation on this rule; when arbitrators were successful in accommodating a dispute, the difference simply disappeared from the records or was noted as ended. Announcing who won the claim was less important than repairing a tear in the fabric of the community. The long and bitter dispute between Arthur Cooke and Symon Charles involving both the Falls and Burlington meetings showed the value placed on nonpublic settlement. Despite both parties' accusations that the other had trampled on proper accommodative procedures, and despite Cooke's demand for "a publick end to it," a slew of important Friends from both sides of the Delaware River prevailed on Charles to go to Cooke's house to "end it between selves."[43] Unlike the courts, which announced publicly who won and lost in unsettled cases, the meeting records reflected the private nature of Quaker dispute resolution. The dual goals of restoring community peace and concealing intra-Quaker conflict meant no official acknowledgment of a victor in most differences.

Just as the resolution did not have to be public, a Gospel Order defendant did not have to confront the aggrieved personally, because the meeting's emissaries could intercede and take on that burden. Not specifically described by the Gospel Order, this procedure handled differences that on their face clearly established a plaintiff in the right and a defendant in need of persuasion. Applied primarily to debts in a manner resembling uncontested judgments in court, this method often produced a sense of the meeting even before the defendant knew of a complaint. For instance, Stephen Beakes complained that Samuel Burges (who was not present) would not pay what he owed; the Falls Meeting ordered two emissaries to tell Burges to pay.[44] Similarly, merely on the strength of Christopher Wetherill's complaint, the Burlington Meeting appointed two emissaries to convince Isaac Horner to pay his debts.[45] When John Curtis and Evan Oliver owed their respective meetings money, the proceedings were extremely short and to the point in arranging for a repayment schedule.[46] Though the vast majority of such nonarbitrated orders involved debts,[47] John Worrall was summarily told to "take speedy course for the cure of his servant man's legg and not to dispose of him till it be effected."[48] Failing to comply with trustees' demands or refusing arbitration were also differences that meetings ended swiftly and summarily.

Before the meeting as a whole would pass judgment, arbitrators were to tackle grievances that came to the monthly meeting and were not amenable to summary orders to the offender. This arbitration process differed from that employed sparingly in the legal system in two significant ways. First, the legal system did not require an arbitration attempt before a full, in-court hearing on the case's merits. In the Gospel Order, if informal mediation by concerned Friends had failed, the next step required the appointment of arbitrators to "hear and determine" (the same phrase used in law) the dispute and report their findings back to the next monthly meeting. As the Chester Quarterly Meeting pointed out to the Chester Meeting, this step was not optional. The Quaker leader Walter Faucett brought his allegation of a fraudulent land sale against his fellow Quaker leaders Samuel Levis and Francis Yarnall to the Chester Meeting. With the parties bitterly unable to agree on how to proceed, the monthly meeting asked the next quarterly meeting to end the conflict. That quarterly meeting noted the difference had not been referred first to arbitrators, and it rebuked the monthly meeting, demanding "that So proceeding without arbitration be not made precedent." The quarterly meeting then rectified the mistake by appointing four weighty Friends "to hear and determine" the dispute and to report their decision.[49]

Second, the way in which arbitrators were chosen was different. In the legal system, court-sponsored arbitration required that parties choose two or three individuals each and that the parties agree on one additional man to act as umpire in case the arbitrators reached a tie vote. Failure to agree on the arbitrators or umpire ended an attempted arbitration. For Quaker dispute resolution, however, the choice of arbitrators could be taken out of the disputants' hands. Meetings expected the parties to choose their own arbitrators, and many followed such a path.[50] If the party-selected arbitrators failed to agree or if the parties could not make a choice, the meeting would appoint arbitrators with the power to end the dispute. In the early years, the meeting chose ad hoc arbitrators for each dispute. Another land dispute involving Walter Faucett, this time against Edward Pritchett, utilized twelve arbitrators (a jury?), while a defamation dispute between David Ogden and John Worrall needed only two appointees.[51] Over time, some meetings regularized this process. The Darby Meeting ordered disciplining overseers to be chosen as arbitrators, while the Radnor Meeting appointed two-man teams as standing arbitration committees in each township.[52] The Gospel Order limited disputants' options by requiring arbitration and appointing the arbitrators regardless of the parties' preferences.

Despite these differences, Quaker arbitration and legal arbitration shared one crucial element: the requirement that the parties "stand and confirm" the arbitrators' award. Although it was not initially specified, in practice Quakers required disputants to sign a penal bond, the same document used by the legal system and a formal symbol that the disputants had a serious commitment to arbitrate. In Faucett and Pritchett's land difference, each signed a large conditional bond (a hundred pounds) to the other, which would be good only if the signer refused to implement the arbitrators' award. The bond amount varied according to the value at stake; John Buzby and Robert Heaton's land difference required only twenty pound bonds. If arbitration had proceeded without a bond and one party had not performed the award, the meeting could now order the recalcitrant party to seal a bond drafted to satisfy the other party.[53] Like arbitration itself, doctrine eventually mandated such bonds; the London Yearly Meeting's authoritative epistle in 1697 required parties to "bind themselves to stand to [the arbitrators'] award and determination."[54] Beyond such formalities lay the irony that the bond conformed to legal, not Quaker, rules, because the only possible function for such a bond was to be able to enforce it in court. This irony recurred as the Quaker alternative fell back on the language and substance of the law to frame and resolve disputes.

Yet the penal bond, backed by the law, dealt with only one sort of arbitration failure, that of a recalcitrant party's refusing to perform an adverse award. Another common failure occurred when arbitrators could not reach a decision. The twelve appointed to resolve Faucett and Pritchett's land dispute could not agree; arbitrators in the previously discussed dispute between Arthur Cook and Symon Charles could not achieve a reconciliation.[55] With either sort of failure, the full meeting then took responsibility for ending the dispute and restoring unity. The procedures in the full meeting that followed arbitration failure revealed a conflict—a struggle for the soul of Quaker dispute resolution—between procedural regularity, exemplified by the language and substance of the law, and informal, flexible resolutions demanded by the doctrinal goal of reconciliation.

Legal principles infiltrated every phase of the Gospel Order. Plaintiffs would phrase their complaint to the meeting in legal terms. Thomas Stackhouse used the legal formula "bargained and sold" in describing how John Eastborne refused to turn over the land Stackhouse had bought. Lydia Wharmley's complaint against John Brock read like a declaration in trover and conversion. Wharmley reported that Brock had taken goods sent to her from England and had not only "refused delivery" of them but also "convert[ed] them to his own use."[56] Once a complaint came to the meeting's attention, the meeting itself phrased its actions in legal language. In a will fight, a defendant was summarily ordered to pay the executors a rent due or, employing the language of equity, "show cause the contrary" at the next meeting. Similarly, the Middletown Meeting took up a deathbed oral will and rephrased it into the legally correct "non-cupative will." When the Chester Meeting successfully resolved Joseph Richard's complaint against William Woodmanson for "comparing him to a London pickpocket," the meeting recorded the "End of Strife from the Beginning to this Day," language that tracked the legal arbitration formula.[57] Yet this adoption of legal language was less important than the adoption of certain legal principles regarding evidence and process.

Circumstantial evidence was inadequate for Quaker meetings, which followed the two-witness rule of the Bible and the law. Caleb Pusey complained that his fellow Quaker leader Robert Wade had shot his horse, but after hearing both sides, the meeting refused to decide, "having no positive proof by whom the said hors was Shott only Surcomstance." The meeting instead tried to persuade Wade to placate Pusey, but when Wade, despite the meeting's clear suspicion of his guilt, continued to maintain that he was "Cleare," the matter was dropped.[58] To meet the standard of proof, complainants obtained the functional equivalent of depositions from distant witnesses or produced "writings of concern" for the meeting to review.[59] Once the complainant had satisfied the burden of proof, the meeting shifted the burden onto the defendant in the same way that a court would. Thomas Ollive produced a letter by Thomas French that Ollive said was gross abuse. Once French conceded that the letter was his, the meeting shifted the burden, requiring that French prove his written accusations by "plain evidence."[60] Finally, quarterly meetings enforced the Gospel Order's procedural regularity by hearing appeals from parties dissatisfied with decisions of a monthly meeting. Like an appellate court, the quarterly meeting reviewed the monthly meeting's performance and declared precedent for future cases. In 1710, this power was exercised to allow persons involved in differences to have copies of the meeting records, a procedural regularity akin to legal requirements that parties receive copies of such legal documents as pleadings.[61] When combined with the use of penal bonds, these legalisms effectively made Quaker dispute resolution less different from civil procedure in practice than it was supposed to be.

Nevertheless, Quaker process possessed greater flexibility and informality than legal process did. Meetings wished to do more than just declare a winner; they also wished to restore community harmony through a resolution of the underlying conflict. The most obvious examples occurred when the Gospel Order plaintiff's behavior was found culpable, a turnabout not easily accomplished in the courts. When Edward Pritchett charged John Simcock with taking eight acres of land but could not make good his charge "by witnesses or otherwise," the meeting turned on Pritchett, finding him guilty and forcing him to acknowledge his error. In Faucett's dispute against Levis and Yarnall, the meeting found Faucett blameworthy for saying Levis and Yarnall had cheated him because such public accusations tended to raise strife. Faucett willingly acknowledged this fault because the meeting condemned the defendants who "did not deal friendly" with him concerning the land.[62] Unlike the courts, meetings looked at the totality of the relationship at issue and could require self-condemnation by either or both parties to heal the breach.

Even when the guilty party was clear, Quaker dispute resolution sought to do more than assess blame. In the dispute between Joseph Kirkbride and Peter Webster and his wife, Mary, a defamation case would have ended in the courts with Peter Webster's confession at the first hearing, for the husband spoke for both in legal proceedings. The Quaker community's goal, however, was to effect a reconciliation between all parties, male and female. For more than a year, the meeting "labored" with Mary Webster until she finally produced a sufficient paper of self-condemnation.[63] Thomas Minshall's defamation complaint against Elizabeth Vernon was strong. Many had heard Vernon's accusations that Minshall's wife murdered a child and was a whore. Yet the meeting found Vernon not culpable, being "so farr discomposed in her mind that there is no credit or heed to be given to what she says." This mercy left Minshall holding only a certificate stating the charges were false.[64] This flexibility in crafting a settlement specific to the individuals involved reflected Quakers' ideal of community.

Quakers were trying to do more with less; they were trying to compel unity through limited and weak community sanctions, which was harder than the legal system's task of enforcing narrow verdicts. Informal and in some cases prolonged "laboring" provided the only weapon short of disownment for keeping Quaker disputes out of reach of the law. Disputants risked little to manipulate the Gospel Order, imposing a double bind on meetings that sought both efficient dispute resolution and control over disputes.

Evaluating the Gospel Order's Success

One way to measure the success of the Quaker alternative was the pace with which disputes passed through the process to a resolution satisfactory to the parties and the meeting. Disputes that lingered longer than three meetings usually involved a large number of participants and were often destructive to community peace because Quaker neighbors were forced to choose sides. Table 24 uses a combination of the speed of disposition and the type of result (accommodative or otherwise) to evaluate efficacy. Disputes that ended in summary proceedings, arbitration, or acceptable self-condemnation by the offending party within three meetings were considered successfully resolved according to the standard of preserving unity. Disputes were presumed successfully resolved if the last meeting reference to the dispute occurred within three monthly meetings from the difference's first appearance and there were no indications of recalcitrance from either party. For the whole period, nearly two-thirds of all disputes (66.3 percent) were successfully or presumed successfully resolved.

Slightly more than one-third of the differences were not successful by the standard of quickly restoring a harmonious community. Nearly half of these were ultimately accommodated, but these extended cases required four or more meetings. Their case histories revealed unsuccessful arbitration attempts, threats of disownment and legal action, refusals by parties to appear or accept rulings, and long "laboring" until finally an accord was reached. Yet such contentious success was better than no success at all, identified by disownments, appeals, court cases before an accord could be reached, or the meeting's abandonment before a satisfactory agreement between the parties was recorded.[65] The most striking fact about these failures is their percentage increase, particularly from 1691 onward. By 1706 extended and unsuccessful disputes formed the majority of all disputes handled by Quaker meetings. That Quaker meetings were progressively less able to meet their goals in dispute resolution provides substance to anecdotal histories of the declining authority of Quaker meetings.[66]

An examination of the pace with which cases moved through the Quaker alternative reveals an increase in the average time taken to pro-

Table 24. Quaker Meeting Dispute Resolution Efficiency

Outcome	1681–85	1686–90	1691–95	1696–1700	1701–5	1706–10	Total
Successful							
Recorded ended, 3 or fewer monthly meetings	12	16	8	20	24	8	88
Presumed, 3 or fewer and no further mention	11	3	8	6	4	4	36
Total successful	23	19	16	26	28	12	124
Percentage	82.2	65.5	80.0	72.3	63.6	40.0	66.3
Extended							
4 or more monthly meetings, but ultimately ended	2	5	1	6	8	8	30
Unsuccessful							
No accommodation, disown, appeal, went to law, etc.	2	4	0	2	8	6	22
Presumed, last entry indicated continued grievance	1	1	3	2	0	4	11
Total extended and unsuccessful	5	10	4	10	16	18	63
Percentage	17.8	34.5	20.0	27.7	36.4	60.0	33.7

cess disputes. The average number of meetings to resolve disputes rose dramatically, nearly tripling from 3.03 months per difference in 1681–85 to an average of 8.57 months in 1706–10.[67] Nonetheless, most disputes were still handled within three meetings. The leap in the average occurred because of the growing number of cases that required nine or more meetings. From 1680 to 1695, only three cases took so long, while from 1696 to 1710 eighteen cases were prolonged, including seven that meetings labored over for two or more years. Although the increased duration of such differences might have been caused by meetings' success in attracting more difficult disputes to resolve, as a result of increased doctrinal diligence, that seems unlikely because the overall number of differences did not increase. The real cause of both the decline in successful resolutions and the increase in time it took to make a final determination was manipulative behavior by Quaker disputants who were willing and able to exploit the weaknesses of the process to their own personal advantage.

Direct confrontation and public opposition to the process were ineffective strategies for manipulative recalcitrants, because meetings possessed sufficient power to force a rapid recantation or a quick disownment. Quaker arbitrators awarded Nathaniel Mullineaux money from Isaac Horner, but the minutes of the Burlington Monthly Meeting indicated Horner would "not stand to what they have Done" because he felt "there is no justice to him here." At the next meeting, Horner was again ordered to pay and give the meeting satisfaction or face both disownment and a Mullineaux lawsuit. Within a month, Horner had paid off the award and publicly acknowledged himself blameworthy.[68] Jacob Chandler's case against Robert Eyre foundered on the "disorderly manner" in Chandler's paper of charges, and arbitration cleared Eyre. Nonetheless, Chandler continued his charges, and the meeting refused to hear him until he was "orderly," behavioral advice that Chandler defied. The meeting immediately began disciplinary proceedings that culminated in Chandler's disownment for having been litigious.[69] The community could not tolerate such defiance if it hoped to control intra-Quaker disputes. More subtle resistance could be effective, however, since the meeting would "labor" and "discourse" with each recalcitrant seemingly forever, to pursue its goal of harmony and to keep the dispute out of court.

As in the courts, delay became a manipulative choice for defendants as a low-risk strategy to postpone and possibly avoid unpleasant judgments. When Lydia Wharmley brought the Quaker leader John Brock to the meeting for "conversion" of her property, Brock delayed referring the matter for arbitration for five monthly meetings until he received a letter from England that supported his claim. Though justice might have been served in Brock's case, John Hollinshead strained the integrity of the process in his defense against Peter Fretwell. The first tactic Hollinshead employed was refusing to sign the arbitration papers, followed two months later by a "slight" to the meeting's order to sign. Nonetheless, the meeting was "willing to favor him as much" as they could, but when Hollinshead, in "deliberate time," still refused arbitration, the meeting drew up a paper of disownment, giving Fretwell permission to sue. Having stalled for six months, Hollinshead finally relented and complied fully, causing the meeting to drop proceedings against him.[70]

Yet Fretwell did better than John Tatham in his long-running dispute with Joseph Growden. In 1687, four years before the court case appeared regarding what Phineas Pemberton called "the most railing reviling business yt ever I saw" (discussed in chapter 3), Tatham sought the aid of the Middletown Meeting in his complaint against one of its leading members, Growden. Growden first avoided the emissaries, then gave a paper pronounced unsatisfactory, then avoided answering again, and then promised to write to satisfy the meeting but did not. After more than a year of laboring, Growden had worn down both the meeting and Tatham—no accommodation was ever reached, a successful strategy for Growden, who won ultimate victory in court eleven years later.[71] This strategy of delaying submission to the meeting's decision did entail the risk of pushing the meeting's patience too far and being disowned. Perhaps that accounts for the disproportionate number of Quaker leaders like Brock, Hollinshead, and Growden, who used delay, for they could judge better how far they could push. When John Eastborne, who was not a leading Quaker, tried this strategy, his recalcitrance led to his disownment.[72]

By the early 1700s, the better strategy for the average Quaker who disliked a meeting decision was to accept the judgment passively but quietly neglect to comply. Such inaction forced the plaintiff to return to the meeting to seek enforcement, in effect beginning the dispute again. A most competent manipulator of this kind was Jonathan Cooper, the defendant in a complaint by John Rutledge. After not appearing at first, Cooper accepted arbitration, which apparently ended the difference. One year later, Rutledge complained Cooper had failed to perform the award, and after further delays and under threat of disownment, Cooper promised to perform within three months. Eight months later, Cooper still had done nothing, was again threatened, again promised to pay, and again did not perform, finally pushing beyond the meeting's forbearance. Recognizing that disownment was imminent, Cooper paid Rutledge, and, although the meeting waited a month to "see how far they can believe the reality of it," Cooper's "sorrow" combined with Rutledge's testimony satisfied the meeting. Cooper's strategy had bought him twenty-eight months of respite from paying his debt.[73]

Some of his contemporaries were even bolder than Cooper in their disputes. Samuel Gibson was given a summary order to pay his debt in early 1706, but only after three-and-a-half years of Gibson's pleading poverty and making empty promises to pay did the meeting give leave to his creditor to take Gibson to court if he failed to pay by the next meeting. In Robert Heaton's debt, over two years of discourse and refusals to comply with an arbitration award passed before Heaton was threatened with disownment for stating that he "never intended to perform." Yet the meeting stayed its hand in subsequent months in what became a futile hope that the difference might yet be ended successfully.[74] Lack of specific, easily executed penalties for passive noncompliance was thus the great weakness of the Gospel Order as a dispute resolver.

A vicious spiral developed in a system that depended on voluntary compliance enforced by community pressure: as fewer disputes were resolved successfully, recalcitrants were emboldened to delay still further, producing still fewer successes. Since meetings were obviously reluctant to disown except for severe and continuing misbehavior, the Gospel Order possessed few sanctions beyond moral suasion. The goal of truly ending conflict within the bounds of the Quaker community required deeper changes in parties' attitudes than attitudinal changes required by a legal case. Given such limited options and ambitious goals, it is not surprising that Quaker plaintiffs might break ranks and sue to gain more certain recovery, undermining the meetings' claim of control over intra-Quaker disputes. Furthermore, the overwhelmingly Quaker composition of bench and jury had made suing less like going before the world's people. Given such tangible disadvantages of the Gospel Order process relative to its intangible strengths of informality and adherence to doctrinal norms in the name of community harmony, the real surprise may be that so many, rather than so few, intra-Quaker disputes came before meetings for resolution. Those causes that were brought to meetings reveal what conflicts members of the Quaker community believed the Gospel Order might resolve better than legal process.

The Types of Differences

While the issues brought to meetings were similar to those on the civil docket of the legal system,[75] the proportions of each type varied considerably. If indeed "parties generally choose that method [of dispute resolution] which appears most appropriate and cost efficient" and if for all dispute forums "resource limitations are perceived and acted upon by the clientele population,"[76] then docket variance reflected the disputants' evaluation of the relative strengths of the two forums. The legal docket contained a far higher percentage of cases involving a debt or a contract (82.3 percent in case, debt, and other) than did the Quaker docket. Such issues when brought to the meeting, including differences over servants' conditions as well as debts, contracts, arbitration awards, fraud, and defective workmanship, constituted only 43.4 percent of the Gospel Order's civil business. Differences involving nondebt/contract issues analogous to the common-law causes of trespass, assault and battery, defamation, and trover and conversion, plus issues of tort, land possession, and land boundaries, all of which involved intangible or difficult to assess damages, formed 44 percent of the Quaker docket, compared with 17.7 percent of the legal docket. Finally, the Quaker community treated certain disputes, such as those over roads and probate, as potential disruptions to the community (10.5 percent of their docket), while the legal system placed such issues in administrative rather than civil forums (0.0 percent of the legal civil docket).[77] Such differences between the Quaker and the civil dockets accurately reflected the respective strengths and weaknesses of the two processes.

The ostensible moral purpose behind resolving indebtedness disputes was to ensure that Quakers kept their word. Prudence, honesty, and order in business were virtues backed by the Book of Discipline, which counseled against commitments beyond one's abilities to pay. Quaker bankrupts could face disownment. Those who owed were warned to "be carefull to pay their debts seasonably" by balancing their accounts every quarter. Those who had tried to escape Old World debts by moving to the Delaware Valley would be dealt with by meetings that would collect for the accounts of distant creditors.[78] In principle, monthly meetings were not to be collection agencies. Their desire was to avoid conflict by remedying moral error and demanding that obligations be fulfilled, lest financial "misconduct cast a reflection on the Society." Occasionally such principles did result in discipline, as when William Biles condemned himself for not admitting that he had signed a bond or when the "backwardness" of Evan Lewis, Jr., was condemned when he did not keep his word to creditors.[79] In practice, however, the creditor, not the meeting, initiated and drove the process, and creditors usually wanted money more than they wanted a confession. Meetings therefore altered principles to meet creditors' needs, becoming a type of collection agency.

To do so, meetings expedited their processes. Debts were most likely to call forth summary proceedings, since creditors' initial presentations were often accepted and emissaries immediately sent to the debtors requiring them to satisfy their adversaries (see the earlier section on Quaker dispute procedures). Similarly, creditors who faced recalcitrant debtors obtained faster recourse to the meeting's sanctions, to wit, threats of disownment or permission to take the case to court.[80] As discussed earlier, meetings incorporated the mutual signing of penal bonds into Gospel Order arbitration, bonds whose practical value arose in an action of debt. When the meeting itself lent money, it required the debtor to sign bonds to reinforce the promise to pay.[81] These actions suggest that Gospel Order authorities sought a higher level of predictability for creditors to encourage them to use the Quaker system.

Furthermore, the meeting's flexibility gave creditors some advantages. Arbitration awards lacking bonds were unenforceable at common law, but meetings regarded unperformed arbitration awards as just debts unpaid and invoked summary proceedings and quick threats of sanctions to enforce them.[82] Where the debtor was in financial difficulty, meetings had two options less available to courts, options designed to maximize return to the creditor without destroying the debtor. First, the meeting could work out a schedule of payments, granting the debtor extra time to raise the cash in return for a firm promise to pay. Creditors would accept such an agreement because of the opportunity to avoid the problems of a costly legal execution on a judgment, which was often useless against asset-poor defendants.[83] Second, the meeting itself might pay the creditor as an act of charity. A sick Roger Smith was tended by William Clayton, whose costs of over three pounds could not be paid by the indigent Smith. The Concord Meeting took up a collection and paid Clayton for his tenderness. In similar circumstances, the Falls Meeting in effect cosigned John Siddall's loan from Joseph Kirkbride.[84] In certain disputes, creditors had better chances of recovering their debt in the meeting than in the court.

Nonetheless, this flexibility created risks to creditors because Quak-

ers deemed harmony and morality more important than the mere recovery of money. In court, the fairness of a bond sued for in debt was
not at issue, and statutes detailed how both written and verbal contracts
were to be enforced.[85] Meetings, however, regularly refused to enforce
bargains deemed unfair by Quaker standards. When Thomas Stackhouse
hired Henry Mitchell, just off the boat, at substandard wages, the Middletown Meeting ordered Stackhouse to raise his wages up to "the method of this country" or set Mitchell free. The widow Williams bound out
her son as security for money lent her deceased husband, but the Radnor Meeting refused to enforce this sort of contract. Moses Key accused
John Martin of "unjust dealing" in the sale of a plantation, and the Concord Meeting made Martin forego going to court to enforce his unfair
contract and settled the dispute.[86]

Even if the bargain did not violate Quaker standards, meetings scru-
tinized the performance for moral lapses. For example, enforcing servants' rights concerned the Quaker forum far more than it concerned
the courts. Meetings enforced the "custom of the country," forcing masters to turn over promised tools, clothes, cattle, and money, to pay for
medical care for sick servants, and to live up to the indenture's terms.[87]
Examining the whole transaction also denied plaintiffs the recovery they
might have had in the courts. Building contractors had detained work-
men's wages to get recompense for a poor job of housebuilding. They
sought either to gain thirty shillings compensation or to make the work-
men finish the house according to the bargain, but the Middletown
Meeting found a fair price to be ten shillings withheld and a mere acknowledgment of defective work. Hugh Durborow recovered his wages
according to contract, but the Chester Meeting forced him to rebate his
employer for lost time.[88] For a potential plaintiff in a contract or debt
case there was far less predictability in the Quaker forum than in the
legal system. The courts had established a clear consensus that granted
disputants clear, enforceable entitlements if the contract or debt conformed to legal requirements, while meetings achieved no such clarity,
instead examining transactions on a case-by-case basis for their conform-
ance to morality. Quaker meetings also suffered from having fewer enforcement options against recalcitrant defendants. From the standpoint
of a creditor, Quaker or otherwise, the courts offered a far better chance
for actual recovery, and the docket distribution reflected that fact.

The Quaker docket did reflect Gospel Order advantages over the legal system in areas where the courts had established no consensus: dis-

putes not involving a debt or a contract. As opposed to voluntary transactions, the law of negligence (torts) was in its infancy, and meetings
searched for fair resolution of such accidents. Ann Johnson broke John
Worrall's gun, and the Chester Meeting awarded Worrall eighteen shillings damage plus possession of the gun for Johnson's negligence. When
David Davis's dog damaged several of his neighbor's hogs, the Middletown Meeting ordered Davis to pay the widow Boone eight shillings for
damage to her sow. Similarly, when John Woolman's inadequate fence
let his "creatures" roam over Joshua Humphries's corn, the Burlington
Meeting required Woolman to compensate Humphries and to fix his
fence.[89] Case-by-case analysis and ad hoc judgments were all courts could
offer these disputants. Quaker meetings' flexibility and their ability to
craft awards that could command respect in the Quaker community
would at least match the predictability of the law. Moreover, these resolutions probably would be cheaper, would be less public, and would be
in conformity with Quaker doctrine.

Similarly, defamation cases brought to court were far more unpredictable than were causes in debt or case. As chapter 3 showed, such
character disputes provoked fewer settled cases, more contested cases,
and more jury trials with witnesses and had far less likelihood of a plaintiff victory than debts or contracts did. Furthermore, defendants could
attempt to prove the truth of the alleged defamatory statement, broad-
casting to the court day crowd further attacks on the plaintiff's reputation. Even plaintiff victories could be pyrrhic, since juries compromised
issues of liability and damage by awarding plaintiffs only two pence, a
symbolic outcome to clear their names while mocking what the name
was worth. In the Quaker forum, the aggrieved could obtain the same
result—clearing the name and placing blame on the opponent—while
using the secrecy of the process to avoid further public airing of the slander. Precisely because such differences had such potential for community disruption, the flexible Gospel Order was better able to address the
real values at stake.

For the simplest defamations, such as when Joseph Richards was compared with a London pickpocket or when James Harrison's letter was
said to be "stuff full of lyes," the meeting could declare the plaintiff innocent and order the defamer to apologize and clear the plaintiff's
name.[90] Summary awards could quickly clear falsely accused defamers
as well, such as when the Falls Meeting discovered that Edmund Lovett
and his wife had never spread defamatory reports against William Dun-

can's wife.[91] In more ambiguous cases, Gospel Order arbitration could more likely produce either reconciliation or a clearing of the charge than could the confrontational processes prescribed by law. When Robert Heath reported "grievous things" concerning Joseph Kirkbride, arbitrators found Heath's charges "dubious" but ended the dispute with a conciliatory paper from Kirkbride. John Worrall complained that John Bowater "had done him wrong," but the meeting found both to blame and ordered that "they should forgive each other all occasions of Ofence that is past."[92] Finally, the sanction of disownment served to restore a community's harmony and an individual's reputation better than a money award did. Henry Hollinsworth said Randall Vernon's family "is as likely as any to be Guilty of a Bastard child" and added, "What if I can Bring you to the Grave and show you the Bones of itt." Hollinsworth later compounded the abuse by calling Vernon an "old pimp" and accused the Chester Meeting of acting "like Jesuites." The eviction of this irritant from the community solved this discord better than cash damages awarded in a court case that would have further broadcast such bile.[93] For issues of character as opposed to money, the Gospel Order possessed advantages over the law.

That the Quaker docket attracted twenty-five land disputes, more than the legal system attracted from all groups, is probably explained better by the weaknesses of land law in the Delaware Valley than by the strength of meeting processes. West Jersey and Pennsylvania proprietors experienced a complete breakdown in their systems of tenths and townships as settlers engaged in rampant land speculation, squatting, and dispersal without regard to plan. Legal requirements for land titles were routinely ignored, resulting in court inquests and alterations of records and adverse possession laws. These futile attempts to maintain accurate land records were followed by efforts with more teeth in them, such as William Penn's "Court of Inquiry" in 1700. This measure to collect back quitrents aroused such opposition that authorities were forced to back down. Further complicating the legal resolution of conflicts over boundaries and rightful possession was the uncertainty of the form of action available. The legal wrangling over whether the fictions used in ejectment were appropriate for the Delaware Valley left potential plaintiffs uncertain about how to frame their complaint.[94] This confusion may explain why settled cases were so few and contests so fierce for trespass and land/ejectment cases. Since results were so unpredictable, informal dispute resolution that was less concerned with the niceties of title and more concerned with a fair result might well have attracted the high number of land cases to the Quaker docket.

Quaker land disputants might have found the Gospel Order desirable because of its flexibility and its mingling of procedures similar to law. Whereas at law a jury from the neighborhood would determine a disputed border, the Quaker approach appointed at least four from the neighborhood to "inspect" the land by using the same procedure a jury would use—examining landmarks as described in deeds ("walking of the bounds").[95] Meetings could also arrange compromises difficult at law; when Robert Pile and Joseph Bushell differed over ten acres, the meeting awarded Bushell that land and gave Pile a Bushell plot closer to Pile's field.[96] Self-help was also easier under the Gospel Order than through a legal order. When arbitrators approved William Yardley's boundary line rather than Ellenor Pownall's, Pownall refused to place her fence on the new line. The Falls Meeting then gave permission for Yardley to build his own fence on the correct line.[97] Finally, when small quantities of land were at stake and one's claim was uncertain, potential legal costs could influence the choice of the forum. In Edward Pritchett's unsuccessful attempt to prove that John Simcock stole eight acres of his land, the costs of losing in meeting—a grudging self-condemnation "that the sd charge is more than I can make out to be true"—hurt less than a court defeat assessing several pounds in court costs.[98] As with differences over accidents and personal character, land issues showed the advantages of the Quaker alternative for those disputes that had no legal consensus. The Gospel Order was not a substitute for the law, for Quakers sought out the law's certainty to enforce their dealings with other Quakers; rather, it was a supplement to the law, filling in the cracks, in a society where Quaker leaders controlled both forums.

The Demography of the Gospel Order's Disputes

As earlier chapters indicated, Quakers in the legal population gained some advantages in garnering authority positions and in winning litigation. Within the meeting, the attribute of membership in the Society of Friends obviously carried no advantage—all were equal on that score. A comparison between the two systems regarding the impact of other attributes on forum use and dispute-resolution outcomes creates two logical possibilities. If an attribute appeared at a similar rate in both systems, the influence of forum values and practices mattered less than the common influence of that attribute did. Where distributions of attributes substantially differed between forums, however, the logical inference is that the forum influenced that group's behavior. To examine behavior within the Quaker forum, attributes of Gospel Order plaintiffs and defendants are compared with those of the overall Quaker population and the Quaker leadership population examined in chapter 1. To be perfectly accurate, this baseline should include all Quakers whether in the legal system or not, but lack of good membership lists makes such an undertaking impossible. However, 80 percent of Gospel Order disputants were also part of the legal population, making this demographic analysis a good approximation for comparing Quaker disputants with nondisputants.[99]

Compared with this Quaker population, plaintiffs in the Quaker forum were considerably more likely to be high officers and Quaker leaders, they were somewhat more likely to be wealthy and to be involved in the legal system as plaintiffs, defendants, criminal defendants, and witnesses, and they were about as likely as the average Quaker to serve on a jury or own land (see table 25). Those who were plaintiffs more than once were even more likely to be high officers, Quaker leaders, plaintiffs, defendants, criminal defendants, witnesses, jurors, landowners, and wealthy at death. Those who were defendants in a Quaker forum showed a similar pattern. Their indices of status (high office, Quaker leadership, wealth) and participation in legal processes were all higher than for those in the general Quaker population and were similar to those of plaintiffs. In contrast to multiple-difference plaintiffs, however, defendants in two or more differences showed only slightly higher rates in these categories than did Gospel Order defendants as a whole.

These findings parallel the relationships discovered about legal litigants. In both systems, participation in dispute processes went hand in hand with higher status and higher participation in other processes. In both systems, this relationship was especially strong for those who brought multiple disputes to the forum, although megaplaintiffs had far higher rates of high officeholding than those who brought more than one difference. Remarkably, such increased use of the processes also seemed to increase one's risk of negative events, such as being sued or criminally prosecuted. Demands on, demands by, status within, and voluntary participation in a dispute-resolution system were mutually reinforcing regardless of the type of system. Though ostensibly open to all, both systems disproportionately responded to the needs and the behaviors of these repeat players.

Table 25. Population Comparisons, Individuals

Attributes	Quaker Population in Legal Population	Quaker Leaders	"Plaintiffs" in Monthly Meetings	"Plaintiffs" (2+ times)	"Defendants" in Monthly Meetings	"Defendants" (2+ times)
N	1282	374	151	25	164	30
Quaker leaders (%)	29.2	100.0	44.4	72	40.2	43.3
Average Quakers (%)	70.8	0	55.6	28	59.8	56.7
Landowners (%)	83.0	94.4	76.8	92	81.7	90.0
Nonlandowners (%)	17.0	5.6	23.2	8	18.3	10.0
Occupations (males only)						
Farmer (%)	53.4	57.4	51.1	31.5	48.6	46.2
Artisan (%)	17.0	9.6	21.3	36.8	20.2	15.4
Farmer-artisan (%)	12.5	17.9	12.8	26.3	11.9	19.2
Merchant (%)	8.0	7.2	7.4	0	1.8	0
Self-described gentry (%)	3.9	3.8	3.2	0	4.6	0
All others[a] (%)	5.2	4.1	4.3	5.3	12.8	19.2
1693 Pennsylvania tax assessment (in pounds)						
100+ (%)	15.5	18.1	17.4	14.3	23.1	20.0
50–99 (%)	18.6	20.8	19.6	28.6	17.3	10.0
1–49 (%)	65.9	61.1	63.0	57.1	59.6	70.0

Inventoried wealth (in pounds)						
500+ (%)	24.2	33.8	36.6	37.5	32.7	12.5
100–499 (%)	57.3	55.6	53.7	50.0	53.8	62.5
1–99 (%)	18.4	10.6	9.8	12.5	13.5	25.0
Legal roles						
High officer (%)	19.7	40.1	29.8	40	26.2	26.7
Lesser officer (%)	35.3	42.3	31.8	36	39.6	43.3
Nonofficer (%)	44.9	17.7	38.4	24	34.1	30.0
Grand juror (%)	55.3	81.3	57.6	84	60.4	76.7
Trial juror (%)	50.2	71.9	54.3	80	56.7	40.0
Plaintiff (%)	30.1	30.5	35.1	44	34.1	36.7
Defendant (%)	26.3	23.5	32.5	44	36.0	36.7
Criminal Defendant (%)	25.9	31.6	30.5	60	36.0	43.3
Witness (%)	24.3	35.4	33.8	40	35.3	36.7

a. "All others" includes the category "servant/slave/laborer" as well as the category "other" from the occupational analysis in chapter 1.

The two systems diverged most dramatically in the area of disputants' occupations. In the legal population, farmers were less likely to be plaintiffs, and farmers and farmer-artisans were less likely to be megaplaintiffs (see tables 10–12). Merchants and the self-described gentry disproportionately brought suits to court, dominating the megaplaintiff category. In the Quaker system, farmers and farmer-artisans brought differences at near or above their population rates, and farmer-artisans were the group most likely to bring more than one difference. Even more striking was the total absence of merchant and self-described gentry among those who brought differences to the meeting more than once. Recall that merchants brought disproportionately more debt cases to court and disproportionately fewer nondebt/contract cases, while farmers sued less in debt and more in nondebt/contract causes. It was therefore no surprise that merchants avoided the Quaker forum, which was weak in deciding and enforcing debt differences and where the docket reflected that fact. It was also unsurprising that farmers and farmer-artisans, whose nondebt/contract disputes the Gospel Order handled better than the law did, disproportionately returned to that forum.

Usage, as defined in chapter 2 for civil litigation, examined disputants aggregate position in lawsuits by way of a ratio that divided the number of times plaintiffs possessed an attribute by the number of times defendants possessed that attribute. A ratio of greater than 1.0 indicated relative invulnerability to suits while less than 1.0 indicated greater vulnerability. In court, members from high-status groups (high officers, Quaker leaders, merchants, and self-described gentry) sued more often than they were sued (ratios well above 1.0), while lower-status members suffered suits more often than they launched suits. Applying the same method to plaintiffs and defendants in Gospel Order disputes reveals that those using the Gospel Order differed from those using the law in that their usage did not vary significantly depending on their attributes (see table 26). With the exception of merchants (who as already noted were rarely involved in the Quaker forum), each attribute is within 0.16 of 1.00, the unity ratio indicating neutral vulnerability. Comparing these ratios with those found in court, the Gospel Order vulnerability ratios were closer to 1.0 for every attribute except farmer-artisan. Each group's members found themselves roughly equally in offensive and defensive positions regarding disputes in front of the meeting, a far cry from the legal system's docket that tilted toward the leading members of society in usage. This comparison with the law suggests that the Quak-

Table 26. Comparison of Meeting and Court
Usage, by Selected Attributes[a]

Attribute	Quaker Differences	Civil Lawsuits
Quaker leaders	1.16	2.13
Average Quakers	.87	1.04
Landowners	1.01	1.08
Nonlandowners	.80	.77
Occupations		
Farmer	.97	.82
Artisan	1.13	.62
Farmer-artisan	1.09	1.06
Merchant	2.80	4.27
Self-described gentry	.88	2.65
Legal roles		
High officer	1.07	2.24
Lesser officer	.83	.79
Nonofficer	1.16	.79

a. The numbers reflect a ratio determined by dividing the
number of appearances as plaintiff by appearances as defendant for each attribute; 1.0 is neutral (i.e., the same
number of plaintiff and defendant cases for individuals
possessing that attribute).

er forum was more open to complaints from lower levels of society, less
welcoming to complaints from the elite, or some combination of both.

An analysis of the matchups, or who had a dispute with whom, reveals another critical difference in usage between the law and the Gospel Order. Although Quakers sued other Quakers with abandon and used
the courts more often than the meeting for such intra-Quaker disputes,
who sued whom revealed that some conflicts occurred more often than
others in court. Quaker leaders sued other Quaker leaders disproportionately rarely, only 12 times, or 4 percent of all intra-Quaker cases.
In the Gospel Order, Quaker leaders brought 46 differences with other
Quaker leaders, roughly 25 percent of all differences and nearly four
times as many differences as cases. Quaker leaders kept to doctrine well
(though not perfectly) when facing equals and thus kept most such in-

tra-elite battles out of the public's sight. This pattern follows behavior predicted by anthropologists of law.[100] Quaker leaders were not so observant of doctrine when their opponent was only an average Quaker, however; 93 suits, a statistically significant number, and only 47 differences before the meeting occurred with this matchup. Suing someone below you apparently troubled leaders' consciences less than suing an equal in court.

Average Quakers might also have had one eye on doctrine and the other on their opponent's standing in the Society of Friends when choosing a forum. Average Quakers brought 34 differences against Quaker leaders to the meeting and sued such Quaker leaders 47 times. Clearly average Quakers did not cower from disputing with their elite, regardless of forum. However, average Quakers brought only 52 differences with other average Quakers to the meeting, although they sued average Quakers nearly three times as often (150 suits). In these results, as with the law, the status of the defendant seems to have been the major determinant of disputing strategy. Going to court was more prevalent when the aggrieved Quaker, of any status, faced an average Quaker than when the defendant was a Quaker leader. The no-litigation doctrine clearly influenced the choice of forum and protected some aggrievors from lawsuits more than others.

Unlike the legal system, the Gospel Order did not characterize its players as winners and losers at the end of a dispute, which precludes an analysis of outcomes precisely parallel to that of chapter 3. However, the percentage of successful resolutions for disputants with certain attributes can indicate which, if any, Quaker subgroups were more contentious than others. Overall, variations from the 66.3 percent success rate were not statistically significant for any group of plaintiffs, although there were some suggestive results. Compared with other subgroups, high officers were the least likely to end their disputes successfully, regardless of whether they were plaintiff or defendant. Quaker leaders successfully ended their disputes as plaintiffs more often than average Quakers, but when such leaders were defendants, harmonious resolutions became much harder to obtain.[101] The lower level of success for high officers and Quaker leaders when they were in a defendant role (rather than a plaintiff role) is congruent with the behavior of these groups in settling or arbitrating cases in legal forums (see table 18 in chapter 3). In short, high status defendants behaved in more disputatious ways regardless of the forum. When placed in a vulnerable role, high officers and Quaker leaders became far more contentious than the average disputant in court or meeting did.

Nonetheless, the most significant determinant as to whether differences were resolved successfully was the geographic location of the parties. First, 72 percent of all Quaker disputes for which both parties' townships can be identified occurred within a township or neighboring townships; the comparable figure for lawsuits was 36 percent. Propinquity thus helped to head a dispute toward the Quaker docket rather than the legal docket. Second, 69 percent of all disputes between those living relatively close to each other were successfully resolved, while only 41 percent of disputes involving more distanced parties were successful. In other words, a majority (59 percent) of disputes between those living more than one township apart dragged on beyond three meetings or reached no final accommodation. Compromise in the Quaker forum seemed most likely when disputants lived near their adversaries, since they knew each other fairly well and could hardly avoid running into each other, at the meeting if nowhere else. If one rarely saw one's opponent, the incentive to gain victory at the expense of a harmonious future relationship was greater.

Quaker doctrine did not control Quaker disputes, and the basis on which Quaker dispute resolution rested could not make Gospel Order accommodation equally possible for all intra-Quaker differences. Successful resolutions depended on geographically close relationships within particular Quaker meetings; these results showed little sense of community between disputants from different Quaker meetings. Meetings' calls for accommodation had maximum persuasive authority over only those parties that had propinquitous and continuous relationships with each other. When combined with varying levels of diligence in keeping Quakers out of court, clearly Quaker central authority did not control actual Quaker practice. Quaker processes, in turn, suffered penetration by legal procedures that made controlling disputants even more difficult. Despite the relative equality of usage and despite Quaker leaders' relatively good adherence to doctrine when facing other leaders, the Quaker dispute alternative suffered. Quaker disputants, who recognized relative strengths in the forums, saw plenty of saints in court who faced no sanctions for breaching doctrine, and dealt with people beyond their neighborhood, chose courts over the Gospel Order in most circumstances. The Gospel Order became merely another contributor to the development of a legal culture of accommodation within a legal system whose success relegated the Gospel Order to a supporting role.

FIVE

Accused Deviants and Their Offenses

On August 8, 1692, a court of quarter sessions met in Burlington to consider criminal activity that had occurred in the county since the last quarterly court in May. Coming before the court was a charge "against Harry the Negro man servant of Isaac Marriott" (Marriott was a prominent Quaker leader in Burlington) for "buggering a cow." Before the thirteen-man grand jury (eleven of whom were Quakers), a mother and a daughter attested to what they had seen. The grand jury found their testimony sufficient to "find the bill" true, sending Harry to trial for this morals offense, this sexual deviance.[1] In the history of colonial criminals, Harry's crime might have been rare (though hardly unknown), but Harry stands together with other outcast, low-status members of society whom historians have seen as the most likely targets for prosecution.[2]

If Harry was one type of criminal deviant, John Hollinshead was another. This Quaker leader, a justice of the peace, a grand and trial juror, and a frequent litigator, faced criminal sanctions three times. In May 1691, the grand jury presented (today it would be termed indicted) Hollinshead for the crime of "damming up the Highway," which limited his neighbors' access to markets. In March 1699, Hollinshead was prosecuted for failing to testify against his fellow Quaker Emanuel Smith when Smith was accused of clipping coins, a silence that resulted in Smith's being freed. Hollinshead also was charged with "contempt of Authority" for conducting a warrantless and thus illegal search of Daniel Sutton's house.[3] Here is the face of a recidivist criminal offender rarely seen in accounts of colonial crime, the face of a well-connected, successful member of the dominant group in the community.

No one would contend that Harry's and Hollinshead's actions were equally significant breaches of this society's mores. Closing a highway was not bestiality, just as today shoplifting is not armed robbery is not murder. What links these offenses together is that they all bring the unwanted attention of the criminal justice system on the accused; they all call individuals to account in front of a court for deviating from norms. Historians have long examined (and grouped together for analysis in tables and text) the wide variety of criminal prosecutions that colonial trial courts heard. The interest of New England courts in morals prosecutions, ranging from fornication to breaking the Sabbath to drunkenness, has been evaluated side by side with murder, rape, assault, slander, fraud, and contempt of authority. Analysis of Virginia's grand juries included breaches of the peace together with breaches of public duty and placed regulatory and tax violations with crimes involving morals, property, and violence. Colonial North Carolina's criminal courts recognized at least forty-five different crimes; of the nine categories into which these were grouped, "other" was the second largest. The historian of colonial New York's crime classified charges into eight groups, ranging from crimes of violence and theft to disorderly houses, violations of public order, and fraud.[4] Although historians have yet to agree on the proper number and definition of categories for analyzing colonial crime, the literature suggests they have all agreed to consider all the crimes and all the accused that came before these county courts. Although the spectacular charge against Harry may seem more significant than the charges against Hollinshead, the difference between them was one of kind, not that one was an accused deviant and the other was not.

In the Delaware Valley, as in other colonies, a criminal defendant could face a wide range of accusations, processes, and results, ranging from a summary fine for missing jury duty to grand jury presentment, testimony, conviction by a trial jury, and a court-imposed sentence of fine, imprisonment, whipping, or, as in Harry's case, death.[5] Nonetheless, all prosecutions reflected an attempt to control behavior. Public discipline creates, pronounces, and maintains a boundary between the permissible and the impermissible. Singling out certain individuals for particular violations of established norms impresses upon them and upon the public viewing the proceedings on court day the nature and risk of deviating from those norms. Those accused have tested the content and importance of certain values as well as the control a society has established over those issues. Criminal law is thus a hinge that links societal values to particular behavior.[6]

Yet calling some behavior "criminal" cannot obscure the discretion present in any legal system; what was on the books might not have corresponded to the behavior that actually triggered prosecutions. Historians of criminal law cannot know the true frequency of criminal acts in a society, the actual distribution of criminal behavior among groups, the fraction of offending actions represented by prosecutions, or whether that fraction changes over time or between types of offenses. Nonetheless, the criminal docket did reflect, in some unquantifiable fashion, the values that the society wished to protect as well as the underlying pattern of deviant transactions.[7] What can be known—the demography of those accused, the charges lodged against them, and the disposition of such charges—can be analyzed as disputes, using the same methods employed in previous chapters regarding civil cases. Use of courts to remedy private disputes also involved behavior that might have violated social norms. The claims made here, as with civil litigation, relate not to unknowable rates of behavior but to known experiences of individuals whose behavior brought them into court.

Characterizing criminal prosecutions as disputes reflects certain parallels between civil and criminal justice in early modern Anglo-American societies. In civil cases, plaintiffs were solely responsible for pursuing their grievances; their remedies, if any, were awarded to compensate and redress a violation of transactional expectations. Similarly, before the king's attorneys appeared to professionalize prosecutions, alleged victims often instigated and controlled the presentation of criminal cases to both grand and trial juries. West Jersey law explicitly gave victims the right to control the criminal prosecution, including the power to forgive the wrongdoer and end the case, akin to settling a civil case. Pennsylvania's high monetary penalties in its reformed criminal laws provided a parallel to civil damages, because victims in the role of informers could instigate *qui tam* prosecutions, wherein they were entitled to a share in any fines collected.[8] Yet, at least symbolically and often in actuality, an accused faced more than just an individual in a criminal prosecution. A criminal dispute was, in various formulations, an offense against the court, the king's peace, God, the people as a whole society, and the state. Constables, sheriffs, and justices reported criminal violations and launched prosecutions on their own, regardless of the victim. Before any trial, the alleged victim's case was most often filtered through a grand jury, which could "no bill" and clear the defendant before a trial. Finally, the penalties awaiting an accused at the end of trial, though reduced from English levels, often involved physical penalties (incarceration or whipping) imposed by the state that a victorious civil plaintiff could not invoke.

In criminal cases, the role of plaintiff therefore often became embodied—perhaps disembodied is more accurate—in the institutions of the criminal justice system; the criminal defendant's opponent possessed not just the attributes of an individual but the weight of the society. With an alleged crime, the aggrieved need not be an individual (although certain crimes, such as assault, robbery, and defamation, do have particular victims), and there need not have been a transaction where the parties' expectations were violated (e.g., victimless crimes like Harry's). The penalty imposed, if any, involved not merely the satisfaction of the victim but also notions of deterrence, retribution, incapacitation, and rehabilitation. In criminal cases, more than in civil cases, judgments about prosecutions, guilt, and punishments reflected inherently collective decisions about the significance of behavior and norms.

Criminal law claimed authority over all transgressions against its standards by all inhabitants in its jurisdiction. Yet this criminal justice system had neither the resources nor the intention to enforce its claimed monopoly. Covering a subset of the society, Quaker meetings prescribed their members' behavior on subjects covered by the criminal law as well as subjects of concern only to the meetings. Quaker norms and procedures relied on their ultimate boundary-setting mechanism—disownment and banishment from the community—to serve as a sanction against recalcitrant violators. As with the comparisons between civil processes and the Gospel Order for dispute resolution, comparisons between legal discipline and Quaker discipline reveal differences in the attributes of the accused and in the types of cases brought to each forum, illustrating the relative strengths and weaknesses of each forum.

This chapter explores the threshold, decisions made regarding who was prosecuted and for what offenses in both forums, drawing a parallel to the examination of civil litigants in chapter 2 and Quaker disputants in chapter 4. Chapter 6 considers the interplay of accusation, choices, and defendant attributes in processing those charged, as chapter 3 did for civil cases. Both the courts and the Quaker system of discipline are further examined to see whether those forums conflicted with or collaborated in efforts at social control. As with civil disputes, this analysis entails, first, a comparison between the individuals accused and the whole legal population and, second, an exploration of who faced which charges. Although the distinction between public and private law was not always clear, cases brought in a county court of quarter sessions according to criminal procedure were classified as criminal, while cases in common pleas were regarded as civil.[9] There were 1,177 criminal cases begun in these years, less than 60 percent of the number of civil cases brought in the same time period. Meanwhile, Quaker men's meetings heard 339 disciplinary cases, almost twice the number of Gospel Order differences brought to that forum. Quaker women's meetings, for whom records are less complete, heard at least 77 disciplinary actions that men's monthly meetings did not record. The distribution of accused and accusations reveals a multitiered approach within and between forums for controlling deviance.

The Accused at Law

Criminal charges were filed against 28 percent of the legal population; that is, 1,057 individuals felt the sting of the criminal process (see table 27). At first glance, it is apparent that those accused were not very different from the rest of the participants in the legal system. Criminal defendants were more likely to hold office, possess more taxed and inventoried wealth, own land, and be a leading Quaker than were others in the legal population. There were also higher percentages of women, servants/slaves/laborers, and non-Quakers in the criminal population than in the legal population. This overrepresentation may reflect these groups' circumscribed participation in public life (especially in decision-making roles), which proportionately decreased their percentage of the noncriminal membership in the legal population.[10] What is most startling is how slight the differences in attributes were between criminal defendants and the legal population at large. Clearly, the criminal law touched in some way every level of this society; just as clearly such accusations did not ostracize the defendant from further participation in public life.[11]

Further evidence of not only the broad sweep of criminal accusations but also the positive link between such accusations and higher status comes with an examination of recidivists (see table 27). A recidivist was defined as a person who suffered two or more criminal accusations during the period of this study; no attempt was made to identify those who might have suffered a second accusation after 1710.[12] Twenty-six percent of Delaware Valley criminals returned to face a subsequent charge,

Table 27. Attributes of Those Accused

Attributes	Criminal Defendants	Recidivists	Legal Population
Total *n*	1057	272	3782
Percentage of total population	27.9	7.2	100
Male (%)	87.6	94.5	90.1
Female (%)	12.4	5.5	9.9
Quakers (%)	36.1	39.5	39.1
Quaker leaders (%)	12.8	12.0	11.4
Average Quakers (%)	23.3	27.5	27.7
Non-Quakers (%)	63.9	60.5	60.9
Landowners (%)	60.0	73.9	58.0
Nonlandowners (%)	40.0	26.1	42.0
Occupations (males only)			
Farmer (%)	47.5	50.3	49.0
Artisan (%)	17.3	18.0	18.3
Farmer-artisan (%)	10.8	10.4	8.9
Merchant (%)	3.6	3.3	8.5
Self-described gentry (%)	6.4	6.0	5.6
Servant/slave/laborer (%)	9.1	7.1	5.1
Other (%)	5.3	4.9	4.6
1693 Pennsylvania tax assessment (in pounds)			
100+ (%)	15.3	21.1	14.2
50–99 (%)	22.7	28.1	17.8
1–49 (%)	62.0	50.9	68.0
Inventoried wealth (in pounds)			
500+ (%)	19.4	20.3	19.0
100–499 (%)	58.2	59.4	56.8
1–99 (%)	22.4	20.3	24.2
Legal roles			
High officer (%)	12.8	17.3	10.4
Lesser officer (%)	24.8	32.4	22.7
Nonofficer (%)	62.4	50.4	66.9

a significantly higher rate than in colonial North Carolina, New York, and probably Massachusetts.[13] Recidivists were more likely to be male, high officers, lesser officers, landowners, wealthy by whichever measure, and Quaker than were the average criminal defendant and the average member of the legal population. Those lower-status groups with percentages of criminal defendants higher than their population rate—women, servants/slaves/laborers, and non-Quakers—had a lower percentage of recidivism, meaning they were less likely to suffer a second charge. In other legal roles, such as litigating, witnessing, or serving on a jury, recidivists were more likely to participate than noncriminals.[14] Recidivists, like the overall criminal defendant population, were not marginal but in some ways were rather central figures in this society.

That status and office did not protect one from accusations and that even repetitive charges did not carry a disqualifying stigma can be seen in the records of three prominent members of the community who, like Hollinshead, were recidivists. Gilbert Wheeler was elected to the Provincial Assembly from Bucks County in 1685, was a justice of the peace there from 1693 to 1695, and served on two trial juries in the 1690s. As an important landowner, his tax assessment and inventoried wealth at death placed him among the wealthiest in the county. He was a prodigious litigator, suing fourteen times, being sued sixteen times, and appearing as a witness in three other cases. He also achieved the unique distinction of being a recidivist in two counties, Bucks and Burlington. In 1682 and again in 1688, Wheeler was convicted of selling rum without a license in Burlington County and was fined on both occasions. On the other side of the river, Wheeler not only continued his operations and was brought before Bucks County courts for liquor law violations in 1686 and 1687 but also was accused of turning a road and fencing it off in 1685, disrupting a court in 1686, and charging extortionate ferry fees in 1693, the year he first became a justice.[15] That Wheeler's crimes occurred before, during, and after his serving in high offices clearly indicates an attitude toward the relationship among wealth, status, and crime that differed from that held by later generations of Americans.

Two other examples reinforce the human dimension behind these surprising recidivist statistics. That Chester County's George Foreman had engaged in a one-man crime spree did not seem to hinder him in the slightest. Foreman, a landed merchant of great wealth (his three-hundred-pound property valuation in the 1693 tax list tied for highest in the county), was accused in 1687 of running an ordinary (tavern) without a license, of rescuing a prisoner from the custody of a constable, and of withholding information from other members of the grand jury about the "disorder" Samuel Rowland had committed against Woley Rosen and his wife.[16] Nonetheless, Foreman, whose only previous involvement with the legal system had been on juries and in suits, became sheriff in 1690 for three years and assumed the roles of justice of the peace and provincial councillor in 1693. Finally, John Hugg, Jr., not only became a justice in Gloucester County despite failing to appear for jury duty in 1690 and riding another's horse without permission in 1691 but also kept that position from 1693 to 1703 despite being accused of taking, killing, and converting to his own use five swine belonging to Matthew Medcalfe in 1698.[17] Running afoul of the law could happen to anyone, and such charges apparently did not stigmatize these deviants or prevent them from holding high office.

The impressions created by these descriptive statistics are confirmed by tests for statistical significance, which compared the attributes of those who experienced a criminal accusation with the attributes of those who did not (see table 28). There was no statistically significant relation be-

Table 28. Demography of Criminal Defendants and Recidivists

Attributes	Criminal Defendant	Never Criminal Defendant	Once Criminal Defendant	Recidivist Criminal Defendant
Total *n*	1057	2725	785	272
Percentage of total population	27.9	72.1	74.3	25.7
Male (%)	27.2	72.8	72.2	27.8
Female (%)	34.9	65.1	88.5	11.5
Chi-square probability	= .001		= .000	
Quakers (%)	25.9	74.1	72.3	27.7
Quaker leaders (%)	31.6	68.4	76.3	23.7
Average Quakers (%)	23.6	76.4	70.1	29.9
Non-Quakers (%)	29.4	70.7	76.0	24.0
Chi-square probability	= .032		= .217	
Landowners (%)	28.9	71.1	68.3	31.7
Nonlandowners (%)	26.6	73.4	83.2	16.8
Chi-square probability	= .121		= .000	

Table 28, continued

Attributes	Criminal Defendant	Never Criminal Defendant	Once Criminal Defendant	Recidivist Criminal Defendant
Occupations (males only)				
Farmer (%)	30.6	69.4	64.8	35.2
Artisan (%)	29.8	70.2	65.3	34.7
Farmer-artisan (%)	38.1	61.9	67.8	32.2
Merchant (%)	13.5	86.5	70.0	30.0
Self-described gentry (%)	35.7	64.3	68.6	31.4
Servant/slave/laborer (%)	56.8	43.2	74.0	26.0
Other (%)	36.3	63.8	69.0	31.0
Chi-square probability	= .000		= .921	
1693 Pennsylvania tax assessment (in pounds)				
100+ (%)	42.6	57.4	47.8	52.2
50–99 (%)	50.0	50.0	52.9	47.1
1–49 (%)	35.9	64.1	68.8	31.2
Chi-square probability	= .093		= .083	
Inventoried wealth (in pounds)				
500+ (%)	32.2	67.8	69.6	30.4
100–499 (%)	32.2	67.8	70.3	29.7
1–99 (%)	29.1	70.9	73.6	26.4
Chi-square probability	= .735		= .883	
Legal roles				
High officer (%)	34.3	65.7	65.2	34.8
Lesser officer (%)	30.5	69.5	66.4	33.6
Nonofficer (%)	26.1	73.9	79.2	20.8
Chi-square probability	= .001		= .000	

tween landownership, tax bracket, and inventoried wealth and experiencing a turn in the criminal dock. In other words, owning land or being relatively well off did not insulate one from charges, while being landless or relatively poor did not significantly increase one's likelihood of facing criminal justice. There was a statistically significant relationship between holding office and becoming a criminal defendant, but the direction of that relationship showed high and lesser officers disproportionately *more* likely to be charged, while nonofficers were *less* likely to become a criminal defendant than expected. These patterns reveal that having wealth and holding office did not protect one from answering for an alleged offense.

Several attributes were statistically significant in ways that favored those of higher status over lower status. Women were significantly more likely to be charged criminally than were men. Servants/slaves/laborers and self-described gentry were hauled before court disproportionately more often, while merchants successfully avoided that trip. Finally, Quakers disproportionately avoided being charged; however, the greatest beneficiaries of that pattern were not Quaker leaders. On the contrary, Quaker leaders, like high officers, were more likely to become criminal defendants than were average Quakers or non-Quakers. This last pattern suggests the interplay between the Quaker disciplinary forum and the courts because, as will be shown, the Quakers brought before meetings to account for their behavior were precisely the average Quakers who avoided legal condemnation. In general, those with higher levels of power, wealth, and status either were not protected from criminal prosecution or were more often the targets of it.

The comparison of those who were criminal defendants only once and those who were recidivists reveals a similar pattern (see table 28). Wealth and occupation had no statistically significant effect on an accused's chances of being accused again; merchants, who generally avoided being charged, had no special protection from subsequent charges if they had already been a criminal defendant. Men were disproportionately more likely to be recidivists than women were, landowners more likely than nonlandowners, high and lesser officers more likely than nonofficers. Quakers and Quaker leaders were not significantly different from non-Quakers in their likelihood of being charged again. Recidivism touched all levels of society, especially the higher levels. However, recognizing this surprisingly egalitarian distribution of the criminal defendant experience is but the first step in understanding the meaning of those experiences; the second step is understanding the distribution of charges.

The Distribution of Criminal Accusations

As described in the Introduction, Delaware Valley Quakers' law reforms implemented new conceptions of justice. One primary concern for criminal justice was proportionality, in other words, that the punishment fit the seriousness of the offense to avoid, in George Fox's words, laws and lawyers "that will throw men into Prison for a thing of nought."[18] Quaker beliefs went beyond penal reform to influence the pattern of prosecutions in the New World. First, English prosecutions of Quakers, especially for their failure to remove hats and to take oaths, led Quakers to view all legal institutions as potential oppressors and made them suspicious of any legal authority. Legitimating this legal system would require the consent and participation of a querulous people.[19] Second, Quakers saw the causes of crime in poverty and in such vices as greed and envy. Changing legal institutions to focus on prevention, reconciliation, and individual reform ideally would combine with improved economic opportunity in the Delaware Valley to reduce crime.[20] Finally, Quakers believed moral law, grounded in the Bible, should be the basis for criminal law. In the *Laws Agreed upon in England* and in the subsequent revisions in Pennsylvania, criminal statutes focused on morality with near-Puritanical zeal. Biblical definitions of deviance increased the potential number of crimes and criminals.[21] These approaches, when combined with actual behavior, fused with the ideology of law reform to create a pattern of criminal accusations unique in the colonies.

Eight major categories of prosecutions have been culled from the nearly twelve hundred criminal accusations filed between 1680 and 1710.[22] The most common criminal charge was the offense against morality, constituting 22.4 percent of all accusations and reflecting the statutory interest (see table 29). The most numerous morals charges were alleged breaches of sexual morality, which made up 45 percent of this category. Fornication accusations, evidenced by a bastard or cohabitation, and improper marriages made up the bulk of these, although there were isolated prosecutions for abortion, adultery, bigamy, incest, and, of course, bestiality (Harry was one of two so accused).[23] The next most common morals offenses involved liquor, including the running of a "disorderly house," an ambiguous charge that could also involve illicit sex. Liquor prosecutions (39 percent of morals charges) also included consumption offenses (i.e., drunkenness) and distribution offenses—selling rum to Indians, selling liquor illegally by the drink, operating a tavern without a license.[24] The remainder of morals prosecutions (16 percent) involved offenses equating sin with crime, including swearing, breaking the Sabbath, gambling, and practicing geomancy.[25]

The docket share for morals violations was not consistent over time

Table 29. Criminal Accusations, Overall and by Five-Year Periods

Accusation Type	Overall Percentage	Percentage of Known Causes	N
Morals	22.4	24.8	264
Contempt	21.4	23.7	252
Civic	12.7	14.1	150
Authority	8.7	9.6	102
Recognizance	14.8	16.4	174
Property	12.6	13.9	148
Violence	12.3	13.7	145
Economic exploitation	4.8	5.4	57
Defamation	1.9	2.1	22
Others/unknown	9.8	—	115
Totals	100.0	100.0	1177

	1680–85	1686–90	1691–95	1696–1700	1701–5	1706–10
Morals (%)	15.9	24.0	27.9	29.8	21.1	11.0
Contempt (%)	13.4	20.1	30.5	22.5	19.6	18.4
Civic (%)	1.2	11.1	17.8	11.9	14.1	14.4
Authority (%)	12.2	9.0	12.7	10.6	5.5	4.0
Recognizance (%)	6.1	12.5	7.1	9.6	19.6	29.9
Property (%)	14.6	15.1	13.2	9.6	11.6	11.4
Violence (%)	15.9	11.1	7.6	15.1	12.6	13.9
Economic exploitation (%)	11.0	6.1	4.6	2.8	6.5	1.5
Defamation (%)	1.2	3.9	1.0	1.4	1.5	1.0
Others/unknown (%)	22.0	7.2	8.1	9.2	7.5	12.9
N	83	279	197	218	199	201

and across colonies. Pennsylvania, beginning with Penn's *Laws Agreed upon in England* and *The Great Law* of 1682, regularly legislated against moral deviance as defined by the Bible. Even though the crimes were sins, the laws enumerated non-Biblical penalties for "all such Offences against God, as Swearing, Cursing, Lying, Prophane Talking, Drunkenness, Drinking of Healths, Obscene words, Incest, Sodomy, Rapes, Whoredom, Fornication and Other uncleanness (not to be repeated) . . . All Prizes, Stage-Plays, Cards, Dice, May-games, Gamesters, Masques,

Revels, Bull-baitings, Cock-fightings, Bear-baitings, and the like, which excite the People to Rudeness, Cruelty and Irreligion."[26] West Jersey legislators never engaged in such codification but rather irregularly enacted statutes forbidding clandestine marriages, whoredom, adultery, cursing, and drunkenness and empowering single justices to administer punishment in certain cases (e.g., liquor violations) that could be brought before them outside the quarterly court sessions.[27] Because of this innovation, West Jersey's courts saw fewer liquor cases and thus had a lower overall percentage of morals prosecutions on their dockets than Pennsylvania did (18.4 percent compared with 25.6 percent).

Differences between provinces on morals charges was nothing compared with variation over time. The region showed a rising docket share for morals offenses, increasing from 16 percent to nearly 30 percent of the docket in the period 1696–1700. The next ten years saw a precipitous decline to an 11 percent docket share for morals cases for the period 1706–10, or 22 cases compared with 65 ten years earlier (see table 29). The most common explanation for this decline has been that the criminal justice system shifted its attention to crimes of violence and property, evidenced by complaints of a crime wave and the harsh Pennsylvania code of 1700.[28] Yet both the absolute number of prosecutions and the docket share of property/violent crimes stayed roughly the same between 1700 and 1710, refuting the crime wave explanation, at least outside Philadelphia. The statistics instead reveal a corresponding increase in recognizances, a preventive criminal process discussed later.

Even at the height of its interest in morals offenses, Delaware Valley courts never approached the 40–60 percent docket share seen in colonial New England, Maryland, or Virginia. Even at the lowest point of its interest, Delaware Valley courts never dropped to the 3–8 percent docket share seen in colonial New York, North Carolina, and South Carolina.[29] The overall docket share for morals offenses (22.4 percent) placed these middle colonies in the middle of colonial interest in morals, which continued virtually unchanged in Chester County from 1726 to 1755.[30] The biblical roots of Delaware Valley law could not allow officials to ignore such offenses, but other goals, such as the need to legitimate authority and to prevent crime rather than punish it, channeled legal resources in ways not seen in other colonies.

After morals, the next most common accusation was contempt, which accounted for 21.4 percent of all prosecutions and related directly to the problem of legitimacy. Contempt was defiance, implicitly political—

the defiance of particular court rules and responsibilities, of the authority and dignity of the entire court system. A majority of all contempt
citations (58 percent) were for failure to perform a particular duty, denoted in table 29 as civic contempt. Constables and overseers, required
to attend each court session during their time in office, were cited for
their absence. Those who failed to appear when called for jury duty, who
failed to perform in their office, or who failed to work on highways on
their assigned days were similarly fined. Although other historians have
suggested that such citations revealed an unwillingness to serve,[31] these
citations also reflected the courts' hope that particular individuals ("good
men") would participate in the process and perform their duties in accord with the rule of law.

Although individual motivations for failure to perform varied widely, such failures could involve popular passive resistance to unwanted
changes in court personnel. In 1698 after a complete turnover of Gloucester County's justices, no constables appeared for the September session, and trials ground to a halt because not enough men showed up
for jury duty. Similarly, after the royal takeover of New Jersey in 1703
reduced Quaker influence, many Burlington County Quakers refused
to serve on juries or as constables or overseers, often to avoid swearing
the newly required oaths.[32] A court's authority diminished and its political base narrowed when "good men," whose participation could legitimize the proceedings, refused to do so. Successful use of civic contempt, to deter nonperformance and enforce participation, would control
the refractory and enhance court authority.

Direct affronts to the court, verbal or physical resistance to legal authority outside court, or subversion of the legal process constituted contempt of authority, 42 percent of all contempt cases. Some were political challenges that courts could not afford to let pass. The political
statement Quakers made in refusing to doff their hats in the new royal
courts of New Jersey represented a symbolic challenge that British courts
had regularly punished.[33] Blunt statements challenging a court's legitimacy were even more threatening. Samuel Jennings, the ex-governor of
West Jersey who declared that the new government's commission was
unlawful, and Jeremiah Bates, who claimed that the sheriff who summoned him for jury duty was not a lawful sheriff, faced contempt charges.[34] Sometimes the contempt rested not in politics but on anger, at times
amplified by inebriation. Calling justices rogues, drunks, or felons, describing grand jurors as liars, spitting in an opponent's face in court, or

stating "thou the Sheriffe, thou a turd" while thrusting a fist in his general direction brought swift prosecution.[35]

Cases involving contempt of authority also focused on violations of procedural norms. John Hollinshead's warrantless search was a contempt of authority. Hung jurors who flipped a coin to decide a case suffered for their "illegal proceedings," even though the parties in the case said they had not been hurt by the chance verdict. Constables who refused to execute warrants of arrest, who delayed in pronouncing the hue and cry, who failed to prosecute felons before the grand jury, or who refused to pursue an escaping prisoner were similarly accused of offenses that thwarted impartial justice. Tax collectors who attempted to give preferential treatment to their neighbors were prosecuted and replaced by others who would do the job fairly.[36] The hint of ineptitude or favoritism could undermine the fragile authority courts possessed as much as derogatory statements did.

These prosecutions, as with all contempt prosecutions, indicated the high value these courts placed on proper participation and behavior in accord with the rule of law by "good men." The Delaware Valley's docket share of 21.4 percent of all contempts was higher than for any other colonial jurisdiction.[37] In 1691–95, a period of political instability in both colonies, contempt peaked at almost a third of all prosecutions, with more than one-sixth of all prosecutions for civic contempt (see table 29). The statistic on civic contempt reflects local elites' struggles to maintain authority in the face of provincial political upheaval through the personnel selected for legal jobs; courts would not let such men duck their duties. The combination of law reforms, which focused attention on the quality of justice; querulous Quakers, who needed to be brought into line and into roles; and the pluralistic nature of Delaware Valley society made contempt a useful tool to enhance legitimacy. Contempt was not merely reactive prosecution but was also a proactive assertion of the Quakers' powerful legal ideology.

The third most common criminal category reflected another part of this ideology pertaining to crime, that of preventing crime before a prosecution became necessary. The "recognizance," which summarily required people with alleged criminal tendencies to post bond even before any crime occurred, was one of the most powerful weapons of the justices of the peace in Britain and the colonies, but Delaware Valley justices raised its use to new heights. Recognizances constituted 14.8 percent of the criminal docket in these four counties. These recognizances were not bail (or its equivalent) to ensure a defendant's appearance to face a specific charge (that kind of bond was not included here but instead was tallied under the crime for which bail was posted). Rather, these "peace bonds" required the defendant to find sureties who promised to pay a specific sum if the defendant violated the conditions of the bond before the next court. Recognizances either bound the defendant to keep the peace after someone who feared injury made a complaint (the bond would name the individual the defendant must avoid harming) or, merely on the suspicion of a defendant's general criminal intent, bound the defendant to good behavior. Having to post a recognizance was a minor punishment in itself, and inability to come up with sufficient sureties resulted in the defendant's imprisonment. At the next court of quarter sessions, the court would determine whether the defendant had adhered to the conditions of the recognizance; if not, the bond either continued in force or was forfeited, with the sureties then having to come up with hard cash.[38]

The recognizance was thus an ideal weapon to implement Quaker precepts of law reform. The amount of the peace bond varied, depending on the feared offense and the potential criminal. A seedy tavern owner's bond to keep a civil house of entertainment and run no unlawful games was forty pounds, while Nehemiah Yeamain, "a free Negro," had to find sureties for five hundred pounds to keep the peace around Sarah Harrison, a white woman.[39] Yet the short time period covered (the bond was evaluated at the next court session) and the use of a money pledge (credit) rather than up-front cash reduced the chances for judicial oppression. Though such bonds had common-law precedent and had been statutorily authorized as early as 1683 in Pennsylvania, the recognizance's docket share increased markedly after 1700 (see table 29), with most of the increase occurring in West Jersey.[40] There have been no counts of these types of recognizances in any other history of a colony's criminal law, suggesting that other colonies did not utilize them at the rate of 20–30 percent of the docket found in the Delaware Valley between 1701 and 1710. Peace bonds were a vital part of this legal system's approach to preventing criminal behavior.

The unlawful taking of another's property and violent offenses each constituted approximately one-eighth of the criminal docket (12.6 percent and 12.3 percent, respectively; see table 29). Property crimes included theft, breaking and entering for the purpose of theft (burglary), trespassing on another's land to carry off products of that land, and taking property not yours (e.g., marking ranging animals). Prosecuted thefts more often involved animals than money, crops, or other personal property, revealing both the economic importance of animals as well as the problems of identification that were unresolved even with the registration of ear marks and brands.[41] Crimes of violence prosecuted included general breaches of the peace (fights and simple assaults) as well as such felonies as aggravated assault (denoted by blood spilling), rape and attempted rape, murder (although trial responsibilities were lodged in provincial courts), riot, breaking down the prison door, aiding escape, and armed robbery.[42] It was these crimes, 25 percent of the docket, that penal reformers were most concerned about in the Delaware Valley.

Pennsylvania, following the notions of law reform, initially enacted the mildest criminal code in the English-speaking world, while West Jersey, less comprehensive in its reforms, reduced punishment of violent crimes to match "the nature of the offence." Pennsylvania prescribed the death sentence only for murder and treason and for all other offenses eliminated branding and mutilation as well. Penalties for theft, burglary, and robbery required the offender to pay multiple restitution (following West Jersey's lead), while rape and violent assault brought fines, whipping, and imprisonment. Less severe breaches of the peace saw lesser fines and whippings, depending on the severity of the offense and whether the defendant was a recidivist.[43] Between 1683 and 1698, Pennsylvania's criminal law had only minor alterations, closing loopholes regarding property conversion and creating a sliding scale of punishment for the repeated theft of "living goods," again reflecting the importance of animals.[44] Yet by the late 1690s, citizens complained that crime was increasing, and Penn called his colony "the greatest refuge and shelter for pirates and rogues in America," "overrun with wickedness."[45] Prosecutions in Pennsylvania for violence peaked at 24.8 percent in 1696–1700, reflecting this concern. The legislature responded in 1698, declaring that "Laws being so easie that they have not answered the good end proposed in making thereof, for that many dissolute persons, not withstanding ye said Laws, have Committed Divers thefts and robberies."[46] Pennsylvania's penal revisions of 1700 reflected a desire for more prosecutions, implemented a deterrence theory, and established, for almost every property and violent offense, harsher penalties, including mutilation, branding, extra whippings, and longer prison terms. The new code was so draconian that the Privy Council in 1705 disallowed many statutes for being unusually cruel and repugnant to the laws of England.[47]

The criminal docket for West Jersey reveals neither a crime wave before 1700 nor a prosecutorial explosion after 1700. The docket share for combined property and violent crimes peaked in the earliest period, at 37.2 percent, and generally declined over the remainder of the period. In Pennsylvania, prosecutions for violence and property offenses actually declined from 34.7 percent in 1696–1700 to 27.2 percent in 1701–5, only to rise again in 1706–10 to 36.6 percent. The reason for this prosecutorial pattern might have lain in exactly what reformers contended: harsh penalties make enforcement more difficult because indictments and convictions become harder to obtain. Or there might have been fewer crimes as a result of deterrence under the harsh code of 1700. Regardless of the reason, these Delaware Valley courts' dockets involved property and violent crimes at a rate that was far less than that of colonial South Carolina, North Carolina, Maryland, and New York; was comparable to that in various Massachusetts jurisdictions; and was slightly higher than that of Virginia and Connecticut.[48] The impact of law reform on these offenses seems to have been marginal.

Three more categories rounded out the criminal docket. Nearly 10 percent of all prosecutions either revealed no cause for the accusation or fell into a miscellaneous group that included tying straw to a horse's tail, having a biting dog, failing to pay a tax levy, and being a runaway servant.[49] Almost 5 percent of the cases involved crimes of economic exploitation, where the offense involved neither force nor larceny. Such crimes included mistreating a servant or holding him past his indentured time; fencing, turning, or felling trees on the highway; extorting excessive ferry or clerk fees; and committing various acts of fraud, such as clipping coins, counterfeiting, cheating Indians out of land, or selling an animal one did not own.[50] Finally, almost 2 percent involved criminal defamation. By choosing to initiate a criminal prosecution, the allegedly defamed avoided the difficulty and expense of gaining a civil victory, which might produce little compensation. Whether the slandered was accused of being a witch or engaging in various sexual improprieties (e.g., having sex with a mare, sleeping with a slave's wife),[51] convincing a grand jury to indict might begin to clear one's name.

The other major component of defamation cases was political. Pennsylvania law demanded severe punishment for all "Scandalous and Malitious Reporters, Defamers, and Spreaders of false news, whether against magistrates or private persons." This provision formed the backdrop to Pennsylvania's sedition law, paralleling West Jersey's, making it a crime to incite hatred of the governor or proprietor or to utter any statement that tended to subvert established government.[52] Though few, such cases revealed what the legal elite felt were some of its greatest threats, such as being called a papist. It was a defamation charge that brought the Quaker schismatic George Keith, his publisher William Bradford, and other of his supporters to the bar in Philadelphia.[53]

Analysis of this distribution of accusations throws into relief the interplay of law reform, Quaker attitudes about authority and morality, and actual behavior. The Delaware Valley courts were unique in their focus on contempt prosecutions, their extraordinary usage of peace bonds, and their middling interest in morals prosecutions. These jurisdictions also produced a relatively constant docket share of property and violent crimes, a share similar to that of other northern colonies. But any defendant's experience in the criminal justice system depended not on overall trends but rather, in part, on the charges he or she faced. Each accused brought before the bar his or her bundle of status, wealth, and power attributes, which might influence the result. This matchup between accusations and attributes brings into focus the role of criminal justice in maintaining the authority and legitimacy of the "good men" who ran the legal system.

Who Was Charged with What

Understanding the criminal justice experience of the 28 percent of the legal population charged with offenses depends on first understanding the accusations each group faced. As with civil causes, eight different attributes of defendants—gender, landownership, officeholding status, religion, Quaker leadership, occupation, wealth (taxed and inventoried), and number of cases—were matched against the categories of accusation. Chi-square analysis of these matchups identified where the pattern of prosecution differed significantly depending on the defendant's attributes. The results are presented in table 30. Of the attributes studied, only wealth, whether measured by tax assessment or inventory at death, was not significantly related to the pattern of criminal charges. For all other attributes, the pattern of charging revealed a two-level criminal justice system. One level was designed "to maintain the legitimacy of a system of domination and to restrain those with power from acting in their unbridled self-interest." These charges—contempt, economic exploitation—set standards for elite behavior that the public could ob-

Table 30. Criminal Accusations, by Criminal Defendant Attributes

Attributes	Morals	Contempt		Recog-nizance	Property	Violence	Economic Exploitation	Defamation	Others/Unknown
		Civic	Authority						
Total n	264	150	102	174	148	145	57	22	115
Percentage of accusations	22.4	12.7	8.7	14.8	12.6	12.3	4.8	1.9	9.8
Male (%)	19.9	13.9	9.0	15.5	12.3	12.6	5.1	1.7	10.0
Female (%)	50.0	0.0	5.1	7.1	15.3	9.2	2.0	4.1	7.1
Chi-square probability = .000									
Quakers (%)	17.1	24.0	8.9	11.1	6.0	11.4	8.0	1.7	11.7
Leaders (%)	9.3	32.0	9.3	3.1	8.2	11.3	12.4	2.1	12.4
Average (%)	20.2	20.9	8.7	14.2	5.1	11.5	6.3	1.6	11.5
Non-Quakers (%)	26.8	4.6	8.1	16.4	15.1	13.0	3.9	2.3	9.8
Chi-square probability = .000									
Landowners (%)	21.6	17.5	9.8	12.8	9.8	11.4	6.2	1.6	9.3
Nonlandowners (%)	23.8	4.6	6.7	18.2	17.3	13.9	2.5	2.3	10.6
Chi-square probability = .000									
Occupations (males only)[a]									
Farmer (%)	24.6	19.0	7.8	12.2	11.8	8.7	7.2	0.3	8.4
Artisan (%)	18.2	12.1	11.4	14.4	6.8	18.2	3.8	3.8	11.4
Farmer-artisan (%)	15.3	23.7	18.6	10.2	6.8	11.9	1.7	3.4	8.5
Merchant (%)	30.0	30.0	10.0	10.0	0.0	10.0	10.0	0.0	0.0
Self-described gentry (%)	11.9	16.7	7.1	9.5	11.9	21.4	9.5	2.4	9.5
Servant/slave/laborer (%)	22.4	4.7	6.5	11.2	24.3	14.0	3.7	2.8	10.3
Chi-square probability = .000									

Table 30, continued

Attributes	Morals	Contempt		Recog-nizance	Property	Violence	Economic Exploitation	Defamation	Others/ Unknown
		Civic	Authority						
1693 Pennsylvania tax assessment (in pounds)									
100+ (%)	25.0	27.5	15.0	5.0	0.0	5.0	15.0	0.0	7.5
50–99 (%)	20.0	16.4	7.3	12.7	9.1	12.7	7.3	5.5	9.1
1–49 (%)	26.0	21.2	8.7	8.7	9.6	11.5	11.5	1.9	1.0
Chi-square probability = .179									
Inventoried wealth (in pounds)									
500+ (%)	15.8	14.0	14.0	7.0	8.8	12.3	12.3	5.3	10.5
100–499 (%)	24.5	18.2	8.2	11.3	11.3	9.4	5.7	1.9	9.4
1–99 (%)	30.0	13.3	5.0	8.3	10.0	15.0	1.7	1.7	15.0
Chi-square probability = .346									
Legal roles									
High officer (%)	15.7	23.3	11.3	4.4	6.9	9.4	9.4	3.1	16.4
Lesser officer (%)	20.6	21.2	9.8	15.5	9.8	8.9	6.7	1.0	6.7
Nonofficer (%)	24.8	6.6	7.6	16.8	15.1	14.5	3.0	2.0	9.7
Chi-square probability = .000									
Number of accusations									
1 (%)	23.0	13.9	7.4	15.1	13.2	11.8	4.1	1.5	10.0
2+ (%)	22.5	11.1	9.7	14.4	13.9	13.2	3.7	2.3	9.5
Chi-square probability = .729									

a. The category "other" has been omitted to ensure that chi-square is a valid test. Criminal analysis will use only six occupational categories.

serve and allowed the subordination of individual elite interests.[54] A second level of charges—recognizances, property, morals, and violence—disproportionately involved nonelite groups, whose members were relatively powerless. The combined force of these two levels produced the unique demography of criminal defendants discussed in the first section and helped legitimize the entire legal system.

Gender significantly influenced the pattern of criminal prosecutions. Women's circumscribed opportunities for public life limited their opportunities to offend. Women were never charged with civic contempt simply because jurors and officers were male. Contempts against authority by women were rare and so unimportant that when Martha Wearing and Anne Vanculine spoke evil words against magistrates, they received little punishment.[55] Similarly, male control over economic life meant that there were few chances for, and thus charges of, illegal economic exploitation by women. That few women had to face accusations of violence or had to post a recognizance reflected male dominance in the use or threat of use of illegal force. An unwed woman's pregnancy, however, constituted visible and public evidence of her breach of moral law. Women disproportionately faced morals charges, most often for fornication; half of all women defendants confronted morals charges. Delaware Valley women's criminal prosecutions followed the tendency of other colonial jurisdictions to focus disproportionately on female morals offenses. However, the level of morals prosecutions experienced by women here (50 percent) exceeded that in other comparable colonial jurisdictions.[56]

The only other charge Delaware Valley women faced significantly more often than men was defamation. Fear of women's tongues, a stereotypically male concern, led Pennsylvania to pass laws against "Scolding & Railing." Slander by women could be just as damaging to reputations as slander by men, John Woolston, Jr., and John Tonkan separately realized eight years apart when they were on the receiving end of Susanna Reeves's barbs.[57] The crimes that were disproportionately male required a certain level of social or physical power, while illicit uses of one's body and tongue were offenses available to the powerless. Men disproportionately experienced one level of accusation, while women faced another.

There was a similarly significant relationship between landownership and types of accusation. A situation nearly opposite to that of women existed here—landowning was a virtual prerequisite to officeholding and to full participation in economic life. Accordingly, landowners were disproportionately accused of civic contempt, economic exploitations, and contempt of authority. Yet this disproportionate impact was even greater than expected since courts charged landowners with these crimes far more often than their population percentage would have suggested. Landowners were 58 percent of the legal population, suggesting that they should have had about that percentage of opportunity for economic exploitation and contempt of authority. Yet they were accused of 81 percent of the economic exploitation crimes and 71 percent of the contempts of authority. If we examine civic contempt charges, landowners constituted 87 percent of those accused of missing jury duty, neglecting official duties, and the like, revealing the courts' definition of "good men" for such jobs overwhelmingly concentrated on the landed. This level of criminal charges focused on disciplining those most likely to have power in this society, those whose participation was most needed, those whose defiance was most dangerous.

Conversely, landowners had greater economic security and thus less incentive to steal blatantly (as opposed to stealing by fraud), meaning that the landless were disproportionately likely to be charged with property offenses. Landowners were also less likely than the landless to have to post a recognizance, but the incidence of morals and violence offenses was virtually identical for both groups. In the latter cases, owning land did not improve one's morals or temper, nor did it carry enough power in a society where 58 percent owned land to insulate an individual from such accusations. Landownership made one especially vulnerable to the upper level of criminal accusations—those concerned with power and participation—but reduced such owners' vulnerability to only two crimes from the lower level—those crimes associated with powerlessness, immorality, and frustration.

A clear demarcation between these two levels of criminal accusations was apparent for officeholders. High officers were disproportionately accused of civic contempt, economic exploitation, defamation, and contempt of authority; they were disproportionately absent from those required to post recognizances and those accused of property, morals, and violence offenses. Interestingly, high officers also had more charges in the "unknown" category than would be expected, perhaps indicating a disproportionate power to suppress the recording or prosecution of some charges. Lesser officers were also disproportionately subject to civic contempt and economic exploitation citations and were relatively immune to prosecutions for violence and property offenses. Unlike high officers, however, lesser officers had to post recognizances and face morals accusations at rates comparable with the overall prosecution rate. This difference was undoubtedly related to the fact that lesser officers, especially constables, were from the lower ranks of society more often than high officers were (described in chapter 1). Finally, those who never served in office were underrepresented among those charged with civic contempt and economic exploitation and disproportionately called on to answer to property, violence, and, to a lesser extent, recognizance and morals issues.

Defamation and contempt of authority cases among high officers illustrated how criminal prosecution disciplined the legal elite to maintain authority for that elite. In 1698, Christopher Wetherill, a Burlington County justice, had to account for calling his fellow justice John Tatham a "Papist," and Andrew Robeson, a Gloucester County justice, had to defend his "Severall Dangerous Words" and threatening language against the government.[58] Such words were particularly unsettling to courts struggling to maintain legitimacy under a newly installed and unpopular governor. When Israel Taylor, surveyor and sheriff of Bucks County, was convicted of defaming the wife of John Swift, a justice and assemblyman, his response that jury members were all "Sworn Rogues" brought Taylor back into court on a second defamation charge.[59] The Gloucester County elite demanded that its sheriff, John Wood, be prosecuted for betraying and perverting justice by conveying a Gloucester County criminal to Burlington County for trial, thus undermining the rights and privileges of the county.[60] Legal jurisdictions demanded the unswerving loyalty of their officers.

Courts also demanded the strict appearance of procedural regularity and fairness. High and lesser officers disproportionately faced those civic contempt charges, which were based not on mere nonappearance but on malfeasance in the performance of duty. Justices George Foreman in Chester County and William Biddle and John Hollinshead in Burlington County were disciplined for failing to prosecute or give evidence against an accused criminal. Foreman's rescue of a prisoner from a constable's custody and former Chester County justice Edward Beazer's assault on a constable might have allowed miscreants to go free, but such acts resulted in their own prosecution.[61] Constables who refused to present information to the grand jury, execute warrants of arrest, or pursue an escaping prisoner thwarted impartial justice, as did tax collectors who bypassed their neighbors.[62] Even when the offense was not motivated by preferential treatment, such as when the hung Bucks County jury flipped a coin to decide a case, preserving the integrity of the process demanded that the whole jury and the constable who sat with them be punished.[63] Civic contempt citations attempted to force elites to subordinate their private agendas of preference to the public agenda of regular process and equal justice.

The final type of upper-level prosecutions, necessary to enhance the courts' legitimacy, attempted to rein in officer arrogance in economic exploitation, disciplining those who attempted to use their power for excessive gain. The Burlington County justice William Emley purchased Indian land for himself in contravention of legal prohibitions against such private dealings. The Chester County clerk Robert Eyre overcharged court fees, which were set by law, in at least three instances. The Chester County justice John Bristow used his position as head ranger to corral wild horses that by law belonged to William Penn. Four of Bucks County's first officeholders—Thomas Brock, Gilbert Wheeler, Joseph Growden, and William Beakes—either extorted ferry fees or built illegal fences in the first ten years of the county's existence. Lesser officers might not have had as many opportunities as high officers had, but constables could and did divert water courses and block roads illegally for economic advantage.[64] By disciplining its elite, the legal system could plausibly claim to be protecting the whole society, thus enhancing its legitimacy. Such prosecutions might have softened the psychological blow nonofficers felt when morals, property, and violence prosecutions fell disproportionately on them; at least, they might say, elites must answer for their offenses as well.

As seen in their participation in legal roles and as litigants, Quakers and Quaker leaders dominated civil processes. It is therefore no surprise to find these groups disproportionately present in crimes of the first level (civic contempt and economic exploitation) and disproportionately absent from prosecutions of the second level (property, recognizances, morals). Because high officers were disproportionately Quakers and Quaker leaders, the analysis on the need to discipline legal elites applies here as well. Thirteen of the sixteen prosecuted high officers examined above were Quakers, and seven were Quaker leaders; some of the alleged preferential treatment was to help fellow Quakers avoid prosecution. Yet there were three additional factors explaining this pattern of prosecution. First, Quakers had emerged from an English legal system in which an antagonistic posture toward the courts was a matter of both conscience and survival.[65] In the Delaware Valley, however, Quaker control of the law required disciplining Quakers to guarantee proper participation by their own "good men," to control their own ingrained opposition to authority, and to counteract the atomistic tendencies of their own religious belief.[66] For example, although Quakers constituted 56 percent of the landowners who dominated the jury pool and 62 percent of all jurors, 79 percent of civic contempt citations for jury duty violations were against Quakers. Quakers as a whole and Quaker leaders in particular thus faced such contempt charges at rates far beyond their percentage of officeholders or jurors.

Second, Quaker trading practices made them vulnerable to accusations of economic exploitation. Before arriving in the Delaware Valley, Quaker businessmen had acquired reputations for shrewdness that shaded toward trickery and deceit, for taciturnity that implied secrecy, and for keeping their trade within the Society of Friends that implied unfair advantage.[67] Since Quakers enjoyed landownership, legal power, and wealth above that of the non-Quaker majority of the population, the legitimacy of Quaker rule would be undermined if those already privileged were allowed to overreach. Prosecution of Quakers by Quakers for dealings that illegally gained Quaker business an extra advantage was an effective means of refuting the corrosive stereotypes while maintaining the Quakers' own self-image of scrupulous honesty in business.

Finally, the disproportionate prosecution of non-Quakers in property, recognizance, and morals cases may reflect not only the privileged position enjoyed by Quakers and Quaker leaders but also Quaker meetings' disciplinary powers. As the next section shows, the criminal system and the Quaker system rarely subjected a Quaker miscreant to double jeopardy by prosecuting the same offense in both forums. Accusations of offenses that both the court and the meeting claimed to control (e.g., illicit sexual relations) were not filed in court when the meeting had already taken action. This division of labor accounts for the lower than expected level of Quaker criminal defendants and illustrates how the Quaker meeting worked together with the court as an adjunct disciplinary system. Crimes of violence, however, constituted an exception to this division of criminal responsibilities. Quakers were prosecuted nearly as often as non-Quakers for such serious crimes. In general, the parallel disciplinary system and their social standing reduced Quakers' chances of standing in the dock accused of a second-level crime.

Whereas gender, land, officeholding, and religion were consistent indicators of a criminal defendant's vulnerability to first- or second-level accusations, occupation had a more ambiguous impact. Although chi-square revealed a statistically significant pattern, the low number of cases identified renders that conclusion suspect.[68] Some relationships between occupation and types of accusation were clear, such as with servants/slaves/laborers, who were disproportionately charged with property offenses and rarely charged with civic contempt. Yet the self-described gentry disproportionately faced violence charges, while farmers saw more civic contempt accusations and fewer accusations of violent offenses. Farmer/artisans disproportionately faced more contempt and fewer violence charges, while artisans faced disproportionately more violence and defamation charges but fewer property offenses. All occupational categories had similar percentages of recognizances. This pattern of charges across levels reveals that occupation, like wealth, had little to do with prosecution rates.

To summarize, two levels of criminal prosecutions explain the demography of the criminal defendant population. The first level included crimes of civic contempt, contempt of authority, and economic exploitation. For each of these charges, those whose gender, land, office, and religion accorded them higher status were disproportionately accused. This differential prosecution—of males more than females, the landed more than the nonlanded, high officers and lesser officers more than nonofficers, and Quakers and Quaker leaders more than non-Quakers—brought those groups before the bar, reined them in, and helped produce legitimacy and authority for the system. The second-level offenses involving property, violence, recognizances, and morals focused more on females, the nonlanded, nonofficers, and non-Quakers. Here the traditional role of criminal law as social control over those of lesser status could be clearly seen. Accusations, however, were not convictions; nor did all offenses follow the same path to ultimate judgment. Rather, the experience of criminal defendants, like civil litigants, emerged from choices made by both the accused and their judges. Chapter 6 shows how such choices solidified elite control of the Delaware Valley through "good laws" and "good men."

The Accused in Quaker Meeting Discipline

The Society of Friends defined deviance and provided their communities with tools for dealing with those who ran afoul of such proscriptions, just as criminal law did. Justifications for Quaker discipline drew on the theology of creating a community of visible saints as well as on the pragmatic need to unify that community in the face of individualistic tendencies. Recognizing that even saints could sin, Quakers believed that disciplining sinners who would reform and disowning sinners who would not were necessary to keep the truth from being tainted and to preserve the Society's image of godliness. Yet the specter of moral relativism, contained in Quaker beliefs in the "Inner Light" and the primacy of individual conscience, threatened to make common behavioral standards impossible. The solution George Fox and other leading Quakers promulgated was a forum in the monthly meeting, both men's and women's, that would test moral judgments and thus supersede individual consciences. "Scripture, right reason, and the meeting's definition of truth," with collective judgments determining the last two, would set standards for behavior. Therefore, Quakers' Christian duty to care for one another also became a duty to watch each other's behavior carefully; men's and women's monthly meetings appointed overseers, but all Quakers had the responsibility to report sinful beliefs and actions. Because there was but one truth to be found, any disputes regarding this oversight would be resolved through consensus decisions at monthly meetings.[69]

Delaware Valley Quaker men and women held separate monthly meetings for the purpose of caring for and watching over their members. Like men, women would become leaders in their meetings by serving in offices (e.g., overseer) or by serving on committees appointed to help the poor, to investigate women accused of offenses, or to write certificates of "clearness" for those who planned to move or marry. In terms of jurisdiction over deviance, the workload was to be divided, with women's meetings responsible for contacting women Quakers accused of violations for the purpose of "laboring" with them to acknowledge their fault. Only for the recalcitrant accused were men's meetings to be involved; if a violator was found to be so resistant to ministrations as to be out of unity, only the men's meeting had the formal authority of disownment. Partly because George Fox intended women's meetings not to be subordinate to the men's meetings, women gained real authority in the Society of Friends.[70]

The records of women's meetings are less complete than those for the men's meetings in this period,[71] and information about women is much less available than for the overwhelmingly male legal population. Nonetheless, certain broad outlines were visible regarding the discipline of women. First, men's meetings did not always refer disciplinary problems with women to the women's meetings. In Chester, Radnor, Darby, Falls, Middletown, and Burlington meetings (for times when both men's and women's records are available), men's meetings held disciplinary hearings for twenty-one women that did not appear in the women's records and heard fourteen cases that also appeared in women's meetings. Of these thirty-five, there were only five disownments. Women's meetings never examined a man who was not also examined by the men's meetings. Though women's meetings handled accused women far more often, men's meetings did exercise control over some women below the level of disownment. Second, women's meetings were overwhelmingly concerned with issues of marriage to non-Quakers, potential marriages to non-Quakers, fornication and bastardy, and the appearance of sexual impropriety. Women's meetings held substantial authority, but they exercised it over a fairly narrow range of issues.

In terms of process, Quakers suspected of deviating from Society norms were reported to their respective monthly meeting, which would then appoint a committee of leading Friends to inform them of the charges against them.[72] Quaker men's meetings spent far more time and effort on discipline cases than on private differences, and Quaker women did not handle private differences at all. In the courts, criminal cases constituted only 37 percent of the docket and civil cases 63 percent of the docket. In the Quaker system, the percentages were reversed; 64 percent of the issues brought to the men's meetings were for the purpose of discipline (339 versus 187 differences). Women's meetings saw 91 disciplinary cases, of which 77 appeared only before the women and 14 went before both meetings. The overall docket covered 416 different disciplinary cases, or 69 percent of all Quaker meeting cases. Meetings would begin the disciplinary process by recording the charge and the charged, along with the names of those who would visit and discover the suspect's attitude toward the charge—confession, denial, or recalcitrance. How meetings resolved disciplinary cases is discussed in chapter 6; this section covers the demography of those accused by the men's meeting and the kinds of charges filed. Both patterns reveal a Quaker system working not just for the good of the community but also as an auxiliary to the criminal legal system.

The attributes of those accused of violating Society norms reveals a pattern distinct from that described for criminal defendants overall and Quaker criminal defendants in particular (see table 31). Whereas crim-

Table 31. Statistical Description of the Quakers Disciplined by Men's Meetings

Attributes	Quakers Disciplined	Quakers Disciplined 2+ Times	Quaker Population in Legal Population	Criminal Defendants	Legal Population	Quaker Criminal Defendants
Total *n*	320	73	1282	1057	3782	332
Male (%)	81.2	97.3	93.7	87.6	90.1	94.3
Female (%)	18.8	2.7	6.3	12.4	9.9	5.7
Quaker leaders (%)	22.2	30.1	29.2	12.0	11.4	35.5
Landowners (%)	74.1	78.1	83.0	60.0	58.0	87.3
Nonlandowners (%)	25.9	21.9	17.0	40.0	42.0	12.7
Occupations (males only)						
Farmer (%)	54.5	46.0	53.4	47.5	49.0	52.7
Artisan (%)	21.2	22.0	17.0	17.3	18.3	18.0
Farmer-artisan (%)	10.3	12.0	12.5	10.8	8.9	14.7
Merchant (%)	2.4	2.0	8.0	3.6	8.5	3.3
Self-described gentry (%)	2.4	4.0	3.9	6.4	5.6	4.9
Servant/slave/laborer (%)	4.2	4.0	2.4	9.1	5.1	2.9
Other (%)	4.8	12.0	2.8	4.9	4.6	3.7

Table 31, continued

Attributes	Quakers Disciplined	Quakers Disciplined 2+ Times	Quaker Population in Legal Population	Criminal Defendants	Legal Population	Quaker Criminal Defendants
1693 Pennsylvania tax assessment (in pounds)						
100+ (%)	26.4	22.7	15.5	15.3	14.2	16.5
50–99 (%)	19.4	22.7	18.6	22.7	17.8	25.2
1–49 (%)	54.2	54.5	65.9	62.0	68.0	58.3
Inventoried wealth (in pounds)						
500+ (%)	20.3	18.2	24.2	19.4	19.0	26.0
100–499 (%)	70.3	72.7	57.3	58.2	56.8	58.3
1–99 (%)	9.4	9.1	18.4	22.4	24.2	15.8
Legal roles						
High officer (%)	15.3	20.5	19.7	12.5	10.1	27.1
Lesser officer (%)	33.1	49.3	35.3	25.1	22.9	41.6
Nonofficer (%)	51.6	30.1	44.9	62.4	67.0	31.3
Grand juror (%)	46.9	71.2	55.3	37.5	33.4	69.3
Trial juror (%)	45.0	61.6	50.2	35.2	30.1	63.0

inal defendants generally held higher status than the legal population as a whole, such was not the case in the Quaker system. If we use the Quakers in the legal population as a baseline for comparison with men's meeting cases (as was done with Quaker differences),[73] those disciplined were less likely than other Quakers to own land, to be a leader in the meeting, or to serve as a high legal officer, a grand juror, or a trial juror. Furthermore, those disciplined avoided other aspects of public life, since they were less likely than the average Quaker to have been a litigant.[74] Most significant, Quaker criminal defendants were far more likely to have been high or lesser legal officers, Quaker leaders, landowners, and male than were those disciplined in the men's meetings. Women, who made up 18.8 percent of those accused in the men's meeting, constituted 34.3 percent of all those who faced disciplinary action by either men's or women's meetings (136 of the 396 accused). Criminal law thus focused on higher-status Quakers, while Quaker discipline focused on average Quakers. A division of responsibility between the two systems based on the alleged deviant's status and participation in public/legal life was apparent.

The types of deviance that concerned meetings explains at least part of this different profile of offenders. Whereas statutes and common law addressed a limited number of offenses, Quakers' desire to preserve the truth and a godly community included those violations and more. Of the 300 men's meeting disciplinary actions that noted a cause, 196 (65.3 percent) concerned deviance from Quaker norms that was criminal or possibly criminal; women's meetings dealt with 42 offenses (54.5 percent) that were criminal or possibly criminal (see table 32). Fighting; shooting servants; stealing; defaming or scandalizing with rumors; drinking to excess; fornicating or producing bastards; swearing; running a disorderly house; selling rum to Indians; passing counterfeit money; rioting; engaging in astrology and other "black" arts; resisting an officer of the law; committing perjury; flipping a coin to produce a jury verdict; laying wagers; playing cards; and trespassing on public land were clearly indictable offenses, which also produced Quaker disciplinary action. Other cases possibly involved criminal liability, including absenting oneself from meetings, which might have meant breaking the Sabbath, and other offenses referred to vaguely as "disorderly walking," "evil carriage," and "unclean practices," which might have referred to sexual violations or disturbing the peace. Women's meetings also included such "disorderly" offenses as not marrying when the marriage had been ap-

Table 32. Types of Accusations in Quaker Meetings

| Accusations | Percentage Accused[a] | | |
	By Men's Meetings	By Women's Meetings	Overall[b]
Sectarian offenses, not illegal			
Disorderly marriages	18.3	22.1	18.7
Separating/bad testimony	6.0	9.1	6.3
Abuse of meeting	5.0	5.2	5.2
Certificates/appeals	2.7	3.9	3.0
Taking arms	1.7	0.0	1.4
Disputes with husband	0.0	5.2	1.1
False meeting records	0.7	0.0	0.6
Dispute with non-Quaker	0.3	0.0	0.3
Subtotal	34.7	45.5	36.6
Sectarian offenses, possibly illegal			
Disorderly walking	17.7	40.3	21.8
Absenting meetings/Sabbath	11.3	2.6	9.9
Subtotal	29.0	42.9	31.7
Overall sectarian offenses	63.7	88.4	68.3
Offenses without victims, probably illegal			
Liquor violations	6.7	0.0	5.5
Swearing/words	3.7	0.0	3.0
Sexual offenses	3.0	11.7	4.1
Wagers/cards/etc.	1.3	0.0	1.1
Magic arts	0.3	0.0	0.3
Subtotal	15.0	11.7	14.0
Offenses with victims, illegal			
Economic (bankruptcy, exploitation)	5.7	0.0	4.7
Violence	5.3	0.0	4.4
Defamation/scandal	5.3	0.0	4.4
Against legal system	2.3	0.0	1.9
Theft/embezzlement	1.3	0.0	1.1
Misdemeanors	1.3	0.0	1.1
Subtotal	21.2	0.0	17.6
Total identified (n)	99.9 (300)	100.1 (77)	99.9 (363)

a. Percentages do not add to 100 because of rounding.
b. Overall *n* counts only once the fourteen cases that appeared in both meetings.

proved, keeping company with non-Quaker males, and keeping company with males without informing one's parents. These accusations also suggested sexual misconduct that might have been prosecutable.[75] These offenders potentially faced a kind of double jeopardy for these acts, since both systems claimed jurisdiction over such violations.

Although the courts and meetings might have had overlapping jurisdictions, in practice few defendants faced such double jeopardy. Only 16 deviant events involving 21 disciplinary actions by meetings had the same defendant(s) prosecuted for the analogous crimes at law. Most of these cases involved morals offenses, such as fornication, liquor violations, and the practice of astrology and geomancy (10 events). The coin flip jurors, those who built on public land, thieves, and brawlers also drew the attention of both forums.[76] Nonetheless, 94 men's and women's disciplinary actions that clearly covered indictable events never produced analogous criminal charges, nor did 123 other cases that might have been covered by criminal law.

Similarly, Quakers could face significant criminal charges yet remain untouched by the meeting. John Woolston, a Burlington Meeting leader, was charged with leading a riot that broke open the county's prison door. Yet he was not one of the eight disciplined (but not criminally prosecuted) for that event by Burlington County's meetings. Rioters faced the law or the meeting, but not both. Joseph Coborne faced criminal charges in Chester County for verbally and physically abusing Thomas Lassey and for illegally fettering and riding a horse that was not his, but no meeting discipline was ever begun against this Quaker leader. Samuel Beakes, a Falls Meeting leader who was acquitted of hog theft but convicted of selling liquor without a license and ordered to close down his "disorderly house," never had to "clear the truth" through a paper of self-condemnation that meetings demanded of sinners.[77] All told, 73 percent of Quaker criminal defendants never faced any Quaker disciplinary proceeding for any offense, and only 4 percent ever faced both the court and the meeting for the same event. The effect was a de facto comity that recognized verdicts in the other forum as sufficient control of deviance. Quaker and criminal law institutions held complementary, not competitive, proceedings.

More than a third of the identified causes for Quaker discipline were either not criminal or actually sanctioned legally. Most prominent were meeting attempts to control marriage practices. Discipline was required for marrying a non-Quaker or attending a non-Quaker wedding. Quakers also had to explain secret marriages, marriages without parental con-

sent, "too hasty" marriages after a spouse's death, or marriages to relatives allowed by law but not by the Bible (e.g., a dead wife's sister). Similarly, such sectarian crimes as joining schismatics, preaching without
meeting approval, making "bad testimony," wearing a hat during prayer,
making groundless accusations, arguing with or living apart from your
husband, or falling away from the truth (e.g., listening to a priest) were
not illegal.[78] Quakers who sought certificates of "clearness" either to
marry or to move to another meeting found themselves forced to "clear
the truth" to gain such permission. The investigation following a request
for a certificate that turned up sectarian violations could not have occurred under criminal law.

Quakers disciplined members for doing things encouraged by law.
Royal New Jersey encouraged those whose conscience would allow them
to bear arms in defense of the colony to do so, but five Quakers who
did were disciplined for violating the peace testimony. Writing verses
or printing almanacs containing a "superfluity" in language brought
meeting reproach. Given Quaker reforms against debtors' prison, engaging in improvident dealings that might lead to bankruptcy could at
most have produced civil liability, but the meeting regarded such debts
as offensive to the Quaker community.[79] Conversely, not every crime
was a moral violation requiring meeting attention; not once did Quakers discipline a defendant convicted of not appearing for jury, constable, or overseer duty. With that one exception, Quaker discipline en-
compassed the whole of secular criminal law as well as a slew of offenses
against religious beliefs. This broader charge explains why meetings gave
much more attention to disciplinary action than to differences between
members.

A closer look at particular types of accusations reveals other aspects
of the complementary nature of criminal and Quaker disciplining (see
table 32). The most common charge (21.8 percent overall, and 40.3
percent in women's meetings) involved the charge of "disorderly walking" or an equivalent euphemism, such as "loose living," "unchristian
practices," or "unclean carriage," with women's meetings especially concerned with keeping Quaker women away from non-Quaker men. The
most common accusation in men's meetings and second most common
overall was disorderly marriage (18.3 percent in men's meetings, 18.7
percent overall), which included marrying a non-Quaker, attending a
Quaker marriage that was doctrinally irregular, or attending a non-Quaker wedding.[80] Not attending meetings was the third most common

charge (9.9 percent). Of these discipline cases totaling nearly half of the Quaker docket, only failure to attend meetings might have been construed as illegal breach of the Sabbath, but the legal system showed extreme reluctance to prosecute this offense. There were no prosecutions for breach of Sabbath in Bucks County, and, despite the justices' desires, there were no successful prosecutions in Burlington County, because grand juries refused to prosecute, defendants pleaded necessity, or presentments were not pursued. Only in Chester County, in four cases, did the legal system show any interest in enforcing the Sabbath. Chester County's meetings, however, pursued seventeen discipline cases for such offenses.[81] In this area of great interest to Quakers, the legal system deferred to the meeting.

In instances where the legal system and the meeting clearly overlapped, Quaker discipline had different thresholds regarding who warranted confrontation. Quakers seemed to have a higher tolerance for liquor violations than the legal system did. Unlike the legal system, Quakers would discipline only for flagrant drunkenness, those who were "too frequently overtaken in drink" or "overtaken so farr that ye Liqour offending my Stomack, I was forced to cast it up again to my great shame and confusion."[82] Sexual offenses (4.1 percent of the cases) showed Quakers had a lower threshold for discipline than the courts had. Some were clearly engaged in sinful and illegal sex, such as Edward Boulton's "disorderly and unseemly" relationship with his maid or Mary Runford's giving birth to a full-term baby only twenty-six weeks after her marriage. Most charges, however, revealed only the appearance of impropriety that would not have stood up in a criminal court. For example, Jean Worrilow condemned herself before Chester Women's Meeting for having a man "lie close to her upon a bed part of one night."[83] This complementary pattern of different thresholds existed for the rest of the overlapping discipline docket. Economic cases, such as improvident dealing and bankruptcy, were not crimes unless they involved fraud, but Quaker views on economic truth set higher standards than the law did. In defamation cases, Quakers also set a lower threshold for violations because the Society viewed scandalous rumors as disruptive of community peace. Finally, offenses against the legal system had to be more threatening than breaking down the prison door or flipping a coin to decide a case for meetings to take notice, while the law attacked Quakers for civic contempt and contempt of authority with abandon.

Quaker meetings thus constituted a third level of discipline that integrated its approach to deviance with the dual-level approach of the legal system. Quaker discipline focused on the average Quaker, especially average Quaker women, while the law focused on the top Quakers. Quakers disciplined in the courts would only occasionally suffer penalties in the meeting, and vice versa. Such double jeopardy could be avoided because of the different interests of the two systems and the different evidentiary thresholds for deviant events where the two systems overlapped. Criminal and Quaker dockets reflected an informal allocation of responsibility between forums, which produced a coordinated system of accusations that covered all levels of society and all types of deviance with remarkably little duplication. How well this system could work for the Quaker elite would depend on how well each part of the system processed the charges, a process open to manipulation by both the deviant and those in charge.

SIX

Dispositions of the Deviant

Harry, the "Negro man servant" accused of cow buggery and indict-ed by Burlington County's grand jury in 1692, tried to avoid con-viction and punishment. Harry pled not guilty and, with the assistance of his master, "referre[d] the Tryall to God and the Countrey," the re-quired legal formula for requesting a jury trial. When the defendant ac-cepted the jury called for that session, the mother and daughter who had testified in secret to the grand jury revealed their evidence in open court. The mother, Mary Myers, attested that she had seen "the Prison-er was gott upon a Cow, And that her Children saw the same, And called her to see." In greater detail, Myers related that "she then saw him ride upon the Cow, And that hee was in Action as Buggering the Cow. . . . And that after the Cow had the usuall Motions of Cows when they had taken the Bull." The daughter, also named Mary Myers, confirmed her mother's testimony, satisfying the two-witness rule established both bib-lically and by Delaware Valley procedure as necessary for criminal con-viction. The jury found Harry guilty, and the justices, without any stat-utory authorization, sentenced both Harry and the cow to death. Immediately, "Many of the Freeholders and Inhabitants of this County preferre a Petition to the Bench for Spareing the Negroes life," which "The Bench say they will Consider," staying the execution. At the next court, the sheriff reported that Harry had escaped, apparently forever avoiding the noose; the records were silent as to whether the cow simi-larly avoided its fate.[1]

This case followed the popular conception of criminal justice in ac-tion—charge, grand jury indictment, a jury trial, witnesses, conviction, penalty. Yet only 12.3 percent of all Delaware Valley criminal charges involved a jury trial; most cases, less sensational, followed different paths.

The recidivist John Hollinshead never was tried for damming the highway, even though a grand jury presented him (akin to indictment). Hollinshead's two other charges, contempts for illegal search and for not giving evidence against a defendant, resulted in summary guilty verdicts and fines that did not involve a grand jury, trial jury, or witnesses.[2] Between criminal accusation and judgment lay a host of decisions for both the legal system and the defendant, and, as shown with Harry, the public paid close attention to many cases, the choices, and the quality of justice meted out.

Before employing the full extent of the law, prosecuting parties and justices had wide discretion in resolving the dispute between society and the defendant. Such choices included ignoring the problem, negotiating or mediating the conflict out of court, or dropping the case for lack of evidence. Defendants could choose to flee, negotiate with the court or their alleged victim for a nontrial resolution, plead guilty or submit to the court, or fight with all available legal options, including a jury trial. As with civil litigation and Quaker disputes, the interplay among the type of charge, type of proceedings, and prosecutorial and defendant choices helped produce a system that, on court day, appeared fair and procedurally legitimate. At the same time, those same choices produced a less visible but nonetheless real pattern of results that spared many higher-status defendants from the worst indignities of the criminal law.

Processing the Accused prior to Trial or Conviction

Two broad types of criminal procedures were used to initiate prosecutions in the Delaware Valley—summary and grand jury. Summary procedures gave justices of the peace, either singly or *en banc,* the power to impose a penalty without indictment or trial and were therefore immense reservoirs of magisterial power.[3] All demands for recognizances and most contempts in the Delaware Valley involved justices' using their own knowledge or information presented to them and imposing criminal liability without further review. With some exceptions, the remainder of the criminal accusations went through the grand jury system of presentments made on information from individual justices who had bound over an accused to appear in court, from constables, from witnesses who appeared before the grand jury, or from the jurors' own knowledge. The practice on both sides of the river was to have a grand jury in attendance at every court of quarter sessions, that is, four times a year. At the start of each session, the thirteen to twenty-three grand jurors summoned by the sheriff from the freemen of the county would be called and attested to "Diligently Inquire and true presentment make" of matters charged or brought to their attention. The grand jury then retired to consider in secret the witnesses and evidence proffered. A majority of the grand jury could then agree to return a formal presentment of a charge, called "billa vera" (true bill); lacking such agreement, the jury endorsed the bill "ignoramus," effectively ending that prosecution.[4]

Regardless of how prosecutions began, formal adjudication accounted for barely half of all criminal cases begun. Six broad categories of outcomes for criminal charges have been assembled: not completed, pretrial cleared, discharged, ordered, in-court judgment of guilty, and in-court judgment of not guilty (see table 33). For those defendants who reached an in-court verdict, there were further choices among the types of verdicts, which offered opportunities for mitigating the public humiliation or the penalty and which will be dealt with in the next section. Of the 1,177 cases, 19.5 percent were not completed, that is, no final outcome of the charge was recorded. Whether a case began with summary or grand jury process did not affect whether it would be completed. The percentages of recognizances and contempts (summary) that remained incomplete were virtually identical with the percentage of morals, property, and violence charges (primarily grand jury) that were incomplete. Most unfinished prosecutions reflected either an unexplained disappearance of the case from the records or the unexpected disappearance of the defendant, such as John Ward's escape while wearing leg irons.[5]

Yet some accusations were disproportionately likely to disappear, while others rarely fell between the cracks. Table 33 reveals that crimes of economic exploitation, which disproportionately involved upper-status defendants, were the type most often not completed, while crimes attacking personal status (defamation) were disproportionately completed. The reason for such a differential probably lay in the victim's interest in seeing the case to a final resolution. In economic exploitation cases, such as diverting water courses, fencing land illegally, or abusing servants, victimization was either diffused throughout society or the victim was in a clearly inferior bargaining position. The failure to prosecute Hollinshead for damming the highway fits this pattern. In contrast, defamation was specific and vivid to an individual, which, when combined with the lower status of most accused of defamation, created incentives for completing a case.

Table 33. Criminal Outcomes, by Accusation Type

Accusations	Without Trial				Court Verdicts		N
	Not Completed	Pretrial Cleared	Discharged	Ordered	Guilty	Not Guilty	
Morals	18.6%	4.2%	3.0%	10.6%	61.4%	2.3%	264
Contempt	19.0	2.4	1.6	4.8	71.8	0.4	252
Civic	17.3	1.3	0.7	4.7	76.0	0.0	150
Authority	21.6	3.9	2.9	4.9	65.7	1.0	102
Recognizance	19.5	13.2	58.6	2.3	5.8	0.6	174
Property	18.2	7.4	3.4	3.4	56.1	11.5	148
Violence	20.7	9.7	6.9	6.2	49.0	7.6	145
Economic exploitation	26.3	8.8	12.3	26.3	22.8	3.5	57
Defamation	4.6	9.1	0.0	9.1	77.3	0.0	22
Other/unknown	22.6	22.6	7.0	13.0	28.7	6.1	115
Total percentage	19.5	8.3	12.2	7.6	48.4	3.8	100
N	230	98	144	90	570	45	1177

Completing a case was not, however, the same as reaching an in-court verdict; 8.3 percent of all defendants were cleared of charges, and another 12.2 percent were discharged from their bonds or from custody before trial. To clear the defendant implied a likelihood of innocence that a mere discharge did not, but courts used the terms almost interchangeably, and neither involved a public trial. One of the first places where systemic discretion to clear a defendant could be exercised was in the grand jury room, where an ignoramus (no true bill found) would end the prosecution. Only one county saw grand juries weed out a substantial number of charges, however. Eight percent of Burlington County's prosecutions ended with an ignoramus, compared with 1 percent or less in each of the other counties. The majority of Burlington County's ignoramuses occurred between 1705 and 1709, undoubtedly reflecting the tension between the new Anglican magistracy and the continuing Quaker presence on grand juries. Except for this period of struggle over prosecutions, grand juries were instruments for prosecution and only very rarely for exoneration.[6] Defendants who hoped to avoid trial would have to angle for intervention by the justices or the alleged victim.

The next method of prosecutorial discretion involved justices' clearing or discharging the defendant irrespective of any grand jury proceeding. Courts could formally strike down the presentment by quashing it as legally insufficient because it lacked proper form or did not state critical details, such as the time and place of the alleged crime.[7] More often, justices would end the prosecution on their own evaluation of the charges, a practice that drove Burlington County's grand jury in 1702 to complain that "several presentments of former Grandjuries have not been duly prosecuted."[8] For example, two witnesses charged Samuel Taylor with being "a Comon perturber of the peace," which resulted in Taylor's imprisonment until justices cleared him without trial. Samuel Scholey, a suspect in John Powell's drowning, was discharged when no witnesses appeared against him (not surprising considering that only Scholey and Powell were in the canoe when Powell met his end). Mary Fryley, along with two other witnesses, accused Seth Hill of attempted rape after she had rejected his plea to "do let me try but one inch"; following three continuances, the court cleared Hill even before a grand jury evaluated the evidence.[9] If the justices could be convinced, defendants could avoid a risky and potentially embarrassing public trial.

Such magisterial discretion cut unevenly across the range of presentments, and such choices revealed certain biases within the system. Chester County's grand jury presented William Collett and Edward Beazer, eminent Quakers, for fighting and shedding blood, a serious offense. Chester County's justices, without trial and on their own examination, cleared Beazer and let Collett post bond to face trial at the next court, a trial that never occurred. A Bucks County grand jury presented Samuel Beakes, a Quaker ex-sheriff, for keeping "an ill and disorderly house" that countenanced gambling, quarreling, and drunkenness, even on Sunday. Though the court revoked his ordinary license, it discharged him from criminal liability. The Quaker landowner John Thomas, presented for erecting unlawful fences and disturbing his neighbor's cattle, was cleared when he promised to make amends.[10] Other than recognizances (discussed later), offenses of an economic nature were most likely to be cleared or discharged by the court (21.1 percent of economic offenses). Adding in the not completed percentage reveals that defendants charged with economic exploitation, who were disproportionately of higher status, avoided public confrontations nearly half the time. In contrast, those cases least likely to be cleared or discharged were morals offenses, whose defendants, like Harry, generally held lower status (only 7.2 percent of moral charges were cleared or discharged).

Furthermore, if the victim could be convinced to drop the prosecution, defendants again would be cleared without having to contest any facts pointing to their guilt. West Jersey explicitly guaranteed that "any persons who prosecute or prefer indictment against others for any personal injuries, or matter criminal, or shall prosecute for any other criminal cause (treason, murder, felony excepted) shall be master of his own process" with full power to forgive and remit the offender either before or after judgment.[11] Pennsylvania at the beginning of this period followed the same rule de facto. The lack of an attorney general at most sessions led to victims' managing the case against defendants, with the corollary that prosecutions were dropped if victim and offender reached an accommodation.[12] Whereas this aspect increased the likelihood that certain crimes, like defamation, would not slip through the cracks, it also gave defendants opportunities to soothe the complainant. The accused could thus avoid the expense and uncertainty of trial in much the same way that litigants settled civil cases.

This mingling of civil case principles in criminal matters reflected overlapping legal categories in common law. Such civil actions as assault and battery, trover and conversion, trespass, and defamation all might be charged as crimes of violence, theft, breaking and entering, and criminal defamation, respectively. Quaker law reform's encouragement of accommodating civil disputes carried over to criminal disputes. Bethell Langstaffe's indictment of Richard Arnold and Arnold's tit-for-tat indictment of Langstaffe were turned over to an arbitrator, as was Samuel Harrison's charge against Elizabeth Tomlinson for felonious entry and theft of goods.[13] Though any case could be arbitrated, the parties usually reached an agreement directly, especially for crimes of violence. Edward Marshall, presented for assault and theft, and his accuser agreed to withdraw (discharge) the jury even after witnesses had begun testifying. Francis Stanfield and his servant, John Hurst, prosecuted each other for physical abuse, beatings, and drawing knives; when each promised to live in peace and quiet with the other, both cases ended. John Collins was presented for violently assaulting and robbing Gilbert Wheeler. Wheeler, stating that Collins had confessed to stealing ten pounds and a mare and had made full satisfaction, obtained the court's forbearance against any further prosecution, and Wheeler even paid the fees.[14] Such agreements, combined with cases when the victim simply failed to prosecute, made violent offenses next most likely after economic exploitation to be cleared or discharged (16.6 percent of violent charges).

Finally, the courts' summary power to require suspected criminals to post peace bonds accounted for the vast majority of discharges, although through a more formal process than other methods of clearing charges. By the terms of the recognizance, defendants had to appear at the next court of quarter sessions to determine whether they had observed the conditions of their bonds. Because Quaker justices hoped these peace bonds would prevent misconduct, discharging the bond and clearing the defendant of any prior accusations lodged meant that the recognizance had succeeded in its preventative function. This nontrial determination followed a ritualistic formula designed to impress recognizance defendants, who were primarily of lower status, with a public display of the power of the law even though no offense had occurred.

When the defendant personally appeared at the bar, the court would inquire if there was anyone or any evidence against the defendant. In the vast majority of cases, none appeared, the bond was discharged, and the defendant paid court fees. When a specific individual had requested the bond, such as when Seth Hill "Attest[ed] the peace" against John Neves, the court would ask if the complainant was still under "any fear or terrour." Hill replied that he was "not now afraid," so Neves was cleared.[15] Discharges and clearances accounted for 71.8 percent of all recognizances, while another 19.5 percent were not completed. This meant that only 8.7 percent of peace bonds failed to meet the system's goals. When someone did appear against the defendant, the court could send the case to the grand jury,[16] or it could hear the evidence on its own, continuing the summary procedure. When Richard Bromley still feared John Walker would harm him, the justices jailed Walker until additional security could be found, while George Peacock was discharged when the court's inquiries about what he had done with Martha Powell turned up witnesses who found her alive and well in Maryland.[17]

The essence of the recognizance procedure was this public performance, in which suspects confronted and dispelled suspicions against their character. Public confirmation of the court's power to stifle deviance was evident to the court-day crowd when these lower-status defendants, presumably now cured of their evil tendencies, were returned to normal, unbonded life after their command performance. That this display was the criminal system's goal can be seen in ten recognizances that became specific charges and convictions. In nine of those ten cases, the court forfeited the bond merely for nonappearance, regardless of any breach of the recognizance's substantive terms.[18] The court possessed the discretion to waive forfeiture and either continue the bond or order the sureties to bring the defendant in to save their bail, but courts rarely did so under their summary power regarding forfeitures.[19] These defendants' crime was failure to appear in the play.

One final method, the court order, resolved criminal cases without an in-court finding of guilt or innocence, without any statement of culpability or direct judgment on the defendant's conduct. Orders did not impose any immediate penalty, although failure to comply with an order could lead to sanctions. Some orders were jurisdictional, such as sending a murder or felony burglary to provincial court for trial because county courts were not competent in such matters. Other orders reflected a weakness in the law enforcement machinery, such as when the goods of those who had fled from justice were ordered valued and sold.[20] Most orders, however, reflected the court's desire to avoid criminal sanctions while still asserting immediate control of the situation. Ordinaries that had become "disorderly houses" were ordered closed. When neighbors felt threatened, Chester County's court ordered that Owen MacDaniel's guns be turned over to the sheriff. When Ledea Harris, a servant, accused John Pidcock, a previously convicted assaulter, of assaulting her, the court ordered her out of the house as a solution. Even testimony that Henry Tradway had wanted to hang or drown Thurla Sena merely produced an order that Tradway pay Sena twenty shillings for damages and post a peace bond.[21] Orders were summary assertions of authority that theoretically did not foreclose a subsequent trial but in reality ended the case.

The highest percentage of orders appeared in cases of alleged economic exploitation; 26.3 percent were so ended. Court interest in using orders for those higher-status defendants whose offense did not fall among the economic cases cleared, discharged, or not completed reflected the power relationship between defendant, victim, and court. Four masters in Chester County were indicted for abusing their servants, including holding or selling them unlawfully, beating them, and not allowing them "all things needfull and requisite." None suffered a conviction because all were merely ordered to correct their behavior or sell the servant.[22] Sometimes the public good was as lightly protected as servants were. Gilbert Wheeler, presented in Bucks County for "takeing extortion for ferrige," was merely ordered to appear at his own house on January 1 for a private session of the court to consider the charges. Turning or blocking the road, stopping a water course, ruining an estate, and even creating public nuisances merely resulted in orders that became fines only after noncompliance.[23]

These orders, often issued without the defendant's appearance, allowed defendants to avoid any public confrontation over their behavior and any finding of guilt. Economic cases were the only category of criminal charges in which orders disposed of more cases than did guilty verdicts. Though it was necessary to restrain the well-connected from extreme economic exploitation to maintain overall legitimacy, courts did not deem it necessary to impose the stigma of guilt on many of these upper-tier offenders, let alone punish them with fines, bonds, whipping, or prison. For those economic cases that could not be ignored or cleared, the legal system balanced the offense and the offender by demanding that only the situation, not the individual, be corrected. Overall, orders as well as other nontrial options of disposing of charges were results of choices made by both prosecution and defense, which were influenced by the type of charge, the amount of public exposure (or display), and the attributes of the defendant.

The Pattern of In-court Judgments

If prosecutorial discretion did not remove a case from the quarter sessions docket, defendants had to decide how to confront the accusation

in court. For some, the court removed any option by summarily finding the defendant guilty. The remainder had three basic options: defendants could plead guilty by either confessing or submitting to the court;
they could "traverse" the charge by pleading not guilty and demanding
a jury trial; or they could waive the traverse and refer the case to the
court for a bench judgment. The latter two options involved contesting
the charge, although in practice asking for a bench judgment was tan-
tamount to conceding guilt, since only two of forty-two bench cases resulted in acquittals. Factors influencing defendants' choices, especially
on whether to take a jury trial or submit to the court, included the type
of charge, the system's attitude toward those who contested versus those
who fought, and the likelihood of acquittal. No matter where the accused turned, at this point in the criminal justice decision tree, the odds
were against them.

From the standpoint of obtaining convictions, this system was less
than 50 percent effective, recording guilty judgments in only 48.4 percent of all cases begun (see table 33). This conviction rate was, however, produced not by trial acquittals (only 3.8 percent of all cases) but
by the high percentage of cases with nontrial disposal described earlier.
By way of comparison, the magistrate-driven systems of criminal justice in seventeenth-century Massachusetts and New Haven were extremely effective in garnering convictions; they had rates of well over 80 percent, sometimes over 90 percent, rates unmatched in contemporary
English courts. Conviction rates in seventeenth-century Rhode Island
and Devon and in eighteenth-century New York, Massachusetts, North
Carolina, and Surrey were similar to or less than the Delaware Valley's.
Although such comparisons are inexact, they suggest that the Delaware
Valley's reformed criminal justice system was not abnormally weak in
its prosecutions but rather fell in the middle of conviction rates in the
English-speaking world.[24]

Justices punished the accused summarily in over a third of all guilty
verdicts, leaving no choices for the defendant (see table 34). Some summary fines fell on those accused of serious offenses. Thomas Sidbottom's
crime never went before the grand jury, but the court fined him five
shillings on "suspition of fellony." Thomas Archer, after being confined
to prison, was summarily fined for assault and battery.[25] But 91.2 percent of summary proceedings focused on those accused of contempt or
morals offenses, particularly swearing and violations of liquor regulations (e.g., unlicensed taverns). West Jersey specifically expanded jus-

Table 34. Verdicts, by Accusation Type

	Uncontested		Contested			
Accusations	Summary Fine/Bond Forfeit	Pled Guilty/ Submitted	Bench Guilty	Jury Guilty	Not Guilty[a]	N
Morals	25.6%	51.2%	8.9%	10.7%	3.6%	168
Contempt	73.6	19.2	2.7	3.8	0.5	182
Civic	93.0	6.1	0.9	0.0	0.0	114
Authority	41.2	41.2	5.9	10.3	1.5	68
Recognizance	81.8	9.1	0.0	0.0	9.1	11
Property	3.0	39.0	4.0	37.0	17.0	100
Violence	3.7	52.4	6.1	24.4	13.4	82
Economic exploitation	6.7	40.0	13.3	26.7	13.3	15
Defamation	0.0	47.1	23.5	29.4	0.0	17
Other/unknown	2.5	65.0	12.5	2.5	17.5	40
Total percentage	31.5	39.7	6.5	15.0	7.3	100
N	194	244	40	92	45	615

a. All but two not guilty verdicts (43 of 45) were rendered by a jury; one property case and one violence case returned a not guilty verdict from the bench.

tices' power in 1683, allowing minor punishments against drunks and swearers without a court hearing, while Pennsylvania in 1700 gave justices similarly sweeping authority over misdemeanors with fines less than twenty shillings to limit unnecessary grand jury presentments that resulted in court fees larger than the fines imposed.[26] The effect of these enactments was to remove some morals offenses entirely from court-day consideration. Other offenses, especially civic contempt, were publicly proclaimed and summarily punished in court, yet often without the appearance of the defendant.

The in-court play for those upper-status defendants who filled the civic contempt docket was thus different from the recognizance procedures that also utilized justices' summary powers. Of those found guilty of civic contempt (primarily involving jurymen, constables, highway overseers, and tax collectors who failed to perform their duties), 93 percent were summarily fined (see table 34). In these instances, the charge, conviction, and punishment often fit on a single line of the records, because justices meted out justice to the always guilty. None accused of civic contempt achieved an in-court finding of not guilty; some might have even preferred to pay the fine to avoid having to serve. Yet these miscreants did not have to appear in court to hear their sentence or to pay their fine. These summary convictions avoided any humiliating "play" for these higher-status defendants while showing the crowd that those who avoided their duties to the court, whatever their social status, had to pay a price. (By way of contrast, the mere fact of avoiding the in-court play would result in a forfeiture of the recognizance for those generally lower-status defendants who had been forced to post such a bond.) Even more egregious but less frequent contempts of authority, such as calling the justices "two great rogues," swearing, spitting in a plaintiff's face, or refusing to doff one's hat, also resulted in fines levied through the court's summary power to preserve its dignity and authority.[27] For most contempt accusations, guilt and punishment were foregone conclusions, but for most defendants, that punishment was a fine, often imposed on them in their absence and paid out of public sight. Most upper-status defendants accused of contempt could avoid being part of the quarter sessions' spectacles.

Not all defendants accused of contempt of authority could avoid that confrontation, and not all wanted to. When there was verbal or physical abuse of the court or when the very authority of the legal system seemed undermined, the legal system foreclosed summary judgment and demanded an in-court resolution. The outcome of such confrontations then represented an interplay between the values the court felt threatened and the choices made by the defendant. If the victim of the abuse was a constable, very little seemed to be at stake for courts. In Chester County, Henry Barnes struck a constable, submitted meekly to the court, paid his court fees, and promised to behave. Edward Beazer beat and wounded a constable. He pled not guilty, was convicted by a jury, but was discharged with the same nonpenalty that Barnes was. The court also forced the seven who watched Beazer beat the constable and did nothing to promise to "do so no more."[28] Sheriffs, grand juries, and justices, in that order, received ascending levels of protection from insults, while attacks on the legitimacy of the government itself showed wide variations depending on changing political currents.[29] Justices, sanctioned by common law and local statute, exercised great discretion in penalizing the contemptuous, weighing the amount of submission and repentance shown by the defendant when important values had been scorned.

Defendants who confessed their contempt of authority and submitted to the mercy of the court (41.8 percent of the guilty verdicts) fared far better than those who publicly contested the charges or, even worse, repeated the original contempt. Isaac Brickshaw and Isaac Warner both accused Justice John Simcock of Chester County of being drunk. Brickshaw put himself on the mercy of king and governor and merely had to post security for good behavior; Warner went to trial, and, despite seven witnesses for him, a jury found him guilty, and the court fined him forty shillings. Henry Hastings and Robert Barber appeared before the same Chester County court for verbally abusing the court. Hastings, "humbley submiting himself to their mercey being sory for what he had said and done and desired to be forgiven," was discharged on his promise of good behavior; Barber, "upon his Examination he still persisting in Contempt," was fined twenty shillings.[30] In Burlington County, Mordecai Bowden escaped with only a published confession, stating that he was ashamed and sorry for groundlessly asserting in court that Justice Edward Hunloke was a cheat. Soon thereafter appeared Thomas French, who had impeached the authority of the whole West Jersey government and who stated that he believed his case had been determined beforehand. The court specifically offered French the chance to acknowledge his crime and submit, but he ignored its suggestion, and the jury found him guilty and proposed to fine him as much as five pounds. French, defiant to the end, stated that he "cannot pay it if it was but Two pence," whereupon the court doubled his fine to ten pounds.[31]

With contempt convictions virtually assured (only 1 trial acquittal out of 252 cases), why then were courts so interested in public retraction of the contempt that they initiated plea bargaining? More than any other crime, contempts of authority were rife with implications for the legitimacy of the legal system, since some contained explicit political messages that revealed bald-faced defiance. In 1698, Jeremiah Bates refused to appear for Gloucester County jury duty, claiming the sheriff was unlawful; a pattern of civil disobedience followed by constables and other veniremen, whose absence in the face of contempt citations ground that court to a halt.[32] The Anglican takeover of New Jersey in 1703 provoked not only Quaker absences from juries but also refusals to doff hats in court, a long-standing and well-known affront.[33] In the face of defiance, court-designed incentives to get such defendants to submit illustrated the fragility of legitimacy. Ironically, by plea bargaining, courts could reaffirm their authority through the public retraction of most contempts, thereby husbanding resources to use against the recalcitrant. There were limits on how far those of higher status could be disciplined by the law, limits that those in charge of the legal system well knew.

As with contempt of authority charges, the choice for defendants on charges that required in-court verdicts was whether to fight with all available weapons or to submit. A majority of defendants accused of property, economic exploitation, and defamation offenses chose to fight, contesting 58.0 percent, 53.3 percent, and 52.9 percent of verdicts, respectively (see table 34).[34] Only a minority of defendants charged with other offenses fought in court. Those charged with violence contested 43.9 percent of all verdicts, followed by morals (23.2 percent), recognizances (9.1 percent), and contempts (7.1 percent). Defendants accused of crimes of violence or crimes of immorality submitted to the court more than half the time. This choice, to fight or submit, probably did not depend on a defendant's evaluation of juries per se; there was no statistically significant difference in the probability of jury acquittals among the four most common charges. Juries acquitted 33 percent of defendants charged with violence or economic exploitation, 30 percent of property defendants, and 25 percent of morals defendants. In defamation cases, however, juries convicted every time (five times) that defendants called for them; defendants never won a contested defamation charge. Defamation was an offense that, while rarely prosecuted, aroused both sides' emotions to the point that rational evaluation and compromise resolution of the case became unlikely. Overall, once the case made it to trial, the average defendant chose from among various options, none of which was likely to lead to a not guilty verdict. Explaining the different choices defendants made requires an examination of the signals sent by the legal culture and the attributes of defendants who accepted or rejected such messages.

For some defendants, their skin color dictated their choices. In 1700, Pennsylvania's "Act for the Trial of Negroes" removed black defendants, whether slave or free, from the jury system and sent them to a summary process before two justices and six substantial freeholders. That same law made rape of a white woman by a black man punishable by death, made attempted rape of a white woman by a black man punishable by castration, and forbade blacks from carrying arms or congregating in groups larger than four. In Bucks County, attempted rape charges against the "negro Peter" resulted in his imprisonment until this special panel could meet, while the white servant Thomas Yates, charged with the same crime, remained at large until the next court and received only a twenty shilling fine and nine months added to his service time.[35] In ten of eleven completed cases in which the defendant was identified as black, convictions followed. Even when blacks invoked the law to protect themselves, they were not believed. John Gilbert, accused by a "negro girl" of begetting her child, denied the accusation, and when she became confused in her testimony, the court released him and whipped her. Mingo, a Burlington County slave, reported his wife was raped by John Neves and testified that he saw Neves lying on top of her and heard her cry out. Neves denied the charge and produced an alibi, and, in a bench judgment, the justices ordered Mingo whipped thirty stripes for defamation.[36]

One choice all but seven criminal defendants made was to represent themselves in their defense. Although a king's attorney would, over time, take increasing responsibility for prosecutions, defendants did not employ counselors, and the legal system's antagonism to lawyers did not encourage them to do so. Burlington County's attitude toward defense lawyers was inflexibly antagonistic. At the end of lengthy trial testimony, the accused murderer John Shawe asked that "hee may have Counsell, being ignorant in the Lawe." Burlington County's justices replied that "if hee want to know any particuler in Lawe touching the premisses, hee shall be informed; but if it be in matter of Fact, Counsell against the King cannot be allowed him."[37] The few defendants who obtained counsel did not rely on knowledgeable friends but instead chose such prominent lawyers as David Lloyd, Thomas Clark, and George Lowther. Regardless of any legal advice a defendant might have received beforehand, almost all came to the bar alone.

Just as civil disputants integrated the messages the legal culture sent by not contesting the bulk of their cases, so too did criminal defendants respond to signals. The Quakers' legal system had rejected the harsh deterrence of English law. The law-reform tradition that introduced less draconian criminal punishments authorized courts to encourage all defendants to follow the example of the contemptuous and reconcile themselves with the legal elite. Defendants had rights: they could demand a jury trial in all criminal cases; they could excuse up to thirty-five jurymen on peremptory challenges, with additional challenges for cause; they could require their accuser's name to be placed in the presentment; they could call witnesses and have them fined if they did not appear; and they could not be convicted without the testimony of two witnesses.[38] Yet exercising these procedural rights carried risks, because justices had discretion over the penalty when the statute provided a choice (e.g., between whipping and a fine). Justices also had common-law powers to remit part or all of the punishment, but only if they were so inclined.[39] What John Murrin found for seventeenth-century Massachusetts held true for the Delaware Valley's first settlers: "To ask for a jury signaled a lack of contrition, a dangerous attitude to assume before the magistrates, especially if the jury found the person guilty."[40]

Courts sent unmistakable messages to encourage defendants to submit humbly to the court's judgment. Burlington County's grand jury presented William Jeanes and John Keene jointly for an undisclosed crime; Keene pled guilty, while Jeanes pled not guilty and requested a jury trial. After hearing four witnesses, the jury found both guilty. Though legal liability was identical, Keene, "who referred himselfe to the Bench," was fined five pounds. Jeanes, whom the bench specifically remarked on for requesting the jury, was sentenced to be "whipt till thy body be bloody."[41] Subsequent Burlington County defendants showed they had received this message. Thomas Peachee admitted that he had impregnated his wife before their marriage and was to choose between a fine and having his wife whipped, but "upon his further submission, the Bench remitt their sentence." Henry Tuckness, who at first wanted to plead innocent to his indictment, "Submitts to the Court on Mature Consideration" and was merely fined. At the same session, the court lauded William Bayley for his "Mature Consideration" in his submission, while later, Mary and William Cole escaped with a minimal fine after retracting their desire to stand trial.[42] Burlington County explicitly sought a defendant's public humiliation as part of the Quaker and law-reform goal of reformation, as part of the reinforcement of the majesty of the law by showing mercy toward suitable defendants, and as part of a symbolic exercise designed to convince spectators of both the guilt of the defendant and the legitimacy of the punishers.[43]

Other Delaware Valley courts sent the same signal. In Bucks County, a jury found Randolph Smallwood guilty of defaming Rachel Milner and fined him ten pounds; nine months later, Martha Wheeler submitted to a similar defamation charge and was fined only five shillings. Defendants who swore or cursed in Bucks County would be fined five shillings on submission but would be sentenced to pay fifteen shillings or serve fifteen days hard labor after a contested court judgment.[44] In assault cases in Chester County before 1700 (when criminal penalties stiffened), those who submitted merely had to promise not to assault anyone again, while those convicted by jury trials faced imprisonment or fines up to sixty-three shillings. Getting drunk and abusing court officers gave Chester County courts a golden opportunity to implant publicly the benefits of submission. Jeremiah Collett was fined five pounds for assaulting the undersheriff and for being insolent in court; when Collett threw himself on the mercy of the court, the justices remitted 90 percent of his fine. Samuel Baker's thirty shilling fine for drunken abuse of Justice John Simcock was entirely remitted when Baker acknowledged his guilt and submitted.[45] Justices encouraged submission to reinforce their goals of the deviant's repentance and reform. With such a public display of their power to humble and forgive, justices also reinforced court authority in the minds of the spectators. Defendants, especially in violence, morals, and contempt of authority charges, grasped the bait of lesser sentences, because for many it was the best option of a bad lot.

Criminal juries thus played a smaller role in determining legal liability than did civil juries; 12.3 percent of all criminal cases utilized a jury, compared with 15.5 percent of civil cases. This low level of jury usage was constant across the region,[46] but jury usage did vary according to the type of accusation. Property accusations brought out the most juries (36 percent of all cases) and the highest percentage of all verdicts returned by juries (53 percent). Not coincidentally, sentencing guidelines for property offenses gave justices the least discretion, thus providing less incentive for the defendant to submit. Law reform provided for multiple restitution (two- to four-fold, depending on the type of good stolen) in simple cases of conversion or receiving stolen goods, with whipping added in cases of larceny and robbery.[47] That courts did not remit whipping even for submissive defendants and that defendants could rarely afford the high restitution awards undoubtedly contributed to defendants' decision to take a chance on a jury trial; they had little to lose.

In contrast, morals offenders demanded jury verdicts in only one-seventh of their trials (9.9 percent of all cases). This low rate was probably due to a combination of legal signals and an evaluation of the evidence against the defendant. Statutes, passed by Quakers, reflected Quaker beliefs on the need to discipline sinners through legal processes.[48] Quakers' goal for sinners, as can be seen in the next section, was to employ a ritual of guilt, humiliation, and reintegration of the deviant into good standing. Defendants accused of sexual offenses usually faced daunting evidence (e.g., a bastard or a very premature child following a marriage in fornication cases) and, with that evidence, long odds against acquittal (only one acquittal out of twenty-four contested sexual morality charges). With a guilty verdict virtually certain, submission would fit the Quaker model and perhaps lead to a lesser sentence, in line with ideals of proportionality. For instance, when married couples confessed to clandestine marriages or premarital sex, they were given small fines or no fines.[49] Other morals offenses, such as selling liquor without a license, swearing, or public drunkenness, were less threatening than sexual offenses. Such crimes required less public humiliation and involved many summary judgments or submissions, followed by reduced penalties. The interaction of charge, Quaker interest in symbolic results, and the defendant's evaluation of the evidence and the probable penalty reduced the likelihood of jury trials on morals offenses.

If a case went to a jury, the jury's decision was final and unimpeachable, regardless of the reasoning or procedural irregularities that lay behind the verdict. In thirty-three of the ninety-two guilty verdicts handed down by juries, there was no record that the required two witnesses testified against the defendant at the trial. Yet unlikely acquittals could emerge from a jury's discretion. The jury trying John Rawlins, accused of stealing his master's mare, heard three witnesses testify that Rawlins was headed to Boston on the mare when he was captured. Nonetheless, the jury found him not guilty, even after the court urged jurors to reconsider their verdict, because they did not wish to convict Rawlins of a felony. Similarly, Amos Nichols and Andrew Friend, accused of armed robbery by Thomas Howell and two others, were able to introduce two witnesses' hearsay testimony that impeached Howell's identification of them as the robbers, thus gaining an acquittal. Despite damning testimony from five witnesses, a Chester County jury acquitted the ex-justice John Bristow of marking a horse that was not his.[50] William Penn's jury experience and precedent meant that jurors could not be punished by justices unhappy with the verdict except in the rare case when their decision rested on a coin toss.

Nevertheless, courts could influence juries with interpretations regarding the charge. Such an intervention undoubtedly saved the life of Jannett Monro, who was accused of killing her child. After six witnesses testified to the color and condition of the child's body, the king's attorney invoked an act of Parliament. He argued that the law required the jurors to return a guilty verdict unless the defendant could prove the child was stillborn, which Monro had asserted without corroborating evidence. The court, however, rejected this law as "Ad Terrorem" (designed to terrify, i.e., too harsh) and charged the jury to find her guilty only "if they finde what has beene Evidenced is proofe Sufficient of the Prisoner's murdering or killing the Child." Faced with only circumstantial evidence, the jury acquitted her, whereas a British jury might have convicted her because of the different standard of proof.[51] Jury trials, like Munro's and Harry's, were highly visible and highly risky gambles for many defendants who realistically had no other option. That Munro and Harry both escaped the gallows, one through acquittal and one through crowd intervention after conviction, indicated that Delaware Valley criminal justice responded to many sources of opinion, even in the most heinous crimes. The result was a legal system that achieved its goals, procedurally and substantively, to reach what Quakers believed to be the purposes of criminal justice.

The Defendants' Experiences

While the legal system framed the questions posed for the criminally accused, it was defendants who had to live with the answers. Regardless of the charge, defendants undoubtedly favored some other resolution than a guilty verdict; if the outcome was to be guilty, defendants undoubtedly favored a resolution with the least penalty and the least publicity possible. These postulates allow an evaluation of whether the disposition of criminal cases left different groups with different experiences in the criminal justice system. First, in the most general terms, did individuals in different status, wealth, power, or religious groups experience statistically different outcomes? Second, of those convicted, was the method of finding guilt different for those in different groups? Finally, did defendants facing the same charge receive different treatment that related to their status, wealth, power, or religion? This last question holds the type of offense constant to examine whether, for instance, high officers received the same treatment that lesser officers and nonofficers did when they were accused of property crimes. The answers to these questions will reveal the role of criminal justice in the overall legitimizing of the Quaker legal system.

First, most attributes had no statistically significant relation to the distribution of criminal outcomes (see table 35). Gender, landownership, occupation, wealth as measured by inventory, and recidivism played

Table 35. Demography of Criminal Defendants and Outcomes

Attributes	Without Trial				Court Verdicts		
	Not Completed	Pretrial Cleared	Discharged	Ordered	Guilty	Not Guilty	N
Total n	230	98	144	90	570	45	1177
Percentage of total population	19.5	8.3	12.2	7.6	48.4	3.8	100
Male	19.4%	8.3%	12.9%	7.3%	48.1%	4.0%	1079
Female	21.4	8.2	5.1	11.2	52.0	2.0	98
Chi-square probability = .179							
Quakers	22.6%	9.1%	11.1%	8.6%	45.4%	3.1%	350
Non-Quakers	17.8	7.1	13.3	7.0	51.1	3.6	691
Chi-square probability = .209							
Quaker leaders	30.9%	7.2%	2.1%	10.3%	44.3%	5.2%	97
Average Quakers	19.4	9.9	14.6	7.9	45.9	2.4	253
Chi-square probability = .009 (match included non-Quakers)							
Landowners	20.2%	8.6%	11.0%	8.1%	48.0%	4.2%	744
Nonlandowners	18.5	7.9	14.3	6.9	49.2	3.2	433
Chi-square probability = .523							
Occupations (males only)[a]							
Farmer	17.8%	9.0%	10.0%	9.4%	50.8%	3.1%	321
Artisan	21.2	6.1	11.4	5.3	49.2	6.8	132
Farmer-artisan	27.1	10.2	6.8	13.6	42.4	0.0	59

							n
Merchant	50.0	0.0	30.0	0.0	20.0	0.0	10
Self-described gentry	26.2	7.1	9.5	7.1	40.5	9.5	42
Servant/slave/laborer	15.9	9.4	12.2	5.6	52.3	4.7	107

Chi-square probability = .113[b]

1693 Pennsylvania tax assessment (in pounds)

							n
100+	20.0%	2.5%	5.0%	27.5%	45.0%	0.0%	40
50–99	25.5	0.0	16.4	3.6	45.5	9.1	55
1–49	19.2	1.9	12.5	5.8	57.7	2.9	104

Chi-square probability = .002[b]

Inventoried wealth (in pounds)

							n
500+	28.1%	3.5%	12.2%	8.8%	40.4%	7.0%	57
100–499	20.1	12.6	6.9	4.4	51.6	4.4	159
1–99	26.7	10.0	1.7	11.7	43.3	6.7	60

Chi-square probability = .113[b]

Legal roles

							n
High officer	27.7%	6.9%	6.9%	12.6%	41.5%	4.4%	159
Lesser officer	18.7	8.5	14.6	6.7	48.7	2.9	316
Nonofficer	18.1	8.6	12.4	7.0	49.9	4.1	702

Chi-square probability = .024

Number of accusations

							n
1	19.4%	8.6%	12.4%	8.1%	49.1%	2.6	583
2+	18.8	8.4	12.3	7.5	47.7	5.3	570

Chi-square probability = .345

---

a. The category "other" has been omitted; criminal analysis will use only six occupational categories.
b. May not be a valid test because too many of the cross-tabulation cells have expected n values of less than 5.

no statistically significant role in determining which of the six outcomes a defendant experienced. Even being a Quaker rather than a non-Quaker did not materially affect the outcome. Three attributes—tax level, officeholding status, and Quaker leadership—were statistically related to certain outcomes. Those whose property was assessed at a hundred pounds and above in the 1693 Pennsylvania tax disproportionately received orders to end their charges.[52] High officeholders also disproportionately were able to obtain orders to end their cases, and their cases were disproportionately not completed; they also received fewer discharges. Similarly, Quaker leaders disproportionately saw their cases fall between the cracks and not completed, disproportionately received orders, and disproportionately avoided discharges.

The groups' different experiences did not occur because of statistically significant differences in their chances of being found guilty. Although higher-status groups had slightly lower rates of guilty verdicts, those differences were not statistically significant. In fact, a comparison of guilty judgments and all other completed outcomes (lumping all not guilty verdicts with all pretrial results in one category and guilty verdicts in the other) revealed that no attribute gave a defendant any significantly better chance of avoiding a guilty verdict (see table 36). Neither status, wealth, power, nor religion significantly altered one's overall

Table 36. Distribution of Completed Criminal Cases, by Defendant Attributes

Attributes	Guilty	Other Outcome	*N*
Total *n*	570	377	947
Percentage of total	60.2	39.8	100
Male	59.7%	40.3%	870
Female	66.2	33.8	77
Chi-square probability = .258			
Quakers	58.7%	41.3%	567
Non-Quakers	62.3	37.7	271
Chi-square probability = .319			
Quaker leaders	64.2%	35.8%	67
Average Quakers	56.9	43.1	204
Chi-square probability = .345 (match included non-Quakers)			

Landowners	60.1%	39.9%	594
Nonlandowners	60.3	39.7	353

Chi-square probability = .942

Occupations (males only)[a]

Farmer	61.7%	38.3%	264
Artisan	62.5	37.5	104
Farmer-artisan	58.1	41.9	43
Merchant	40.0	60.0	5
Self-described gentry	54.8	45.2	31
Servant/slave/laborer	62.2	37.8	90

Chi-square probability = .878

1693 Pennsylvania tax assessment (in pounds)

100+	56.3%	43.8%	32
50–99	61.0	39.0	41
1–49	71.4	28.6	84

Chi-square probability = .235

Inventoried wealth (in pounds)

500+	56.1%	43.9%	41
100–499	64.6	35.4	127
1–99	59.1	40.9	44

Chi-square probability = .573

Legal roles

High officer	57.4%	42.6%	115
Lesser officer	59.9	40.1	257
Nonofficer	60.9	39.1	575

Chi-square probability = .781

Number of accusations

1	60.9%	39.2%	470
2+	58.8	41.3	463

Chi-square probability = .512

---

a. The category "other" has been omitted to ensure that chi-square is a valid test. Criminal analysis will use only six occupational categories.

chances of being found guilty. At the macrolevel, once a case required a verdict, this system showed no biases. It was in the pretrial experiences that bias appeared. This pattern reveals that high officers and Quaker leaders avoided in-court verdicts by obtaining orders and by somehow having their cases not completed. They also rarely had to obtain a discharge in front of the court for any sort of suspected offense that might have occasioned a peace bond or a trial. Their experience within the court system and the power structure of the Delaware Valley suggests that they knew how to make their encounters with criminal law a little less painful and a little less public; they knew how to divert the process before a verdict became necessary.

Second, although no group disproportionately escaped guilty verdicts, there were significant differences in *how* groups were found guilty. Defendants who were male, owned land, achieved high or lesser office, were farmers, or were Quakers or Quaker leaders disproportionately experienced summary guilty verdicts, primarily in the form of fines (see table 37). These same defendants disproportionately avoided humiliating in-court guilty pleas and submissions to the bench for mercy. Their expe-

Table 37. Distribution of Guilty Verdicts, by Defendant Attributes

Attributes	Summary Fine/ Bond Forfeit	Pled Guilty/ Submitted	Bench Guilty	Jury Guilty	N
Total *n*	194	244	40	92	570
Percentage of total	34.0	42.8	7.0	16.1	100
Male	36.6%	40.9%	6.4%	16.2%	519
Female	7.8	62.8	13.7	15.7	51
Chi-square probability = .000					
Quakers	48.4%	33.3%	6.9%	11.3%	159
Non-Quakers	23.2	50.4	7.9	18.4	353
Chi-square probability = .000					
Quaker leaders	55.8%	23.3%	9.3%	11.6%	43
Average Quakers	45.7	37.1	6.0	11.2	116
Chi-square probability = .000 (match included non-Quakers)					
Landowners	42.6%	35.6%	6.2%	15.7%	357
Nonlandowners	19.7	54.9	8.5	16.9	213
Chi-square probability = .000					
Occupations (males only)[a]					
Farmer	45.4%	34.4%	4.9%	15.3%	163
Artisan	33.9	44.6	4.6	16.9	65
Farmer-artisan	44.0	28.0	8.0	20.0	25
Merchant	50.0	50.0	0.0	0.0	2

Self-described gentry	41.2	23.5	23.5	11.8	17
Servant/slave/laborer	10.7	57.1	12.5	19.6	56

Chi-square probability = .004[b]

1693 Pennsylvania tax assessment (in pounds)

100+	44.4%	38.9%	5.6%	11.1%	18
50–99	36.0	40.0	8.0	16.0	25
1–49	46.7	30.0	5.0	18.3	60

Chi-square probability = .933[b]

Inventoried wealth (in pounds)

500+	52.2%	21.7%	8.7%	17.4%	23
100–499	46.3	28.1	7.3	18.3	82
1–99	34.6	42.3	7.7	15.4	26

Chi-square probability = .807[b]

Legal roles

High officer	51.5%	33.3%	4.6%	10.6%	66
Lesser officer	44.8	35.1	7.1	13.0	134
Nonofficer	26.0	48.0	7.4	18.6	350

Chi-square probability = .000

Number of accusations

1	32.5%	48.3%	5.6%	13.6%	286
2+	34.6	37.9	8.5	19.1	272

Chi-square probability = .049

a. The category "other" has been omitted; criminal analysis will use only six occupational categories.
b. May not be a valid test because too many of the cross-tabulation cells have expected *n* values of less than 5.

rience of guilt with minimal public confrontation was directly opposite that of women, nonlandowners, nonofficers, servants/slaves/laborers, and non-Quakers. These lower-status groups disproportionately chose to submit to the court to resolve their charges and had relatively fewer summary judgments and fines. When the public saw a defendant in the dock confessing a crime and engaging in the desired repentance that would lead to rehabilitation, that person was most likely from the lower tiers of Delaware Valley society.

Observe carefully how this criminal justice system operated. All groups faced criminal charges at roughly the same rate, although certain charges fell more often on some groups than on others. All groups faced roughly the same likelihood of guilty verdicts. At this level, justice seemed to be blind. Yet in terms of the power of the law to humble a defendant into public surrender and in terms of the defendants the crowd saw (as opposed to heard of) being brought to account, these Quaker courts focused on those of lesser status. Those of higher status who were found summarily guilty paid their fines without necessarily even being seen on court day. It was how a defendant was found guilty that differed. There was a double message—all were vulnerable to criminal prosecution, but some were more vulnerable to public humiliation than others.

What of defendants' final option, to fight the charges with a trial? Because jury trials were the most involved, the most public, and the most sensational of in-court fights, we should look at which defendants chose juries. For most attributes, there was no statistically significant difference in the preference for jury trials. However, three critical attributes—religion, officeholding status, and recidivism—had an impact on whether defendants chose jury trials. Quakers disproportionately avoided jury trials, while non-Quakers disproportionately sought them out, despite the dramatic way Quakers packed the juries. Similarly, recidivists and nonofficers disproportionately used juries, while high officers and one-time criminal defendants avoided them. Those of lower status, wealth, power, or religion thus called for juries as often or more often than those better positioned in this society.[53] These results suggest that defendants with otherwise good reasons to fight the charge were not afraid that the socioeconomic composition of juries would bias the result against them.

Criminal juries seemed to live up to this implicit vote of confidence that non-Quakers and nonofficers gave them. An analysis of criminal jury verdicts shows no statistically significant difference for any defendant attribute in the distribution of not guilty verdicts.[54] Despite the fact that Quakers and Quaker leaders overwhelmingly dominated the jury pools, they appear to have lived up to their oath to "well and truly try the issue" and did not overtly slant their verdicts to protect Friends.[55] This even-handedness paralleled the results of civil jury trials and matched the Quaker ideal of "good men," who, by their fair decisions, could imbue the regime with legitimacy. Jury verdicts were the most visible justice the crowd could see; any perversion of jury process, such as the Bucks County jury's deciding the case with a coin flip, had to be punished severely.[56] That even apparently fair-minded juries were not used very often suggests that factors other than the jury pool determined defendants' choices: their evaluation of the case against them, the chances for prosecutorial discretion ending the case, and the legal culture that pushed for submission.

Finally, when faced with the same type of charges, did different defendants receive different justice? A more focused picture of any bias in the system emerges by comparing the verdicts for, for example, Quakers and non-Quakers charged with morals offenses. Since the number of cases for a particular charge divided by the different groups among the outcomes often gives such small numbers for each box of the cross-tabulation that chi-square analysis is not valid, the following conclusions are statistically speculative, except where noted.

As in table 36, two categories of completed cases—guilty and other outcomes—were matched against the various attributes to test whether certain groups were found disproportionately guilty of certain charges. Most charges followed the overall pattern; that is, for particular charges, findings of guilt were not statistically skewed to favor certain groups over others. In three match-ups, however, the results did show a statistically significant bias; the groups favored were the Delaware Valley's legal and religious favorites. In property cases, high officers and lesser officers disproportionately avoided being judged guilty (chi-square probability = .022). High officers suffered guilty verdicts half as often as nonofficers (37.5 percent to 75.6 percent), while lesser officers fell in between, with 55.6 percent found guilty in property accusations. An examination of how those results occurred reveals that much of the variance was because defendants opted for juries. High officers chose to fight property charges more often with jury trials (54.6 percent of all charges) and never submitted; lesser officers and nonofficers used juries less frequently and submitted more often.[57] Those juries found high officers guilty in only 33.3 percent of the cases, as opposed to jury findings of guilt for lesser officers at 69.2 percent and for nonofficers at 74.3 percent. At every branch of this decision tree, officeholding status influenced the path and the result of property charges; high officers came out ahead.

Similarly, Quakers were significantly less likely to be convicted on two other charges. Quakers were found guilty in only 50 percent of the violence cases, compared with a 71.8 percent guilty rate for non-Quakers; in morals cases, Quakers were guilty 65.9 percent of the time, non-Quakers 81.7 percent.[58] Within the Society of Friends, Quakers and Quakers leaders suffered guilty verdicts in violence charges at virtually the same rate (49.4 percent for leaders, 52.0 percent for average Quakers), but in morals charges, 100 percent of Quaker leader defendants were found guilty, compared with only 60.5 percent of average Quakers. For morals offenses, perhaps Quaker justices and juries expected meetings to discipline a Quaker deviant who was not prominent, thus backing off from imposing a kind of double jeopardy. Courts also made certain that Quaker leaders, who might avoid discipline in the meeting through their influence, received legal punishment. Regardless of the reason, this legal system clearly skewed results in favor of high officers in cases involving property and in favor of Quakers in cases involving violence and morals.

Most charges and most attributes did not show this statistically significant bias, although the patterns are suggestive of certain sorts of manipulations. The tendency of higher-status defendants to end their charges before they led to an in-court confrontation persisted across four of the five most common charges (see table 38). Quakers and Quaker leaders avoided in-court verdicts more often than non-Quakers did in civic contempt, contempt of authority, accusations of violence, and morals offenses. Quakers, for instance, were twice as likely as non-Quakers to end morals charges before a formal verdict. Similarly, high officers avoided in-court verdicts more often than lesser officers and nonofficers for charges of civic contempt, contempt of authority, violence, and morals offenses. The only charge that both Quakers and high officers did not end more often before a verdict—property charges—saw both groups achieving significantly higher acquittal rates.[59] That this pattern persisted across charges reinforces the inference that higher-status defendants could disproportionately avoid the possibility of the humiliation of an in-court guilty verdict, and, when they could not do so, they could more often gain acquittals.

Other types of defendants also received skewed results when faced with certain charges. Women defendants saw violence and property accusations disposed of before verdicts more often than men did, suggesting that women's theft and aggression posed less need for public condemnation than the same acts done by men. The two sexes did, however, have nearly identical rates of guilt and pretrial outcomes in morals cases, the most often charged crime against women. While on the surface these outcomes appeared similar for men and women, the types of guilty verdicts varied greatly. In morals cases, women disproportionately submitted to the court (73.3 percent for women versus 48.5 percent for men), while men were disproportionately fined (31.1 percent for men

Table 38. Cases Completed without In-court Verdict

Attributes	Contempt Civic	Contempt Authority	Property	Violence	Morals
Total *n*	124	80	121	115	215
Male (%)	8.1	15.6	16.7	27.8	21.6
Female (%)	—	0.0	23.1	42.9	23.1
Quakers (%)	12.9	17.4	13.3	35.3	31.8
Non-Quakers (%)	0.0	14.9	17.4	22.5	15.7
Quaker leaders (%)	20.8	33.3	16.7	33.3	0.0
Average Quakers (%)	8.7	11.8	10.0	40.0	36.8
Landowners (%)	0.0	14.0	17.5	23.9	24.8
Nonlandowners (%)	9.4	17.4	17.2	35.4	17.4
Occupations (males only)[a]					
Farmer (%)	7.8	13.0	28.1	13.0	23.8
Artisan (%)	8.3	7.7	12.5	10.0	17.7
Farmer-artisan (%)	15.4	33.3	0.0	60.0	37.5
Merchant (%)	0.0	0.0	0.0	100	50.0
Self-described gentry (%)	0.0	0.0	33.3	28.6	0.0
Servant/slave/laborer (%)	20.0	25.0	8.7	27.3	23.8
Legal roles					
High officer (%)	12.9	25.0	12.5	36.4	42.1
Lesser officer (%)	11.3	11.5	33.3	26.1	15.4
Nonofficer (%)	0.0	14.3	12.8	28.4	21.5

a. The category "other" has been omitted; criminal analysis will use only six occupational categories.

versus 6.7 percent for women). These submissions occurred despite the fact that submission did not often reduce the penalty for morals offenses, which usually involved fines for men and whipping for women.[60] The difference may lie in men's access to financial resources that single women accused of fornication might not have had; perhaps only men had the money to pay when given a choice between a whipping and a fine.[61] Alternatively, women's sexuality might have been seen as more threatening than men's, requiring a public court-day condemnation.[62] Women, who were unlikely to be recidivists, sought to perform the Quaker ritual of repentance in order to pass through the legal gauntlet with the least amount of public humiliation and the most rapid reintegration. Since a jury trial would involve even greater publicity, would not likely lead to an acquittal, and would probably result in the same sentence, a submission to the court on a morals charge was a woman's best option.

Defendants who owned land and belonged to certain occupation groups were more likely to try to secure better deals from the courts. Of the three most common occupation groups (where a substantial number faced each charge), farmer-artisans, an occupation previously noted to be preferred by Quakers, disproportionately avoided in-court guilty judgments. On civic contempt, contempt of authority, violence, and morals charges, these farmer-artisans succeeded in avoiding verdicts far more often than either farmers or artisans did (see table 38). While landowners showed no greater talent than nonlandowners for obtaining pretrial settlements, they did follow different in-court strategies for property and morals charges. In property charges, the landed disproportionately refused to submit to the court, while the nonlanded disproportionately threw themselves on the mercy of the court. In morals charges, the landed were fined significantly more often than the nonlanded, while again the nonlanded found it in their best interests to submit.[63] Defendants, facing the same charges, chose among their legal options in ways that revealed the impact of social power in this legal system.

The experience of criminal defendants in the Delaware Valley and how that experience appeared to the court-day audience reflected the old maxim "where you stand depends on where you sit." Those who sat well in this society stood on ground designed to minimize their public exposure, even when the integrity of the system demanded their prosecution and conviction. Through legal and extralegal strategies—getting their charges to fall between the cracks, obtaining orders instead of verdicts, or receiving fines instead of having to submit in court—the upper tier of this society could reduce the risk of public humiliation. The "good men" would be held accountable for their behavior but could avoid the harshest penalties. Those who sat somewhat lower in this society found themselves forced to stand in open court to resolve the charge. Often their best option was humble submission in a court-day drama that fit Quaker ideals of criminal rehabilitation and reinforced court authority. Those who sat in the audience saw the high and mighty charged as often as the lowly; they heard the high and mighty convicted as often as the lowly. But they *saw*, parading before the court, defendants from the lower levels of society disproportionately forced to confront accusations of their deviance in face-to-face encounters. Such apparently even-handed criminal justice, especially when combined with a social control message, could not help but reinforce the legitimacy of Quaker "good men" enforcing Quaker "good laws." It was what—and whom—the crowd could not see that gave "good men" their advantage.

Processing Deviants through the Quaker Meeting

If the Quaker legal system sought to induce submission and the public humiliation of defendants as a means to reinforce court legitimacy, Quaker meetings sought such confession and public repentance as ends in themselves. Those accused of offenses against Quaker norms (as described in chapter 5) had to satisfy the meeting by "clearing the truth" or else face disownment. The process was deceptively simple. All Quakers as part of their duty of care were responsible for confronting transgressors privately to persuade them to reform. Delaware Valley's meetings institutionalized oversight after 1695 (even before London's Yearly Meeting had advocated it) by designating overseers, who were to visit each family monthly to care for sinners and to ensure conformity. Probably most offenses were handled at this private level and went unrecorded. If an individual resisted these suggestions, the monthly meeting would then appoint a special committee to give the miscreant "tender council" in a "labor of love"; this appointment produced the first record of the 416 disciplinary cases considered here. The committee sought to persuade the deviant to appear at a subsequent meeting, where he or she would admit fault, condemn it, and submit a written confession for the meeting's consideration. As with differences, no judgment regarding a deviant passed by default—at least one face-to-face confrontation was deemed essential to the process. To strengthen its arguments with the miscreant, a committee could investigate and gather evidence from witnesses, but guilt was not an issue. Only one accused, Phineas Pemberton, was ever cleared of charges.[64] The only real issue was the sinner's attitude toward the offense and toward the meeting.

Most accused exhibited the proper confession, repentance, and humiliation without much prompting. Nathaniel Lamplue confessed at his first opportunity that he had been "insnared or overtaken in drink . . . to my shame"; Richard Farr took his admonishment to attend meetings "very kindly" and promised to be more careful. Giving "good satisfaction" to the meeting through self-condemnation became formulaic in expressions of sorrow and repentance. Edward Boulton's self-condemnation for having sex with his maid used typical euphemisms—"want of watchfulness," "unseemly and immodest words and actions," "unruly spirit," "wishes to withstand such temptations in the future." Anne Knight got married without her meeting's permission; she acknowledged that she had "done much contrary to the truth," but her paper had to be rewritten when the meeting found it "somewhat short." Detailed descriptions of offenses provided the linguistic framework for the humble acknowledgment of fault. Thomas Withers said that members of the Concord Monthly Meeting were "cheats" but later acknowledged that he himself was the cheat.[65] When the meeting found the confession satisfactory and the attitude proper, the disciplined had cleared the "Truth," and the case ended with no further sanction.

For those whose attitudes and responses were unsatisfactory, Quaker discipline proceeded by reiterating until the accused either adopted the proper attitude or was disowned. Meetings meticulously examined the self-condemnation papers to see if they were "pretending Love" or giving "quibbling answers." If so, the disciplined had to rewrite the paper, which was often redrafted by committees appointed by the meeting, so that the response would be "fully pertinent."[66] Such rewrites provided future miscreants with examples of acceptable formulas for self-condemnation. If the accused continued to resist signing an acceptable paper, the meeting engaged in "long labors" to persuade them to submit and avoid disownment. For example, John Eastborne had "disorderly and unfairly cast [Ann Hanby] off" from their engagement and then had "rendered her ridiculous" in a defamatory speech. Eastborne, confronted privately, was "hard relying" and "leaning on his own judgment," which provoked meeting intervention. He appeared at the next meeting with a certificate from Ann Hanby clearing him, but because he remained "in his former mind," the meeting continued the case to seek his humiliation. Over a year later, Eastborne produced a paper of self-condemnation; the meeting found it "not full enough to clear truth" and appointed a committee to draw up a satisfactory paper, which Eastborne then signed to end the matter.[67] The length of this case was hardly anomalous. Meetings pursued a dozen cases for a year or more, including seven years on one couple's "disorderly carriage." The goal was to have even the worst sinners repent and promise to amend their behavior in front of the meeting.

Though the couple accused of disorderly carriage was "hard and obstinate," they ultimately submitted.[68] For the accused who refused to confess and be humbled, meetings had some choice words. Francis Harrison's paper "came not from a right motion," and the meeting wished to send Harrison's attitude "to the Pitt from whence it came." Humphrey Johnson's spirit—"headdy highminded, unruly, willful, stubborn"—had treated the meeting's labor "like water spilt upon the Ground trampling itt underfoot turning like the Dogg to the vomit again." Meetings also condemned passive resistance, as in the case of John Vernon, whose promised amendment of his life was discovered to have been "ineffectual" fifteen months later.[69] While recalcitrants might have salved their pride and avoided humiliation, disownment provided meetings with a suitably humiliating substitute treatment for those beyond the pale. When a meeting abandoned this reiterative process as hopeless, it ordered a paper of condemnation and disownment drafted. This litany of sins was then read to the offender and to the full monthly meeting, entered in the meeting records, and posted at the meetinghouse for all to see. One way or another, the truth would be cleared through the humiliation or the expulsion of the offending Quaker.

Unlike judging criminal justice, evaluating the effectiveness of Gospel Order discipline relies not on who was found guilty (all but one were) or who received different processes (all followed roughly the same path). Rather, the success of Quaker discipline can be ascertained from the pattern of its failures. Who were the Quaker offenders who refused to abase themselves to the meeting and incurred disownment; for what offenses were they disowned; how often did disownment occur? Was the number of discipline cases rising or falling, and how long did it take to end a case? Meetings obviously desired fewer deviants and speedy resolution, and achieving those goals would reflect well on the power of the Society over its members' behavior. These patterns, along with the causes for discipline, the demography of the accused, and subtle changes in the process itself, reflected the complementary relationship between the Gospel Order and the law.

The disowned were of lower status than the population of those accused (see table 39), and the accused were of lower status than the average Quaker (see table 31 in chapter 5). The percentages of high officers, Quaker leaders, and landowners in the disowned population were even lower than the disproportionately low rates among those ever charged by a meeting. Farmers suffered disownment disproportionately

Table 39. Statistical Description of Quakers Disowned by
Men's Meetings

Attributes	Quakers Accused	Quakers Disowned
Total *n*	320	42
Male (%)	81.2	88.1
Female (%)	18.8	11.9
Quaker leaders (%)	22.2	19.0
Landowners (%)	74.1	66.7
Nonlandowners (%)	25.9	33.3
Occupations (males only)		
Farmer (%)	54.5	68.2
Artisan (%)	21.2	18.2
Farmer-artisan (%)	10.3	4.5
Merchant (%)	2.4	0.0
Self-described gentry (%)	2.4	0.0
Servant/slave/laborer (%)	4.2	4.5
Other (%)	4.8	4.5
Legal roles		
High officer (%)	15.3	7.1
Lesser officer (%)	33.1	52.4
Nonofficer (%)	51.6	40.5
Grand juror (%)	46.9	54.8
Trial juror (%)	45.0	42.9

often when they were brought before the meeting, while farmer-artisans were disowned less often, and merchants and the self-described gentry were never disowned. The offenses that these Quakers of lesser status fought so hard that they incurred disownment were predominantly sectarian offenses for which there was either no criminal prosecution or only the possibility of criminal prosecution (see table 40, second column). The most commonly given reason for disownment was "disorderly marriage," which usually meant a marriage between a Quaker and a non-Quaker. The next two most common reasons for disownment were for "separating" or giving bad testimony, indicating a breach of dogma, and for "disorderly walking" (a euphemism, usually for sexual offens-

Table 40. Accusations and Disownments in Quaker Meetings

Offenses	Overall Percentage Accused	Percentage Disowned	Percentage of Accused Who Were Disowned
Sectarian offenses, not illegal			
Disorderly marriages	18.7	27.0	14.7
Separating/bad testimony	6.3	13.5	21.7
Abuse of meeting	5.2	8.1	15.8
Certificates/appeals	3.0	—	—
Taking arms	1.4	—	—
Dispute with husband	1.1	—	—
False meeting records	0.6	—	—
Dispute with non-Quaker	0.3	—	—
Subtotal (*n*)	36.6 (133)	48.6 (18)	13.5 (18)
Sectarian offenses, possibly illegal			
Disorderly walking	21.8	13.5	6.3
Absenting meetings/Sabbath	9.9	8.1	8.3
Subtotal (*n*)	31.7 (115)	22.6 (8)	7.0 (8)
Overall sectarian offenses	68.3	70.2	10.5
Offenses without victims, probably illegal			
Liquor violations	5.5	10.8	20.0
Swearing/words	3.0	—	—
Sexual offenses	4.1	2.7	6.9
Wagers/cards/etc.	1.1	—	—
Magic arts	0.3	—	—
Subtotal (*n*)	14.0 (51)	13.5 (5)	9.8 (5)
Offenses with victims, illegal			
Economic (bankruptcy, exploitation)	4.7	2.7	5.9
Violence	4.4	—	—
Defamation/scandal	4.4	8.1	18.8
Against legal system	1.9	2.7	14.3
Theft/embezzlement	1.1	—	—
Misdemeanors	1.1	2.7	25.0
Subtotal (*n*)	17.6 (64)	16.2 (6)	9.4 (6)
Total identified (*n*)	99.9 (363)	99.9 (37)	

es).[70] Sectarian offenses that contravened no law resulted in the highest rate of disownments for any group of charges (17.3 percent; see table 40, third column). Meetings clearly focused their harshest disciplinary attention on those offenses that the law could not handle, on those offenders who were less important in their community, and on those issues that mattered most to the leadership of the Society of Friends.[71]

Over the whole period, 10.1 percent of the disciplinary cases (42 out of 416) ended in disownment. There was, however, a startling change in both the number of cases and the rates of disownment after 1695, which marked the end of the divisive Keithian schism.[72] Between 1696 and 1710, there were nearly twice as many cases in the men's meetings as there had been in the previous fifteen years; in the women's meetings, the number was almost three times as great. Delaware Valley men's meetings overall averaged 8.3 disciplinary cases per year up through 1695, while after 1695 they averaged 14.3 cases per year. The average number of meetings to resolve a case increased 18 percent, from 3.3 meetings through 1695 to 3.9 meetings between 1696 and 1710. The period 1706–10 showed the longest average (4.3 meetings to end disciplinary proceedings), indicating a worsening of this trend. The pace of disownments also increased. From 1680 to 1695, only 2.4 percent of the cases resulted in disownment; from 1696 to 1705, 18.5 percent of the cases ended in disownment, and the figure rose to over 25 percent in the last five-year period. In absolute numbers, thirty-nine Quakers were disowned between 1696 and 1710, thirteen times as many as had been disowned between 1680 and 1695; twenty were disowned between 1706 and 1710 alone. Clearly, the pattern of Quaker discipline changed after 1695 to involve more deviants, more meeting attention, more offender recalcitrance, and more disownment than in the halcyon first years of Quaker settlement.

Compared with Quaker disciplinary patterns of the mid-eighteenth century, when hundreds of offenders per year appeared before Pennsylvania meetings, this increasing level of discipline might seem insignificant. Jack Marietta, whose massive research on Pennsylvania Quaker discipline up to the 1780s covered over thirteen thousand cases, suggested that Quakers had little problem enforcing discipline prior to 1720.[73] His analysis, however, rested on the assumption that Quakers retained a majority status in the population and that this Quaker-dominated environment offered few competing lifestyles to comfort disowned offenders. My analysis has shown Quakers had in all probability lost their majority well before 1720. Another analysis, which focused on the Burlington Monthly Meeting, found meeting authority over discipline challenged after 1694 because of the increasing heterogeneity of Delaware Valley society. This population change diminished Quaker religious authority and made offenders more reluctant to submit to the meeting when alternative life-styles offered freedom from such controls.[74] The pluralistic nature of Delaware Valley society contributed to disciplinary problems faced by Quaker leaders long before the explosion of cases after 1720.

This study argues that the increase in cases and disownments after 1695 resulted from attempts to strengthen meeting control over behavior; these attempts were using as a model the successful process and substance of the criminal law. Such an analysis has been suggested by Jon Butler, who argues that a "disciplinary renascence" followed the Keithian schism, as Quaker leaders "moved to cleanse their own membership after suppressing his [Keith's] challenge to their authority."[75] Quaker meetings inaugurated new institutions and procedures designed to regularize and thus enhance their disciplinary mechanisms. The appointment of overseers, begun in 1695, mimicked the role of constables in the legal system. The reporting of disciplinary offenses became overseer driven in the same way that reporting of crime fell to constables.[76] Other new institutional structures included youth meetings, established in 1694–95 to stamp out all "Loosness and Vanity," and preparatory meetings, begun in 1700 to set the agenda for monthly meetings. Preparatory meetings focused especially on specific offenses, such as not keeping one's word in business dealings, not keeping to plain language and fashion, sleeping in meetings, and not keeping to Quaker marriage rules.[77] As such, they set the docket for discipline and served as a grand jury.

As these new institutions sought to eliminate offenses, Quakers began to rely less on general principles and more on specific definitions of the offenses to be controlled. Irregularly issued epistles specified these offenses and procedures—servant behavior was to be controlled, overseers were to be stricter, there was to be no superfluity in marriages or burials, astrology and geomancy were condemned. Quakers codified the welter of regulations in 1704 with the issuance of their first Book of Discipline. The conclusion of that code favorably noted that it paralleled the legal rules and practices Quakers were now embracing: "as it's necessary for the good Governmt of a Nation to have good Laws and yet to little Purpose with putting them as occasion offers in Execution, So will Rules of Discipline as necessary in the Church be also to little purpose if due Care be not taken to Put them in Practice."[78]

As Quaker institutional structures and rules became more clearly delineated, behavior in specific cases showed the influence of legal principles. Quarterly meetings took appeals as a supreme court would, reviewing and occasionally reversing decisions of monthly meetings. Ann Beazer's unsavory words to the monthly meeting regarding its refusal to consent to her marriage was excused by the Chester Quarterly Meeting, which found that the monthly meeting "did beare a little too hard upon the young couple." Offenders used the appeals process and the increasing tendency to legalism to obtain copies of the meeting minutes against them. In some cases, monthly meetings used the appellate hierarchy for advisory opinions, as the Middletown Meeting did when it sought the "advise and assistance" of the Bucks Quarterly Meeting to confirm that Robert Heaton needed to strengthen his self-condemnation and that George Holme should not marry his dead wife's sister.[79] In particulars as well as in structure, the increased discipline and disownments after 1695 sought the legitimacy generated by specific charges and regular procedures; Quaker meetings strengthened their positions against miscreants in adopting a legal model.

Quaker disciplinary substance as well as process began to coordinate with the law. Four monthly meetings and one quarterly meeting issued pronouncements condemning the sale of rum to Indians, reinforcing Pennsylvania's statute. Two meetings would not give permission to marry unless the law's strictures had been followed. The Radnor Meeting ordered its members' fences to meet the law's requirements and assigned its own fence-viewers to supplement the county's fence-viewers. The Bucks Quarterly Meeting found some Quakers "remiss in answering" the legal requirement of recording births, marriages, and burials and ordered its monthly meetings to see that the law was "answered." Similarly, in 1704 the Falls Meeting proclaimed its desire to "keep to Royal Laws" regarding the queen's proclamation for the regulation of money so that Quakers would avoid charging "extortion upon Interest" above the legal limit.[80] Quaker meetings incorporated legal strictures into their religious discipline.

These meetings cooperated not only in reinforcing particular laws but also in enhancing the general efficacy of the law. The Chester Quarterly Meeting aided the tax collector in 1702, concluding that "whereas wee have been allwayes Ready and willing to assist and support Civill government, do order that all be advised not to Refuse the paying of any Levey Lawfully demanded." Stubborn tax evaders were to "be speedily dealt with according to Gospel order so our holy profession may be quit of them and Truth kept clear." By 1706, the Chester Meeting made support for the regime a disciplinary issue, pronouncing against "seditious words and practices, Insinuations and turbulent behavior" to the "great disturbance both of Church and State."[81] Although the Society of Friends and its Gospel Order alternative had been grounded in opposition to the law in England, Delaware Valley's Quaker meetings did their best to support the law once they were in control of it.

Meetings did more than just issue proclamations; particular cases also reinforced legal interests. Those Quakers on the Bucks County jury who decided the issue by flipping a coin were first prosecuted not in court but in the Falls Monthly Meeting, which ultimately required seven of the jurors (five of whom were leaders) to condemn themselves.[82] Four Quakers accused by the Burlington Meeting of rioting and breaking open the prison door at first gave a "slight answer" and did not appear. After the threat of disownment, two confessed to "not understanding their wicked intentions but being unwarily drawn into that tumultuous company" and declared their sorrow.[83] The very legitimacy and authority of the Quaker rule of law was at stake; that both forums attacked the miscreants despite the general avoidance of such double jeopardy indicates the serious nature of the offenses.

In many instances, meetings upheld legal process without a parallel court action, seemingly holding Quakers to higher standards in their interactions than courts did. Cited neither for contempt nor perjury, William Biles was brought before the meeting for failure to acknowledge (admit to signing) a bill in court and stating that "the court had neither done him Law nor Justice." Thomas Harding's resistance to a court officer and Thomas French's and Seth Hill's improper court behavior produced Quaker discipline but not legal action. The Chester Meeting upheld the grand jury's decision to set land aside for public use by disciplining Robert Wade and Henry Hollinsworth for building on the land. The meeting accepted Thomas Taylor's and Jonathan Taylor's papers of self-condemnation for drinking only if they paid fines in open court. Meetings avoided legal probate fights by settling such issues as guardians, inventory, and property division before allowing parties to go to court.[84] In what appears to have been a de facto division of labor, courts seem to have authorized Quaker meetings to guard the authority of the legal system from Quaker infractions that might have undermined the belief that, in matters of law, Quakers were indeed "good men."

Quaker meetings thus laid the institutional foundation for the disciplinary explosion of the mid-1700s by borrowing from the law in both process and substance and by collaborating closely with a court system that achieved popular acceptance. This system bore some resemblance to the relationship between church and state in Puritan New England. In both regions there was a great overlap between the personnel in legal and church roles—members of the dominant denomination controlled the legal levers. Furthermore, there was a strong similarity in goals— repentance and humble submission, with guilt not usually in question. Both locales evidenced close yet informal cooperation between lay and religious authorities. The church came to the aid of the state in a coalition designed to reinforce a religious duty to obey duly constituted civil authority. Both regions were able to achieve, at least at the local level, a measure of social stability and consensual acceptance of institutions for defining and controlling deviance.[85]

Yet the Quaker accomplishments were even more remarkable than those of the Puritans because of the diversity of the population and the rapid loss of a Quaker majority. Delaware Valley's state apparatus, because of its guarantees of freedom of religion, the memories of legal persecution in England, and the precarious population base for Quaker power, was weaker than that of Puritan New England. Furthermore, despite overlapping jurisdiction, Quakers rarely used "double jeopardy" against offenders, again unlike New England's use of coequal punishments.[86] Quaker meetings complemented the law, but the reverse was not true. The division of docket responsibilities and of types of defendants disciplined worked to reinforce the law's legitimacy, especially as meetings borrowed more and more legalistic practices to reinforce their own disciplinary authority. As with dispute resolution, the law both used and absorbed its alternative. "Good laws," covering deviance as well as private disputes, triumphed and left Quakers, those whom Penn described as "good men," secure in power for the next half-century.

Conclusion:
A People of Process

Quakers asserted their authority over the Delaware Valley upon their arrival, authority that they kept in Pennsylvania until the 1750s, despite becoming a minority in the population within the first generation and despite a further shrinking of their proportion in the next thirty years. Authority is more than just the naked assertion of power, whether by a majority or a minority; it involves legitimation under a theory of rightness, internalized by those over whom power is exercised. A regime with authority needs to use little coercive force, which suited colonial elites, who sought authority without the institutional capacity for much coercion.[1] The source of Quakers' continuing authority has been variously located: successful family life (domesticity), individualistic market forces, and Quaker political culture, among others. Perhaps because of the obvious political turmoil of the founding generation, the role of law has not received credit for Quaker authority. Yet this study has shown that Quakers, despite provincial political upheavals, established the rule of law in their colonies and installed Quakers as decision-makers in county courts. There are five main reasons why the rule of law established in the first generation should be preferred over other hypotheses on the primary source of Quaker authority.

First, beginnings matter. Historians have noted that the first generation of English settlers left indelible impressions on the regions where they settled. These impressions were not immutable, but they did limit the cultural, social, economic, and political options available for the generations to come. From the Chesapeake's first generation came patterns of high deathrates, uneven sex ratios, exploitation of labor, reliance on tobacco cultivation, and individualistic migration. These aspects inhibited social cohesion throughout the seventeenth century. For the first generation of New England settlement, historians have rightly analyzed patterns of town and church formation in establishing high levels of social cohesion. Town control over the distribution of land, the exclusion of heterogeneous elements, and the resolution of disputes, when combined with religious fervor and family migration, resulted in demographically successful and economically sustainable communities. Neither of these first generations relied on the rule of law as the primary method for resolving disputes or legitimating the authority of elites.

The Delaware Valley was a third such "cultural hearth" in British North America. With the exception of New York, no other initial group of English settlers would confront already established colonists from other European nations. Without exception, the Delaware Valley migrants would be the most religiously and ethnically diverse in the first generation of British settlement, a level of diversity that would only increase with time. Quakers, the dynamic element among the initial British settlers, were committed to controlling the Delaware Valley colonies. Such Quaker authority would protect and nourish their beliefs and their communities in their attempts at a radical restructuring of British life. The economic, social, and familial restructurings would take time to establish amidst the hardships and diversity of their settlement, but Quaker restructuring of the legal system could be implemented immediately. Law reforms, mere proposals developed in England by Quakers and others, were quickly adopted and were enforced by Quakers appointed to virtually all offices and packed onto juries. Of all the colonial elites, only Quakers placed such great reliance on laws and legal personnel for initial control.

Second, perspectives matter. In unpacking the relationships between individuals and groups in any society, one must identify both the perspectives individuals carry with them (e.g., religion, occupation, wealth) and the perspectives different roles in particular economic and social transactions bring. People in small colonial societies like the early Delaware Valley knew each other in multiple ways and settings—as friend, relative, neighbor, competitor, laborer, trader, petty legal officer, church member, etc. Individuals adopt different personas and strategies, depending on their background and the particular role they play in a transaction. A certain percentage of all transactions go sour in any society; because of its diversity, the Delaware Valley had perhaps a greater potential for the misunderstandings that create sour economic and social transactions than did other colonial societies.

The legal system does not deal with all transactions; it deals with those that have gone sour and might have crossed a legal boundary by violating a legally established expectation about social and economic behavior. The spectrum of perspectives then becomes focused on the question of which boundaries and expectations will be upheld. Clearly, from a systemic perspective, these transactions provide the gravest potential for social disorder and thus, if resolved peaceably, the greatest potential for establishing legal authority. The legal system allows the individuals involved to express their perspectives on the transaction—the aggrieved transform themselves into plaintiffs, and the accused must defend themselves in the role of criminal defendant. Other parties, outsiders to the transaction, may be called on to express their perspectives and render their judgments—justices, witnesses, jurors. Furthermore, others involved in the legal system will be observing. Spectators make decisions about their own future behavior and their future participation in the legal system based not only on their personal experiences with the law but also on what they see and hear they can expect from the Quaker legal system in action. Only the law in Delaware Valley society had the potential to coordinate its residents' diverse perspectives on these most troublesome transactions.

Third, choices matter. At the most basic level, legitimate government rests on the consent of the governed, and consent rests on opinions and is a choice, granted or withheld in countless daily decisions.[2] Individuals and groups had a choice whether to assent voluntarily to Quaker rule by obeying and participating in the Quaker legal system. For example, law is but one method for resolving interpersonal disputes; the choice of Delaware Valley individuals coming from a wide variety of perspectives to become plaintiffs in large numbers empowered the legal system with decision-making authority. Once a case, civil or criminal, began, the legal system offered a set of choices to the parties. By matching the parties' perspectives with the choices they made at various points and in different legal roles, we can draw inferences about the underlying shape of power relationships within the society. For example, the choices Quaker leaders made as plaintiffs versus the choices they made as defendants reflected their view of the power they had in society and resulted in more favorable nontrial outcomes. How criminal charges ended reflected other choices: the desire and ability of the elite accused to arrange a resolution that protected them from public humiliation. Before trial, in both civil and criminal cases, the choices made reflected the bargaining power of the parties involved and tilted the results in favor of those with the greater bargaining power.

The choices made by decision-makers reflected a different set of perspectives. The choices made about who was to be charged with criminal offenses reflected one priority: the need for the criminal law to reach all levels of Delaware Valley society. Contempt charges reinforced Quaker control over the legal system's personnel while conveying the message that no one was above the law. The choices juries made in deciding the few cases that went to trial reflected another priority, that of dispensing even-handed treatment to all groups, rich and poor, Quaker and non-Quaker alike. From the perspective of an observant spectator, the statistically neutral pattern of verdicts and judgments would create the opinion that the Quaker legal system was in fact producing justice. Such a conclusion would, by creating confidence in the system, increase both usage of the law and obedience of the law's dictates. The political consequences would be an increase in the regime's legitimacy.

Fourth, process matters. All modern institutions rely on procedures that circumscribe and direct the choices available in resolving disputes and questions of deviance. These processes are linked to issues of authority and the role legitimacy plays in establishing authority. Legitimacy and authority have been the focus for the sociology of law, a topic Max Weber introduced. Weber posited a shift from traditional authority in premodern societies to rational-legal authority in modern ones. According to Lawrence M. Friedman,

> rational-legal authority rejects the person in favor of the process. Legitimacy (and authority) rest on procedural norms, in contrast to the legitimacy of charisma and tradition. But what is so special about procedures? Procedures are nothing in themselves, but everything insofar as they are instruments for ascertaining, measuring, and aggregating choice. . . .
>
> Reduced to its essential elements, the modern state rests on the authority of law, and law rests on the authority of personal choice.[3]

Legal process is therefore the funnel through which perspectives and choices can be channeled to produce legitimacy and authority.

Not all processes succeed in that translation; some regimes do not achieve legitimate authority in the eyes of the population. The question therefore becomes, Which processes will most likely succeed in garnering a positive response from the population, in attaining the consent of the governed? In examining procedures for their effects on legitimacy, modern social scientists have arrived at two conclusions relevant to this study. First, procedures are more likely to be viewed as fair when the participants themselves can control the presentation of their case. This idea of *process control* means that if the parties have the opportunity to present evidence and state their position, they will conclude that there is procedural justice and that the authorities in the system thus deserve legitimacy. This effect persists regardless of *decision control,* that is, regardless of whether their presentation influences the outcome favorably.[4] Second, "assessments of procedural fairness are strongly linked to judgments about whether the authorities being dealt with are trying to be fair." To make such a judgment, individuals must make judgments about the motives and personal qualities of the authority. Such a normative judgment operates regardless of whether the result is favorable.[5] If the procedures are judged to be fair, they operate to legitimize authorities and grant them discretionary power, a "cushion of support against the potentially damaging effects of unfavorable outcomes."[6]

The social psychology of procedural justice in the late twentieth century cannot be simply and directly applied to the legal behavior of the seventeenth century. Nonetheless, these results do offer clues about why the colonial Delaware Valley legal system achieved legitimacy. Quaker legal procedures excelled on both counts. On the first, law reforms helped place more control of cases in the hands of the parties themselves. Simplification of procedures and language, which resulted in reducing the need for lawyers; reduction of fees, which increased access and reduced frustration; and emphasis on settling disputes before trial, which encouraged more direct negotiation between the parties, all increased process control in civil cases. In criminal prosecutions, the accused had opportunities to present their cases under circumstances in which the cost of losing the case had generally been reduced from the draconian common-law penalties. On the second issue, Quaker authorities' conspicuous attention to the rule of law, plus the fact that many civil and criminal cases were resolved by agreement, led parties to conclude that the system was treating them fairly. When this was combined with the statistically neutral performance of juries, it seems likely that spectators and participants alike could easily conclude that Quaker authorities were trying hard to be fair and thus deserved that "cushion of support" that comes from legitimacy.

Despite the centrality of procedures in assessing system performance, for individuals and groups there was also a fifth issue that mattered: outcomes. As seen in the Delaware Valley civil and criminal cases, the choices participants made before the trial began significantly affected the results. Those pretrial decisions tilted in favor of those with greater socioeconomic power (not higher levels of wealth in and of itself)—the legal and Quaker leadership. Differentials in bargaining power also could relate to differences in legal knowledge, negotiating skill, and the strength or weakness of one's case, but certain social attributes clearly influenced pretrial outcomes. In these nontrial resolutions, however, the parties exercised process control through their choices, suggesting that the parties would accept the result as legitimate even if the result was unfavorable. Legal process thus sanctioned these differences in bargaining power as legitimate, while at the same time convincing those with less bargaining power that the result was fair. By rewarding those with bargaining power advantages, these outcomes reinforced and augmented such advantages in future disputes. The powerful manipulated the choices to stay powerful, while the losers accepted the results; the court-day crowd, however, saw and heard only those aspects of the process and outcomes that were even-handed.

Authority legitimated by the choices, processes, and outcomes made by individuals and groups who possessed diverse perspectives was the Quakers' first great achievement in the Delaware Valley. This achievement occurred despite the Quakers' anti-authoritarianism, despite their divisions over religious issues, and despite their own, potentially competing institutions. This achievement was even more impressive because of the setting: a religiously and ethnically diverse population, with few preexisting links between the immigrants and few strong communities established after their arrival. This achievement did not rely on the traditional or inherited authority manifested in English society; from the beginning, it was the function of law.

Pennsylvania, the dominant colony in the Delaware Valley, maintained social peace until the revolutionary crisis in the 1760s, despite a growing population of increasing diversity. Quakers retained control of Pennsylvania's political and legal life until the 1750s, despite their ever-dwindling percentage of the population. The legitimated legal system gave individuals and families, regardless of their backgrounds, stable expectations for their social and economic transactions. Such stability was a precondition for full exploration of economic opportunities in a region noted for its booming growth. That legitimacy lingered despite the dwindling influence of law reform, a process that began in the early 1700s. With population and economic growth came more cases; to handle them, the law became more complex and more laden with technicalities and legalese, which meant that to navigate the system successfully, it became increasingly necessary to obtain legal counsel. Alternatives, such as the Quaker meeting for disputes and deviances, also became more technical, more narrowly used, and more ancillary to the law.

Whether these changes ultimately eroded the early pillars of legitimacy—accessibility and process control—is for another study to determine. What is clear is that the early "good laws" had built, through their processes and through Quaker adherence to them, a reservoir of legitimacy that provided Quaker authorities with long-lasting support from non-Quakers. This support manifested itself in the majority's selection of Quaker politicians at the ballot box and its use of courts controlled by Quaker justices and juries. At the same time that Quakers established themselves as "good men," they found ways to manipulate the processes and use their early bargaining-power advantages to enhance their economic and social position.

The diverse population of the middle colonies has sometimes been said to foreshadow the future pattern of all American societies; the success of the Delaware Valley in terms of economic and population growth has been said to rest on economic individualism and privatistic family relations that also anticipated the future.[7] The keeping of social peace in the Delaware Valley, the precondition for such development, foreshadowed another modern feature: the use of legal processes to accommodate divergent interests and groups. In their rejection of traditional means of English authority in favor of law, Quakers had become a people of process, basing their control of their colonies on experimental legal procedures. By the end of the first generation of Quaker settlement, the success of those reforms had made Quaker rule legitimate and had convinced non-Quaker residents to join as people of process. This connection continued even as the processes themselves mutated and even as the Quaker elite used those processes more effectively than the rest of the population did. This outcome—processes that appeared fair, integrated a diverse population, and legitimized authority but at the same time were manipulated to produce unfair results based on the socioeconomic power of the parties involved—would also foreshadow the American future.

Notes

Abbreviations

Court Records

Bucks Courts
Records of the Courts of Quarter Sessions and
Common Pleas of Bucks County, Pennsylvania,
1684–1700 (Meadville, Pa., 1943)

Bucks Dockets
Bucks County Combined Common Pleas and
Quarter Sessions Docket, 1684–1731, Histori-
cal Society of Pennsylvania, Philadelphia

Burlington Courts
H. Clay Reed and George Miller, eds., The Burlington Court Book: A Record of Quaker Jurispru-
dence in West New Jersey, 1680–1709 (Washington, D.C., 1944)

Chester Courts I
Records of the Courts of Chester County, Pennsylvania, 1681–1697 (Philadelphia, 1910)

Chester Courts II
Records of the Courts of Chester County, Pennsyl-
vania, vol. 2, transcribed by Dorothy Lapp
(Danboro, Pa., 1972)

Gloucester Courts
Transcription of the Minute Book, Quarter Ses-
sions/Common Pleas, no. 1, 1686–1713,
Gloucester County, N.J., Gloucester County
Historical Society, Woodbury, N.J.

Gloucester Documents
Transcriptions of the First Quarter Century Documents of Old Gloucester County, New Jersey,
vol. 1, Gloucester County Historical Society,
Woodbury, N.J.

Statutes and Legislative Records

Minutes of Council, I
Minutes of the Provincial Council of Pennsylvania, from the Organization to the Termination of

	the Proprietary Government, vol. 1 (Philadelphia, 1852)
Minutes of Council, II	*Minutes of the Provincial Council of Pennsylvania, from the Organization to the Termination of the Proprietary Government,* vol. 2 (Philadelphia, 1852)
New Jersey Concessions	Aaron Leaming and Jacob Spicer, eds., *The Grants, Concessions, and Original Constitutions of the Province of New Jersey* (Philadelphia, 1752)
Pennsylvania Laws, 1682–1700	Staughton George, Benjamin Mead, and Thomas McCamant, eds., *Charter to William Penn, and Laws of the Province of Pennsylvania Passed between the Years 1682 and 1700* (Harrisburg, 1896)
Statutes at Large II	James Mitchell and Henry Flanders, eds., *The Statutes at Large of Pennsylvania from 1682 to 1801,* vol. 2 (Harrisburg, 1896)

Quaker Meetings

All of the following sources were found at the Friends Historical Library, Swarthmore, Pa. Citations are according to date of the entry, as recorded in the Quaker system of numbering months (e.g., March = 1, April = 2, and so on).

Bucks QM	Bucks Quarterly Meeting Minutes, 1684–1710
Burlington MM	Burlington Men's Monthly Meeting Minutes, 1678–1710
Burlington WM	Burlington Women's Monthly Meeting Minutes, 1681–1710
Burlington QM	Burlington Quarterly Meeting Minutes, 1686–1710
Chester MM	Chester (Pa.) Men's Monthly Meeting Minutes, 1681–1710
Chester WM	Chester (Pa.) Women's Monthly Meeting Minutes, 1695–1710
Chester QM	Chester/Concord Quarterly Meeting Minutes, 1684–1710
Chesterfield MM	Chesterfield (N.J.) Men's Monthly Meeting Minutes, 1684–1710
Concord MM	Concord Men's Monthly Meeting Minutes, 1684–1710
Darby MM	Darby Men's Monthly Meeting Minutes, 1684–1710

Darby WM	Darby Women's Monthly Meeting Minutes, 1684–1710
Falls MM	Falls Men's Monthly Meeting Minutes, 1680–1710
Falls WM	Falls Women's Monthly Meeting Minutes, 1683–1710
Middletown MM	Middletown Men's Monthly Meeting Minutes, 1683–1710
Middletown WM	Middletown Women's Monthly Meeting Minutes, 1685–1710
Radnor MM	Radnor Men's Monthly Meeting Minutes, 1684–1704
Radnor WM	Radnor Women's Monthly Meeting Minutes, 1685–1710

Archives and Journals

HSP	Historical Society of Pennsylvania
PMHB	*Pennsylvania Magazine of History and Biography*
WMQ	*William and Mary Quarterly*, 3d ser.

Introduction

1. Carl Bridenbaugh, "The Old and New Societies of the Delaware Valley in the Seventeenth Century," *PMHB* 100 (1976): 145–63; Barry Levy, *The Quakers and the American Family* (New York, 1988), 124–27; Jon Butler, *Power, Authority, and the Origins of American Denominational Order* (Philadelphia, 1978), 28–29; John Pomfret, *Colonial New Jersey: A History* (New York, 1973), 36–48; Gary Nash, *Quakers and Politics: Pennsylvania, 1681–1726* (Princeton, N.J., 1968), 4–8; Sally Schwartz, "Society and Culture in the Seventeenth-Century Delaware Valley," *Delaware History* 20 (1982): 98–122.

2. Peter Charles Hoffer, *Law and People in Colonial America* (Baltimore, 1992), 30–31; Levy, *Quakers and Family,* 110–11.

3. Nash, *Quakers and Politics,* 10–23; Jack Greene, *Pursuits of Happiness: The Social Development of Early Modern British Colonies and the Formation of American Culture* (Chapel Hill, N.C., 1988), 48 (quote).

4. David Hackett Fischer, *Albion's Seed* (New York, 1988), 428–31, 459, 597–99; Nash, *Quakers and Politics,* 48–49; Levy, *Quakers and Family,* 110–11; Stephanie Grauman Wolf, *Urban Village* (Princeton, N.J., 1976), 12–13.

5. Richard S. Dunn and Mary Maples Dunn, eds., *The Papers of William Penn,* vol. 1 (1644–79) (Philadelphia, 1981), 387–410; Richard Dunn and Mary Maples Dunn, eds., *The Papers of William Penn,* vol. 2 (1680–

84) (Philadelphia, 1982), 137–227; Nash, *Quakers and Politics,* 28–47; Caroline Robbins, "Laws and Governments Proposed for West New Jersey and Pennsylvania, 1676–1683," *PMHB* 105 (1981): 373–92. The epigraph is in Dunn and Dunn, *Papers of Penn,* vol. 2, 213.

6. Craig Horle and Marianne Wokeck, eds., *Lawmaking and Legislators in Pennsylvania: A Biographical Dictionary,* vol. 1 (1682–1709) (Philadelphia, 1991), 48.

7. Dunn and Dunn, *Papers of Penn,* vol. 2, 144 (quote), 214; William Penn, "Some Account of the Province of Pennsilvania," in *Narratives of Early Pennsylvania, West New Jersey, and Delaware, 1630–1707,* ed. Albert Cook Myers (New York, 1912), 208.

8. Horle and Wokeck, *Lawmaking and Legislators,* 45; Dunn and Dunn, *Papers of Penn,* vol. 2, 347–48

9. Fischer, *Albion's Seed,* 455; Butler, *Power and American Denominational Order,* 30; Jon Butler, *Awash in a Sea of Faith: Christianizing the American People* (Cambridge, Mass., 1990), 118–19.

10. *New Jersey Concessions,* 488; Dunn and Dunn, *Papers of Penn,* vol. 2, 539; *Pennsylvania Laws, 1682–1700,* 168–69.

11. James Lemon, *The Best Poor Man's Country* (New York, 1972), 27, 125–27; Pomfret, *Colonial New Jersey,* 118; Alan Tully, *William Penn's Legacy: Politics and Social Structure in Provincial Pennsylvania, 1726–1755* (Baltimore, 1975), 71; Joseph Illick, *Colonial Pennsylvania: A History* (New York, 1976), 108–9; Levy, *Quakers and Family,* 125, 127, 151; Frederick Tolles, *Quakers and the Atlantic Culture* (New York, 1960), 117; Fischer, *Albion's Seed,* 455; D. W. Meinig, *The Shaping of America: A Geographical Perspective on 500 Years of History,* vol. 1, *Atlantic America, 1492–1800* (New Haven, Conn., 1986), 443–44.

12. Horle and Wokeck, *Lawmaking and Legislators,* 11–15, 38–55, 797–99; Fischer, *Albion's Seed,* 463–64.

13. Richard McCormick, *New Jersey from Colony to State, 1609–1789* (Newark, N.J., 1981), 46–49, 60–66; Edwin Tanner, *The Province of New Jersey* (London, 1908), 120; *Burlington Courts,* xxxi–xxxix.

14. "The Present State of the Colony of West Jersey, 1681," in Myers, *Narratives,* 191–92.

15. William Penn, "A Further Account of the Province of Pennsylvania," in *Narratives,* ed. Myers, 203, 262, 264, 267, 269.

16. Gabriel Thomas, "An Historical and Geographical Account of Pensilvania and of West-New-Jersey," in *Narratives,* ed. Myers, 325 (first quote), 326 (second quote), 328 (third quote). Michael Zuckerman, "Identity in British America: Unease in Eden," in *Colonial Identity in the Atlantic World, 1500–1800,* ed. Nicholas Canny and Anthony Pagden (Princeton, N.J., 1987), 122–27, has noted contradictions in the extremes with which pro-

motional literature like Thomas's painted England's New World colonies. One such contradiction, the "effortless indolence" versus the "exemplary industry" needed for New World survival, is reason for the caveats on believability.

17. Bridenbaugh, "Old and New Societies," 159–60.

18. Lemon, *Best Poor Man's Country,* xiii.

19. Levy, *Quakers and Family,* 151–52.

20. Fischer, *Albion's Seed,* 567, 560.

21. Edmund Morgan, *American Slavery, American Freedom* (New York, 1975), 180–362; David Konig, *Law and Society in Puritan Massachusetts: Essex County, 1629–1692* (Chapel Hill, N.C., 1979), 160–85; Gary Nash, *Urban Crucible* (Cambridge, Mass., 1979), 44–49, 88–90.

22. Sharon Salinger, *"To Serve Well and Faithfully": Labor and Indentured Servants in Pennsylvania, 1682–1800* (New York, 1987), 35, 38; Illick, *Colonial Pennsylvania,* 57, 63, 108–9; Lemon, *Best Poor Man's Country,* 5, 27; Greene, *Pursuits of Happiness,* 47; Fischer, *Albion's Seed,* 541.

23. Salinger, *"To Serve Well and Faithfully,"* 2; Fischer, *Albion's Seed,* 421; Bridenbaugh, "Old and New Societies," 161; Marion Balderston, ed., *James Clapoole's Letter Book, London and Philadelphia, 1681–84* (San Marino, Calif., 1967), 223–24 (quote).

24. Penn, "A Further Account," 260.

25. Fischer, *Albion's Seed,* 431; Greene, *Pursuits of Happiness,* 49; Levy, *Quakers and Family,* 155.

26. Nash, *Quakers and Politics,* 171–74, 179; Horle and Wokeck, *Lawmaking and Legislators,* 259; Craig Horle, *The Quakers and the English Legal System* (Philadelphia, 1988), 15; Fischer, *Albion's Seed,* 574–75; Jon Butler, "Into Pennsylvania's Spiritual Abyss: The Rise and Fall of the Later Keithians, 1693–1703," *PMHB* 101 (1977): 153 (quote).

27. Horle and Wokeck, *Lawmaking and Legislators,* 41 (quote), 44; J. William Frost, *The Keithian Controversy in Early Pennsylvania* (Norwood, Pa., 1980), i–xix; J. William Frost, "Religious Liberty in Early Pennsylvania," *PMHB* 105 (1981): 432; Butler, *Power and American Denominational Order,* 33–40; Butler, *Awash in Faith,* 119; Butler, "Pennsylvania's Spiritual Abyss," 154–55.

28. Nash, *Quakers and Politics,* 48–49, 163, 174 (first quote); Fischer, *Albion's Seed,* 590 (second quote); Horle and Wokeck, *Lawmaking and Legislators,* 38–43.

29. On Penn's hopes, see *New Jersey Concessions,* 425; Dunn and Dunn, *Papers of William Penn,* vol. 1, 396–97; Dunn and Dunn, *Papers of William Penn,* vol. 2, 225; J. William Frost, *A Perfect Freedom: Religious Liberty in Pennsylvania* (New York, 1990), 13–14, 16; and Butler, *Awash in Faith,* 105.

30. Horle and Wokeck, *Lawmaking and Legislators,* 45–55; Frost, *Perfect Freedom,* 22–24; Frost, "Religious Liberty," 430–40.

31. Greene, *Pursuits of Happiness,* 49; Butler, *Awash in Faith,* 120–21 (Baptists), 123–24 (Presbyterians); Thomas, "An Historical Account," 347.

32. Richard Vann, "Quakerism: Made in America?" in *The World of William Penn,* ed. Richard S. Dunn and Mary Maples Dunn (Philadelphia, 1986), 165–68.

33. Frost, *Perfect Freedom,* 19.

34. Fischer, *Albion's Seed,* 422, 424.

35. Levy, *Quakers and Family,* 123–89.

36. Fischer, *Albion's Seed,* 578–80; Lemon, *Best Poor Man's Country,* 49–51, 55–56, 98–101, 110; Nash, *Quakers and Politics,* 90–93; Levy, *Quakers and Family,* 150; Greene, *Pursuits of Happiness,* 49, 137–38; Zuckerman, "Identity in British America," 138 (quote).

37. James Lemon, "The Weakness of Place and Community in Early Pennsylvania," in *European Settlement and Development in North America,* ed. James R. Gibson (Folkestone, England, 1978), 206; Wayne Bockelman, "Local Government in Colonial Pennsylvania," in *Town and County: Essays on the Structures of Local Government in the American Colonies,* ed. Bruce Daniels (Middletown, 1978), 216; Lemon, *Best Poor Man's Country,* 24, 130; Herbert Fitzroy, "Richard Crosby Goes to Court, 1683–1697," *PMHB* 42 (1938): 12–14; Laura Becker, "The People and the System: Legal Activities in a Colonial Pennsylvania Town," *PMHB* 105 (1981): 138.

38. Sidney Webb and Beatrice Webb, *The Development of English Local Government, 1689–1835* (London, 1963), 8–10, 22; Cynthia Herrup, *The Common Peace* (Cambridge, 1987), 195.

39. Lois Green Carr, *County Government in Maryland, 1689–1709* (New York, 1987), 479, 609–75; Darrett Rutman and Anita Rutman, *A Place in Time: Middlesex County, Virginia, 1650–1750* (New York, 1984), 144; David Konig, "Country Justice: The Rural Roots of Constitutionalism in Colonial Virginia," in *An Uncertain Tradition: Constitutionalism and the History of the South,* ed. Kermit Hall and James Ely, Jr. (Athens, Ga., 1989), 72; Gordon S. Wood, *The Radicalism of the American Revolution* (New York, 1992), 82 (quote).

40. Norma Landau, *The Justices of the Peace, 1679–1760* (Berkeley, Calif., 1984), 15, 38–39, 61; A. G. Roeber, *Faithful Magistrates and Republican Lawyers* (Chapel Hill, N.C., 1981), 74–75, 85; Rhys Isaac, *The Transformation of Virginia* (Chapel Hill, N.C., 1982), 92–93; Gail Sussman Marcus, "'Due Execution of the Generall Rules of Righteousnesse': Criminal Procedure in New Haven Town and Colony, 1638–1658," in *Saints and Revolutionaries,* ed. David Hall, Thad Tate, and John Murrin (New York, 1984), 129–31; Konig, *Law and Society in Puritan Massachusetts,* xiii–xv,

65–71, 88, 112–19, 190; Hoffer, *Law and People,* 25–26; Rutman and Rutman, *Place in Time,* 87–93.

41. Fischer, *Albion's Seed,* 461, 585; Horle, *Quakers and the English Legal System,* 192.

42. Warren Billings, "The Transfer of English Law to Virginia, 1606–1650," in *The Westward Enterprise: English Activities in Ireland, the Atlantic, and America, 1480–1650,* ed. K. P. Andrews, N. P. Canny, and P. E. H. Hair (Liverpool, 1978), 215–36; George Haskins, *Law and Authority in Early Massachusetts* (New York, 1960), 191–93, 212–13; G. B. Warden, "Law Reform in England and New England, 1620 to 1660," *WMQ* 35 (1978): 676–83.

43. *Bucks Courts; Bucks Dockets; Chester Courts I; Chester Courts II; Burlington Courts; Gloucester Courts; Gloucester Documents.*

44. *Pennsylvania Laws, 1682–1700,* 167, 176, 184, 225; *Statutes at Large II,* 134, 148–49; Richard Field, *The Provincial Courts of New Jersey, with Sketches of the Bench and Bar* (New York, 1849), 43; *Burlington Courts,* xl–lv; Bockelman, "Local Government," 217–23; A. G. Roeber, "Authority, Law, and Custom: The Rituals of Court Day in Tidewater Virginia, 1720 to 1750," *WMQ* 37 (1980): 30–31, 36; Hendrik Hartog, "The Public Law of a County Court: Judicial Government in Eighteenth Century Massachusetts," *American Journal of Legal History* 20 (1976): 317–22.

45. *Burlington Courts,* 96, 99, 122; *Pennsylvania Laws, 1682–1700,* 285–86.

46. *Pennsylvania Laws, 1682–1700,* 136; *Statutes at Large II,* 74; *Burlington Courts,* 27, 83, 129, 136; *Chester Courts I,* 163, 225, 370; *Chester Courts II,* 5, 70, 82, 94, 107, 122; *Gloucester Courts,* 189, 213, 230; *Bucks Courts,* 298–99, 370.

47. Richard Lempert, "Grievances and Legitimacy: The Beginnings and End of Dispute Settlement," *Law and Society Review* 15 (1981): 713.

48. *Gloucester Courts,* 198–215, 211 (first quote), 215 (second quote); *Burlington Courts,* xxxv.

49. Alan Hyde, "The Concept of Legitimation in the Sociology of Law," *Wisconsin Law Review* (1983): 398; Yash Ghai, "The Rule of Law, Legitimacy and Governance," *International Journal of the Sociology of Law* 14 (1986): 183; H. Andrew Michener and Martha R. Burt, "Components of 'Authority' as Determinants of Compliance," *Journal of Personality and Social Psychology* 31 (1975): 613; Becker, "People and the System," 148; Wayne McIntosh, "A State Court's Clientele: Exploring the Strategy of Trial Litigation," *Law and Society Review* 19 (1985): 421–22; Wayne McIntosh, "Private Use of a Public Forum: A Long-Range View of the Dispute Processing Role of Courts," *American Political Science Review* 77 (1983): 1003–5; Lynn Mather, "Dispute Processing and a Longitudinal Approach to Trial Courts," *Law and Society Review* 24 (1990): 367.

50. Konig, *Law and Society in Puritan Massachusetts,* 162–64, 186–91, 163 (first three quotes), 189 (last quote).

51. Douglas Hay, "Property, Authority and the Criminal Law," in *Albion's Fatal Tree,* ed. Douglas Hay, Peter Lineburgh, John G. Rule, and E. P. Thompson (New York, 1975), 29 (first quote), 33 (second quote); John Brewer and John Styles, *An Ungovernable People: The English and Their Law in the Seventeenth and Eighteenth Centuries* (New Brunswick, N.J., 1980), 14 (last quote).

52. John Langbein, "Albion's Fatal Flaws," *Past and Present* 98 (1983): 96–120; Hyde, "Concept of Legitimation," 420–21.

53. *Gloucester Courts,* 140, 145, 170, 174, 230, 358, 363; *Burlington Courts,* 11, 72, 80, 83, 92, 117, 129–30, 136, 146, 168, 201, 304; *Chester Courts I,* 85, 263, 270, 276, 302, 306, 365–66; *Chester Courts II,* 62, 66, 73, 82.

54. Horle, *Quakers and the English Legal System,* 187–244; Thomas A. Green, *Verdict according to Conscience: Perspectives on the English Criminal Trial Jury, 1200–1800* (Chicago, 1985), 200–249.

55. Dunn and Dunn, *Papers of Penn,* vol. 2, 89.

56. Christopher Hill, *The Century of Revolution, 1603–1714* (New York, 1961), 129–30, 177–78, 188, 225–27; Christopher Hill, *The World Turned Upside Down* (London, 1972), 269–76; Robbins, "Laws and Governments Proposed," 375, 389–91; Richard Morris, *Studies in the History of American Law* (New York, 1974), 45–62. See also Donald Veall, *The Popular Movement for Law Reform: 1640–1660* (Oxford, 1970).

57. Veall, *Popular Movement for Law Reform,* xvii, 95, 98, 112, 121, 143–44, 214; Robbins, "Laws and Governments Proposed," 373–74; Green, *Verdict according to Conscience,* 200–249; Horle, *Quakers and the English Legal System,* 162–63, 215.

58. J. William Frost, "The Affirmation Controversy and Religious Liberty," in *The World of William Penn,* ed. Dunn and Dunn, 307–12; Horle, *Quakers and the English Legal System,* 11, 49; *Pennsylvania Laws, 1682–1700,* 247–48; *New Jersey Concessions,* 397, 548.

59. Hill, *World Turned Upside Down,* 271 (quote); Veall, *Popular Movement for Law Reform,* 104, 107; Horle, *Quakers and the English Legal System,* 167.

60. Veall, *Popular Movement for Law Reform,* 113 (land registry), 36, 104, 168–69 (decentralized), 171 (election of judges); Green, *Verdict according to Conscience,* 159, 232–33 (neighborhood jury), 159, 229 (law and fact juries).

61. Dunn and Dunn, *Papers of Penn,* vol. 1, 393–94, 396–400; Dunn and Dunn, *Papers of Penn,* vol. 2, 218, 221 (first quote), 222–25; *Pennsylvania Laws, 1682–1700,* 117, 129; *New Jersey Concessions,* 398 (second quote), 427–29.

62. *Pennsylvania Laws, 1682–1700,* 132, 163, 226; *Statutes at Large II,* 155–56.

63. Veall, *Popular Movement for Law Reform,* 114, 172; *New Jersey Concessions,* 455; *Pennsylvania Laws, 1682–1700,* 128, 131.

64. Veall, *Popular Movement for Law Reform,* 201–2; Horle, *Quakers and the English Legal System,* 165 (first quote), 167; Hill, *World Turned Upside Down,* 270–71 (second quote); Frederick Tolles, *Meeting House and Counting House* (New York, 1948), 50 (third quote).

65. Veall, *Popular Movement for Law Reform,* 40, 43, 187; *New Jersey Concessions,* 426, 455, 530, 538–41; *Pennsylvania Laws, 1682–1700,* 100, 117, 147–50, 187, 199, 235–36.

66. Veall, *Popular Movement for Law Reform,* 114, 118, 184–85, 188; *Pennsylvania Laws, 1682–1700,* 128, 167.

67. *Pennsylvania Laws, 1682–1700,* 131; on Quakers' not suing other Quakers, see chapters 2 and 4, herein.

68. Tolles, *Meeting House,* 50 (quote); Veall, *Popular Movement for Law Reform,* 128; Herbert Fitzroy, "The Punishment of Crime in Provincial Pennsylvania," *PMHB* 60 (1936): 242–43.

69. Barbara Shapiro, "Law Reform in Seventeenth Century England," *American Journal of Legal History* 19 (1975): 286, 296.

70. Veall, *Popular Movement for Law Reform,* 132; Kathryn Preyer, "Penal Measures in the American Colonies: An Overview," *American Journal of Legal History* 26 (1982): 336–37; Lawrence Gipson, "Crime and Its Punishment in Provincial Pennsylvania," *Pennsylvania History* 2 (1935): 6; Robbins, "Laws and Governments Proposed," 388; Fitzroy, "Punishment of Crime," 243–44; Dunn and Dunn, *Papers of Penn,* vol. 1, 399, 402; *Pennsylvania Laws, 1682–1700,* 108–12; Dunn and Dunn, *Papers of Penn,* vol. 2, 222.

71. Dunn and Dunn, *Papers of Penn,* vol. 1, 398; *Pennsylvania Laws, 1682–1700,* 116.

72. Dunn and Dunn, *Papers of Penn,* vol. 1, 397–98; *Pennsylvania Laws, 1682–1700,* 117.

73. Dunn and Dunn, *Papers of Penn,* vol. 1, 399; *New Jersey Concessions,* 429 (quote). Pennsylvania also saw victim control of process, although the procedure was not codified.

74. Paul Lermack, "Peace Bonds and Criminal Justice in Colonial Pennsylvania," *PMHB* 100 (1976): 174–77.

75. Fischer, *Albion's Seed,* 424 (quote), 584–89. See also Tolles, *Meeting House,* 11–13, 109–12; Tully, *Penn's Legacy,* 77–80; and Illick, *Colonial Pennsylvania,* 49–61.

76. Lemon, *Best Poor Man's Country;* Mary Schweitzer, *Custom and Contract: Household, Government and Economy in Colonial Pennsylvania* (New

York, 1987); Meinig, *Shaping of America,* vol. 1, 134, 140; Alan Tully, "Quaker Party and Proprietary Politics: The Dynamics of Politics in Pre-Revolutionary Pennsylvania, 1730–1775," in *Power and Status: Officeholding in Colonial America,* ed. Bruce C. Daniels (Middletown, 1986), 75–105; Wayne Bodle, "Themes and Directions in Middle Colonies Historiography, 1980–94," *WMQ* 51 (1994): 365 (first quote), 359–60, 369; Levy, *Quakers and Family,* 140 (second quote), 152 (third and fourth quote), 189 (last quote).

    77. Roberto Unger, *Law in Modern Society* (New York, 1976), 47.

    78. Bruce Mann, *Neighbors and Strangers: Law and Community in Early Connecticut* (Chapel Hill, N.C., 1987), 10; Konig, *Law and Society in Puritan Massachusetts,* 186–91; William E. Nelson, *Dispute and Conflict Resolution in Plymouth County, Massachusetts, 1725–1825* (Chapel Hill, N.C., 1981), 3–75.

Chapter 1: The Demography of the Law

    1. *Burlington Courts,* 1–242 passim.

    2. Rhys Isaac, *The Transformation of Virginia* (Chapel Hill, N.C., 1982), 88–94; A. G. Roeber, *Faithful Magistrates and Republican Lawyers* (Chapel Hill, N.C., 1981), 73–94; David Konig, *Law and Society in Puritan Massachusetts: Essex County, 1629–1692* (Chapel Hill, N.C., 1979), xiii, 124, 188–91; *New Jersey Concessions,* 448–49; *Pennsylvania Laws, 1682–1700,* 167, 225.

    3. *Bucks Courts,* 180, 275–77, 347, 353, 356–413 passim; *Bucks Dockets,* 386.

    4. *Bucks Courts,* 326, 336, 347, 352, 353, 359, 365, 377, 379, 383, 384, 388, 389, 400.

    5. *Chester Courts I,* 19; *Chester Courts II,* 143.

    6. *Burlington Courts,* 142–43, 148.

    7. Chester County Tax List 1693, Chester County Miscellaneous Papers, 1684–1847, folio 17, HSP; *Bucks County Tax Records, 1693–1778,* ed. Terry McNealy (Doylestown, 1983), 1–2; Chester County Tax List 1699, in *Chester County Treasurers Book 1699–1749,* MS # 76212, Chester County Historical Society, West Chester, Pa. A total of 381 members of the legal population for Bucks and Chester counties appeared on the 1693 tax list, while the total legal population for the whole period was 1,995. I am deeply indebted to Lucy Simler, who discovered the previously unknown 1699 Chester County tax returns and shared this knowledge with me.

    8. Chester MM 5/1688; Burlington MM 10/1683.

    9. A chi-square probability value of 1.00 indicates a perfectly normal distribution of results; if the probability is between .05 and 1.00, the re-

sults are regarded as within the range of likely random outcomes, revealing no statistically significant variations from expected results. I have chosen the .05 line, although some statisticians prefer probabilities of less than .01 (a 99 percent plus likelihood that differences are not random). Konrad Jarausch and Kenneth Hardy, *Quantitative Methods for Historians* (Chapel Hill, N.C., 1991), 104–18. For landholding matched with religion, see table 5.

10. For the roles of officers and jurors in the Delaware Valley, see Wayne Bockelman, "Local Government in Colonial Pennsylvania," in *Town and County: Essays on the Structures of Local Government in the American Colonies,* ed. Bruce Daniels (Middletown, 1978), 216–37; Frank Eastman, *Courts and Lawyers of Pennsylvania,* vol. 1 (New York, 1922), 91–106, 151–55; Lawrence Lewis, "Courts of Pennsylvania in the Seventeenth Century," *PMHB* 5 (1881): 141–90; and William Loyd, *The Early Courts of Pennsylvania* (Boston, 1910). For a study of Middlesex County, Virginia, from 1650 to 1750, which breaks down legal offices similarly, see Darrett Rutman and Anita Rutman, *A Place in Time: Middlesex County, Virginia, 1650–1750* (New York, 1984), 143–52.

11. Alan Tully, *William Penn's Legacy: Politics and Social Structure in Provincial Pennsylvania, 1726–1753* (Baltimore, 1975), 80–92; David Hackett Fischer, *Albion's Seed* (New York, 1989), 424; Barry Levy, *The Quakers and the American Family* (New York, 1988), 157.

12. J. William Frost, *The Quaker Family in Colonial America* (New York, 1973), 3, 53–55, 67–69. For my study, active participation or conformity to Quaker norms was required to qualify as a Quaker: producing a certificate from a previous meeting, being a party to a dispute or a disciplinary procedure brought before the meeting, signing a meeting decree, filling a leadership position. Sources included the men's minutes of the Chester (Pennsylvania), Bucks, and Burlington Quarterly Meetings, and the monthly (men's and women's) meetings of Chester, Concord, Radnor, Darby, Falls, Middletown, Burlington, and Chesterfield from each meeting's first records to 1710, found in the Friends Historical Library, Swarthmore College, Swarthmore, Pa.; W. W. Hinshaw, *Encyclopedia of Quaker Genealogy* (Ann Arbor, Mich., 1938); Hinshaw's card files on individuals who appeared in the records of the above meetings, also at the Friends Library; and *Burlington Courts,* 347–72, index also identified Quakers.

13. Fischer, *Albion's Seed,* 422–24, 430–31. See Introduction, herein, for analysis that rejects the Quaker sympathizer notion.

14. Quaker records do not always use the titles of positions; thus, a collector of funds for the poor has been classified a treasurer, trustees of the land for the meetinghouse were called elders, a regular transcriber of documents was identified as a clerk, and so on. My identification of Quaker lead-

ers was checked against lists of "weighty" (most involved and important) Friends in the Chesterfield and Chester Men's Meetings, which Jean Soderlund generously provided me when she worked at the Friends' Historical Library, Swarthmore College. The correspondence between our lists helped confirm my method of identifying Quakers. See also Jean Soderlund, "Women's Authority in Pennsylvania and New Jersey Quaker Meetings," *WMQ* 44 (1987): 727; Jean Soderlund *Quakers and Slavery: A Divided Spirit* (Princeton, N.J., 1985), 190; Levy, *Quakers and Family,* 141, 301–2; and Fischer, *Albion's Seed,* 515.

15. The court records were *Records of the Court at Upland in Pennsylvania, 1676–1681,* in HSP, *Memoirs VII* (Philadelphia, 1860; repr. 1959), 9–203; and *Records of the Court of New Castle,* vol. 2 (1681–1699) (Meadville, Pa., 1935). For land, wills, and estate information, published sources included William Wharton, *Land Survey Register, 1675–1679,* ed. Albert Cook Myers (Wilmington, 1955); *PMHB* 9 (1885): 223–33; *PMHB* 24 (1900): 182–86; *New Jersey Archives,* series 1, vol. 23 (Abstracts of Wills, 1670–1730); and *New Jersey Archives,* series 1, vol. 21 (West Jersey Land Records). Unpublished sources included Burlington County Wills, Inventories and Administrations, 1688–1728, microfilm rolls 5a and 6, and Gloucester Wills, Inventories and Administrations, 1691–1733, microfilm rolls 350 and 351, New Jersey Archives, Trenton; Survey Book A, 1686–1745, Sharp's Book B, 1688–1723, Bull's Book, 1700–1744, and Leeds Survey Book, HSP for West Jersey; Pennsylvania Deed and Survey Books, Bucks County Books 1–3, Chester County Book 1, Philadelphia County Wills and Inventories Books A–E (through 1730), Exemplification Index Chester and Bucks County grantees, 1683–1803, Miscellaneous Chester County Papers 1684–1847, folio 123, HSP for Pennsylvania; and Wills and Administration Records, 1714–1730, Chester County Archives, West Chester, Pa..

16. Ibid. An examination of the roles of self-described planters in West Jersey indicates that the term *planter* did not denote high status in the Delaware Valley. Of the twenty-two planters in Gloucester, none held high office or had exceptional wealth; similarly, of the twenty-four planters in Burlington, none held high office or was possessed of goods above the population's average at death. *Self-described gentry* were those who defined themselves as gentleman, esquire, or colonel.

For purposes of this study, *artisans* were defined as those who produced products from materials other than land. The artisan list included carpenters, glaziers, hatters, joiners, websters, shipwrights, shoemakers/cordwainers, tailors, bricklayers, woolcombers, brewers, malsters, distillers, and curriers. *Servants/slaves/laborers* included all indentured servants, slaves, and free workers describing themselves as "laborers." Small numbers of each type forced me to use an unwieldy category for statistical purposes. I was influenced by the classification schemes in Carville Earle, *The Evolution of a Tidewater Settlement System* (Chicago, 1975), 80; Jean Russo, "Free Workers in a Plantation Economy: Talbot County, Maryland, 1690–1759" (Ph.D. diss., Johns Hopkins University, 1983), 137–51; Richard Vann, "Quakerism: Made in America?" in *The World of William Penn,* ed. Richard S. Dunn and Mary Maples Dunn (Philadelphia, 1986), 161; and Cynthia Herrup, *The Common Peace* (Cambridge, 1987), 211; and by discussions with Lucy Simler regarding artisans and biooccupationalism at the Philadelphia Center for Early American Studies.

17. See notes 7 and 15; and James Lemon and Gary Nash, "The Distribution of Wealth in Eighteenth-Century America: A Century of Change in Chester County, Pennsylvania, 1693–1802," *Journal of Social History* 2 (1968): 8–10. The groupings, especially for inventory values, reflect the basic categories Aubrey Land, "Economic Behavior in a Planting Society: The Eighteenth-Century Chesapeake," *Journal of Southern History* 33 (1967): 472–73, used in evaluating eighteenth-century Maryland. Biases for both tax lists and wealth include undervaluation deriving from attempts to hide assets, changing monetary values, the lack of a standard valuation scheme, and skewed coverage toward the wealthy. Because the categories used here were so broad, no attempt has been made to account for such biases.

18. Gary Nash, *Quakers and Politics: Pennsylvania, 1681–1726* (Princeton, N.J., 1968), 203n.48; *New Jersey Archives,* series 1, vol. II, 305 (account of the inhabitants of West Jersey in 1699); Craig Horle and Marianne Wokeck, eds., *Lawmaking and Legislators in Pennsylvania: A Biographical Dictionary,* vol. 1 (1682–1709) (Philadelphia, 1991), 49; Vann, "Quakerism," 165.

19. Lemon and Nash, "Distribution of Wealth," 12; Valerie Gladfelter, "Power Challenged: Rising Individualism in the Burlington, New Jersey, Friends Meeting, 1678–1720," in *Friends and Neighbors: Group Life in America's First Plural Society,* ed. Michael Zuckerman (Philadelphia, 1982), 118–19; Richard McCormick, *New Jersey from Colony to State, 1609–1789* (Newark, N.J., 1981), 52; Frederick Tolles, *Meeting House and Counting House* (New York, 1948), 12–13; Joseph Illick, *Colonial Pennsylvania: A History* (New York, 1976), 82; Fischer, *Albion's Seed,* 422–24; Frost, *Perfect Freedom,* 19 (quotes). Part of the acceptance of such estimates came from contemporaries. For example, two non-Quaker attorneys felt there would be a failure of justice in Bucks County "being for ye greatest pt settled wth Quakers there cannot be a sufficient number of jurors" who could take an oath in a murder case. James Logan Collection, vol. 3, 120, HSP.

20. Fischer, *Albion's Seed,* 424.

21. Nash, *Quakers and Politics,* 50 (one-third to one-half of the adult males arrived as servants); Sharon Salinger, *"To Serve Well and Faithfully": Labor and Indentured Servants in Pennsylvania, 1682–1800* (Cambridge, 1987), 21 (the size of the unfree labor population was difficult to determine); Fischer, *Albion's Seed,* 435 (the largest occupational group in immigration registers was servants).

22. Levy, *Quakers and Family,* 176–89.

23. Ibid., 123–52; Tolles, *Meeting House,* 65, 89. Note this claim modifies Fischer, *Albion's Seed,* 435–37 (which contends most immigrants were servants or husbandmen), and Levy, *Quakers and Family* (which claims that land and farming were the core goals of Quaker domesticity). Lois Carr suggested to me the possibility that Quakers might have arrived with more assets to enable them to gain land more rapidly than non-Quakers could. She also suggested some of the variation may be due to differences in ages between Quakers and non-Quakers, a factor this study did not investigate.

24. Levy, *Quakers and Family,* 140–44; Fischer, *Albion's Seed,* 462–67.

25. Levy, *Quakers and Family,* 123–52.

26. John Conley, "Doing It by the Book: Justice of the Peace Manuals and English Law in Eighteenth Century America," *Journal of Legal History* 6 (1985): 258; Norma Landau, *The Justices of the Peace, 1679–1760* (Berkeley, Calif., 1984), 1–2, 6–11, 21–23, 25, 71–80; John Dawson, *A History of Lay Judges* (Cambridge, Mass., 1960), 134, 136–41, 181, 183, 254, 272; Roeber, *Faithful Magistrates,* 6–7, 22; Konig, *Law and Society in Puritan Massachusetts,* 13–14; J. A. Sharpe, *Crime in Early Modern England, 1550–1750* (New York, 1984), 28–30; J. M. Beattie, *Crime and the Courts in England, 1660–1800* (Princeton, N.J., 1986), 59–60.

27. Bradley Chapin, *Criminal Justice in Colonial America, 1606–1660* (Athens, Ga., 1983), 89; Konig, *Law and Society in Puritan Massachusetts,* 33–34, 15–18; Lois Carr, "The Foundations of Social Order: Local Government in Colonial Maryland," in *Town and County: Essays on the Structures of Local Government in the American Colonies,* ed. Bruce Daniels (Middletown, 1978), 87, 98; Edmund Morgan, *American Slavery, American Freedom* (New York, 1975), 149–53, 247–49; Bernard Bailyn, "Politics and Social Structure in Virginia," in *Seventeenth-Century America,* ed. James Morton Smith (Chapel Hill, N.C., 1959), 98–102; Roeber, *Faithful Magistrates,* 31; Conley, "Doing It by the Book," 260; Gail Sussman Marcus, "'Due Execution of the Generall Rules of Righteousnesse': Criminal Procedure in New Haven Town and Colony, 1638–1658," in *Saints and Revolutionaries,* ed. David Hall, Thad Tate, and John Murrin (New York, 1984), 109; John Murrin, "Magistrates, Sinners, and a Precarious Liberty: Trial by Jury in Seventeenth-Century New England," in *Saints and Revolutionaries,* ed. Hall, Tate, and Murrin, 167, 173, 184; George Haskins, *Law and Au-*

thority in Early Massachusetts (New York, 1960), 76–78; Donna Spindel, *Crime and Society in North Carolina, 1663–1776* (Baton Rouge, 1989), 21, 25–26, 30–31.

28. Michael Dalton, *The Countrey Justice* (London, 1622); Richard Chamberlin, *The Complete Justice* (London, 1681); Conley, "Doing It by the Book," 261–62, 272. Chamberlin's work was found in the 1708 inventory of John Guest, a Pennsylvania judge. Edwin Wolf II, "The Library of a Philadelphia Judge, 1708," *PMHB* 83 (1959): 188.

29. *New Jersey Concessions,* 428; *Burlington Courts,* 214, 134; *Pennsylvania Laws, 1682–1700,* 247–48 (quotes), 164; *Statutes at Large II,* 39–40, 268–69.

30. *Bucks Courts,* 92 (no trial due to the lack of a quorum; referred to arbitrators); *Burlington Courts,* 202; *Pennsylvania Laws, 1682–1700,* 133, 176; *Chester Courts I,* 192, 264–66, 313–14. Justice John Simcock was "abused" by those who said he was drunk. Justice John Bristow was accused of marking an already marked horse (he was acquitted despite damning evidence) and, in his job as head ranger, of taking a horse that should have belonged to the governor (the charges were dropped).

31. For causes ruled on, see *Chester Courts II,* 97, 133, 168; aid to juries, *New Jersey Concessions,* 427–8; courts lacking copies of laws, *Chester Courts I,* 236, and *Gloucester Courts,* 178; and equity, *Chester Courts I,* 293.

32. *Gloucester Courts,* 215.

33. Samuel Smith, *The History of the Colony of Nova-Caesaria or New Jersey, Containing an Account of Its First Settlement, Progressive Improvements, the Original and Present Constitution, and Other Events to the Year 1721* (Burlington, 1765), 209; George Odiorne, "Arbitration and Mediation among Early Quakers," *Arbitration Journal* 9 (1950): 161.

34. *New Jersey Concessions,* 408; *Burlington Courts,* lii; Smith, *History of New Jersey,* 225–26; Dunn and Dunn, *Papers of Penn,* vol. 2, 218–19; Bockelman, "Local Government," 220.

35. The justices' average inventory, in pounds valued, compared with the population's average in Chester County was 541 versus 347; Burlington County, 705 versus 345; and Gloucester County, 489 versus 260.

36. *New Jersey Concessions,* 534; *Pennsylvania Laws, 1682–1700,* 235; *Statutes at Large II,* 137–38.

37. *Bucks Courts,* 288; Phineas Pemberton to John Swift, October 19, 1695, Pemberton Papers, vol. 2, 119, HSP; *Burlington Courts,* 326 (reviling the clerk as one who would "write as he pleases" and write "nothing as a body did give in").

38. Bockelman, "Local Government," 222, 232; Pemberton Papers, vol. 1, 19, 27, 35, 57, 58, Etting Collection, HSP.

39. For document forms, see *Pennsylvania Laws, 1682–1700,* 131–32,

163; *Statutes at Large II,* 154–55; David Lloyd to Phineas Pemberton, February 21, 1686, Pemberton Papers, vol. 1, 28. Compare with the attorney clerks in Carr, "The Foundations of Social Order," 75.

40. John Tatham to Phineas Pemberton, July 26, 1695, Pemberton Papers, vol. 2, 112.

41. Samuel Bowne to Phineas Pemberton, October 29, 1695, Pemberton Papers, vol. 2, 120; David Lloyd to Phineas Pemberton, November 20, 1698, Pemberton Papers, vol. 1, 82; Joseph Growden to Phineas Pemberton, February 9, 1698, Pemberton Papers, vol. 1, 75.

42. Phineas Pemberton to Alice Pemberton, March 18, 1700, Pemberton Papers, vol. 2, 164; William Rakestraw to Phineas Pemberton, January 24, 1701, Pemberton Papers, vol. 2, 176b; Phineas Pemberton to Jacob Hall, December 18, 1695, Pemberton Papers, vol. 2, 121a.

43. Bockelman, "Local Government," 219–20; *Pennsylvania Laws, 1682–1700,* 235; *Statutes at Large II,* 138; *Bucks Dockets,* 389.

44. *Burlington Courts,* 176–77.

45. Ibid., 236.

46. Tully, *Penn's Legacy,* 105, 112; Bockelman, "Local Government," 229.

47. Bockelman, "Local Government," 220; *Pennsylvania Laws, 1682–1700,* 235; *Statutes at Large II,* 138–39; *Bucks Dockets,* 393; *Burlington Courts,* 303.

48. *Burlington Courts,* 71–72, 206, 213; *Bucks Courts,* 263 (quote).

49. *Bucks Courts,* 25, 59; *Chester Courts I,* 39, 56 (Caleb Pusey, Walter Fausett, and Robert Vernon were peacemakers in Chester County in 1685); *Pennsylvania Laws, 1682–1700,* 128.

50. Among the short-term attorneys general were Thomas Revell in Burlington County in 1695, David Lloyd in Bucks County in 1687–88, John White in Chester County in 1690, John Moore in Chester County in 1700, Thomas Clark in Chester County in 1708, and Alexander Griffith in Burlington County in 1709.

51. Bockelman, "Local Government," 218–22; *Burlington Courts,* xl–xli.

52. Complete analysis of Pennsylvania legislators from this period has been done by Horle and Wokeck, *Lawmaking and Legislators.*

53. Chapin, *Criminal Justice in Colonial America,* 96 (quote); Bockelman, "Local Government," 224; *Chester Courts II,* 73, 154.

54. *Pennsylvania Laws, 1682–1700,* 236; *New Jersey Concessions,* 541; *Burlington Courts,* liv, 117 (quote). Pennsylvania required constables to attest that they would continue to serve "until another be attested in thy Room." *Pennsylvania Laws, 1682–1700,* 248; *Statutes at Large II,* 40.

55. *Burlington Courts,* liv, 213, 180.

56. *Gloucester Courts,* 368; *Chester Courts I,* 362–63 (first quote); *Chester Courts II,* 2 (second quote).

57. *Burlington Courts,* 301; Chapin, *Criminal Justice in Colonial America,* 96.

58. Konig, *Law and Society in Puritan Massachusetts,* 12, 119; Robert Wheeler, "The County Court in Colonial Virginia," in *Town and County: Essays on the Structures of Local Government in the American Colonies,* ed. Bruce Daniels (Middletown, 1978), 123; Spindel, *Crime and Society in North Carolina,* 35–36. English historians have recently challenged this view. Sharpe, *Crime in Early Modern England,* 34; Beattie, *Crime and Courts,* 70–71.

59. Bockelman, "Local Government," 225; *Pennsylvania Laws, 1682–1700,* 136, 233; *Burlington Courts,* 117.

60. *Burlington Courts,* 27, 30, 148, 271, 321–22; *Bucks Courts,* 298; *Pennsylvania Laws, 1682–1700,* 136, 233.

61. Lesser officers also include other participants in minor offices who were not constables or highway overseers: tax assessors, collectors, and receivers; packers; fence-viewers; overseers of the poor; boundary-line supervisors; and hogbeadles.

62. Roger Thompson, *Sex in Middlesex* (Amherst, Mass., 1986), 5, 31; Rutman and Rutman, *Place in Time,* 90–91, 144–47; Carr, "The Foundations of Social Order," 91; Wheeler, "County Court in Colonial Virginia," 115; Konig, *Law and Society in Puritan Massachusetts,* 164; David Konig, "Country Justice: The Rural Roots of Constitutionalism in Colonial Virginia," in *An Uncertain Tradition: Constitutionalism and the History of the South,* ed. Kermit Hall and James Ely, Jr. (Athens, Ga., 1989), 72–73; David Williams, "The Small Farmer in Eighteenth-Century Virginia Politics," in *Colonial America: Essays in Political and Social Development,* 3d ed., ed. Stanley Katz and John Murrin (New York, 1983), 417, 419, 421; Spindel, *Crime and Society in North Carolina,* 19; Murrin, "Magistrates, Sinners, and a Precarious Liberty," 188, 197; Laura Becker, "The People and the System: Legal Activities in a Colonial Pennsylvania Town," *PMHB* 105 (1981): 140, 149. For a comparison of English jury practices of the time, see Beattie, *Crime and Courts,* 320–21, 379, 385, 392.

63. Roeber, "Authority, Law and Custom," 45 (first quote); Gwenda Morgan, "Law and Social Change in Colonial Virginia," *Virginia Magazine of History and Biography* 95 (1987): 456 (second quote).

64. Landau, *Justices of the Peace,* 51 (quote); Dawson, *A History of Lay Judges,* 121–27; Chapin, *Criminal Justice in Colonial America,* 33–34; Sharpe, *Crime in Early Modern England,* 37; Walter Shumaker and George Longsdorf, *The Cyclopedic Law Dictionary* (Chicago, 1912), 453.

65. Chapin, *Criminal Justice in Colonial America,* 34; Wheeler, "County Court in Colonial Virginia," 115; Carr, "The Foundations of Social Order," 76; Dawson, *A History of Lay Judges,* 217–18; Spindel, *Crime and Society in North Carolina,* 37.

66. *Bucks Courts,* 321; *Pennsylvania Laws, 1682–1700,* 233; *New Jersey Concessions,* 528; *Burlington Courts,* 234–35; *Gloucester Courts,* 162; *Chester Courts I,* 270, 276, 283, 302, 358; *Bucks Courts,* 298.

67. Carr, "The Foundations of Social Order," 76; Wheeler, "County Court in Colonial Virginia," 115; Morgan, "Law and Social Change," 453.

68. *Burlington Courts,* 115 (presentment from their own knowledge); *Burlington Courts,* 206 (ignore instruction to look into breaking the Sabbath); *Chester Courts I,* 264 (charge an officer for ranging horses). 1707 saw an increase in ignoramus findings in Burlington, and no true bills were found at several courts. *Burlington Courts,* 112, 322–23; *Chester Courts II,* 99.

69. For previous presentments not prosecuted, see *Burlington Courts,* 261; for quashed indictments, *Chester Courts II,* 176; and for attestations for grand jurors quoted, *Pennsylvania Laws, 1682–1700,* 248, and *Statutes at Large II,* 40.

70. *Pennsylvania Laws, 1682–1700,* 100, 117, 127, 129; *Statutes at Large II,* 128–29; *New Jersey Concessions,* 395–98; *Burlington Courts,* 118.

71. Dawson, *A History of Lay Judges,* 122–27; William Nelson, *Dispute and Conflict Resolution in Plymouth County, Massachusetts, 1725–1825* (Chapel Hill, N.C., 1981), 25; Craig Horle, *The Quakers and the English Legal System, 1660–1688* (Philadelphia, 1989), 11, 49, 107–17, 223–24; Thomas Green, *Verdict according to Conscience* (Chicago, 1985), 200–208, 221–49; *New Jersey Concessions,* 395, 427–28; *Statutes at Large II,* 241–42.

72. *Bucks Courts,* 358–60 (fifty shilling fine); Falls MM 10/1698–3/1699; Middletown MM 12/98; Winfred Root, *The Relations of Pennsylvania with the British Government, 1696–1763* (Philadelphia, 1912), 238.

73. *Freeman* was defined in Pennsylvania in a complicated scheme based on landownership, land cultivation, or payment of scot and lot to the government. Laws were passed to punish "everie person being a Freeman" who was summoned to serve but did not appear. *Pennsylvania Laws, 1682–1700,* 99, 127, 215. Regarding jury packing in England, see Landau, *Justices of the Peace,* 52–53; and Beattie, *Crime and Courts,* 320–23.

74. Beattie, *Crime and Courts,* 320–22, 379, 392; Lois Green Carr, *County Government in Maryland, 1689–1709* (New York, 1987), 658–61.

75. For grand juries, 60.7 percent of Quaker landowners were called, compared with 27.8 percent of non-Quaker landowners. For trial juries, 56.5 percent of Quaker landowners were called, compared with 28.1 percent of non-Quaker landowners.

Chapter 2: Litigants and Their Causes

1. William Felstiner, Richard Abel, and Austin Sarat, "The Emergence and Transformation of Disputes: Naming, Blaming, and Claiming," *Law*

and Society Review 15 (1981): 647, 651; William Felstiner, "Influences of Social Organization on Dispute Processing," in *Law and the Behavioral Sciences*, 2d ed., ed. Lawrence M. Friedman and Stewart Macaulay (New York, 1977), 1013–23; Richard Miller and Austin Sarat, "Grievances, Claims and Disputes: Assessing the Adversary Culture," *Law and Society Review* 15 (1981): 527; Lynn Mather and Barbara Yngvesson, "Language, Audience and the Transformation of Disputes," *Law and Society Review* 15 (1981): 818–19; Wayne McIntosh, "150 Years of Litigation and Dispute Settlement: A Court Tale," *Law and Society Review* 15 (1981): 824; Maureen Cain and Kalman Kulcsar, "Thinking Disputes: An Essay on the Origins of the Dispute Industry," *Law and Society Review* 16 (1982): 395.

2. *Pennsylvania Laws, 1682–1700*, 100, 128; *Statutes at Large II*, 128; Richard S. Dunn and Mary Maples Dunn, eds., *The Papers of William Penn*, vol. 1 (1644–79) (Philadelphia, 1981), 397.

3. *Pennsylvania Laws, 1682–1700*, 100, 199; *Statutes at Large II*, 128.

4. *New Jersey Concessions*, 398. Pennsylvania had the same rules about personally pleading one's cause or pleading by "friends": *Pennsylvania Laws, 1682–1700*, 100, 204; *Statutes at Large II*, 128.

5. *New Jersey Concessions*, 509–10; *Pennsylvania Laws, 1682–1700*, 131, 219; *Statues at Large II*, 43, 189. The goal was to reduce the county court's workload of "petty actions" by giving single justices more power to render conclusive judgments.

6. *New Jersey Concessions*, 395; *Pennsylvania Laws, 1682–1700*, 100, 204; *Gloucester Courts*, 2 (May 25, 1686). In West Jersey, if the defendant lived more than forty miles from court, the filing time increased two days for each additional twenty miles.

7. *Pennsylvania Laws, 1682–1700*, 226.

8. Walter Wheeler Cook, *Readings on the Forms of Action at Common Law* (Chicago, 1940), 81; *New Jersey Concessions*, 395; *Bucks Courts*, 4–5; *Gloucester Courts*, 281.

9. *Pennsylvania Laws, 1682–1700*, 289–90.

10. Donald Veall, *The Popular Movement for Law Reform, 1640–60* (Oxford, 1970), 145–46.

11. *New Jersey Concessions*, 395, 547–48; *Pennsylvania Laws, 1682–1700*, 171, 200; *Statutes at Large II*, 249–50.

12. *New Jersey Concessions*, 395; *Pennsylvania Laws, 1682–1700*, 131.

13. *Gloucester Courts*, 266; *Burlington Courts*, 206–7.

14. Lawrence M. Friedman, "Legal Culture and Social Development," *Law and Society Review* 4 (1969): 34; Richard Ross, "The Legal Past of Early New England: Notes for the Study of Law, Legal Culture, and Intellectual History," *WMQ* 50 (1993): 32–33.

15. *Pennsylvania Laws, 1682–1700*, 100, 117, 131, 163, 199, 204, 226;

Statutes at Large II, 128, 136, 149, 154–56; *New Jersey Concessions,* 398. For fees, see *Pennsylvania Laws, 1682–1700,* 100, 117, 148–49, 187, 199; *Statutes at Large II,* 137–40; and *New Jersey Concessions,* 399, 455, 538–41.

16. In English common law, *nihil dicit* meant the defendant had nothing to say to the complaint; *assumpsit* and *quantum meruit* referred to contract and assumed contract terms; *scire facias, capias ad satisfaciendum,* and *fiere facias* were types of executions available under particular circumstances after the plaintiff had a judgment. Walter Shumaker and George Longsdorf, *The Cyclopedic Law Dictionary* (Chicago, 1912), 625, 73, 752, 827, 124, 371. For early usage of these terms, see *Gloucester Courts,* 1–27; *Burlington Courts,* 39, 140, 198, 257; *Chester Courts I,* 344–45; and *Chester Courts II,* 36. For a contemporary discussion, see William Sheppard, *The Faithful Councillor or the Marrow of the Law in English,* 2d ed. (London, 1653).

17. Schumaker and Longsdorf, *Cyclopedic Law Dictionary,* 661, 456. For a short description of the imparlance, see Sheppard, *Faithful Councillor,* 357 (quote). Usage of the oyer and imparlance can be seen throughout *Chester Courts II.*

18. Roy Lokken, *David Lloyd, Colonial Lawmaker* (Seattle, 1959), 104–5, 166; *Statutes at Large II,* 149 (quote). David Lloyd's personal legal career revealed this contradiction as well—while he brought to America a notebook (in HSP) filled with legal Latin and wrote ever-more convoluted judiciary acts, he fought against allowing the action of ejectment (with its fictitious parties and leases) into practice in the Delaware Valley.

19. *Pennsylvania Laws, 1682–1700,* 131, 205; *Statutes at Large II,* 46–47 (against "unjust and vexatious" suits). Barratry was also punished in colonial Massachusetts and Virginia, but, unlike the Delaware Valley, these colonies arrived at their statutes after many years of legal experience (Massachusetts in 1648 and Virginia in 1662). See George Haskins, *Law and Authority in Early Massachusetts* (New York, 1968), 213; and W. W. Hening, ed., *The Statutes at Large, Being a Collection of All the Laws of Virginia,* vol. 2 (Richmond, 1809), 66.

20. *Pennsylvania Laws, 1682–1700,* 101, 181.

21. Ibid., 165.

22. Ibid., 128.

23. Ibid., 148–50; *Statutes at Large II,* 137–40; *New Jersey Concessions,* 538–41; Caroline Robbins, "Laws and Governments Proposed for West New Jersey and Pennsylvania, 1676–1683," *PMHB* 105 (1981): 390.

24. Lawrence M. Friedman, *The Republic of Choice: Law, Authority, and Culture* (Cambridge, Mass., 1990), 213; Kermit Hall, *The Magic Mirror, Law in American History* (New York, 1989), 6. *Legal culture* has been defined by others in similar ways, but its analytical usage has been described as "genuinely elusive," a "catchall," and "a slippery concept." Hall, *Magic*

Mirror, 6 (first quote); Ross, "Legal Past of Early New England," 33 (second quote), 34 (third quote). Ross noted, however, how legal culture allows insights into less specialized premodern legal systems, particularly in terms of interconnections across jurisdictional lines.

25. Frederick Tolles, *Meeting House and Counting House* (New York, 1948), 75; Anton-Hermann Chroust, *The Rise of the Legal Profession in America,* vol. 1, *The Colonial Experience* (Norman, Okla., 1965), 28; David Hackett Fischer, *Albion's Seed* (New York, 1989), 425.

26. Chester MM 1700 (between pages 62 and 63); Chester QM, 9/1702; Friends Yearly Meeting Paper, undated (but pre-1687 because it was signed by James Harrison, who died in 1687), Pemberton Papers, vol. 2, 30, HSP (quote).

27. Morton Horwitz, *The Transformation of American Law, 1780–1860* (Cambridge, Mass.: 1977), 145–48; Jerold Auerbach, *Justice without Law?* (New York, 1983), 32–33.

28. *Bucks Dockets,* 455–56, 459; *Bucks Courts,* 282, 105, 145; *Gloucester Courts,* 146, 157, 301, 303. On rules of coverture, suits, and conveyance, see Marylynn Salmon, *Women and the Law of Property in Early America* (Chapel Hill, N.C., 1986), 14–18.

29. For differing views on the social status of litigants in New England, see David Allen, *In English Ways* (Chapel Hill, N.C., 1982), 226; William Nelson, *Dispute and Conflict Resolution in Plymouth County, Massachusetts, 1725–1825* (Chapel Hill, N.C., 1981), 67; and Christine Leigh Heyrman, *Commerce and Culture* (New York, 1984), 69–73, 236–37.

30. Chester MM, 62 (undated but among notes dated 1700); Chester QM 9/1702; Burlington MM 6/1681; Friends Yearly Meeting Paper, no date, Pemberton Papers, vol. 2, 29–30, HSP; Arnold Lloyd, *Quaker Social History* (London, 1950), 74; *Burlington Courts,* xii; Paul Lermack, "Peace Bonds and Criminal Justice in Colonial Pennsylvania," *PMHB* 100 (1976): 173–74; George Odiorne, "Arbitration and Mediation among Early Quakers, *Arbitration Journal* 9 (1950): 165; Tolles, *Meeting House,* 51, 75–78; Stephen Botein, "The Legal Profession in Colonial North America," in *Lawyers in Early Modern Europe and America,* ed. Wilfred Pratt (New York, 1981), 132; Auerbach, *Justice without Law?* 28–30.

31. McIntosh, "150 Years of Litigation," 825; Thomas Haskell, "Litigation and Social Status in Seventeenth-Century New Haven," *Journal of Legal Studies* 7 (1978): 236–38; Allen, *In English Ways,* 226.

32. *Burlington Courts,* 206, 210–11.

33. *Chester Courts I,* 242.

34. *Bucks Courts,* 126, 129–30.

35. See chapter 4 for a full discussion of the objections to Quakers' going to court against one another.

36. Those allowed to go to court were recorded in Chester MM 4/1703, 4/1704; Chester QM 12/1685; Middletown MM 11/1699, 1/1700, 4/1709; and Burlington MM 4/1700, 1/1707. Those disciplined for going to court appeared in Chester QM 6/1699. Middletown MM 11/1703 ordered all actions at law withdrawn, but no sanction was imposed.

37. Of the cases that occurred between two members of the same meeting in Chester County, members of the Chester Monthly Meeting filed 83.3 percent of the cases, while accounting for only 46.8 percent of the Quakers in the legal population. Similarly, members of the Middletown Monthly Meeting in Bucks County had 75 percent of intrameeting law cases, while accounting for only 41 percent of the Quakers in the legal population, and Burlington Monthly Meeting members had 80 percent of the intrameeting cases in Burlington County, while accounting for 69.7 percent of the Quaker population. At the other extreme, Radnor Monthly Meeting members constituted 15.3 percent of the Quaker population, and Darby Monthly Meeting members were 16.1 percent of the Quaker population; however, they accounted for 0.0 and 4.1 percent, respectively, of the intrameeting cases in Chester County. Falls Monthly Meeting members constituted 59 percent of the Quaker population but only 25 percent of the intrameeting cases in Bucks County.

38. Tolles, *Meeting House,* 89.

39. Sally Falk Moore, *Law as Process: An Anthropological Approach* (London, 1978), 2, 3, 14, 19; Roberto Unger, *Law in Modern Society* (New York, 1976), 49; Lon Fuller, "Law and Human Interaction," *Sociological Inquiry* 47 (1977): 60–64; Bruce Mann, *Neighbors and Strangers: Law and Community in Early Connecticut* (Chapel Hill, N.C., 1987), 21.

40. Edwin Wolf II, "The Library of a Philadelphia Judge, 1708," *PMHB* 83 (1959): 185–91, shows the variety of formbooks, guides, and law reports that were available in the Delaware Valley by 1708. Formbooks that utilized contemporary declarations as models and informed this and the following paragraphs included John Herne, *The Pleader: Containing Perfect Presidents and Forme of Declarations, Pleadings, Issues, Judgments and Proceedings* (London, 1751) (there was a 1657 edition noted in Wolf's library); Creswell Levinz, *A Collection of Select and Modern Entries and Declarations, Pleadings, Issues, Verdicts, Judgments, etc.* (London, 1702); George Townsend, *A Preparative to Pleading, Being a Work Intended for the Instruction and Help of Young Clerks of the Court of the Common Pleas* (London, 1713); Sheppard, *Faithful Councillor.*

41. Cook, *Forms of Action at Common Law,* 12–14, 23–24, 59–60; Sheppard, *Faithful Councillor,* 279–81; Theodore F. T. Plucknett, *A Concise History of the Common Law* (Boston, 1956), 366–67.

42. Plucknett, *Concise History of Common Law,* 372; J. H. Baker, *An Introduction to English Legal History,* 2d ed. (London, 1979), 58–59; John

Cound, Jack Friedenthal, and Arthur Miller, *Civil Procedure: Cases and Materials,* 2d ed. (St. Paul, 1974), 332; Cook, *Forms of Action at Common Law,* 12–13, 137–38.

43. David Thomas Konig, "A Guide to the Use of the Plymouth Court Records," in *Plymouth Court Records, 1686–1859,* vol. 1, ed. David Thomas Konig (Wilmington, 1978), 153–55; Baker, *English Legal History,* 264, 275, 282–85, 306–9; William Nelson, *Americanization of the Common Law* (Cambridge, 1975), 54–55; Cound, Friedenthal, and Miller, *Civil Procedure,* 344–49; Sheppard, *Faithful Councillor,* 124–25.

44. Sheppard, *Faithful Councillor,* 36–37; Konig, "Guide to Plymouth Court," 157–58.

45. Konig, "Guide to Plymouth Court," 156; Cound, Friedenthal, and Miller, *Civil Procedure,* 340–41; Plucknett, *Concise History of Common Law,* 374–75; Cook, *Forms of Action at Common Law,* 24–25; Sheppard, *Faithful Councillor,* 155.

46. Konig, "Guide to Plymouth Court," 150–51; Nelson, *Americanization of Common Law,* 61; Baker, *English Legal History,* 266–70.

47. Cook, *Forms of Action at Common Law,* 110–12; Lawrence M. Friedman, *A History of American Law* (New York, 1973), 18–19; Plucknett, *Concise History of Common Law,* 373–74.

48. Konig, "Guide to Plymouth Court," 151; Cound, Friedenthal, and Miller, *Civil Procedure,* 340–41; Cook, *Forms of Action at Common Law,* 81–83; Schumaker and Longsdorf, *Cyclopedic Law Dictionary,* 12.

49. Konig, "Guide to Plymouth Court," 169–70; Peter Hoffer, *Law and People in Colonial America* (Baltimore, 1992), 68; Mann, *Neighbors and Strangers,* 81–82; *Burlington Courts,* 114–15, 187, 197, 206, 234; *Bucks Courts,* 101–3, 392, 400; *Chester Courts II,* 67; *Gloucester Courts,* 146.

50. *Burlington Courts,* 197–98; *Bucks Courts,* 151, 155, 156, 159, 258. This latter dispute was ultimately withdrawn, but seven years later Tatham sued Growden again in a case that was continued over five court sessions. Growden, perhaps remembering his ineffectual experience with a nonsuit in 1691, could have gotten a nonsuit in 1699 but continued the case instead, a move that paid off when he won a jury verdict at the next court session. *Bucks Courts,* 348, 385, 402–13.

51. *Chester Courts I,* 324; *Chester Courts II,* 15, 54, 179, 191, 195; *Burlington Courts,* 183, 237–38. An example of several different causes of action linked together occurred in Robert Turner's suit against Benjamin White in case. Turner, *Gloucester Documents,* 98, alleged trespass, a cutting of trees, and a conversion of trees to the defendant's use. This one transaction could call forth several different causes of action, yet a strict interpretation of pleading rules would probably not have allowed case. *Chester Courts I,* 226, 232, illustrated a switch in causes from case to debt.

52. *Burlington Courts,* 186, 250.

53. Ibid., 172 (quotes), 174.

54. *Bucks Courts,* 44–45.

55. Ibid., 43, 167; *Chester Courts II,* 9; Lokken, *David Lloyd,* 166; *Minutes of Council,* II, 258–60; *Chester Courts I,* 242. Ejectione firme was allowed where defendants did not challenge the proceedings; see *Bucks Courts,* 43, 47, 380, 386; and *Gloucester Documents,* 155. Defamation, trespass, and case were used to try titles to land; see *Burlington Courts,* 145, 153; and *Chester Courts I,* 214, 232. On David Lloyd in 1705 in Council, see *Minutes of Council,* II, 180–81; Lawrence Lewis, "The Courts of Pennsylvania in the Seventeenth Century," *PMHB* 5 (1881): 150; and Frank Eastman, *Courts and Lawyers in Pennsylvania,* vol. 1, (New York, 1923), 118, 119. David Konig, *Law and Society in Puritan Massachusetts: Essex County, 1629–1692* (Chapel Hill, N.C., 1979), 61, noted the substitution of case for ejectment in Massachusetts procedure.

56. *Chester Courts I,* 254; *Chester Courts II,* 97, 133.

57. *Bucks Courts,* 3–55 passim. Milcome versus Smith and Smith, *Bucks Courts,* 7, was a declaration in case that ran less than a hundred words.

58. *Gloucester Documents,* 84.

59. *Bucks Courts,* 44–45, 264–65; *Gloucester Documents,* 148, 155.

60. *Gloucester Documents,* 83.

61. Ibid., 126; *Bucks Courts,* 317; plaintiffs' declarations, May 1, 1703, January 1, 1704, and May 20, 1707, Chester Narratives, Box q, Chester County Archives, West Chester, Pa.; *Burlington Courts,* 279.

62. Plaintiffs' declarations, February 25, 1699, December 11, 1700, July 29, 1703, March 16, 1703, January 1, 1704, January 20, 1703, March 10, 1703, November 26, 1703, July 25, 1704, Chester Narratives, Box q, Chester County Archives, West Chester, Pa.; *Gloucester Documents,* 111, 103, 92, 93, 94, 115, 131.

63. Konig, "Guide to Plymouth Court," 169; Hoffer, *Law and People,* 68; *Burlington Courts,* 140, 305, 198; *Chester Courts II,* 199, 207, 178 (*non cull*); Sheppard, *Faithful Councillor,* 360 (*nihil debet* and *non cull*).

64. *Burlington Courts,* 250, 257, 296; *Bucks Dockets,* 413; *Chester Courts II,* 97, 179. Sheppard, *Faithful Councillor,* 364 (on negative pregnant), 372–73 (on demurrer).

65. Sheppard, *Faithful Councillor,* 357, 358; *Chester Courts II,* passim.

66. Each segment of the table will indicate the chi-square probability for the statistical significance at the bottom of each set of attributes matched with causes. When the probability number was less than .05 (the standard for indicating that a statistical relationship is significantly skewed from the results expected from population), the largest differences from the expected results are presented in order of their contribution to the chi-square finding.

67. Jean Russo's personal letter to me on May 11, 1985, on Maryland cases stated that "most suits concerned the defendant's failure to repay a debt of some form." The work of Bruce Mann in Connecticut, Lois Green Carr in Maryland, Warren Billings in Virginia, and David Konig and William Nelson in Massachusetts confirms this statement.

68. Tolles, *Meeting House,* 58–60, 73–78, 89–95; Fischer, *Albion's Seed,* 428, 557.

69. For example, these records are not precise enough to determine, for cases of indebtedness, whether a writing was used, which type of writing was more commonly used, and whether there was a change in usage over time. I am therefore unable to compare my results directly with those of Bruce Mann, *Neighbors and Strangers,* which identifies the usage and significance of book debt and its later decline in favor of more standardized bonds and notes.

70. Mann, *Neighbors and Strangers,* 28–30, 171.

71. Helena Wall, *Fierce Communion: Family and Community in Early America* (Cambridge, Mass., 1990), 36–37; Konig, *Law and Society in Puritan Massachusetts,* 81–82.

Chapter 3: Strategies and Outcomes in Civil Litigation

1. Sally Falk Moore, *Law as Process: An Anthropological Approach* (London, 1978), 4; William Felstiner, Richard Abel, and Austin Sarat, "The Emergence and Transformation of Disputes: Naming, Blaming, Claiming . . . ," *Law and Society Review* 15 (1981): 647, 651; Wayne McIntosh, "Private Use of a Public Forum: A Long-Range View of the Dispute Processing Role of Courts," *American Political Science Review* 77 (1983): 992.

2. Moore, *Law as Process,* 3, 9, 18; Roberto Unger, *Law in Modern Society* (New York, 1976), 49.

3. Wayne McIntosh, "150 Years of Litigation and Dispute Settlement: A Court Tale," *Law and Society Review* 15 (1981): 825; Felstiner, Abel, and Sarat, "The Emergence and Transformation of Disputes," 639–54; Richard Abel, "A Comparative Theory of Dispute Institutions in Society," *Law and Society Review* 8 (1973): 289–94; Richard Miller and Austin Sarat, "Grievances, Claims and Disputes: Assessing the Adversary Culture," *Law and Society Review* 15 (1981): 533, 562; Robert Kidder, "Afterward: Change and Structure in Dispute Processing," *Law and Society Review* 9 (1975): 387–90; Barbara Yngvesson, "Law in Pre-Industrial Societies," *Sociological Inquiry* 47 (1977): 145–46; William Felstiner, "Influences of Social Organization on Dispute Processing," in *Law and the Behavioral Sciences,* 2d ed., ed. Lawrence M. Friedman and Stewart Macaulay (New York, 1977), 1013–23; Austin Sarat and Joel Grossman, "Courts and Conflict Resolution: Prob-

lems in the Mobilization of Adjudication," *American Political Science Review* 69 (1975): 1204–9; Laura Nader and Harry Todd, eds., *The Disputing Process—Law in Ten Societies* (New York, 1978), 11–29; Marc Galanter, "Why the 'Haves' Come Out Ahead: Speculations on the Limits of Legal Change," *Law and Society Review* 9 (1974): 95–103; Bruce H. Mann, "Rationality, Legal Change, and Community in Connecticut, 1690–1760," *Law and Society Review* 14 (1980): 193–218.

4. Jerold Auerbach, *Justice without Law?* (New York, 1983), 3–4; Unger, *Law in Modern Society*, 47 (quote).

5. David T. Konig, *Law and Society in Puritan Massachusetts: Essex County, 1629–1692* (Chapel Hill, N.C., 1979), xiii–xv, 65–71, 88, 112–19, 190; Eric Steele, "Review Essay: Morality, Legality, and Dispute Processing: Auerbach's *Justice without Law?*" *American Bar Foundation Research Journal* 189 (1984): 199–205.

6. *Burlington Courts*, 3, 35, 44, 83; *Gloucester Courts*, 165–69; *Chester Courts I*, 17, 92, 105; *Bucks Courts*, 21, 335–36. Detailed descriptions of such examples appear later in the discussion of litigants' adopting an accommodating persona.

7. Calling these cases settled does necessarily imply an amicable resolution between the parties. Cryptic comments in the dockets like "ended" and "discontinued" often followed many court sessions of continuances and may reflect real unhappiness on the part of the plaintiff whose case has been stalled to death. In a few cases, death itself "ended" the case, although such cases could be refiled by or against the estate. The term *settled* will, however, be used throughout because it best conveys the notion of a dispute resolution outside of court.

8. The distinction between contested and uncontested was often a difficult one, made harder by the brevity of the record, and it was sometimes made on a case-by-case basis. Defendants or their representatives often appeared in court but pled "nihil dicit" or "non sum informatus"; though there was a confrontation in court, there was no real conflict on the merits. Similarly, judgments on pleas in abatement were regarded as uncontested (technical pleading failures that could be easily amended and often were); even though clearly the parties were in pleading conflict, the merits were not yet reached. Judgments on demurrers testing whether the facts as stated constituted a sufficient cause of action were labeled contested because they ended the pleading and normally were the final judgment on the dispute. Cases that had been tried before a single justice between sessions (for amounts less than forty shillings) and were then taken to the full bench for confirmation or appeal were contested, even if the court quickly ratified the previous decision. In other difficult instances, ambiguity in the record was resolved in favor of classifying a case contested, especially if the defendant

appeared. Many such cases involved bench judgments where the only information was that there had been a judgment in favor of either the plaintiff or the defendant. To list these cases as contested because a default, confession, or nonsuit was not recorded probably slightly inflates the number
of contested bench judgments (121 counted, or 7.4 percent of completed
cases).

9. *Bucks Courts,* 369. Pennsylvania statutes allowed defendants to be
arrested only in cases where landed defendants, such as Thatcher, were believed about to leave the province or refused to give security for their appearance and performance of any award against them. *Pennsylvania Laws,
1682–1700,* 118, 171; *Statutes at Large II,* 249.

10. *Burlington Courts,* 178, 155; *Gloucester Courts,* 247.

11. J. H. Baker made this suggestion in the New York University Legal
History Colloquium, October 2, 1991.

12. Lawrence M. Friedman and Robert V. Percival, "A Tale of Two
Courts: Litigation in Alameda and San Benito Counties," *Law and Society
Review* 10 (1976): 269–72, 286–87.

13. There were at least fifteen such cases of one-step chancered bonds
after a judgment was made or confessed in Burlington County, ten in Bucks
County, eight in Chester County, and three in Gloucester County.

14. *Burlington Courts,* 276, 278; *Chester Courts II,* 94, *Bucks Courts,*
380. *Chester Courts I,* 323, involved a jury trial where the plaintiff had to
remit the penalty on the bond to obtain a postverdict execution.

15. Richard S. Dunn and Mary Maples Dunn, *The Papers of William
Penn,* vol. 1 (1644–79) (Philadelphia, 1981), 398; *Pennsylvania Laws, 1682–
1700,* 116.

16. All of these contested cases utilized three or more witnesses: for servants conditions and wages, see *Chester Courts I,* 110–11, 129, and *Burlington Courts,* 12, 15; for payment for work performed, *Chester Courts I,*
164–66, 207–8, and *Burlington Courts,* 74, 108–10, 210; and for fraud and
performance questions, *Chester Courts I,* 190–92, *Burlington Courts,* 106–
7, 230–31 (warranty defense against poor performance by a doctor), *Gloucester Courts,* 146–48 (arbitration performance), and *Bucks Courts,* 342–44
(not making a good title in a bargain and sale of land).

17. *Pennsylvania Laws, 1682–1700,* 118, 201 (quotes), 101, 181.

18. This reversal of roles by the use of a civil case was noted regarding
New England's accused witches, who could forestall criminal charges by
bringing scandal and defamation complaints against their accusers. For more
on this point, see John Demos, *Entertaining Satan: Witchcraft and the Culture of Early New England,* (Oxford, 1982), 249; and Helena Wall, *Fierce
Communion: Family and Community in Early America* (Cambridge, Mass.,
1990), 34–35.

19. *Chester Courts I*, 53–54.
20. *Burlington Courts*, 174–75.
21. *Chester Courts I*, 290 (first three quotes), 291 (last two quotes).
22. *Burlington Courts*, 132–33.
23. *Chester Courts I*, 58.
24. *Burlington Courts*, 33–34.
25. For trespass cases, see *Chester Courts I*, 11; *Bucks Courts*, 71–72; *Burlington Courts*, 49–50, 161; and *Gloucester Courts*, 132–34. For cases involving trover/trespass by animals, see *Chester Courts I*, 80–83 (sixteen witnesses), 372–74; *Burlington Courts*, 33, 171–72; and *Gloucester Courts*, 140–43, 255–59.
26. Steele, "Review Essay," 199, 202; Konig, *Law and Society in Puritan Massachusetts*, 117–20, 190, xiii–xv; Laura Becker, "The People and the System: Legal Activities in a Colonial Pennsylvania Town," *PMHB* 105 (1981): 140–41.
27. For arbitration requisites, see Bruce Mann, "The Formalization of Informal Law: Arbitration before the American Revolution," *NYU Law Review* 59 (1984): 447, 459–60; John Dawson, *A History of Lay Judges* (Cambridge, 1960), 164–65; Morton Horwitz, *The Transformation of American Law, 1780–1860* (Cambridge, Mass., 1977), 145; William Loyd, *The Early Courts of Pennsylvania* (Boston, 1910), 48–49; and Gail McKnight Beckman, ed., *The Statutes at Large of Pennsylvania in the Time of William Penn*, vol. 1 (1680–1700) (New York, 1976), 27.
28. *Pennsylvania Laws, 1682–1700*, 128. For references to arbitrations that did not appear as court cases, see the difference between Samuel Cuerton and John Cluse, December 4, 1684, Pemberton Papers, vol. 1, 5, Etting Collection, HSP; David Lloyd to Phineas Pemberton, November 20, 1698, Pemberton Papers, vol. 1, 82; difference between James Harrison and Will Register, September 27, 1686, Pemberton Papers, vol. 1, 18; and Court of Common Pleas, Philadelphia, January 1708, 203, Stauffer Collection, HSP. In the difference between Lawrence Bannor and William Beakes, a case was filed and then arbitrated successfully, but there is no court record of such a resolution (the case was incomplete according to the docket). June 27, 1686, Miscellaneous, 12, Etting Collection, HSP; David Lloyd to James Harrison, August 30, 1686, Pemberton Papers, vol. 2, 11, HSP; Lawrence Bannor's bond to William Beakes, June 25, 1686, Pemberton Papers, vol. 2, 18; *Bucks Courts*, 50–53. "Peacemakers" were suggested and referred to by that name by law reformers during the English Civil War. Donald Veall, *The Popular Movement for Law Reform 1640–60* (Oxford, 1970), 170. Relying primarily on isolated instances, Wall, *Fierce Communion*, 21–29, has claimed that arbitration was a significant force in all colonies, particularly in the Delaware Valley; Bruce Mann, *Neighbors and Strangers: Law and Com-

munity in Early Connecticut (Chapel Hill, N.C., 1987), 104n.10, also believes that the few references to arbitration in Connecticut prior to 1700 reflect "a mark of the success of arbitration." Though arbitration rate is another "dark number" in legal history because many successful arbitrations left no tracks, I believe that the use and success rate of arbitration in the Delaware Valley have been overstated.

29. *Gloucester Courts,* 159–60, 169 (quote).

30. For successful arbitrations, see *Bucks Courts,* 49, 82, 92, 335, 352, 400; *Bucks Dockets,* 377, 447, 448; *Chester Courts I,* 132; *Gloucester Courts* 23, 277, 203, 209; and *Gloucester Documents,* 140.

31. For the peacemakers' award in 1683, see *Chester Courts I,* 39; for the long petition for execution of the award in 1696, see *Chester Courts I,* 376–79. See also Herbert Fitzroy, "Richard Crosby Goes to Court, 1683–1697," *PMHB* 55 (1936): 12–19.

32. *Gloucester Courts,* 122–23, 146–48.

33. Auerbach, *Justice without Law?* 32–33; Mann, "Formalization of Informal Law," 451; Mann, *Neighbors and Strangers,* 101–36; Konig, *Law and Society in Puritan Massachusetts,* 109–11; Wall, *Fierce Community,* 21–29; Barry Levy, *Quakers and the American Family* (New York, 1988), 80–82, 123–89.

34. *Records of the Court at Upland in Pennsylvania, 1676–1681* in HSP, *Memoirs VII* (Philadelphia, 1860; repr. 1959), 9–203; Leon De Valinger, Jr., ed., *Court Records of Kent County, Delaware, 1680–1705* (Washington D.C., 1959); Mann, *Neighbors and Strangers,* 172 (64.3 percent of cases in book debt were contested in the first decade of the 1700s; book debt, bonds, and notes were contested at rates from 42.1 percent to 57.1 percent in the 1710s); David Konig, "Country Justice: The Rural Roots of Constitutionalism in Colonial Virginia," *An Uncertain Tradition,* ed. Kermit Hall and James Ely, Jr. (Athens, Ga., 1989), 73, 81 (Konig indicates 52 percent of his cases were contested in the 1740s); Lois Green Carr, *County Government in Maryland, 1689–1709* (New York, 1987), 183–86 (most cases required a judicial recording even though two-thirds required no judicial wisdom; noncontentious suits declined from the 1690s to 1708–9). John Murrin noted high jury usage (58.6 percent) and a low number of cases withdrawn in Suffolk County, Massachusetts, in the 1670s in a letter to me, which generously authorized me to use these unpublished data.

35. John Smith to Phineas Pemberton, January 18, 1698, Pemberton Papers, vol. 1, 72; Phineas Pemberton to Alice Pemberton, March 18, 1700, Pemberton Papers, vol. 2, 164; William Rakestraw to Phineas Pemberton, January 24, 1701, Pemberton Papers, vol. 2, 176b; Phineas Pemberton to Jacob Hall, December 18, 1695, Pemberton Papers, vol. 2, 121a.

36. *Bucks Courts,* 18, 21; *Burlington Courts,* 13, 21–22, 25; *Gloucester Courts,* 134; *Chester Courts I,* 92–93.

37. Anton-Hermann Chroust, *The Rise of the Legal Profession in America,* vol. 1, *The Colonial Experience* (Norman, Okla., 1965), 213; Lawrence Lewis, "The Courts of Pennsylvania in the Seventeenth Century," *PMHB* 5 (1881): 182–85; *Statutes at Large II,* 41, 270.

38. For John Tatham, see *Bucks Courts,* 150, 158; and *Burlington Courts,* 106, 113. For Edward Hunloke, see *Burlington Courts,* 67, 104, 143; and *Bucks Courts,* 154. For Jeremiah Collett, see *Chester Courts I,* 162. For Phineas Pemberton, see *Bucks Courts,* 172. For Thomas Revell, see *Burlington Courts,* 39, 44. For Patrick Robinson, see *Chester Courts I,* 214, 217, 262, 278; *Bucks Courts,* 139.

39. Chroust, *Rise of the Legal Profession in America,* 209–18; Frank Eastman, *Courts and Lawyers in Pennsylvania,* vol. 1, (New York, 1923), 109–23, 203–10. All the lawyers mentioned appeared in more than one jurisdiction, evidencing the circuit nature of their practice. Regarding the monopolizing of all attorneys, Daniel Pastorious charged his adversary in the Frankfort Land Company case with retaining "the four known Lawyers of this province" to deny Pastorious legal counsel. Roy Lokken, *David Lloyd, Colonial Lawmaker* (Seattle, 1959), 189–90. For estimates of the English ratio of lawyers to population, see C. W. Brooks, "Litigants and Attorneys in the King's Bench and Common Pleas, 1560–1640," in *Legal Records and the Historian,* ed. J. H. Baker (London, 1978), 53–54.

40. See, for example, *Bucks Courts,* 290–91; *Bucks Dockets,* for the year 1702; and David Lloyd to Phineas Pemberton, August 2, 1686, Pemberton Papers, vol. 2, 62.

41. *Burlington Courts,* 84, 318; *Chester Courts I,* 240; *Chester Courts II,* 130; *Gloucester Courts,* 130–31; *Bucks Dockets,* 354.

42. *Gloucester Courts,* 159–61.

43. *Bucks Courts,* 79, 80 (quote).

44. *Burlington Courts,* 193 (quote), 194.

45. Thomas Holme, "Map of Ye Improved Part of the Province of Pensilvania," reproduced in James Lemon, *The Best Poor Man's Country* (New York, 1972), 52–53; Phineas Pemberton to Deare (Wife?), November 27, 1687, Pemberton Papers, vol. 2, 87.

46. *Bucks Courts,* 151, 156, 159, 160, 348, 351, 357, 360, 377, 382, 385, 402–13.

47. David Konig's study of litigation, *Law and Society in Puritan Massachusetts,* xii, also noted that the high level of lawsuits in seventeenth-century Essex County, Massachusetts, "was not the exclusive preserve of a small group of persistently litigious men." Litigiousness might have arrived in the eighteenth century, after the period studied here and after the legitimizing impact of law-reform processes had given way to common-law forms and complexity. Peter Hoffer, *Law and People in Colonial America* (Baltimore,

1992), 50–55. Michael Kammen, *People of Paradox* (New York, 1973), 42, contended that colonial litigiousness, especially an unwillingness to accept court decisions as final, indicated colonial governments lacked "clear criteria of legitimacy." While such litigiousness might have been symptomatic of an eighteenth-century legitimacy problem, appeals were few in the Delaware Valley from 1680 to 1710, judgments were accepted and enforced, and plaintiffs' choices to bring litigation served as a marker for legitimacy, as they did in Massachusetts.

48. For a reference to law that required a jury trial for assaults, see *Burlington Courts,* 107. For cases where reference was made to the bench for decisions when technical legal grounds were not at issue, see *Burlington Courts,* 162, 41; *Bucks Courts,* 140; *Chester Courts II,* 76; and *Gloucester Courts,* 134.

49. *Burlington Courts,* 127; *Chester Courts I,* 355–56; *Chester Courts II,* 20.

50. For this spelling, see *Bucks Courts,* 98, 342.

51. *New Jersey Concessions,* 538–41; *Statutes at Large II,* 137–40.

52. *Chester Courts I,* 289–91; *Bucks Courts,* 353–55, 359.

53. In cases with two to five witnesses, defendants won only 25 percent of cases; however, where there were six or more witnesses and the defendants presented at least one, defendants won nearly 42 percent of the time.

54. Galanter, "Why the 'Haves' Come Out Ahead," 97–103.

55. *Bucks Courts,* 358–60; Falls MM 10/1698–3/1699; Middletown MM 12/1698; Winfred Root, *The Relations of Pennsylvania with the British Government, 1696–1763* (Philadelphia, 1912), 238.

56. Konig, "Country Justice," 73, claims that juries settled almost as many cases as the bench but does not make clear whether the 23 percent jury cases are for all entered cases or only those that went to court. Konig, *Law and Society in Puritan Massachusetts,* used civil case evidence extensively, but only in describing the decline of litigation in the Dominion of New England does he look at numbers. Mann, *Neighbors and Strangers,* is concerned with only debt verdicts, a subset of all civil cases. John M. Murrin, "Magistrates, Sinners, and a Precarious Liberty: Trial by Jury in Seventeenth-Century New England," in *Saints and Revolutionaries,* ed. David Hall, Thad Tate, and John Murrin (New York, 1984), does not examine the distribution of cases and litigants statistically. Colonial historians have focused their statistical talents primarily on criminal cases.

57. Delaware Valley law reforms had favored juries of the neighborhood for all trials and required justices to enforce the jury verdicts. See the Introduction.

58. Konig, *Law and Society in Puritan Massachusetts,* 65–71, 112–16, 190; Becker, "People and the System," 140–41; Rhys Isaac, *The Transfor-*

mation of Virginia (Chapel Hill, N.C., 1982), 93, 134; Gail Sussman Marcus, "'Due Execution of the Generall Rules of Righteousnesse': Criminal Procedure in New Haven Town and Colony," in *Saints and Revolutionaries,* ed. Hall, Tate, and Murrin, 129–31; A. G. Roeber, *Faithful Magistrates and Republican Lawyers* (Chapel Hill, N.C., 1981), 74–75, 85.

59. Those who had been grand jurors chose juries in 19.6 percent of their cases as civil defendants; those who never served on a grand jury chose civil juries in 13.4 percent of their cases (chi-square probability = .000). Those who had been trial jurors chose juries in 18.9 percent of their civil cases, whereas those who were never trial jurors chose civil juries 13.1 percent of the time (chi-square probability = .000).

60. Chi-square probability value of .004, meaning a 99.6 percent chance the distribution was nonrandom.

61. Chi-square probability value of .000, meaning a 99.9 percent chance the distribution was nonrandom.

62. David Hackett Fischer, *Albion's Seed* (Oxford, 1989), 421–24.

63. *Pennsylvania Laws, 1682–1700,* 248; *Statutes at Large II,* 270.

64. Tom R. Tyler, "What Is Procedural Justice?: Criteria Used by Citizens to Assess the Fairness of Legal Procedures," *Law and Society Review* 22 (1988): 103–35.

Chapter 4: Quaker Dispute Processing

1. Sally Falk Moore, *Law as Process: An Anthropological Approach* (London, 1978), 3; Eric Steele, "Review Essay: Morality, Legality and Dispute Processing: Auerbach's *Justice Without Law?*" *American Bar Foundation Research Journal* 189 (1984): 197; Richard Abel, "A Comparative Theory of Dispute Institutions in Society," *Law and Society Review* 8 (1973): 290.

2. The minutes of the following men's monthly meetings were used: Chester, 1681–1710; Concord, 1684–1710; Darby, 1684–1710; Radnor, 1684–1704 (gap from 1704 to 1712); Falls, 1680–1710; Middletown, 1683–1710; Burlington, 1678–1710; and Chesterfield, 1684–1710. Women's monthly meetings did not handle these disputes. The minutes of the following quarterly meetings were used: Chester/Concord, 1684–1710; Bucks, 1684–1710; and Burlington, 1686–1710. Citations will give the name of the meeting followed by the numerical month and year as given according to the Quaker recording method (March = 1, April = 2, years begin in March).

3. On recurring interactions/reciprocal expectations, see Lon Fuller, "Law and Human Interaction," *Sociological Inquiry* 47 (1977): 62–64; and Roberto Unger, *Law in Modern Society* (New York, 1976), 49. Differences appeared in the Quaker records in a stylized fashion, almost always using the

word *difference* to describe the problem between the two named Friends, with references made to "ending" the problem through the use of extra parties. I am indebted to J. William Frost for pointing out such regularities of Quaker styles. Regarding the transformation/choice processes involved, see Richard Lempert, "Grievances and Legitimacy: The Beginnings and End of Dispute Settlement," *Law and Society Review* 15 (1981): 708, 713; Richard Miller and Austin Sarat, "Grievances, Claims and Disputes: Assessing the Adversary Culture," *Law and Society Review* 15 (1981): 526; Lynn Mather and Barbara Yngvesson, "Language, Audience, and the Transformation of Disputes," *Law and Society Review* 15 (1981): 818, 819; and Wayne McIntosh, "150 Years of Litigation and Dispute Settlement: A Court Tale," *Law and Society Review* 15 (1981): 825, 840. For the definition of mediation and arbitration and their functions in setting boundaries, see Laura Nader and Harry Todd, Jr., eds., *The Disputing Process—Law in Ten Societies* (New York, 1978), 8–11, 29, 59, 89–90, 247–48.

4. Moore, *Law as Process,* 26; Nader and Todd, *The Disputing Process,* 18, 38; Wayne McIntosh, "Private Use of a Public Forum: A Long-Range View of the Dispute Processing Role of Courts," *American Political Science Review* 77 (1983): 991–92, 995. On panegyrics to alternative dispute settling, especially Quaker, see Jerold Auerbach, *Justice Without Law?* (New York, 1983), 29–31; William Nelson, *Dispute and Conflict Resolution in Plymouth County, Massachusetts, 1725–1825* (Chapel Hill, N.C., 1981), 13–44; George Odiorne, "Arbitration and Mediation among Early Quakers," *Arbitration Journal* 9 (1950): 161–66; Stephen Botein, *Early American Law and Society* (New York, 1983), 31–49; Frederick Tolles, *Meeting House and Counting House* (New York, 1948), 75–78, 251–52; Paul Lermack, "Peace Bonds and Criminal Justice in Colonial Philadelphia," *PMHB* 100 (1976): 173–74; and Helena Wall, *Fierce Communion: Family and Community in Early America* (Cambridge, Mass., 1990), 21–29.

5. Craig Horle, *The Quakers and the English Legal System, 1660–1688* (Philadelphia, 1988), 16 (quote), 101–49; Tolles, *Meeting House,* 34–36; Lermack, "Peace Bonds," 173; Jon Butler, *Power, Authority, and the Origins of the American Denominational Order* (Philadelphia, 1978), 19–20.

6. Matthew 5:33–37; James 5:12; Horle, *Quakers and the English Legal System,* 11, 49; J. William Frost, "The Affirmation Controversy and Religious Liberty," in *The World of William Penn,* ed. Richard S. Dunn and Mary Maples Dunn (Philadelphia, 1986), 305–12.

7. *Pennsylvania Laws, 1682–1700,* 247; *Statutes at Large II,* 39, 267–68; *Burlington Courts,* 214, 341, 361; Gary Nash, *Quakers and Politics: Pennsylvania, 1681–1726* (Princeton, N.J., 1968), 218, 249–50.

8. Tolles, *Meeting House,* 7, 64–65; Frederick Tolles, *Quakers and the Atlantic Culture* (New York, 1960), 5, 13, 17, 21–22, 29–35, 119; Butler,

Power and American Denominational Order, 17–20, 28–29; Jon Butler, *Awash in a Sea of Faith: Christianizing the American People* (Cambridge, Mass., 1990), 118; Odiorne, "Arbitration and Mediation among Early Quakers," 161; Carl Bridenbaugh, "The Old and New Societies of the Delaware Valley in the Seventeenth Century," *PMHB* 100 (1976): 170–71.

9. Richard Vann, "Quakerism: Made in America?" in *The World of William Penn,* ed. Dunn and Dunn, 165.

10. Valerie Gladfelter, "Caring and Control: The Social Psychology of an Authoritative Group, the Burlington (NJ) Friends Meeting, 1678–1720" (Ph.D diss., University of Pennsylvania, 1983), 16–17; J. William Frost, *The Quaker Family in America* (New York, 1973), 1–3; Butler, *Power and American Denominational Order,* 18–21, 31, 40; Edwin Bronner, "Quaker Discipline and Order, 1680–1720: Philadelphia Yearly Meeting and London Yearly Meeting," in *The World of William Penn,* ed. Dunn and Dunn, 327–30.

11. Harry Todd Jr., "Litigious Marginals: Character and Disputing in a Bavarian Village," Julio Ruffini, "Disputing over Livestock in Sardinia," and Barbara Yngvesson, "The Atlantic Fishermen," in *The Disputing Process,* ed. Nader and Todd, 59–85, 86–121, 209–46.

12. Odiorne, "Arbitration and Mediation among Early Quakers," 161 (quoting George Fox). See also Auerbach, *Justice Without Law?* 28–29.

13. London Yearly Meeting Epistle, dated 1697, in Chester MM, 62–63 (first two quotes); Chester QM 9/1702 (reference to that epistle); Jack Marietta, "Ecclesiastical Discipline in the Society of Friends, 1682–1776" (Ph.D. diss. in history, Stanford University, 1968), 106 (last quote, quoting Philadelphia Yearly Meeting 7/1719).

14. Friends Yearly Meeting Paper, no date (but signed by James Harrison, who died in 1687), Pemberton Papers, vol. 2, 29–30, HSP. Referred to in Concord MM 12/1689.

15. London Yearly Meeting 1697 Epistle; Tolles, *Meeting House,* 251–52; Marietta, "Ecclesiastical Discipline," 106.

16. Burlington MM 6/1681 (first quote), 7/1681 (second quote).

17. Burlington MM 7/1683, 9/1683 (quote).

18. Radnor MM 7/1695, 11/1701.

19. Chester QM 9/1701, 9/1702.

20. London Yearly Meeting 1697 Epistle.

21. Tolles, *Meeting House,* 251–52; Marietta, "Ecclesiastical Discipline," 106–7; Bronner, "Quaker Discipline and Order," 328–29.

22. Tolles, *Meeting House,* 251 (quote); Nelson, *Dispute and Conflict Resolution,* 26–44. Defamation cases, which were also ambiguous in the courts, and cases involving discipline as part of the failure to resolve a private dispute were determined on a case-by-case basis but usually were categorized as "differences."

23. Incidence of usage of Quaker meetings and courts for dispute resolution between Quakers, over five-year periods:

Years	Bucks County		Chester County		Burlington County	
	Meetings	Law	Meetings	Law	Meetings	Law
1680–85	10	6	7	8	11	34
1686–90	6	5	18	18	5	26
1691–95	10	13	5	10	5	17
1696–1700	10	7	21	12	5	15
1701–5	14	7	15	29	15	10
1706–10	21	11	4	23	5	5
Total	71	49	70	100	46	107

24. Jon Butler, "Into Pennsylvania's Spiritual Abyss: The Rise and Fall of the Later Keithians, 1693–1703," *PMHB* 101 (1977): 151–70; J. William Frost, "Unlikely Controversialists: Caleb Pusey and George Keith," *Quaker History* 64 (1975): 16–36; Nash, *Quakers and Politics,* 127–80.

25. Butler, *Power and American Denominational Order,* 40–41; Valerie Gladfelter, "Power Challenged: Rising Individualism in the Burlington, New Jersey, Friends Meeting, 1678–1720," in *Friends and Neighbors,* ed. Michael Zuckerman (Philadelphia, 1982), 116, 122–32; Joseph Illick, *Colonial Pennsylvania: A History* (New York, 1976), 66–69, 88–89, 101–2; Nash, *Quakers and Politics,* 181–240.

26. Concord MM 7/1700; Chester QM 1701, 1702; Radnor MM 11/1701; London Yearly Meeting Epistle 1697.

27. Burlington MM 6/1681, 7/1681, 3/1685.

28. Chester QM 6/1699.

29. Chester QM 12/1696; Middletown MM 9/1699, 11/1699, 12/1699.

30. Middletown MM 7/1697–10/1697.

31. Falls MM 1/1687, 4/1687, 5/1687; *Bucks Courts,* 67, 70, 84.

32. Middletown MM 12/1686, 1/1687.

33. Marietta, "Ecclesiastical Discipline," 136–39. Jack Marietta, *The Reformation of American Quakerism, 1748–1783* (Philadelphia, 1984), 6–7, 48, does show fewer discipline cases in these early years than in the mid-eighteenth century, but only 1 percent overall deal with going to court against other Quakers.

34. Chester MM 4/1703 (first quote), 4/1704 (second quote); Falls MM 7/1704, 8/1704, 9/1704 (third quote), 10/1704; Bucks QM 12/1704, 3/1705.

35. Burlington MM 1/1706, 9/1706, 1/1707, 2/1707, 8/1709.

36. Chester MM 2/1706, 3/1706, 6/1706, 7/1706, 8/1706, 11/1706, 12/1706; Chester QM 12/1706, 3/1707 (quote), 6/1707.

37. Chester MM 4/1687–5/1687; *Chester Courts I,* 200; Chester MM 8/1688; *Chester Courts I,* 129–33; Chester MM 9/1696, 11/1696; *Chester Courts II,* 88, 90, 92, 94; Middletown MM 12/1686, 1/1687; *Bucks Courts,* 70–72; Middletown MM 5/1687–4/1688; *Bucks Courts,* 151, 156, 159, 160; Middletown MM 10/1703–4/1704; *Bucks Dockets,* 407; Burlington MM 12/1691; *Burlington Courts,* 131; Chesterfield MM 11/1685, 12/1685; *Burlington Courts,* 80.

38. Middletown MM 4/1707–7/1707, 6/1708–8/1708, 4/1709–7/1709; 8/1709 (quote), 9/1709.

39. Historians have accepted the directives regarding Quakers' not suing other Quakers as reflecting Quaker reality, at least at first. Every history of colonial Quakers I read that discussed the issue accepted the Quaker claim. The most recent acceptance was in Wall, *Fierce Communion,* 25, 147.

40. Middletown MM 10/1703–4/1704 (quote).

41. Falls MM 3/1706–6/1706, 4/1708–1/1709.

42. Chester MM 2/1684.

43. Burlington MM 7/1687, 11/1687, 2/1688–5/1688 (quote), 7/1688; Falls MM 12/1687–2/1688.

44. Falls MM 5/1692, 6/1692.

45. Burlington MM 7/1688, 8/1688.

46. Chesterfield MM 1/1696–3/1696; Radnor MM 8/1697, 9/1697.

47. For other summary orders regarding debts, see Chester MM 2/1710; Chester MM 4/1703; Radnor MM 11/1696; Radnor MM 8/1693; Concord MM 2/1694; and Middletown MM 7/1689.

48. Chester MM 11/1683.

49. Chester MM 2/1703; Chester QM 3/1703 (quotes). On the duty to arbitrate before the meeting took up the case, see London Yearly Meeting 1697 Epistle; Friends Yearly Meeting Paper, no date, Pemberton Papers, vol. 2, 29–30; and Tolles, *Meeting House,* 251–52.

50. London Yearly Meeting 1697 Epistle; Burlington MM 7/1681; Chester MM 10/1702, 2/1703; Chester MM 6/1703–11/1703; Chester MM 2/1706–12/1706.

51. Chester MM 9/1696, 6/1703, 7/1703. For other examples of appointed arbitrators, see Chester MM 4/1687; Chester MM 2/1706; Concord MM 12/1688; Chester QM 3/1689; Chester QM 3/1703; Falls MM 10/1701; Burlington MM 6/1687; Burlington MM 3/1701; and Tolles, *Meeting House,* 251.

52. Darby MM 4/1704; Radnor MM 7/1695.

53. Chester MM 9/1696; Middletown MM 8/1698; Middletown MM

2/1707. See also Middletown 6/1707; Bucks QM 12/1704; Chester QM 3/1707; Burlington MM 6/1683.

54. London Yearly Meeting 1697 Epistle.

55. Chester MM 9/1696; Falls MM 12/1687–3/1688; Burlington MM 7/1687–7/1688.

56. Middletown MM 9/1692 (first quote); Falls MM 5/1685 (last quotes). Nelson, *Dispute and Conflict Resolution,* 37, noted the phenomenon of disputants' using the common-law pleading style in Congregational church–sponsored dispute resolution and contended that such actions stemmed from individuals' applying a single set of norms to both secular and religious spheres. I find this explanation unsatisfactory for Quakers, whose antagonism to English common law was deep. Such adoptions, I believe, were stopgap attempts to use the regularity of legal procedure to bolster the Gospel Order's flagging stature and authority.

57. Chester MM 4/1692 (first quote); Middletown MM 12/1702 (second quote); Chester MM 9/1686 (third and fourth quotes); Arbitration award, June 27, 1686, Miscellaneous, 12, Etting Collection, HSP.

58. Chester MM 8/1691 (first quote), 9/1691 (second quote).

59. Chester MM 9/1684; Middletown MM 9/1687.

60. Burlington MM 7/1692.

61. On appellate review, see Chester QM 3/1703; Chester QM 12/1706; Burlington QM 6/1701; and Bronner, "Quaker Discipline and Order," 329. On a right to copies of minutes, see Chester QM 9/1710.

62. Chester MM 6/1699–8/1699 (first quote); Chester QM 6/1703 (second quote).

63. Falls MM 7/1697–11/1698.

64. Chester MM 3/1699.

65. Abandonment of the contest was categorized as a failure if the differences were brought before four or more meetings and no outcome was recorded or if the last entry indicated the disputants could not agree to an accommodation.

66. Butler, *Power and American Denominational Order,* 41–42; Gladfelter, "Power Challenged," 116–17, 122–33.

67. Average number of meetings between beginning and end of dispute:

County	1681–85	1686–90	1691–95	1696–1700	1701–5	1706–10	Total
Chester	1.14	1.61	1.60	2.43	4.73	5.75	2.68
Bucks	4.90	5.33	2.60	5.20	4.43	8.90	5.75
Burlington	2.54	4.80	1.40	6.40	6.07	9.40	4.98
Overall	3.03	3.10	1.73	3.75	5.09	8.57	4.42

Median number of meetings between beginning and end of dispute:

County	1681–85	1686–90	1691–95	1696–1700	1701–5	1706–10	Total
Chester	1.0	1.0	2.0	2.0	3.0	4.5	2.0
Bucks	2.5	4.0	2.0	2.5	2.0	3.0	3.0
Burlington	2.0	2.0	2.0	4.0	2.0	1.0	2.0

68. Burlington MM 2/1700, 3/1700 (quote), 4/1700–5/1700.

69. Concord MM 12/1697 (quotes), 1/1698, 10/1698.

70. Falls MM 5/1685–10/1685; Burlington MM 7/1701–2/1702.

71. Phineas Pemberton to Deare (wife?), November 27, 1687, Pemberton Papers, vol. 2, 87; Middletown MM 5/1687–5/1688; *Bucks Courts,* 402–13.

72. Middletown MM 10/1703–7/1704.

73. Ibid., 4/1707–7/1707, 6/1708–8/1708, 4/1709–7/1709, 8/1709 (first quote), 9/1709 (second quote).

74. Burlington MM 1/1706, 9/1706, 1/1707, 2/1707, 6/1709; Middletown MM 3/1708–11/1708, 3/1709–5/1710, 6/1710 (quote), 7/1710–8/1710.

75. Nelson, "Dispute and Conflict Resolution," 34, noted a "striking similarity between the dispute-resolution business of Plymouth County churches" and the county court's docket for the period 1725–74. The records Nelson used did not allow him the "statistical precision" necessary for a full docket comparison that can be done with the relatively complete Quaker records.

76. McIntosh, "150 Years of Litigation," 840 (first quote); McIntosh, "Private Use of a Public Forum," 991 (second quote), 1005.

77. On the Quaker docket, the remainder of differences were appeals to higher meetings (2.2 percent).

78. Tolles, *Meeting House,* 58, 59; Radnor MM 3/1704 (quote), 3/1695.

79. Marietta, "Ecclesiastical Discipline," 125 (first quote); Falls MM 1/1687; Chester MM 2/1710 (second quote).

80. Chester MM 9/1698–11/1698; Chester MM 4/1703, 3/1704, 4/1704; Chester MM 2/1705, 3/1705; Concord MM 2/1694, 3/1694; Middletown MM 4/1697, 5/1697; Chester QM 12/1685.

81. Burlington QM 12/1699, 3/1700, 6/1700, 12/1701.

82. Burlington MM 7/1683, 9/1683.

83. Chester MM 2/1710–6/1710; Falls MM 5/1692–6/1692, 6/1705, 5/1710–7/1710.

84. Concord MM 11/1699–1/1700; Falls MM 1/1709.

85. *Pennsylvania Laws, 1682–1700,* 118.

86. Middletown MM 1/1700 (first quote), 2–5/1700; Radnor MM 5/ 1693; Concord MM 1/1702 (second quote), 8/1702.

87. Chester MM 11/1683, 9/1684, 10/1684; Bucks QM 6/1685; Burlington MM 6/1685–12/1685; Burlington MM 9/1682.

88. Middletown MM 6/1700; Chester MM 1/1686.

89. W. S. Holdsworth, *A History of English Law,* vol. 6 (London, 1924), 636–37; Chester MM 11/1688, 3/1689; Middletown MM 1/1684, 7/1684; Burlington MM 8/1701. On fencing, West Jersey's 1683 law was ambiguous about whether such a case or result was even possible. *New Jersey Concessions,* 459.

90. Chester MM 9/1686; Falls MM 10/1686 (quote).

91. Falls MM 7/1693.

92. Falls MM 11/1707 (first quote), 12/1707 (second quote); Chester MM 9/1700 (third quote), 10/1700 (fourth quote).

93. Chester MM 7/1704, 8/1704 (first two quotes), 12/1704 (last 2 quotes).

94. Nash, *Quakers and Politics,* 90–93, 216, 229; Edwin Tanner, *The Province of New Jersey* (London, 1908), 100–110; Peter Wacker, *Land and People* (New Brunswick, N.J., 1975), 299–300; James Lemon, *The Best Poor Man's Country* (New York, 1972), 49–56, 93; Mary Schweitzer, "Contracts and Custom: Economic Policy in Colonial Pennsylvania, 1717–1755" (Ph.D. diss. in history, Johns Hopkins University, 1983), 123–54; *New Jersey Concessions,* 399–400, 427, 437–39, 478, 541–45; *Pennsylvania Laws, 1682– 1700,* 100, 101, 118–19, 132, 181, 205, 237; *Statutes at Large II,* 21, 131, 206–12, 237; Richard McCormick, *New Jersey from Colony to State, 1609– 1789* (Newark, N.J., 1981), 45; Frank Eastman, *Courts and Lawyers in Pennsylvania,* vol. 1 (New York, 1923), 118–19.

95. Chester MM 4/1687, 5/1687, 9/1696, 11/1696; Falls MM 2/1703, 3/1703; Burlington MM 1/1697–4/1697.

96. Concord MM 8/1687.

97. Falls MM 1/1685, 4/1685, 8/1686, 9/1686.

98. Chester MM 6/1699–8/1699.

99. Since the Quaker subset of the legal population was used as a baseline for comparison, the same distortions and biases noted for that population as a whole come into play here. Specifically, landholding may be underrepresented because of unrecorded land, and wealth in taxation and inventories may be overstated because of a higher propensity of wealthy individuals to show up on those measures. This measure also assumes that Quakers who participated in the legal system were not statistically different from the overall Quaker population in the Delaware Valley.

100. McIntosh, "150 Years of Litigation," 825. Similarly, Delaware Valley high officers faced high officers in only 3.9 percent of all lawsuits.

101. Ratio of successful to contentious/unsuccessful differences:

Attribute	As "Plaintiff"	As "Defendant"
High officer	1.67	1.28
Lesser officer	2.26	1.98
Nonofficer	2.09	2.73
Quaker leader	2.27	1.56
Ordinary Quaker	1.75	2.25
Overall	2.00	2.00

Chapter 5: Accused Deviants and Their Offenses

1. *Burlington Courts*, 142.

2. Kai Erickson, *Wayward Puritans: A Study in the Sociology of Deviance* (New York, 1966), 67–159; N. E. H. Hull, *Female Felons: Women and Serious Crime in Colonial Massachusetts* (Urbana, Ill., 1987), 9; John Demos, *Entertaining Satan: Witchcraft and the Culture of Early New England* (New York, 1982); Lawrence M. Friedman, *A History of American Law* (New York, 1973), 63; Lawrence M. Friedman, *Crime and Punishment in American History* (New York, 1993), 50.

3. *Burlington Courts*, 124, 217.

4. Erickson, *Wayward Puritans*, 171–75; Michael Stephen Hindus, *Prison and Plantation: Crime, Justice, and Authority in Massachusetts and South Carolina, 1767–1868* (Chapel Hill, N.C., 1980), 64; Donna Spindel, *Crime and Society in North Carolina, 1663–1776* (Baton Rouge, 1989), 45–46, 72–73; Gwenda Morgan, "Law and Social Change in Colonial Virginia," *Virginia Magazine of History and Biography* 95 (1987): 464–65; Douglas Greenberg, *Crime and Law Enforcement in the Colony of New York, 1691–1776* (Ithaca, N.Y., 1974), 49–53.

5. *Burlington Courts*, 142–43, 148. Harry's sentence would be protested by many in the courtroom who wished his life spared, and he ultimately escaped custody, never to grace the records again.

6. Greenberg, *Crime and Law Enforcement*, 9; Bradley Chapin, *Criminal Justice in Colonial America, 1606–1660* (Athens, Ga., 1983), 101–2; Erickson, *Wayward Puritans*, 6–12; David Flaherty, "Crime and Social Control in Provincial Massachusetts," *Historical Journal* 24 (1981): 339; Douglas Greenberg, "Crime, Law Enforcement, and Social Control in Colonial America," *American Journal of Legal History* 26 (1982): 321; David Konig, *Law and Society in Puritan Massachusetts: Essex County, 1629–1692* (Chap-

el Hill, N.C., 1979), 124–25; 188–90; Eugene Genovese, *Roll Jordan Roll: The World the Slaves Made* (New York, 1974), 25; Douglas Hay, "Property, Authority and Criminal Law," in *Albion's Fatal Tree,* ed. Douglas Hay, Peter Lineburgh, John Rule, and E. P. Thompson (New York, 1975), 17–63.

7. Michael Hindus and Douglas Jones, "Quantitative Methods or *Quantum Meruit*? Tactics for Early American Legal History," *Historical Methods* 13 (1980): 67–69.

8. *New Jersey Concessions,* 397–98, 429; *Pennsylvania Laws, 1682–1700,* 121, 202.

9. Hindus and Jones, "Quantitative Methods," 66–69; Gail McKnight Beckman, ed., *The Statutes at Large of Pennsylvania in the Time of William Penn,* vol. 1 (1680–1700) (New York, 1976), 26, 27, 53. It is important to note that a case could contain more than one defendant; the difference is significant for both method and interpretation. Two files were kept, one for the roles and attributes for each defendant (the individual file), regardless of whether the defendant was named first or later in the criminal complaint, and one for the cases, which used only the first named defendant. This abridging of the data in the case file was necessary given the capabilities of the statistical package SAS, which worked on the basis of matching names in individual files with names in cases, allowing the case types and outcomes to be correlated with roles and attributes. By choosing to organize the data by case, instead of separating out each defendant to each charge, I have remained faithful to how crime was conceptualized and recorded during this period at the expense of some statistical accuracy. Readers should note when the baseline used is the total of individuals or the total of cases, and the numbers should be regarded not as absolutes but only as indicators of trends.

10. Greenberg, *Crime and Law Enforcement,* 42–44.

11. For similar findings, see Eli Faber, "Puritan Criminals: The Economic, Social, and Intellectual Background to Crime in Seventeenth-Century Massachusetts," *Perspectives in American History* 11 (1977–78): 103, 134–35; Greenberg, *Crime and Law Enforcement,* 120. These findings run contrary to those of Friedman, *Crime and Punishment,* 50–52, and Thomas Haskell, "Litigation and Social Status in Seventeenth-Century New Haven," *Journal of Legal Studies* 7 (1978): 219–41, and contrary to the general thrust of Paul Boyer and Stephen Nissenbaum, *Salem Possessed: The Social Origins of Witchcraft* (Cambridge, 1974), and Demos, *Entertaining Satan,* regarding the subspecies of criminal deviants, witches. Furthermore, contrary to Erickson, *Wayward Puritans,* being ushered into the deviant role in this society was not irreversible.

12. Obviously, this definition means that those who appeared as criminal defendants early in the period had a much longer period in which to

suffer a second accusation than those who first appeared later in the period. Hindus and Jones, "Quantitative Methods," 74. However, this problem is important only if one wishes to trace whether recidivism increases or decreases over time. For the purposes of establishing the relationship between certain attributes and recidivism as well as the percentage of recidivists in a given population, these problems are less severe.

13. Greenberg, *Crime and Law Enforcement*, 210 (16.4 percent recidivism); Flaherty, "Crime and Social Control in Provincial Massachusetts," 356 ("very little recidivism"); Spindel, *Crime and Society in North Carolina*, 145 (17.6 percent recidivism).

14. The participation rate in various legal roles was higher for recidivists than for those in the legal population: 48.4 percent of recidivists were grand jurors (versus 33.5 percent of the legal population); 46.9 percent were trial jurors (versus 30.1 percent in legal population); 46.2 percent were plaintiffs (versus 28.9 percent in legal population); and 59.3 percent were civil defendants (versus 31.1 percent of legal population).

15. *Burlington Courts*, 9, 84; *Bucks Courts*, 60, 77, 24, 70, 281.

16. *Chester Courts I*, 107, 114, 131.

17. *Gloucester Courts*, 66, 85, 192.

18. Herbert Fitzroy, "The Punishment of Crime in Provincial Pennsylvania," *PMHB* 62 (1938): 243; George Fox, "To the Parliament of the Comon-wealth of England" (1659), quoted in Frederick Tolles, *Meeting House and Counting House* (New York, 1948), 50.

19. Craig Horle, *The Quakers and the English Legal System, 1660–1688* (Philadelphia, 1988), 11, 14; Gary Nash, *Quakers and Politics: Pennsylvania, 1681–1726* (Princeton, N.J., 1968), 175, 179.

20. Paul Lermack, "Peace Bonds and Criminal Justice in Colonial Pennsylvania," *PMHB* 100 (1976): 173–74; Fitzroy, "Punishment of Crime," 243–45; Kathryn Preyer, "Penal Measures in the American Colonies: An Overview," *American Journal of Legal History* 26 (1982): 336–37.

21. David Flaherty, "Law and the Enforcement of Morals in Early America," in *American Law and the Constitutional Order*, ed. Lawrence M. Friedman and Harry N. Scheiber (Cambridge, 1978), 55, 56, 59; Lawrence Gipson, "Crime and Its Punishment in Provincial Pennsylvania," *Pennsylvania History* 2 (1935): 5–6; Beckman, *Statutes at Large of Pennyslvania*, 18–24; Barbara Shapiro, "Law Reform in Seventeenth Century England," *American Journal of Legal History* 19 (1975): 296; J. William Frost, *A Perfect Freedom: Religious Liberty in Pennsylvania* (Cambridge, 1990), 16–17.

22. Bradley Chapin, Douglas Greenberg, Eli Faber, David Flaherty, Donna Spindel, and I (among others) have done statistical analyses of colonial crime and criminals (their works cited above). Yet the categories of crimes used in each study differ widely, often because of differences in the

place studied but more likely because each historian has dealt with sources according to what made the most sense. For purposes of comparison, I have rearranged their numbers to fit my categories as closely as possible. Without some standardization, comparative analysis of crime in colonial America will remain difficult.

23. For abortion, see *Burlington Courts*, 69–70, 252; adultery, *Chester Courts I*, 157, *Chester Courts II*, 39, and *Gloucester Courts*, 94; bigamy, *Burlington Courts*, 18, 182; bestiality, *Chester Courts II*, 138, and *Burlington Courts*, 142, 148; and incest, *Burlington Courts*, 72.

24. The drunkenness category included inebriations that resulted in other offenses, such as breach of peace, swearing, or abusing the court. For the disorderly house, see *Chester Courts I*, 354, and *Burlington Courts*, 101, 218, 325; drunkenness, *Chester Courts I*, 380, 391; selling rum to Indians, *Bucks Courts*, 32, 77, and *Gloucester Courts*, 127; selling liquor by the drink, *Chester Courts II*, 129, and *Gloucester Courts*, 246; and selling liquor without a license, *Bucks Courts*, 211, *Chester Courts II*, 125, and *Burlington Courts*, 192, 218.

25. For swearing, see *Bucks Courts*, 20, 78, 116, 204, *Chester Courts I*, 364, and *Chester Courts II*, 76; breaking the Sabbath, *Chester Courts II*, 154, and *Burlington Courts*, 190, 206, 209; gambling, *Chester Courts I*, 380; and practicing geomancy, *Chester Courts I*, 371. On equating sin with crime, see Flaherty, "Law and the Enforcement of Morals," 54.

26. Richard S. Dunn and Mary Maples Dunn, eds. *The Papers of William Penn*, vol. 2 (1680–84) (Philadelphia, 1982), 225 (quote). See also Beckman, *Statutes at Large of Pennsylvania*, 18–21.

27. *New Jersey Concessions*, 446, 460, 477, 528.

28. Fitzroy, "Punishment of Crime," 248–49; Gipson, "Crime and Its Punishment," 8; Greenberg, "Crime, Law Enforcement, and Social Control," 308; Lermack, "Peace Bonds," 183–84.

29. The following table compares, as best as I can determine, the prosecutions in each jurisdiction for each category as I have defined them:

	Morals	Contempt	Property	Violence
New Haven, Conn., 1639–65	45.2%	18.3%	13.7%	5.0%
Middlesex County, Mass., 1650–86	69.2	6.4	3.0	a
Essex County, Mass., 1651–80	41.6	19.4	23.1	a
North Carolina, 1670–1776	8.3	3.5	18.0	34.3
New York, 1691–1776	5.5	5.9	13.7	40.3
Richmond County, Va., 1692–1776	56.8	12.0	6.4	9.7

	Morals	Contempt	Property	Violence
Prince Georges, Md.,				
1696–1706	40.4	7.0	16.9	28.3
Chester County, Pa., 1726–55	26.4	1.3	20.7	33.0
Middlesex County, Mass.,				
1760–74	64.9	11.1	13.2	9.5
Charleston, S.C., 1769–76	3.2	0.0	37.8	53.6
Delaware Valley, 1680–1710	22.4	21.4	12.6	12.3

a. Made no reference to crimes of violence.

M. P. Baumgartner, "Law and Social Status in Colonial New Haven, 1639–1665," *Research in Law and Sociology* 1 (1978): 157; Faber, "Puritan Criminals," 99–127 (used only convictions); Erickson, *Wayward Puritans,* 173–75 (used only convictions); Spindel, *Crime and Society in North Carolina,* 56–57; Greenberg, *Crime and Law Enforcement,* 50; Morgan, "Law and Social Change," 465; Lois Green Carr, *County Government in Maryland, 1689–1709* (New York, 1987), 169–71 (did not include summary contempt or contempt of constables and jurors who failed to appear); Alan Tully, *William Penn's Legacy* (Baltimore, 1977), 190–91; Hindus, *Prison and Plantation,* 64 (both Middlesex and Charleston statistics). This table is more illustrative than conclusive, because each historian has used his or her own definitions of what crimes to count (especially contempt and morals), and some have used accusations as the basis for inclusion whereas others have used convictions.

30. Tully, *Penn's Legacy,* 190–91.

31. Spindel, *Crime and Society in North Carolina,* 24, 95, 144; Morgan, "Law and Social Change," 461.

32. For constables who failed to appear, see *Burlington Courts,* 271, 314, 317; *Gloucester Courts,* 205; *Chester Courts II,* 136; and *Bucks Docket,* 418. For overseers who neglected their duty, see *Burlington Courts,* 334; *Gloucester Courts,* 357; *Chester Courts II,* 155; and *Bucks Courts,* 292, 298. For jurors who failed to appear for duty or left early, see *Burlington Courts,* 181, 195, 209, 317, 324; *Gloucester Courts,* 216; *Chester Courts II,* 138; and *Bucks Courts,* 68, 112. For punishment for jurors' nonappearance, see *Statutes at Large II,* 43. For concerted passive resistance to courts by nonappearances, see *Gloucester Courts,* 195–215. Courts in Burlington County did not field a jury in eight court sessions over a three-year period. Part of Burlington's problems rested on the issue of Quakers' taking oaths under the new royal government. Initially, some jurors were sworn and some attested, but by 1709 when Quakers refused the oath, the sheriff was in-

structed to call a jury of people who could take the oath (i.e., all non-Quakers). *Burlington Courts,* 294, 306, 341.

33. Horle, *Quakers and the English Legal System,* 14; *Burlington Courts,* 293, 299.

34. *Burlington Courts,* 220; *Gloucester Courts,* 207–8.

35. *Chester Courts I,* 265–66, 192; *Chester Courts II,* 1, 43, 50, 92; *Burlington Courts,* 176 (quote).

36. *Gloucester Courts,* 124, 249; *Burlington Courts,* 55, 193, 217, 261; *Bucks Courts,* 319, 339, 358–60, 401. Courts did not always consistently label such offenses "contempts," but all these prosecutions used the summary procedures and punishments of contempt and were so classified.

37. See the table in note 29.

38. Chapin, *Criminal Justice in Colonial America,* 27–28; Norma Landau, *The Justices of the Peace, 1679–1760* (Berkeley, Calif., 1984), 23–24; Lois Green Carr, "The Foundations of Social Order: Local Government in Colonial Maryland," in *Town and County: Essays on the Structures of Local Government in the American Colonies,* ed. Bruce Daniels (Middletown, 1978), 78; Konig, *Law and Society in Puritan Massachusetts,* 14; Lermack, "Peace Bonds," 174–76; Michael Dalton, *The Countrey Justice, Containing the Practise of the Justices of the Peace out of Their Sessions* (London, 1622), 140–75; *Gloucester Documents,* 283–90.

39. Tavern bond, 12/1700, Narratives, Box 1, 1691–1720, Chester County Archives, West Chester, Pa.; *Gloucester Courts,* 213.

40. *Pennsylvania Laws, 1682–1700,* 144–45, 210; Lermack, "Peace Bonds," 176 (time of authorization said to be 1700); Greenberg, "Crime, Law Enforcement, and Social Control," 308 (importance said to be on decline). Of recognizances prior to 1700, 22 of 75 (29 percent) occurred in West Jersey. From 1701 to 1710, 56 of 98 (57 percent) recognizances occurred in West Jersey. West Jersey's recognizances went from 4 percent of all prosecutions in 1680–95 to 24 percent in 1696–1710 (35 percent in 1706–10).

41. On theft, see *Bucks Courts,* 179–80, 283, *Gloucester Courts,* 86, 260–62, and *Burlington Courts,* 35, 52, 63, 64; burglary, *Bucks Courts,* 113, *Chester Courts II,* 130, 132, 137, 165, and *Gloucester Courts,* 77; trespassing, *Chester Courts II,* 125, 189, and *Gloucester Courts,* 34; and conversion, *Bucks Courts,* 340–41, *Chester Courts I,* 346, *Burlington Courts,* 58, 292, 334, and *Gloucester Courts,* 86, 267.

42. On simple assault, see *Burlington Courts,* 26, 69, 92, *Gloucester Courts,* 16, 167, *Bucks Courts,* 58, 60, 330, and *Chester Courts II,* 117; aggravated assault, *Bucks Courts,* 297, 306, *Chester Courts I,* 348, *Chester Courts II,* 183, and *Gloucester Courts,* 365; rape/attempted rape, *Bucks Courts,* 75, *Bucks Dockets,* 375, 385, *Burlington Courts,* 55, 75, 254–55, 314, and *Glouc-*

ester Courts, 52, 53; murder, *Bucks Courts,* 165, 177, *Burlington Courts,* 56, and *Gloucester Courts,* 66; riot, *Burlington Courts,* 20; break prison/aid escape, *Burlington Courts,* 4, 243, 248, 252, 328, and *Gloucester Courts,* 247; and armed robbery, *Bucks Dockets,* 380.

43. *New Jersey Concessions,* 402 (1676, quote), 434 (1681). On the lenient Pennsylvania code, see Beckman, *Statutes at Large of Pennsylvania,* 18–23; Fitzroy, "Punishment of Crime," 247–48; Preyer, "Penal Measures," 336–37; Lermack, "Peace Bonds," 174; and Gipson, "Crime and Its Punishment," 6.

44. Beckman, *Statutes at Large of Pennsylvania,* 23; *Pennsylvania Laws, 1682–1700,* 138 (a three-time hog thief received a fine three times the value of the goods stolen, thirty-nine lashes, and banishment), 170.

45. *Minutes of Council,* I, 527 (quotes); Gipson, "Crime and Its Punishment," 8; Lermack, "Peace Bonds," 183.

46. *Pennsylvania Laws, 1682–1700,* 274.

47. Gipson, "Crime and Its Punishment," 9; Lermack, "Peace Bonds," 183–84; Fitzroy, "Punishment of Crime," 249–50. See, for example, *Statutes at Large II,* 7, 12, 175.

48. See table in note 29.

49. *Bucks Courts,* 377; *Gloucester Courts,* 123, 180; *Chester Courts I,* 364.

50. On servants, see *Chester Courts I,* 43, 49, 76, 84; counterfeiting, *Burlington Courts,* 85–86, 267; fencing highways, *Chester Courts II,* 92, *Bucks Dockets,* 399, and *Gloucester Courts,* 178; fee extortion, *Bucks Courts,* 141, and *Chester Courts I,* 194; and cheating, *Burlington Courts,* 115, 117, 294, and *Chester Courts II,* 100.

51. *Bucks Courts,* 147; *Burlington Courts,* 226, 302, 321.

52. *Pennsylvania Laws, 1682–1700,* 115 (quote), 174, 198; *Statutes at Large II,* 14–15; *New Jersey Concessions,* 483.

53. Samuel Pennypacker, *Pennsylvania Colonial Cases* (Philadelphia, 1892), 117–41; J. William Frost, ed., *The Keithian Controversy in Early Pennsylvania* (Norwood, Pa., 1980), 165–205; *Burlington Courts,* 209.

54. Richard Lempert, "Grievances and Legitimacy: The Beginnings and End of Dispute Settlement," *Law and Society Review* 15 (1981): 712 (quote); Genovese, *Roll, Jordan, Roll,* 27; Hay, "Property, Authority and Criminal Law," 33, 39, 51, 61.

55. *Chester Courts I,* 217; *Burlington Courts,* 226 (no fines collected).

56. Lyle Koehler, *A Search for Power: The "Weaker" Sex in Seventeenth-Century New England* (Urbana, Ill., 1980), 193; Friedman, *Crime and Punishment,* 51; Peter Hoffer, *Law and People in Colonial America* (Baltimore, 1992), 84, quoting Cornelia Hughes Dayton, "Women before the Bar: Gender, Law, and Society in Connecticut, 1710–1790" (Ph.D. diss., Princeton University, 1986), 164; Spindel, *Crime and Society in North Carolina,*

82–85 (31.6 percent of women criminals were charged with morals offenses); Greenberg, *Crime and Law Enforcement*, 50–51 (21.1 percent of women criminals were charged for disorderly houses or illegal relations with slaves).

57. *Pennsylvania Laws, 1682–1700*, 115 (quote), 198; *Burlington Courts*, 64, 160. Women were prosecuted for property offenses slightly more often than men, but at a rate that was not statistically significant (15.3 percent of women, 12.4 percent of men accused). This lack of difference between men and women regarding property accusations also existed in North Carolina (17.0 percent of women, 12.6 percent of men) but not in New York (36.1 percent of women, 11.3 percent of men). Spindel, *Crime and Society in North Carolina*, 83; Greenberg, *Crime and Law Enforcement*, 50.

58. *Burlington Courts*, 209 (first quote); *Gloucester Courts*, 199 (second quote).

59. *Bucks Courts*, 87–88, 116, 211.

60. *Gloucester Courts*, 24, 28, 31.

61. *Chester Courts I*, 114, 131, 362; *Burlington Courts*, 214, 217.

62. *Chester Courts II*, 148; *Gloucester Courts*, 124, 205, 249; *Burlington Courts*, 176; *Bucks Courts*, 319, 339, 401.

63. *Bucks Courts*, 358–59.

64. *Burlington Courts*, 115, 117; *Chester Courts I*, 194, 266; *Bucks Courts*, 141, 281, 32, 211; *Gloucester Courts*, 16; *Burlington Courts*, 209.

65. Horle, *Quakers and the English Legal System*, 16, 25, 101–2.

66. Nash, *Quakers and Politics*, 179, 162–63.

67. Tolles, *Meeting House*, 46–49, 60–61, 89.

68. Chi-square may not be a valid test for statistical significance when more than 20 percent of the cells in the cross-tabulation have expected (or predicted) counts less than 5. Here 31 percent of the cells have expected counts less than 5 cases.

69. Valerie Gladfelter, "Caring and Control: The Social Psychology of an Authoritative Group, the Burlington (NJ) Friends Meeting 1678–1720," (Ph.D. diss., University of Pennsylvania, 1983), 11–24; J. William Frost, *The Quaker Family in America* (New York, 1973), 52 (quote); Jack Marietta, *The Reformation of American Quakerism, 1748–1783* (Philadelphia, 1984), 3–5; David Hackett Fischer, *Albion's Seed* (Oxford, 1989), 428.

70. Jean Soderlund, "Women's Authority in Pennsylvania and New Jersey Quaker Meetings, 1680–1760," *WMQ* 44 (1987): 723–27; Marietta, *Reformation of Quakerism*, 27–31.

71. Burlington WM, Chester WM, Darby WM, Falls WM, Middletown WM, and Radnor WM were used. The following women's monthly meetings records were not available for periods when there were men's records available: Burlington, 1678–81 (no records prior to 1681); Chester, 1681–

95 (women met with men); Chesterfield Women's Monthly Meeting Minutes, 1684–1710 (no records prior to 1688, illegible thereafter); Concord Women's Monthly Meeting Minutes, 1684–1710 (have not survived); Falls, 1680–83 (no records before 1685); Radnor, 1684 (no records prior to 1685). Because of these gaps, comparisons with the men's meetings must be tentative.

72. Marietta, *Reformation of Quakerism,* 5.

73. As noted previously, the legal population is an imperfect proxy for the underlying population. The baseline should be the attributes of all Quakers, not just those in the legal system. Of all the Quakers disciplined by men's meetings, 74 percent were members of the legal population. Women disciplined by only the women's meetings were even less likely to be members of the legal population and thus were not included in this comparison.

74. Thirty percent of the Quakers in the legal population became plaintiffs, whereas 27.2 percent of the Quakers were disciplined.

75. On fighting, see Burlington MM 9/1703; shooting a servant, Burlington MM 2/1690; stealing, Concord MM 3/1689; defamation, Middletown MM 11/1689; drinking, Middletown MM 1/1710, and Chester MM 6/1700; fornicating, Concord MM 4/1688, Middletown MM 4/1700, 4/1701, and Falls MM 4/1701; running a disorderly house, Falls MM 11/1683; selling rum to Indians, Falls MM 11/1683, and Chester MM 5/1688; counterfeiting, Chester MM 7/1689; rioting, Burlington MM 4/1701; practicing astrology, Chester QM 12/1695, and Concord MM 9/1695; resisting an officer of the law, Middletown MM 10/1707; committing perjury, Bucks QM 12/1686; flipping a coin, Falls MM 10–11/1698; making wagers, Darby MM 7/1688; playing cards, Falls MM 3/1705; trespassing on public land, Chester MM 4/1689; breaking the Sabbath, Chester MM 7/1689; disorderly walking and the like, Chester MM 5/1687, 10/1694; not marrying after the marriage date had been set, Chester WM 8/1705, 7/1708; and keeping company with non-Quaker or unapproved males, Chester WM 4/1699, Radnor WM 6/1710, Falls WM 4/1687, Burlington WM 7/1700.

76. For sex, liquor, and other morals offenses, see Chester MM 2/1687, *Chester Courts I,* 94; Chester MM 5/1687, 10/1694, Chester QM 12/1694, *Chester Courts I,* 339–40; Chester MM 12/1696, *Chester Courts I,* 405; Concord MM 9/1695, *Chester Courts I,* 363; Middletown MM 2/1697, Bucks QM 6/1697, Middleton WM 7/1699, *Bucks Courts,* 285; Burlington MM 3/1687, *Burlington Courts,* 71; Chesterfield MM 9/1690, *Burlington Courts,* 123; and Chesterfield MM 4/1691, *Burlington Courts,* 123. For the coin-flip jury verdict, see Falls MM 10/1698, 3/1699, Middletown MM 12/1698, and *Bucks Courts,* 358. For building on public land, see Chester MM 5/1695, *Chester Courts I,* 340. For theft, see Chester MM

2/1704, *Chester Courts II,* 111. For fighting, see Concord MM 9/1706, *Chester Courts II,* 146.

77. *Burlington Courts,* 252; Burlington MM 4–5/1701; Chesterfield MM 4/1701; *Chester Courts,* 131, 133, 215, 227; *Bucks Dockets,* 352, 361, 398, 413.

78. For marrying out of unity, see Chester MM 4/1708, and Burlington MM 7/1707, 7/1708; attending a non-Quaker wedding, Chester MM 7/1697; "stealing" a daughter for a clandestine marriage, Burlington MM 1/1703; marrying too hastily, Burlington MM 7/1689; manifesting the Keithian schismatic, Radnor MM 4/1700, and Chester MM 8/1707; bad preaching/testimony, Middletown MM 3/1694, and Concord MM 12/1689, 2/1698, 4/1699, 6/1701; showing contempt for meeting, Concord MM 7/1685; wearing an inappropriate hat, Burlington MM 12/1704, and Chester MM 2/1703; arguing with or living apart from husband, Burlington WM 5/1708, 9/1708; and listening to a priest, Burlington MM 7/1706.

79. On bearing arms, see Burlington MM 12/1704, 4/1705; writing verses, Concord MM 10/1705; almanac superfluity, Burlington MM 12/1682; and economically improvident deals, Concord MM 1/1707.

80. Marietta, *Reformation of Quakerism,* 6, in his survey of 13,000 Delaware Valley Quaker discipline cases from the mid-eighteenth century also found such "marriage delinquency" the most common accusation, but at twice the rate of this earlier period (37.4 percent). Barry Levy, *Quakers and the American Family* (Oxford, 1988), 132, 141–42, also places tremendous importance on marriage discipline.

81. *Burlington Courts,* 190, 206, 209; *Chester Courts I,* 177, 184, 263, 380, 391; *Chester Courts II,* 154; *Pennsylvania Laws, 1682–1700,* 103, 108, 192 (no analogy found in West Jersey laws).

82. Middletown MM 11/1704 (first quote), 7/1710 (second quote).

83. Burlington MM 12/1704; Middleton WM 2/1700; Chester WM 3/1696.

Chapter 6: Dispositions of the Deviant

1. *Burlington Courts,* 142–43 (quotes), 148.

2. Ibid., 217.

3. Bradley Chapin, *Criminal Justice in Colonial America, 1606–1660* (Athens, Ga., 1983), 27–30; Michael Dalton, *The Countrey Justice, Containing the Practise of the Justices of the Peace out of Their Sessions* (London, 1622), 16–23; Norma Landau, *The Justices of the Peace, 1679–1760* (Berkeley, Calif., 1984), 6–7, 23–25; Douglas Greenberg, *Crime and Law Enforcement in the Colony of New York, 1691–1776* (Ithaca, N.Y., 1974), 112–13.

4. *Pennsylvania Laws, 1682–1700,* 117, 129. On attestations, see *Pennsylvania Laws, 1682–1700,* 248 (quote); *Burlington Courts,* 64; and Chapin, *Criminal Justice in Colonial America,* 33.

5. *Chester Courts I,* 27.

6. This level of "ignoramus" findings is far lower than that of colonial North Carolina (18.6 percent of charges found ignoramus) and Surrey's quarter sessions and assizes from 1660 to 1800 (19.1 percent ignoramus). Donna Spindel, *Crime and Society in North Carolina, 1663–1776* (Baton Rouge, 1990), 92; J. M. Beattie, *Crime and the Courts in England, 1660–1800* (Princeton, N.J., 1986), 402.

7. *Gloucester Courts,* 334; *Chester Courts II,* 117.

8. *Burlington Courts,* 261.

9. *Gloucester Courts,* 110 (first quote), 114; *Chester Courts I,* 295, 301; *Burlington Courts,* 254, 255 (second quote), 259, 264, 267.

10. *Bucks Dockets,* 375, 398; *Chester Courts I,* 213, 216, 224.

11. *New Jersey Concessions,* 397–98, 429.

12. For cases where victims were appointed to prosecute the offender, see *Chester Courts I,* 103, 114, 115, 134, 150; and *Bucks Courts,* 94–95.

13. *Burlington Courts,* 29; *Gloucester Courts,* 161, 163, 168.

14. *Burlington Courts,* 83, 86–87; *Chester Courts I,* 59, 60; *Bucks Courts,* 95, 100.

15. *Burlington Courts,* 256.

16. For criminal charges that grand juries found groundless after evidence had been presented, see *Burlington Courts,* 306, 307, 322–23. For a case that simply disappeared from the records, probably because it was dropped, see *Burlington Courts,* 223. For a case where the whole presentation was laid before the grand jury, which then discharged the defendant, see *Chester Courts I,* 399.

17. *Gloucester Courts,* 236–37; *Chester Courts I,* 357.

18. *Bucks Courts,* 81. For examples of forfeiture of recognizance bond for nonappearance, see *Burlington Courts,* 115; *Gloucester Courts,* 204; and *Bucks Dockets,* 425.

19. *Chester Courts I,* 122, 159; *Bucks Dockets,* 426; *Burlington Courts,* 314, 334. There was one case that had a not guilty jury verdict after evidence had been taken: *Chester Courts II,* 142.

20. *Bucks Courts,* 270, 177, 181; *Chester Courts II,* 137, 147; *Gloucester Courts,* 247; *Chester Courts II,* 60; *Burlington Courts,* 272.

21. *Burlington Courts,* 101; *Chester Courts I,* 393; *Bucks Dockets,* 376; *Burlington Courts,* 73.

22. *Chester Courts I,* 38, 42, 43 (quote), 45, 49, 50, 76, 84.

23. *Bucks Courts,* 281 (quote), 24; *Burlington Courts,* 209, 91; *Gloucester Courts,* 16; *Chester Courts II,* 171, 183.

24. Gail Sussman Marcus, "'Due Execution of the Generall Rules of Righteousnesse': Criminal Procedure in New Haven Town and Colony, 1638–1658," in *Saints and Revolutionaries,* ed. David Hall, Thad Tate, and John Murrin (New York, 1984), 126–27; John Murrin, "Magistrates, Sinners, and a Precarious Liberty: Trial by Jury in Seventeenth-Century New England," in *Saints and Revolutionaries,* 156, 164. Regarding conviction rates, see Greenberg, *Crime and Law Enforcement,* 71 (48 percent convictions in New York); Murrin, "Magistrates, Sinners, and a Precarious Liberty," 169 (30 percent jury verdicts of guilty in Rhode Island prior to 1660, rising to 52 percent in the 1660s); David Flaherty, "Crime and Social Control in Provincial Massachusetts," *Historical Journal* 24 (1981): 340 (51 percent guilty verdicts in Massachusetts); Spindel, *Crime and Society in North Carolina,* 93 (38 percent convictions in the known verdicts in North Carolina); J. S. Cockburn, *A History of English Assizes* (Cambridge, 1972), 96 (44 percent acquitted/dismissed in Devon and 35 percent at quarter sessions); and Beattie, *Crime and Courts,* 411 (49 percent trial jury convictions in Surrey).

25. *Chester Courts I,* 402 (quote), 405; *Bucks Courts,* 330.

26. *New Jersey Concessions,* 460, 477; *Statutes at Large II,* 19, 24. Some basis for this authority already existed in common law; see Dalton, *The Countrey Justice,* 136–40; and Chapin, *Criminal Justice in Colonial America,* 30.

27. *Chester Courts I,* 266; *Bucks Courts,* 24; *Chester Courts II,* 92; *Burlington Courts,* 165, 293, 299.

28. *Chester Courts,* 348, 362, 365.

29. For contempt of government, see *Burlington Courts,* 220; and *Gloucester Courts,* 24, 28, 31. For other contempts, see *Burlington Courts,* 102, 130, 219.

30. *Chester Courts I,* 192, 265, 269 (first quote), 272 (second quote).

31. *Burlington Courts,* 57, 58 (quote), 83, 86.

32. *Gloucester Courts,* 195–210. There was no grand jury available at three of the four sessions in 1699, and no trial juries for any of those sessions.

33. *Burlington Courts,* 293, 299, 327, 339.

34. The contested case percentage was determined by adding jury verdicts, plus all bench verdicts, and dividing by the total number of in-court outcomes.

35. *Statutes at Large II,* 77–79, 233–34; *Bucks Docket,* 375, 385.

36. *Bucks Courts,* 180, 277; *Burlington Courts,* 256. A similar, though less harsh, process was at work if the victim was an Indian or a servant accusing the master of harsh treatment. Though these accusers were not punished, their opponents in all but one case contested the charges in a clear belief that such low-status victims would be unable to obtain convictions.

That belief was almost always borne out by results, which failed to protect these low-status victims by criminal sanctions against their oppressors. On Indians, see *Chester Courts I*, 6; *Burlington Courts*, 115, 117, 218, 294; and *Chester Courts I*, 233 (defendants submitted to the court admitting taking goods from Indian traps). On servants, see *Chester Courts I*, 38, 42, 43, 76, 84, 45, 49, 50; and *Bucks Courts*, 20, 24.

37. On the king's or queen's attorney, see *Burlington Courts*, 138, 177, 307, 310; *Chester Courts I*, 339; and *Chester Courts II*, 59. It is unclear why the county court kept jurisdiction over a murder accusation instead of sending the trial to provincial court. Perhaps the political upheaval of the period (the case was in May 1692) had rendered the provincial court as powerless as the assembly. In any case, Shawe was convicted of murder by misadventure and sentenced to forfeit all his property. *Burlington Courts*, 136–39, 138 (quote).

38. On the right to a jury and challenges, see *New Jersey Concessions*, 427–29, in Richard S. Dunn and Mary Maples Dunn, *The Papers of William Penn*, vol. 1 (1644–79) (Philadelphia, 1981), 398; *Pennsylvania Laws, 1682–1700*, 100, 117, 129, 199; and *Statutes at Large II*, 18, 128–29. In a theft case against Thomas Wright in Burlington County in 1691, Wright successfully challenged twenty-one jurors but still lost. *Burlington Courts*, 118. In the Philadelphia trial of George Keith, he and his codefendant, Thomas Budd, challenged all Quakers as prejudiced, which was disallowed even after specific exceptions were made. Samuel Pennypacker, *Pennsylvania Colonial Cases* (Philadelphia, 1892), 117–41. On requiring the accuser's name in the presentment, see *Statutes at Large II*, 243; compelling witnesses, *Pennsylvania Laws, 1682–1700*, 116, 218, 228, *Statutes at Large II*, 47, and *New Jersey Concessions*, 429; and the two-witness rule, Dunn and Dunn, *Papers of Penn*, vol. 1, 398, and *Pennsylvania Laws, 1682–1700*, 116.

39. *Pennsylvania Laws, 1682–1700*, 121; *Gloucester Courts*, 97. For examples of remission of penalty, in part or full, see *Chester Courts I*, 51, 89, 113; and *Burlington Courts*, 84.

40. Murrin, "Magistrates, Sinners, and a Precarious Liberty," 189 (quote). For trial as a means to secure repentance, see Marcus, "'Due Execution,'" 130.

41. *Burlington Courts*, 43–44.

42. Ibid., 129 (first quote), 295 (second quote).

43. Paul Lermack, "Peace Bonds and Criminal Justice in Colonial Pennsylvania," *PMHB* 100 (1976): 173–74; Kathryn Preyer, "Penal Measures in the American Colonies: An Overview," *American Journal of Legal History* 26 (1982): 336–37; Douglas Hay, "Property, Authority and the Criminal Law," in *Albion's Fatal Tree*, ed. Douglas Hay, Peter Lineburgh, John

Rule, and E. P. Thompson (New York, 1975), 40–49; Marcus, "'Due Execution,'" 129–30.

44. *Bucks Courts,* 58, 77, 78, 204, 20, 116.

45. *Chester Courts I,* 107, 108, 84, 89. On assault, compare convictions in *Chester Courts I,* 97, 101, 134, with *Chester Courts I,* 70, 348, 349, 406, and *Chester Courts II,* 1, 32.

46. In Bucks County, 14.8 percent used juries in criminal cases; Chester, 12.2 percent; Burlington, 11.1 percent; and Gloucester, 13.3 percent.

47. Compare *Pennsylvania Laws, 1682–1700,* 110–15, 138, 144–45. These penalties were stiffened in Pennsylvania's revisions of 1700. See *Statutes at Large II,* 5–15.

48. Penn's *Frame* commanded "Such Offences against God, as Swearing, Cursing, Lying, Prophane Talking, Drunkennes, Drinking of Healths, Obscene words, Incest, Sodomy, Rapes, Whoredom, Fornication and other uncleanness (not to be repeated:)" as well as "Prizes, Stage-Plays, Cards, Dice, May-Games, Gamesters, Masques, Revels, Bull-Baitings, Cockfightings, Bear-baitings and the like . . . shall be respectively discouraged and severely punished." Richard Dunn and Mary Maples Dunn, eds., *The Papers of William Penn,* vol. 2 (1680–1684) (Philadelphia, 1982), 225. The laws passed in 1682 in Pennsylvania covered three different types of swearing and seven different types of sexual offenses. *Pennsylvania Laws, 1682–1700,* 109–10.

49. On improper marriages, see *Gloucester Courts,* 153, 209 (fines remitted); *Chester Courts I,* 363; and *Chester Courts II,* 8 (orders to marry properly). On premarital sex, see *Chester Courts II,* 50 (couple ordered to pay half the court charges and behave themselves); and *Burlington Courts,* 129 (choice of whipping or fine remitted).

50. *Gloucester Courts,* 260–62; *Chester Courts II,* 59–60; *Chester Courts I,* 313–14.

51. *Burlington Courts,* 166–67.

52. Chi-square may not be a statistically valid test for the relation between 1693 tax assessment and outcome because 44 percent of the cells had expected results of less than 5. See chapter 5, note 68, for chi-square requirements.

53. The figures for defendants who chose criminal juries were 8.3 percent for Quakers and 14.2 percent for non-Quakers (chi-square probability .006); 8.8 percent for high officers, 9.5 percent for low officers, and 14.4 percent for nonofficers (chi-square probability .031).

54. The chi-square probability for jury victories/losses matched against sex was .403; officeholding, .302; religion, .262; landowning, .316; occupation, .053; inventoried wealth, .412; and 1693 Pennsylvania tax assessment, .138.

55. *Pennsylvania Laws, 1682–1700,* 248.

56. *Bucks Courts,* 358–60. Quakers on the jury were also punished by their meetings. Falls MM 10/1698–3/1699; Middletown MM 12/98.

57. For property accusations, lesser officers chose jury trials in 41.9 percent of cases, while submitting in 16.1 percent. Nonofficers used jury trials for 33.0 percent of their property charges, while submitting in 32.0 percent. (The chi-square probability was .022.)

58. The chi-square probability was .028 in the comparison between Quakers and non-Quakers found guilty of violence. The chi-square probability was .025 in the comparison of Quakers and non-Quakers found guilty of morals charge.

59. In property cases, high officers were found not guilty 50 percent of the time; lesser officers, 11.1 percent; and nonofficers, 11.6 percent. Quakers were found not guilty of property offenses in 20 percent of their cases, while the non-Quaker acquittal rate was 9.8 percent.

60. Chi-square probability was .039, but chi-square may not be valid due to a low number of cases. See chapter 5, note 68. *Statutes at Large II,* 5–8. For examples of cases where the courts standardized penalties, see *Chester Courts II,* 19, 28, 107, 117, 118, 125, 165, 171, 174; and *Bucks Dockets,* 365, 376, 393. For examples of cases where there were different penalties for men and women who were partners in the offense, see *Chester Courts I,* 158, 184; *Chester Courts II,* 12, 28; *Burlington Courts,* 332–33; and *Gloucester Courts,* 94, 95, 97.

61. *Burlington Courts,* 123, 156, 271.

62. N. E. H. Hull, *Female Felons: Women and Serious Crime in Colonial Massachusetts* (Urbana, Ill., 1987), 11–12; Spindel, *Crime and Society in North Carolina,* 82.

63. The landed submitted in only 27.8 percent of their guilty verdicts in property cases, while the nonlanded submitted in 61.7 percent of theirs (the chi-square probability was .019). The landed were fined in 34.8 percent of their guilty verdicts in morals cases while submitting to 44.6 percent; the nonlanded had only 15.7 percent fines and 64.3 percent submissions (the chi-square probability was .036).

64. Falls MM 10/1695. On Quaker procedures, see J. William Frost, *The Quaker Family in America* (New York, 1973), 53–56; Jack Marietta, *The Reformation of American Quakerism* (Philadelphia, 1984), 3–10; Jon Butler, *Power, Authority, and the Origins of American Denominational Order* (Philadelphia, 1978), 39, 40; Valerie Gladfelter, "Power Challenged: Rising Individualism in the Burlington, New Jersey, Friends Meeting, 1678–1720," in *Friends and Neighbors,* ed. Michael Zuckerman (Philadelphia, 1982), 119–20; and "tender council," Chester QM 6/1695. On investigations, see Burlington MM 4/1707–10/1707, Radnor MM 7/1697, and Falls

MM 10/1695; overseers, Radnor MM 7/1695, Concord MM 8/1695, Darby MM 9/1695, and Middletown MM 10/1695; and "labor of love," Chester MM 12/1709.

65. Concord MM 1/1686 (first quote), 11/1688 (second quote); Burlington MM 12/1704 (Boulton quotes); Falls WM 6/1683, 7/1685 (Knight quotes); Concord MM 7/1685 (last quote), 8/1685.

66. Concord MM 4/1690 (first quote); Middletown MM 5/1700 (second quote); Falls MM 11/1683 (third quote).

67. Middletown MM 11/1689 (first four quotes), 12/1689 (fifth quote), 3/1690, 3/1691 (last quote), 6/1691.

68. Chester MM 5/1687–10/1687, 4/1694 (quote), 5/1694.

69. Concord MM 12/1689–3/1690, 4/1690 (first quote), 6/1690 (second quote), 6/1701–10/1701, 1/1702 (third and fourth quotes); Chester MM 5/1708, 8/1709 (last quote).

70. Marietta, *Reformation of Quakerism,* 6–7, also found "marriage delinquency" the most common offense disciplined (37.4 percent of cases).

71. Barry Levy, *Quakers and the American Family* (New York, 1988), 132, in his survey of one meeting found the condemned were overwhelmingly young (82 percent), which may partially explain why the disowned tended to be of lower status.

72. J. William Frost, "Religious Liberty in Early Pennsylvania," *PMHB* 105 (1981): 432–33; Jon Butler, "Into Pennsylvania's Spiritual Abyss: The Rise and Fall of the Later Keithians, 1693–1703," *PMHB* 101 (1977): 153, 157; David Hackett Fischer, *Albion's Seed* (New York, 1989), 469–70.

73. Marietta, *Reformation of Quakerism,* 48.

74. Gladfelter, "Power Challenged," 116–33.

75. Butler, *Power and American Denominational Order,* 39.

76. For the best example of overseer-driven discipline, see Middletown MM 12/1700, 2/1701, 10/1708, 7/1709, 10/1709.

77. For youth meetings, see Chester MM 9/1694; Radnor MM 1/1694; Concord MM 8/1695; Falls MM 10/1695; Bucks QM 12/1697; Chesterfield MM 7/1697; and Butler, *Power and American Denominational Order,* 39. For preparatory meetings, see Concord MM 7/1700; and Butler, *Power and American Denominational Order,* 40.

78. Edwin Bronner, "Quaker Discipline and Order, 1680–1720: Philadelphia Yearly Meeting and London Yearly Meeting," in *The World of William Penn,* ed. Richard S. Dunn and Mary Maples Dunn (Philadelphia, 1986), 328–29. On servant behavior, see Radnor MM 2/1702; instructions to overseers to be stricter, Radnor MM 1/1703, Concord MM 3/1696, 9/1710, Middletown MM 4/1699, 1/1708, Falls MM 1/1707, and Bucks QM 6/1704; superfluity, Concord MM 3/1696, Darby MM 3/1696, Chester QM 3/1696, Falls MM 4/1710, and Middletown MM 5/1691 ("airy spir-

it" to be disciplined); and astrology/geomancy, Concord MM 9/1695.

79. Chester QM 6/1689 (quote); Bucks QM 6/1706, 6/1710; Burlington QM 9/1703–12/1703. For minutes of meeting to be given to the accused at the discretion of monthly meeting, see Chester QM 9/1710.

80. On selling rum to Indians, see Chester MM 5/1688; Concord MM 1/1688; Falls MM 2/1687–4/1687; Middletown MM 11/1687; Bucks QM 6/1684; and "Testimony of the Philadelphia Quarterly Meeting against Selling Rum to the Indians, 1689," Miscellaneous Mss., Friends Historical Library, Swarthmore College. On marriage, see Concord MM 7/1700, 12/1700; and Falls MM 8/1691. On fence-viewers, see Radnor MM 5/1693. On registry, see Bucks QM 3/1686 (first two quotes). On money, see Falls MM 12/1704 (last quote).

81. Chester QM 6/1702 (first two quotes), 12/1706 (last two quotes).

82. Falls MM 10/1698–3/1699; Middletown MM 12/1698.

83. Burlington MM 2/1701, 4/1701, 5/1701 (first quote), 6/1701 (last quote), 7/1701; Burlington QM 3/1701.

84. Bucks QM 12/1686 (quote); Middletown MM 1/1707; Burlington MM 3/1695, 10/1701; Chester MM 4/1689, 5/1695, 6/1700. On probate, see Chester MM 12/1684; Falls MM 5/1683, 7/1683, 7/1701–10/1701; Middletown MM 1/1701, 3/1701, 9/1702, 1/1703; Burlington MM 9/1682, 12/1691, 1/1696, 5/1696; and Chesterfield 3/1689, 4/1689, 8/1689, 9/1689.

85. William Nelson, *Dispute and Conflict Resolution in Plymouth County, Massachusetts, 1725–1825* (Chapel Hill, N.C., 1981), 36–37, 41; George Haskins, *Law and Authority in Early Massachusetts* (New York, 1960), 17, 25, 48, 60–63, 88–89; Emil Oberholzer, *Delinquent Saints: Disciplinary Action in the Early Congregational Churches of Massachusetts* (New York, 1956), 13, 24, 216; Timothy Breen and Stephen Foster, "The Puritans' Greatest Achievement: A Study of Social Cohesion in Seventeenth-Century Massachusetts," *Journal of American History* 60 (1973): 5–15; Marcus, "'Due Execution,'" 126, 129–30.

86. For discussion of fornication as subject to punishment by church and state in Massachusetts, see Roger Thompson, *Sex in Middlesex: Popular Mores in a Massachusetts County, 1649–1699* (Amherst, Mass., 1986), 55; and Haskins, *Law and Authority in Early Massachusetts,* 89.

Conclusion: A People of Process

1. Lawrence M. Friedman, *The Republic of Choice: Law, Authority and Culture* (Cambridge, Mass., 1990), 211–12.

2. Edmund Morgan, *Inventing the People: The Rise of Popular Sovereignty in England and America* (New York, 1988), 13.

3. Friedman, *Republic of Choice,* 39.

4. E. Allan Lind and Tom R. Tyler, *The Social Psychology of Procedural Justice* (New York, 1988), 208–15; Tom R. Tyler, *Why People Obey the Law* (New Haven, Conn., 1990), 115, 133, 147; John Thibaut and Laurens Walker, *Procedural Justice: A Psychological Analysis* (New York, 1975), 119.

5. Tyler, *Why People Obey,* 138, 146, 151 (quote).

6. Ibid., 101 (quote), 107, 161.

7. Jack P. Greene, *Pursuits of Happiness: The Social Development of Early Modern British Colonies and the Formation of American Culture* (Chapel Hill, N.C., 1988), 138–39.

Index